Arata
THE LEGEND

18

WE ARE MAN, BORN OF HEAVEN AND EARTH,
MOON AND SUN AND EVERYTHING UNDER THEM.

EYES, EARS, NOSE, TONGUE, BODY, MIND...

PURITY WILL PIERCE EVIL AND
OPEN UP THE WORLD OF DARKNESS.

ALL LIFE WILL BE REBORN AND INVIGORATED.

APPEAR NOW.

STORY & ART BY
YUU WATASE

Arata THE LEGEND

HARACTERS

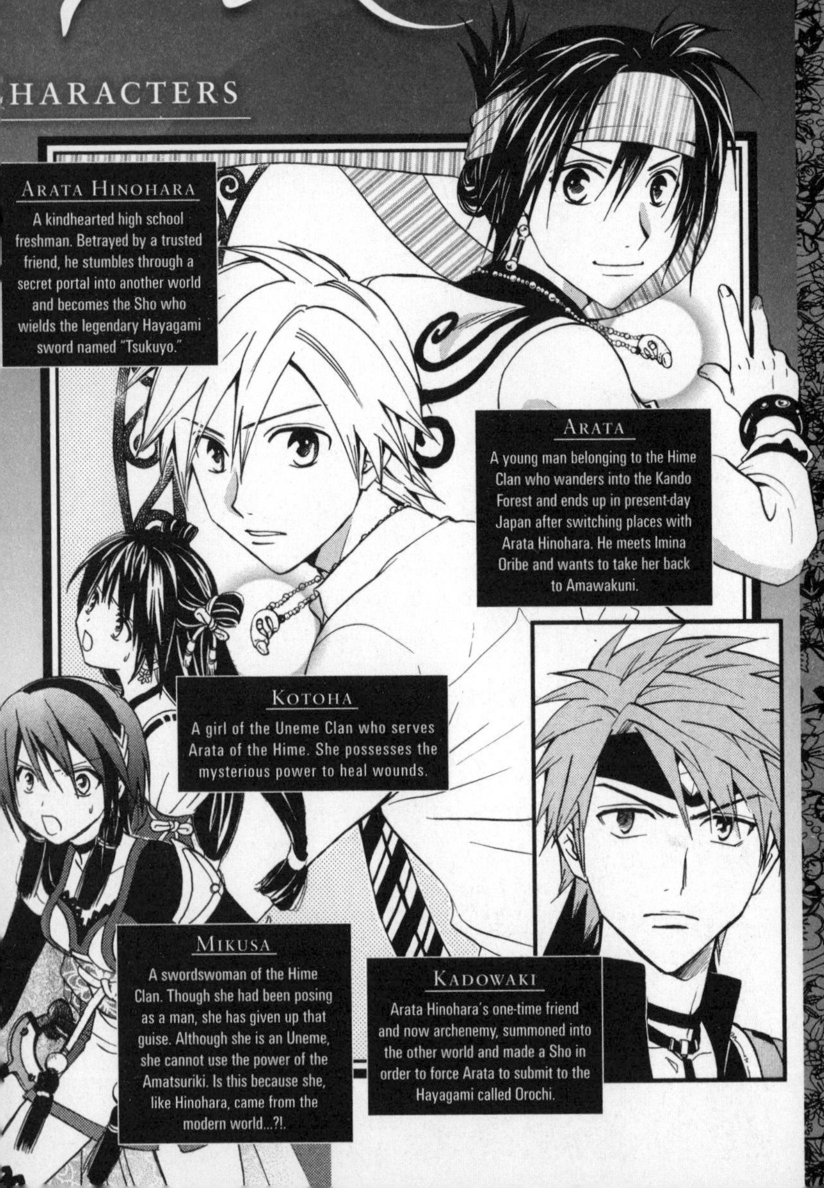

Arata Hinohara

A kindhearted high school freshman. Betrayed by a trusted friend, he stumbles through a secret portal into another world and becomes the Sho who wields the legendary Hayagami sword named "Tsukuyo."

Arata

A young man belonging to the Hime Clan who wanders into the Kando Forest and ends up in present-day Japan after switching places with Arata Hinohara. He meets Imina Oribe and wants to take her back to Amawakuni.

Kotoha

A girl of the Uneme Clan who serves Arata of the Hime. She possesses the mysterious power to heal wounds.

Mikusa

A swordswoman of the Hime Clan. Though she had been posing as a man, she has given up that guise. Although she is an Uneme, she cannot use the power of the Amatsuriki. Is this because she, like Hinohara, came from the modern world...?!.

Kadowaki

Arata Hinohara's one-time friend and now archenemy, summoned into the other world and made a Sho in order to force Arata to submit to the Hayagami called Orochi.

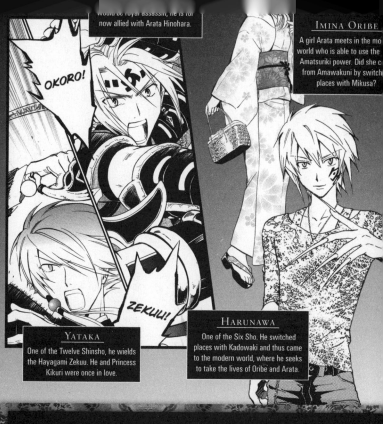

...would be royal assassin, he is for now allied with Arata Hinohara.

OKORO!

ZEKUU!

IMINA ORIBE

A girl Arata meets in the mo... world who is able to use the Amatsuriki power. Did she c... from Amawakuni by switch... places with Mikusa?

YATAKA

One of the Twelve Shinsho, he wields the Hayagami Zekuu. He and Princess Kikuri were once in love.

HARUNAWA

One of the Six Sho. He switched places with Kadowaki and thus came to the modern world, where he seeks to take the lives of Oribe and Arata.

THE STORY THUS FAR

Arata Hinohara, a modern Japanese high school student, finds himself in Amawakuni, a land in another dimension. There he is chosen as the new wielder of the legendary Hayagami Tsukuyo and embarks on a quest to save Princess Hime, who has kept the powers of the various Hayagami in check but now hovers precariously near death.

Arata and his comrades enter the territory ruled by Kikutsune, one of the Six Sho who seeks Arata's submission as well as possession of Tsukuyo. Pushed to the edge in the struggle for these goals, Kikutsune transforms into a powerful demonic form known as an onigami. An intense battle ensues in which Arata manages to defeat Kikutsune, but he is then called away to save the people Kikustune has oppressed. This results in Kikutsune being forced to submit to Kadowaki.

Meanwhile, in the modern world, Arata of the Hime and Imina Oribe visit Oninaki Island for summer break. Harunawa, another of the Six Sho, has come after them and manages to subjugate Oribe's cousin Maya to his will and send her off to do his malicious bidding.

18
Arata
THE LEGEND

CONTENTS

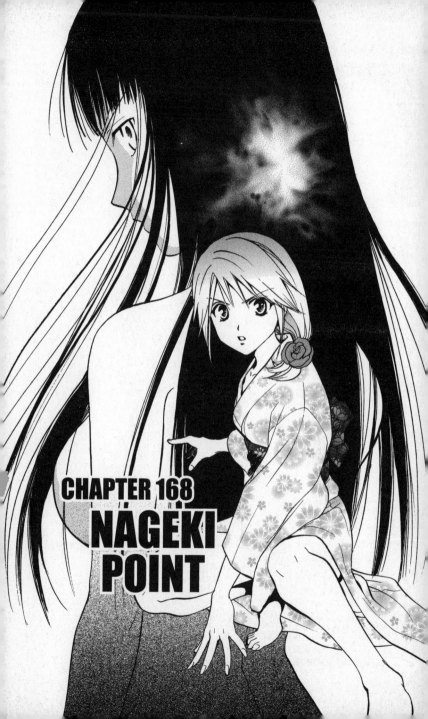

CHAPTER 168
NAGEKI POINT

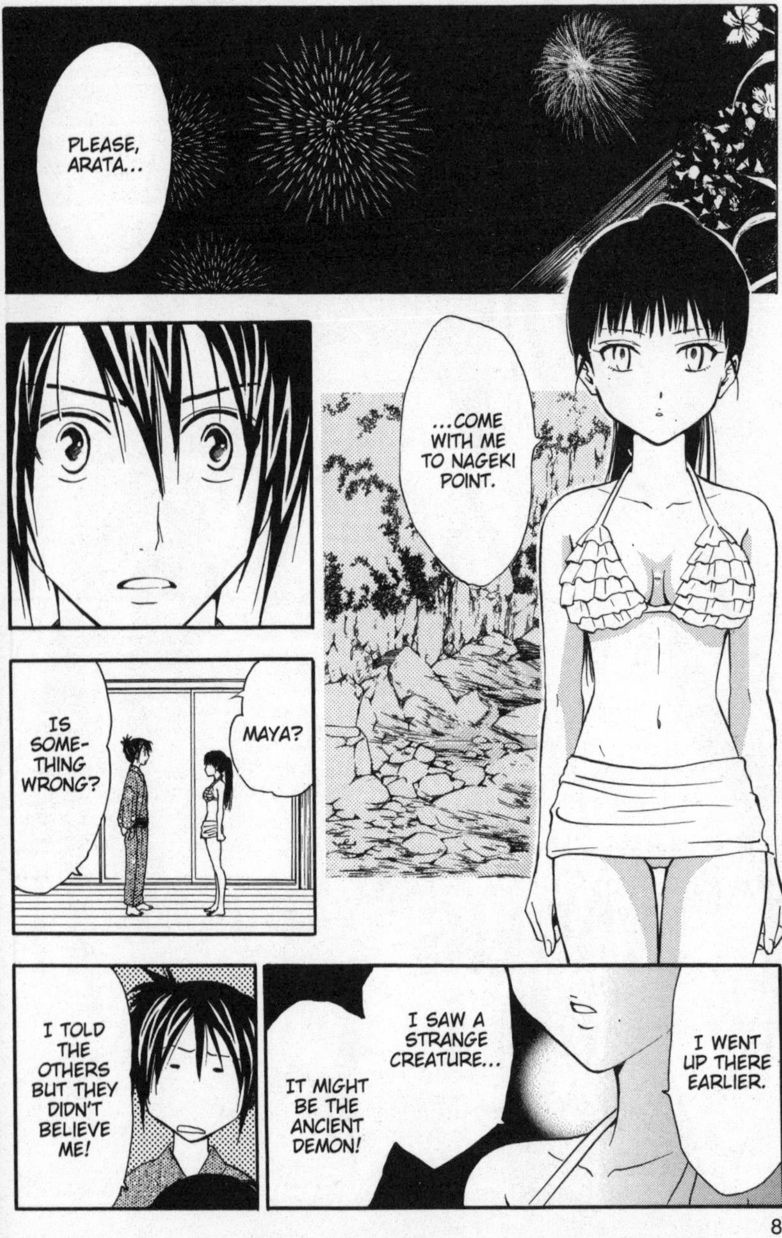

PLEASE, ARATA...
...COME WITH ME TO NAGEKI POINT.
MAYA?
IS SOMETHING WRONG?
I WENT UP THERE EARLIER.
I SAW A STRANGE CREATURE...
IT MIGHT BE THE ANCIENT DEMON!
I TOLD THE OTHERS BUT THEY DIDN'T BELIEVE ME!

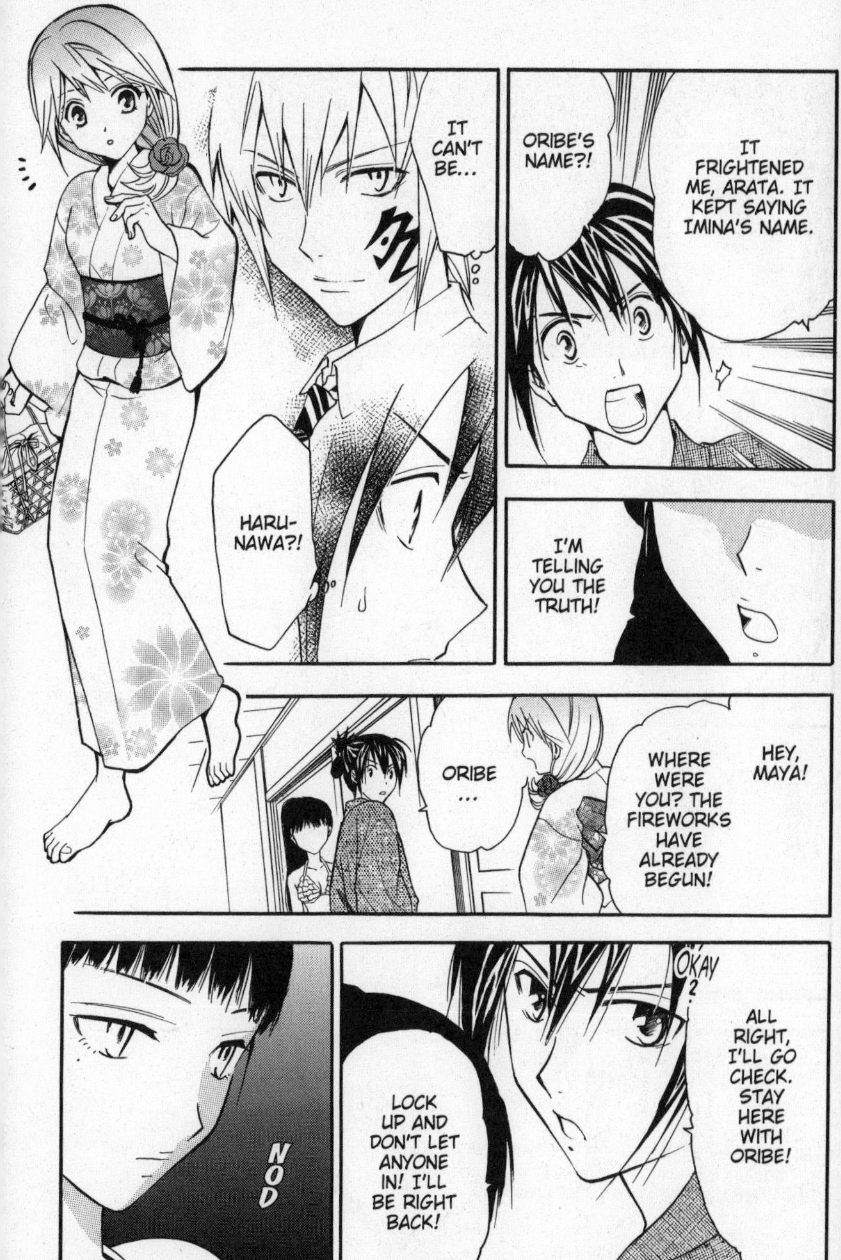

IT FRIGHTENED ME, ARATA. IT KEPT SAYING IMINA'S NAME.
ORIBE'S NAME?!
I'M TELLING YOU THE TRUTH!
IT CAN'T BE...
HARU-NAWA?!
HEY, MAYA!
WHERE WERE YOU? THE FIREWORKS HAVE ALREADY BEGUN!
ORIBE ...
OKAY?
ALL RIGHT, I'LL GO CHECK. STAY HERE WITH ORIBE!
LOCK UP AND DON'T LET ANYONE IN! I'LL BE RIGHT BACK!
NOD

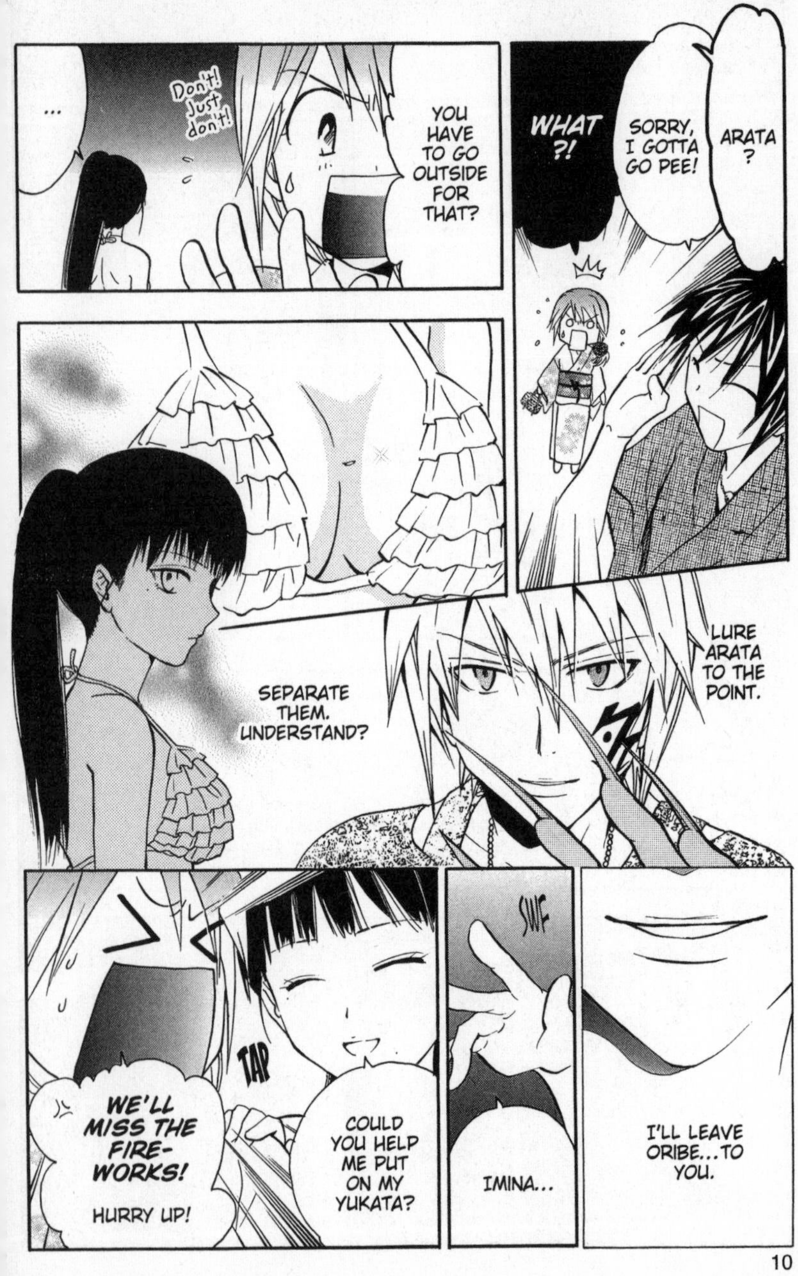
ARATA?
SORRY, I GOTTA GO PEE!
WHAT?!
YOU HAVE TO GO OUTSIDE FOR THAT?
Don't! Just don't!
...
LURE ARATA TO THE POINT.
SEPARATE THEM. UNDERSTAND?
I'LL LEAVE ORIBE...TO YOU.
SWF
IMINA...
COULD YOU HELP ME PUT ON MY YUKATA?
TAP
WE'LL MISS THE FIRE-WORKS!
HURRY UP!

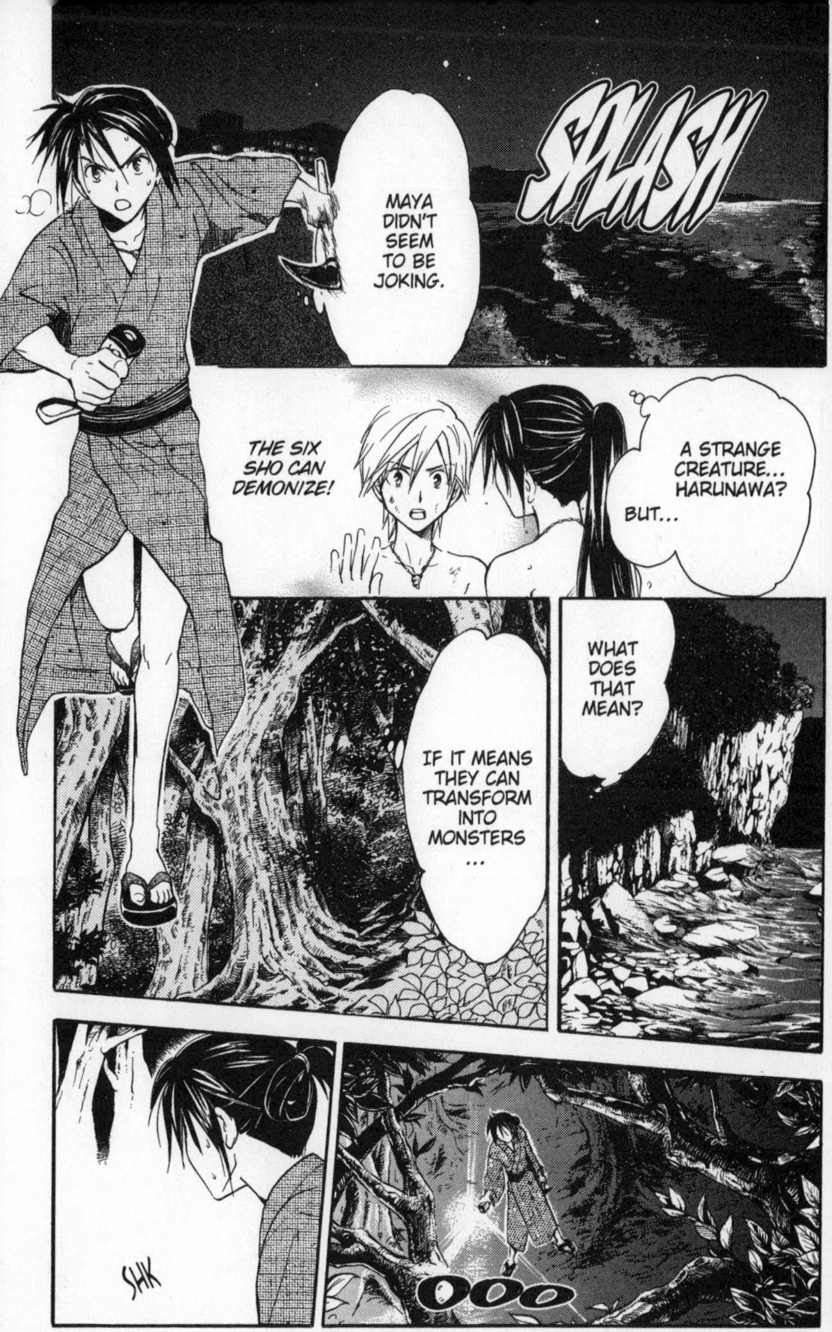
SPLASH
MAYA DIDN'T SEEM TO BE JOKING.
A STRANGE CREATURE... HARUNAWA?
BUT...
THE SIX SHO CAN DEMONIZE!
WHAT DOES THAT MEAN?
IF IT MEANS THEY CAN TRANSFORM INTO MONSTERS ...
OOO
SHK

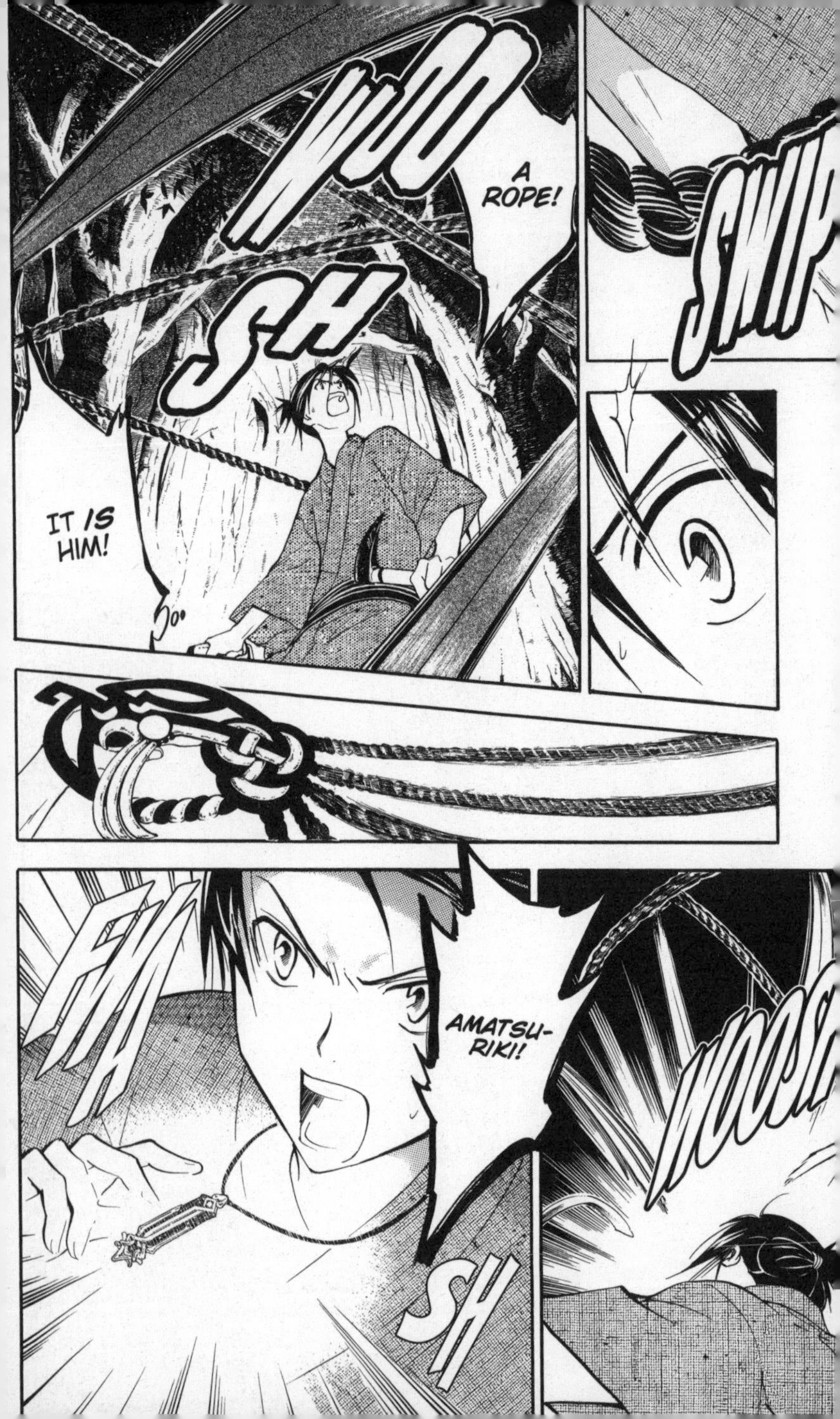
SWIP
A ROPE!
SH
IT IS HIM!
AMATSU-
RIKI!
SH

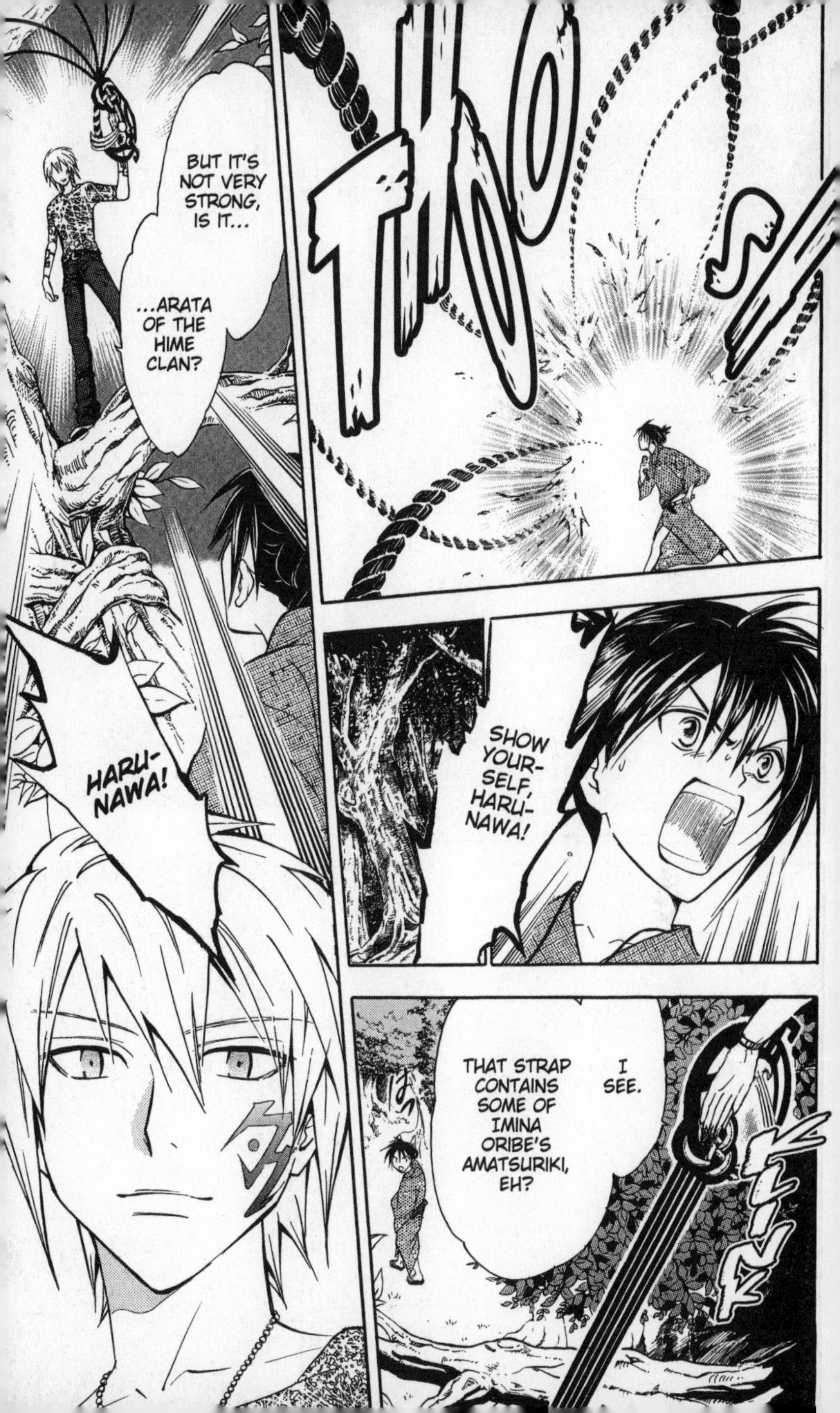
THOOSH
SHOW YOURSELF, HARUNAWA!
I SEE.
THAT STRAP CONTAINS SOME OF IMINA ORIBE'S AMATSURIKI, EH?
BUT IT'S NOT VERY STRONG, IS IT...
...ARATA OF THE HIME CLAN?
HARUNAWA!

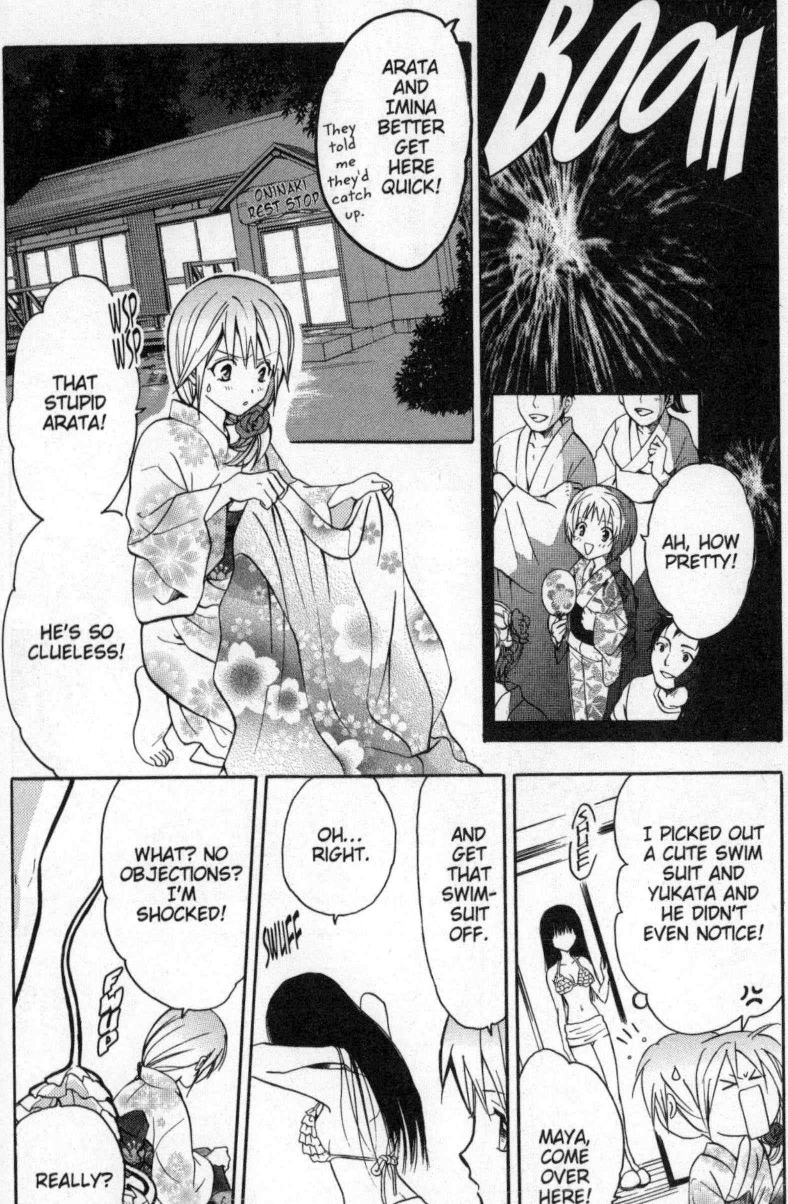
BOOM
AH, HOW PRETTY!
ONINAKI REST STOP
ARATA AND IMINA BETTER GET HERE QUICK!
They told me they'd catch up.
WSP WSP
THAT STUPID ARATA!
HE'S SO CLUELESS!
I PICKED OUT A CUTE SWIM SUIT AND YUKATA AND HE DIDN'T EVEN NOTICE!
SHUFF
MAYA, COME OVER HERE!
AND GET THAT SWIM-SUIT OFF.
OH... RIGHT.
SWUFF
WHAT? NO OBJECTIONS? I'M SHOCKED!
FWUP
REALLY?

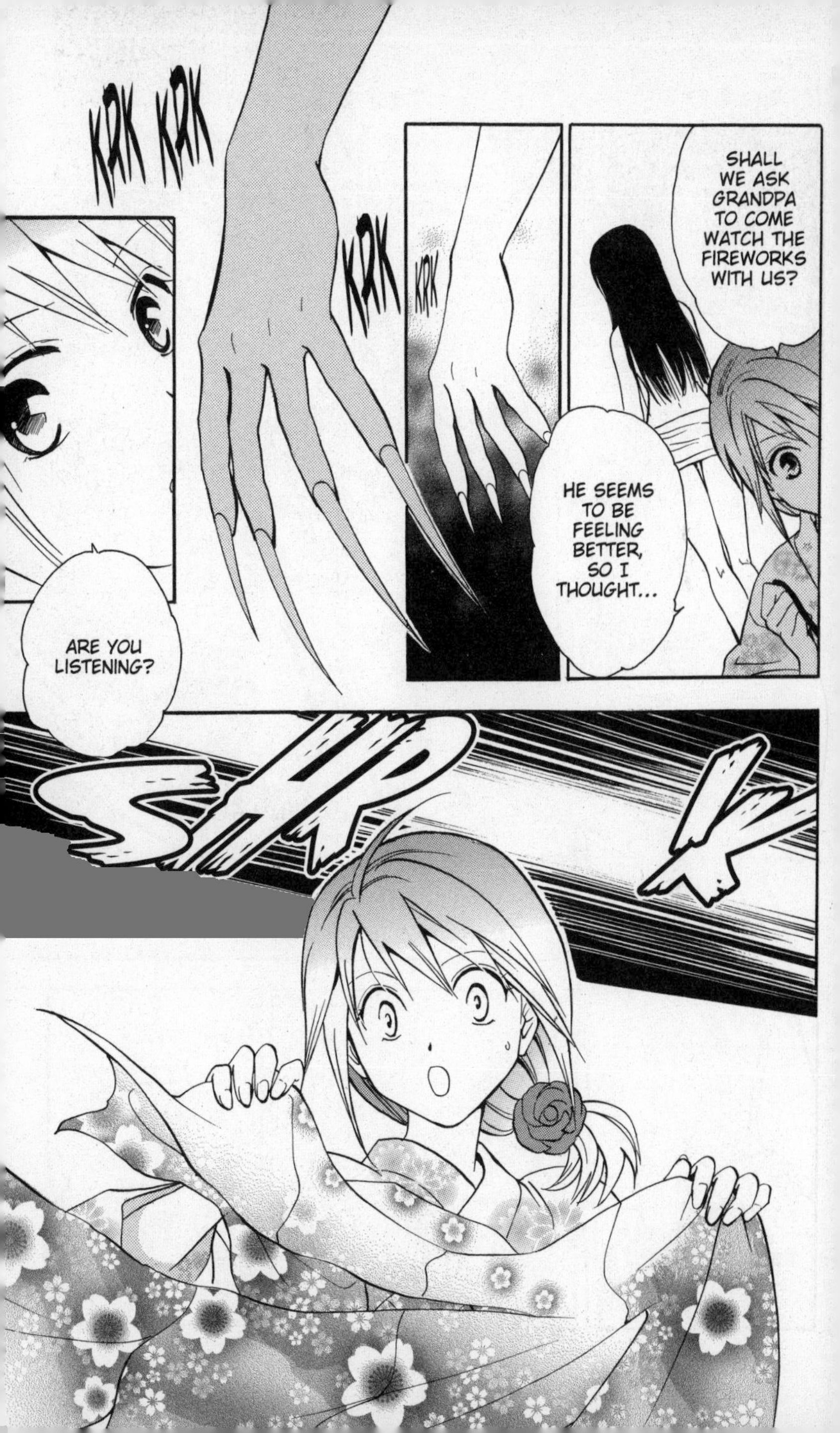
SHALL WE ASK GRANDPA TO COME WATCH THE FIREWORKS WITH US?
HE SEEMS TO BE FEELING BETTER, SO I THOUGHT...
KRK
KRK
KRK KRK
ARE YOU LISTENING?
SHRK

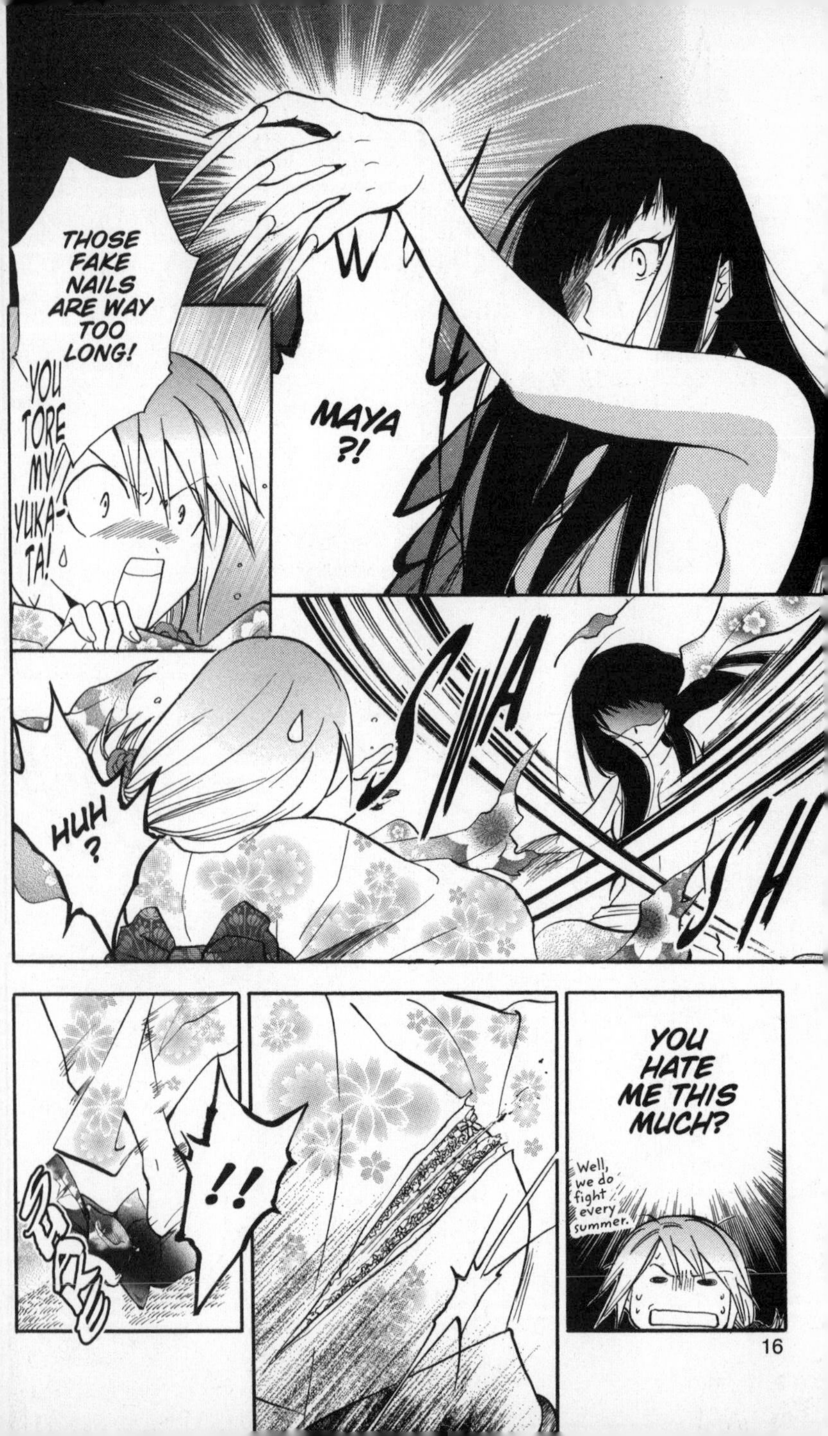
MAYA ?!
THOSE FAKE NAILS ARE WAY TOO LONG!
YOU TORE MY YUKA-TA!
HUH ?
YOU HATE ME THIS MUCH?
Well, we do fight every summer.
!!

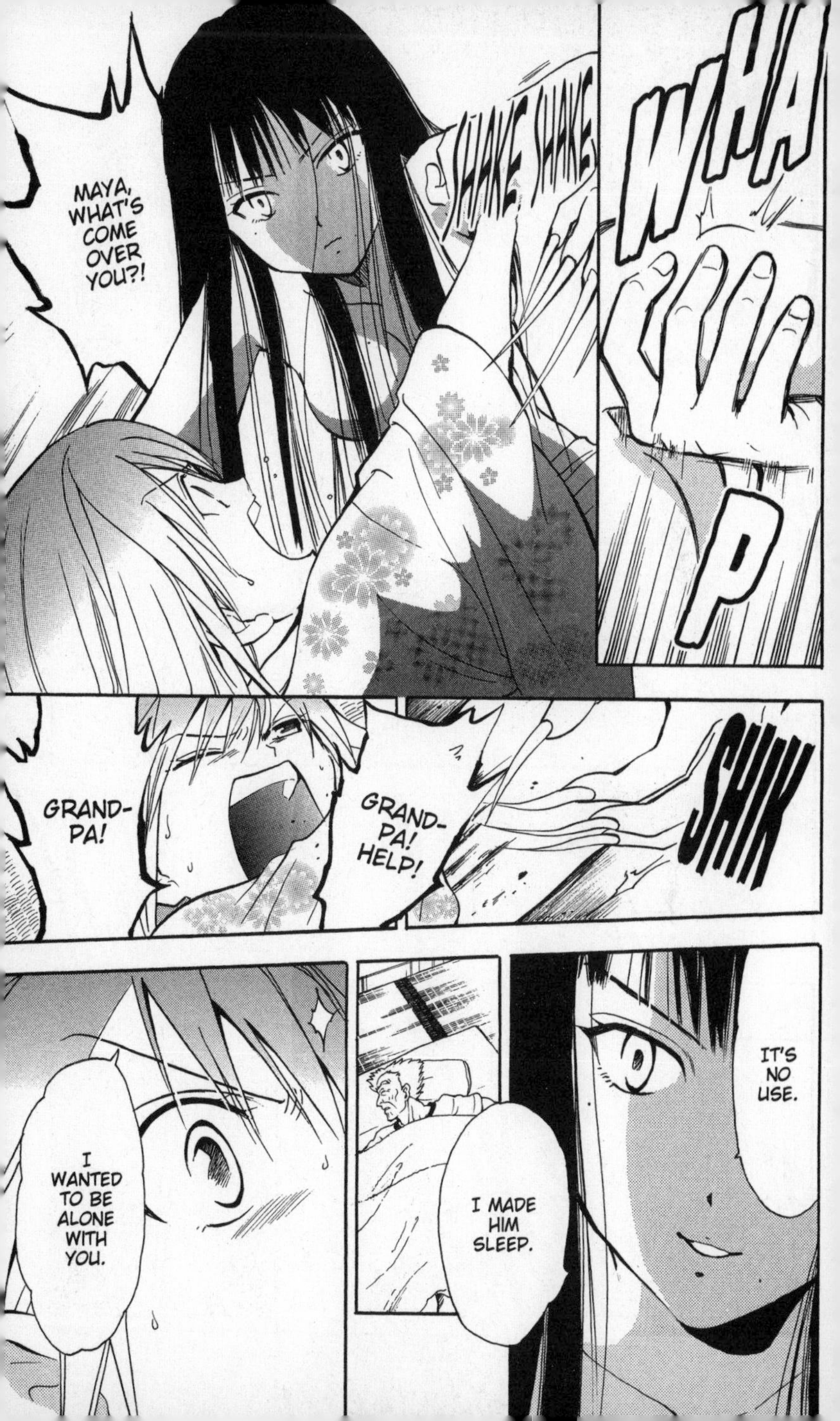
WHAP
SHAKE SHAKE
MAYA, WHAT'S COME OVER YOU?!
SHIK
GRAND-PA! HELP!
GRAND-PA!
IT'S NO USE.
I MADE HIM SLEEP.
I WANTED TO BE ALONE WITH YOU.

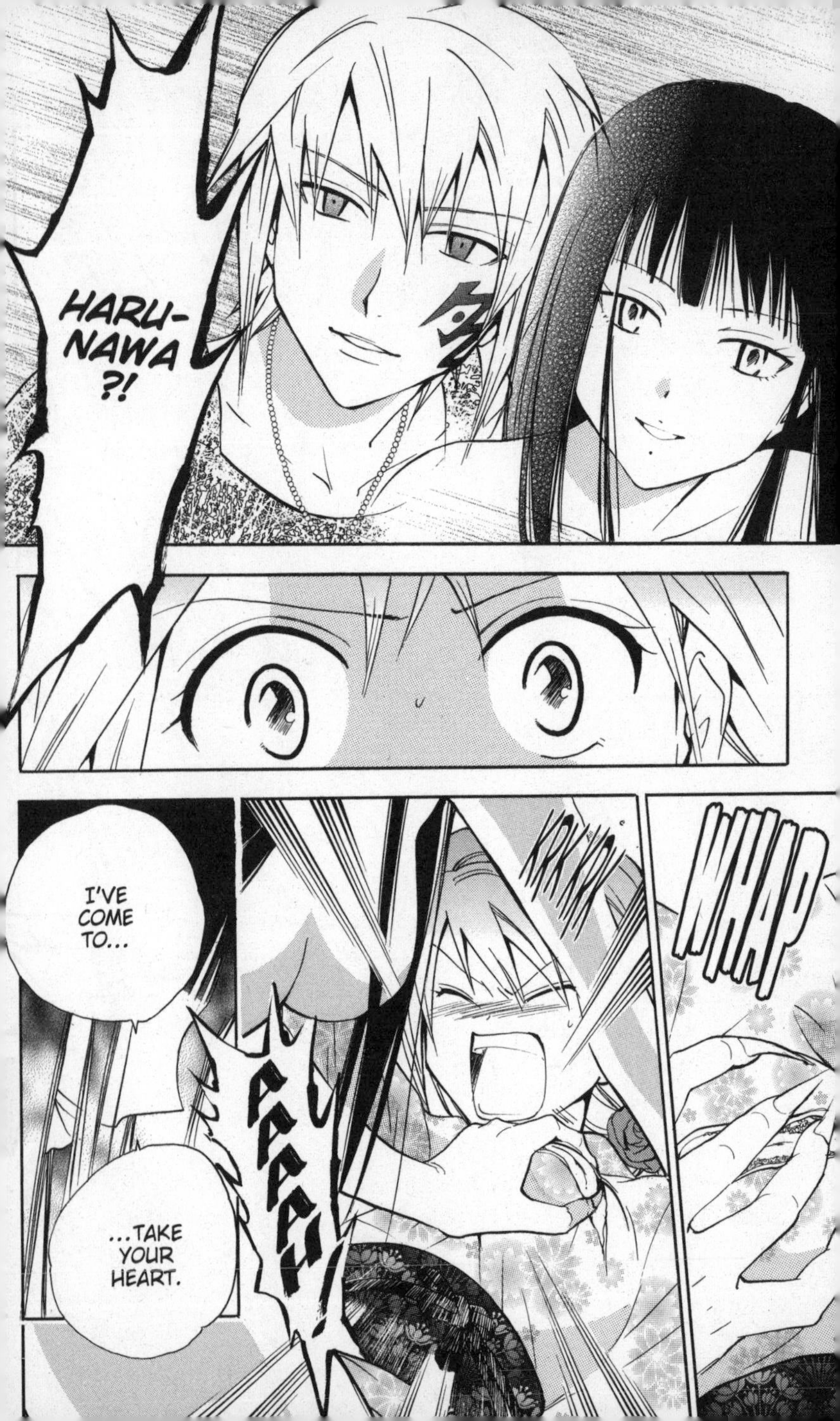
HARU-NAWA?!
WHAP
KRKKRK
I'VE COME TO...
AAAAH!
...TAKE YOUR HEART.

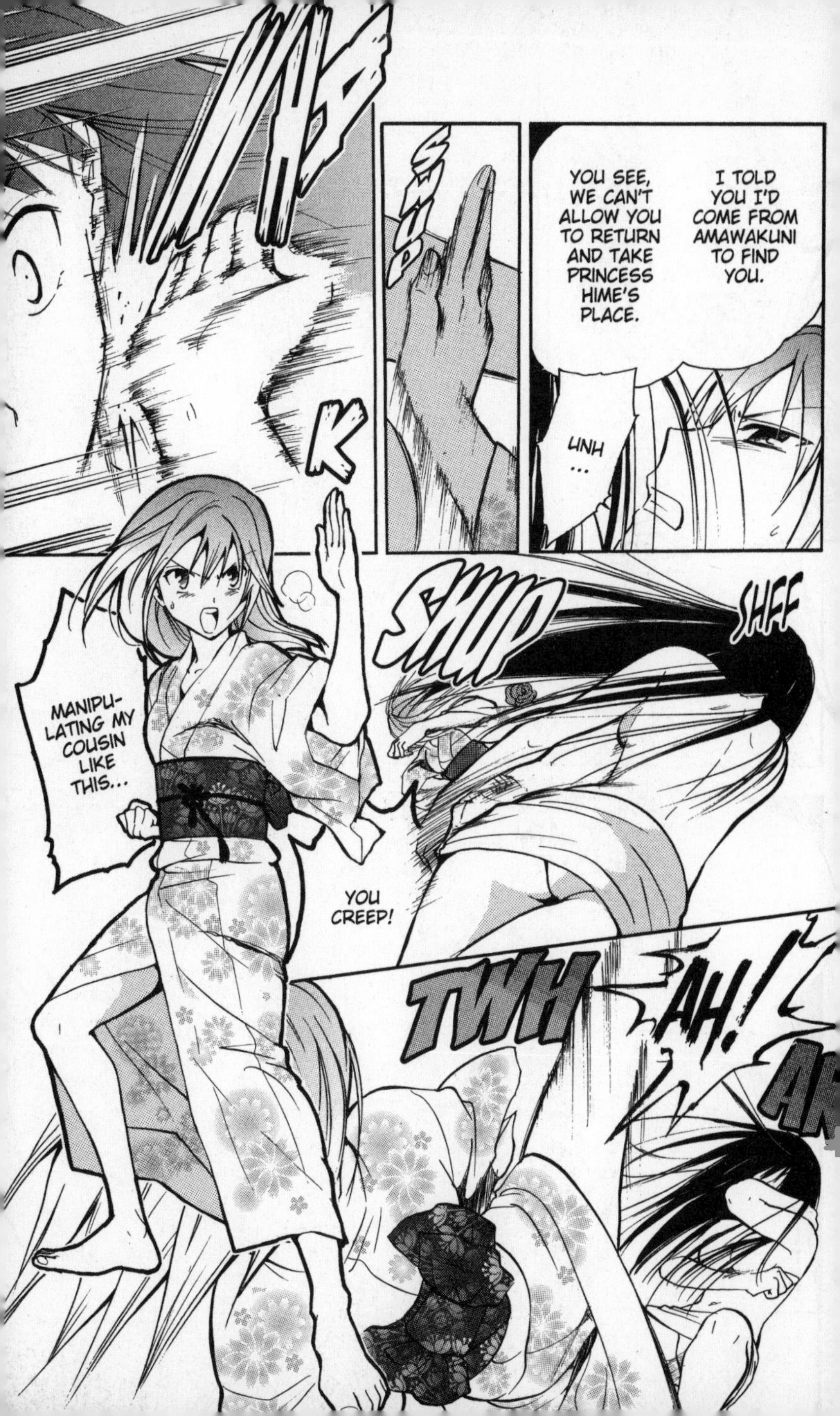
I TOLD YOU I'D COME FROM AMAWAKUNI TO FIND YOU.
YOU SEE, WE CAN'T ALLOW YOU TO RETURN AND TAKE PRINCESS HIME'S PLACE.
UNH ...
SHIP
WHA
K
SHFF
SHUP
MANIPULATING MY COUSIN LIKE THIS...
YOU CREEP!
AH!
TWH
AH

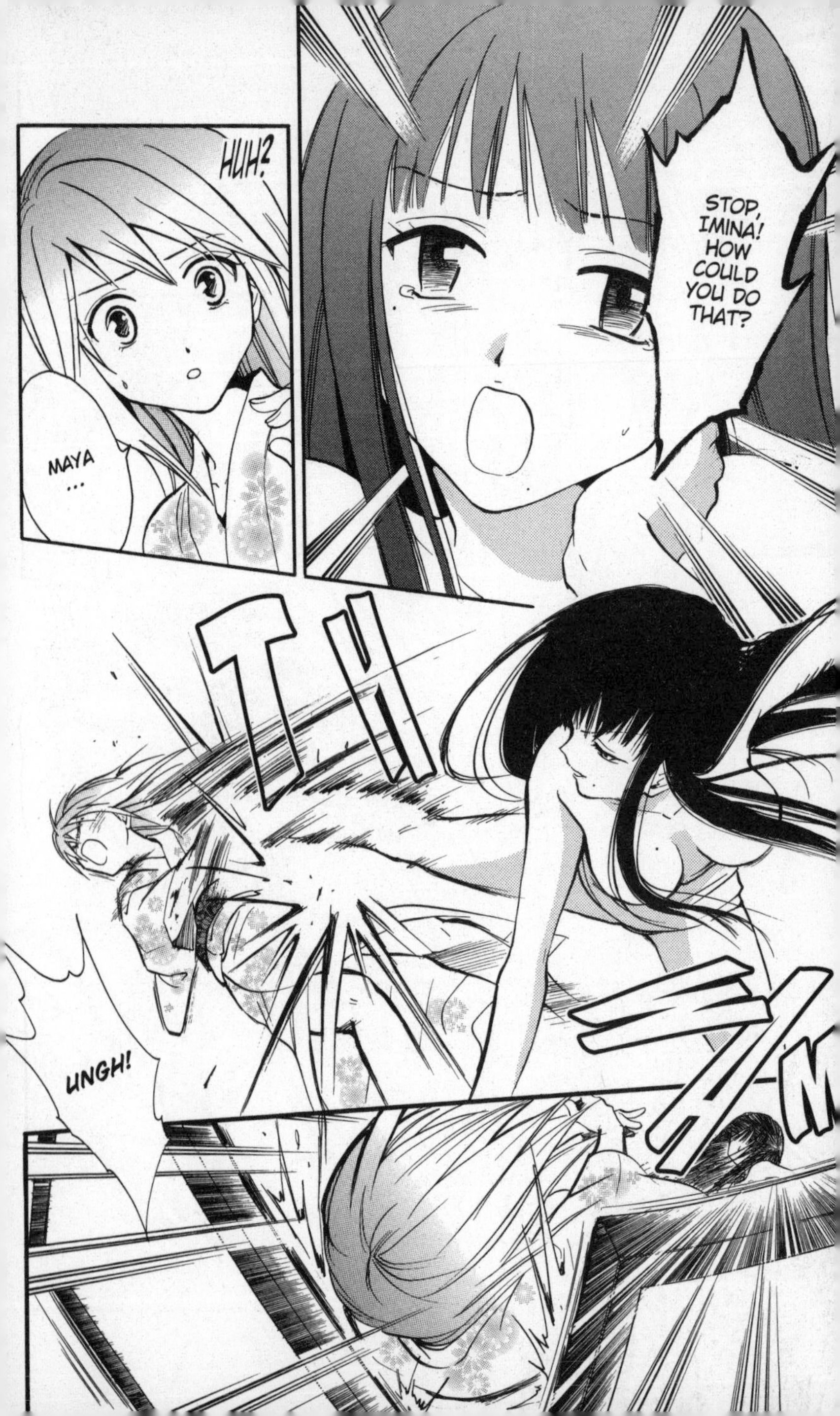
STOP, IMINA! HOW COULD YOU DO THAT?
HUH?
MAYA ...
THWAM
UNGH!

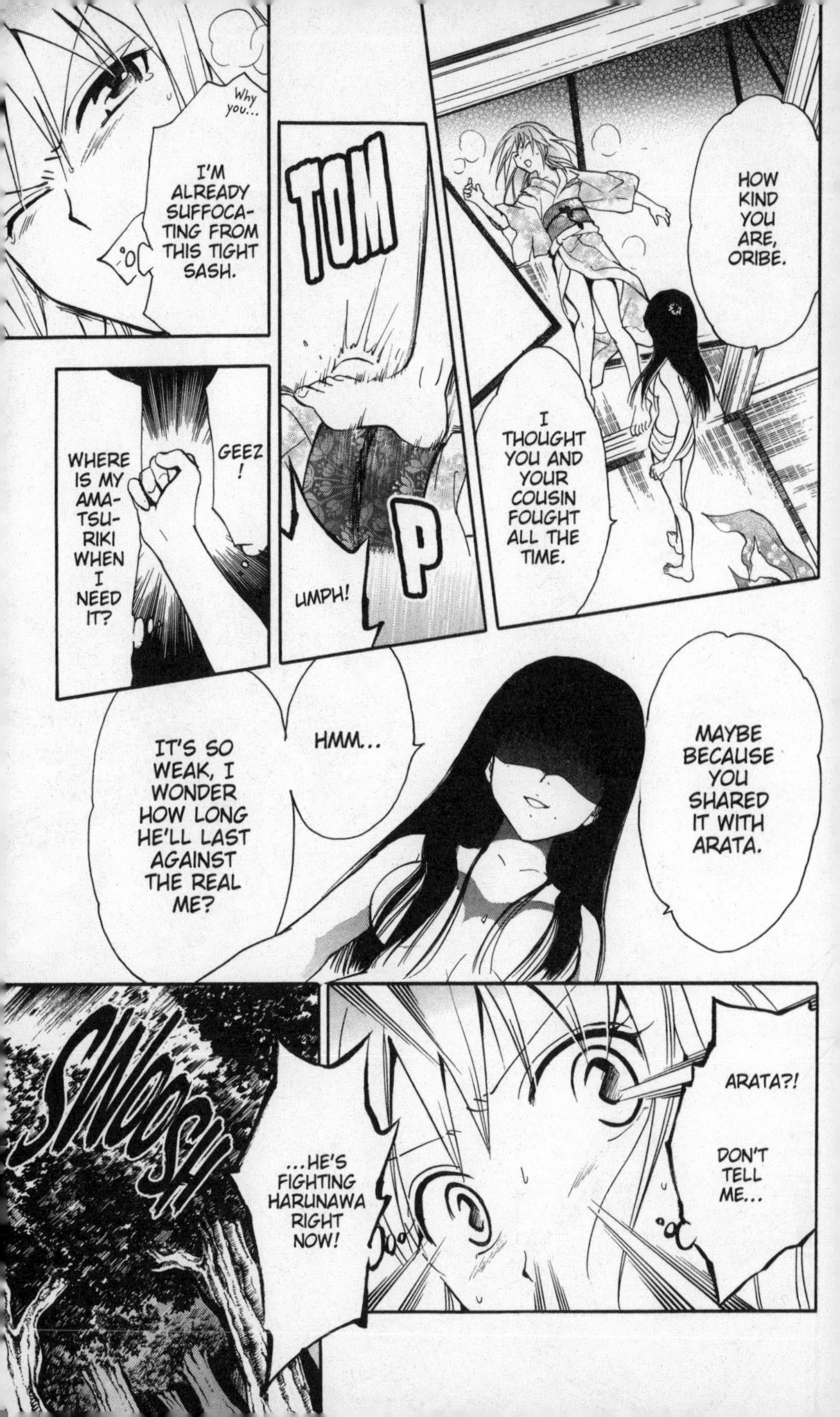
HOW KIND YOU ARE, ORIBE.
I THOUGHT YOU AND YOUR COUSIN FOUGHT ALL THE TIME.
TOM
P
UMPH!
Why you...
I'M ALREADY SUFFOCA-TING FROM THIS TIGHT SASH.
GEEZ!
WHERE IS MY AMA-TSU-RIKI WHEN I NEED IT?
MAYBE BECAUSE YOU SHARED IT WITH ARATA.
HMM...
IT'S SO WEAK, I WONDER HOW LONG HE'LL LAST AGAINST THE REAL ME?
ARATA?!
DON'T TELL ME...
...HE'S FIGHTING HARUNAWA RIGHT NOW!
SHOOSH

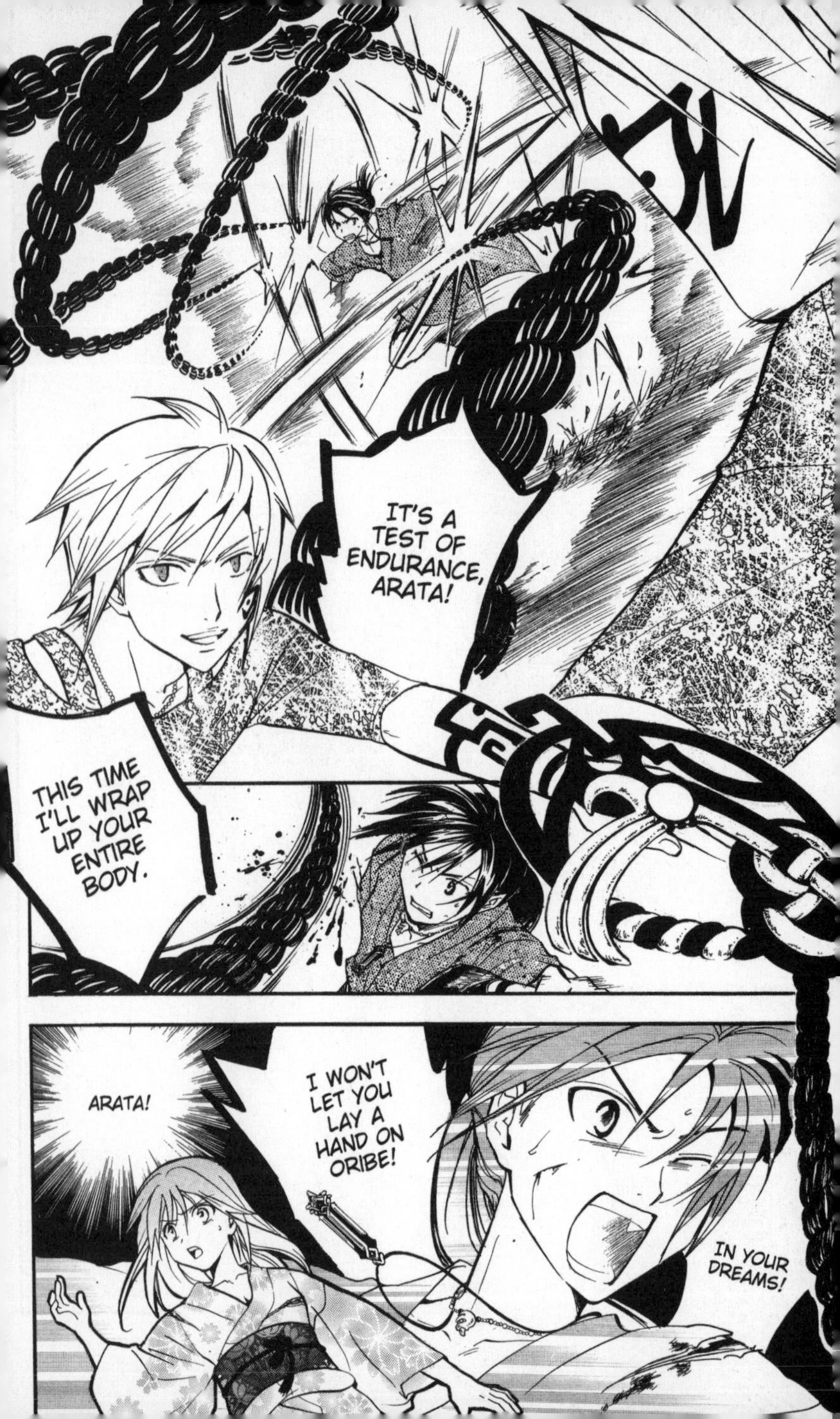
IT'S A TEST OF ENDURANCE, ARATA!
THIS TIME I'LL WRAP UP YOUR ENTIRE BODY.
I WON'T LET YOU LAY A HAND ON ORIBE!
ARATA!
IN YOUR DREAMS!

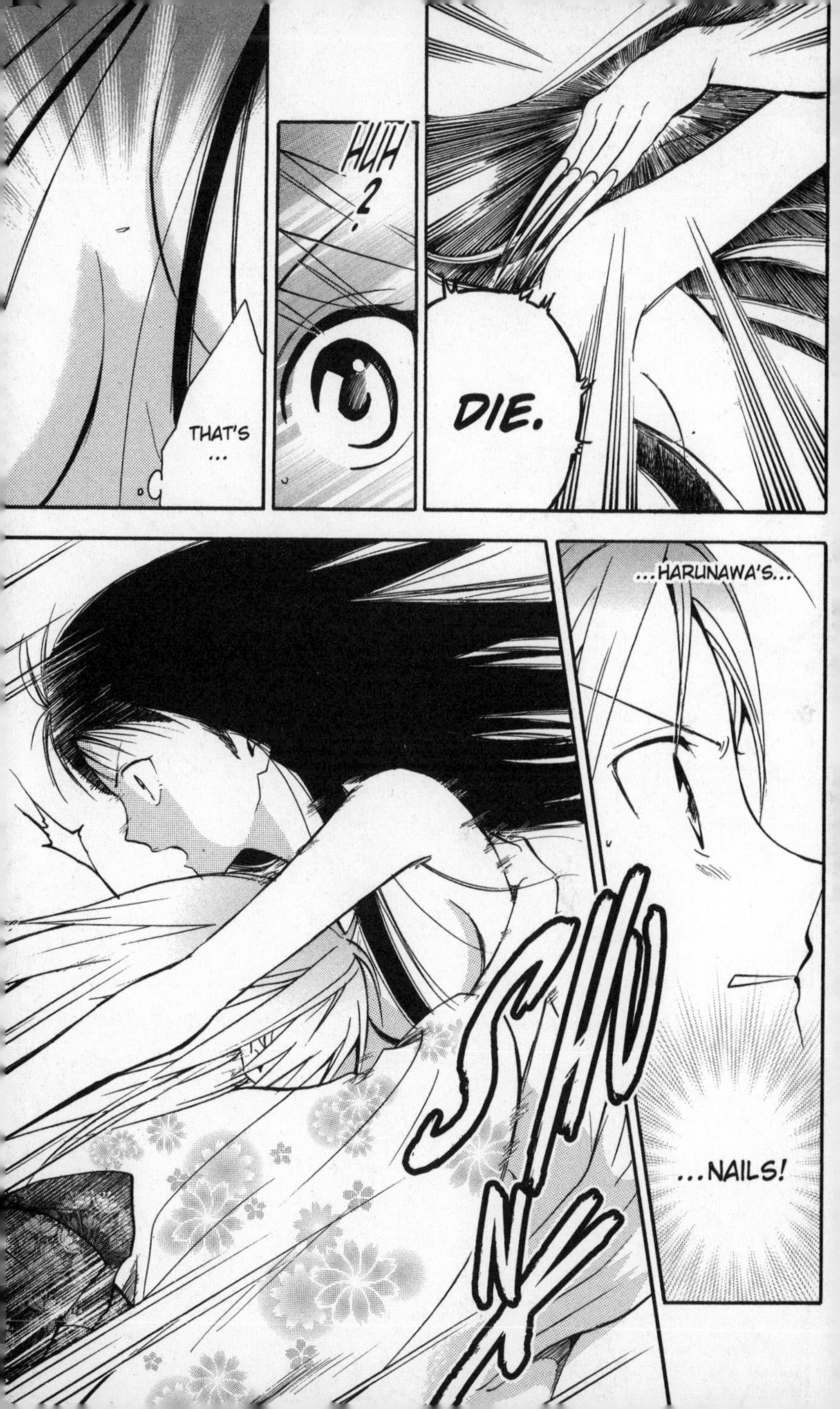
DIE.
HUH ?
THAT'S ...
...HARUNAWA'S...
...NAILS!
SHNK

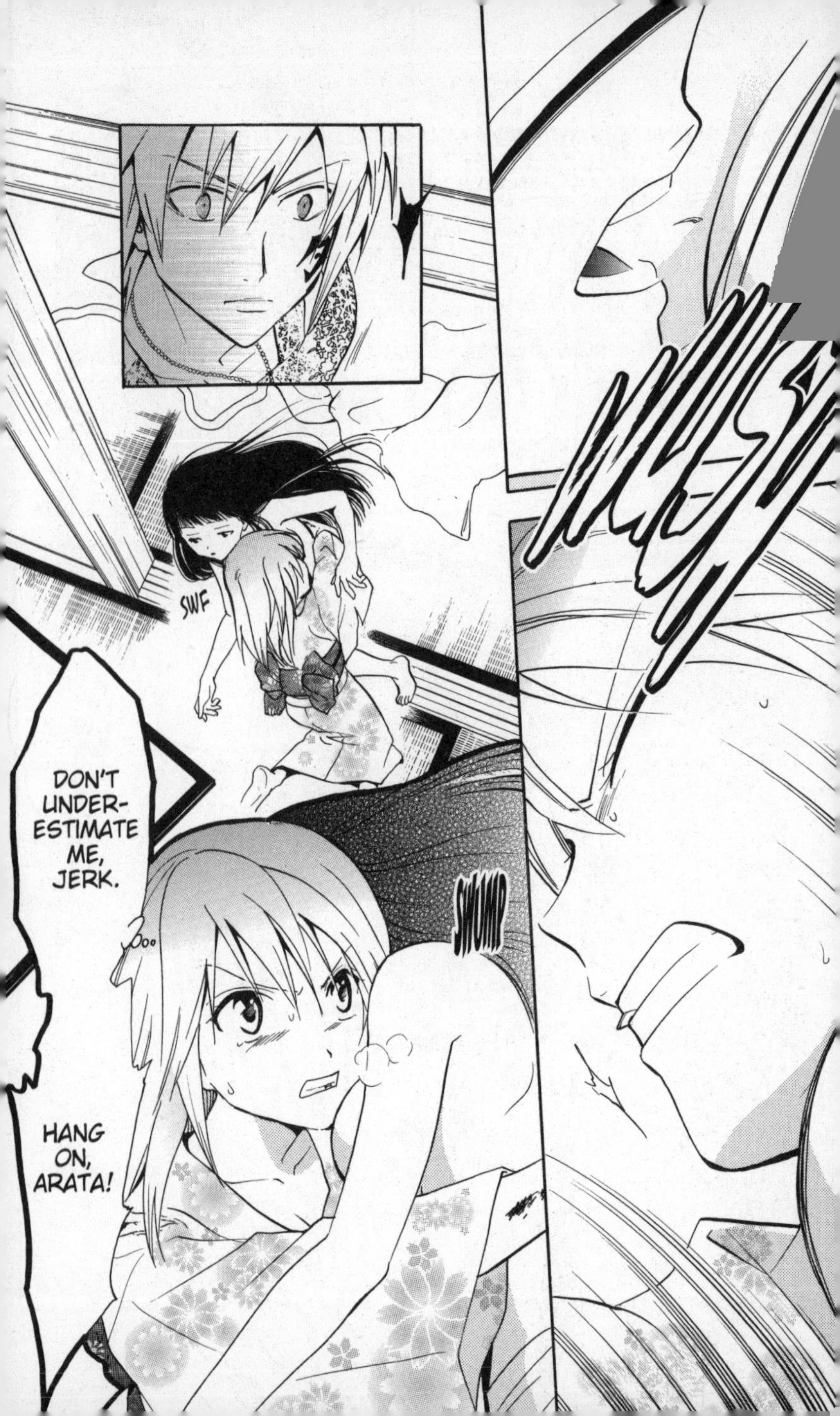
SWF
DON'T UNDER-ESTIMATE ME, JERK.
SWUMP
HANG ON, ARATA!

CHAPTER 169

ROCK AND MEMORY

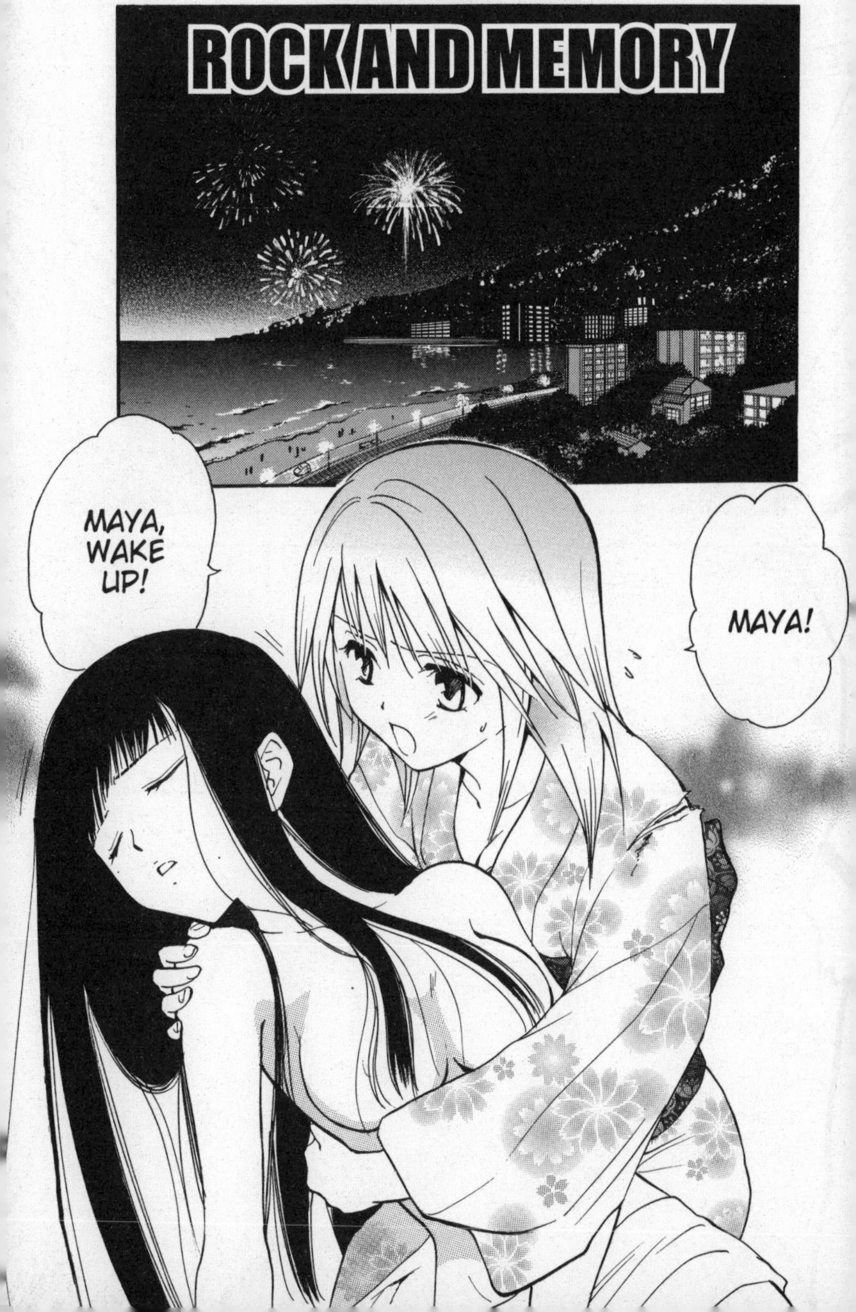
MAYA!
MAYA, WAKE UP!

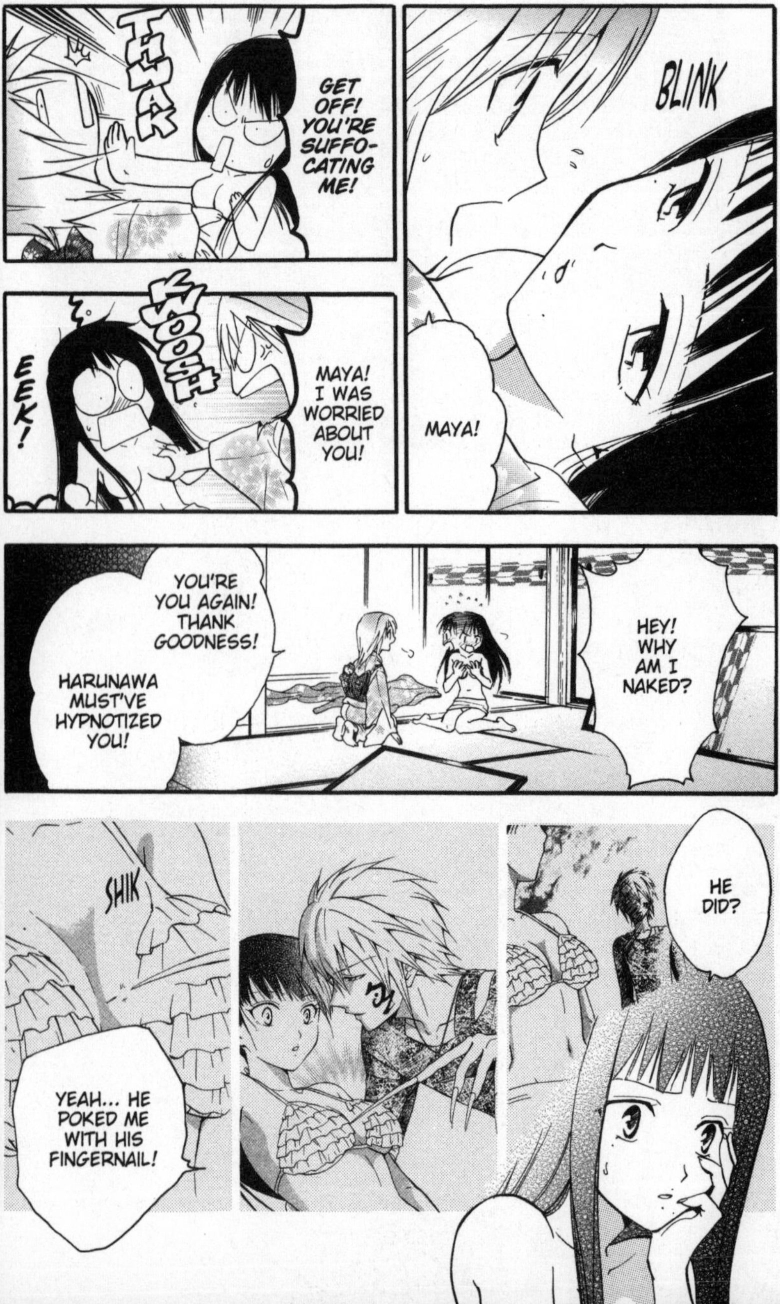
BLINK
MAYA!
THWAK
GET OFF! YOU'RE SUFFO-CATING ME!
MAYA! I WAS WORRIED ABOUT YOU!
KWOOSH
EEK!
HEY! WHY AM I NAKED?
YOU'RE YOU AGAIN! THANK GOODNESS!
HARUNAWA MUST'VE HYPNOTIZED YOU!
HE DID?
SHIK
YEAH... HE POKED ME WITH HIS FINGERNAIL!

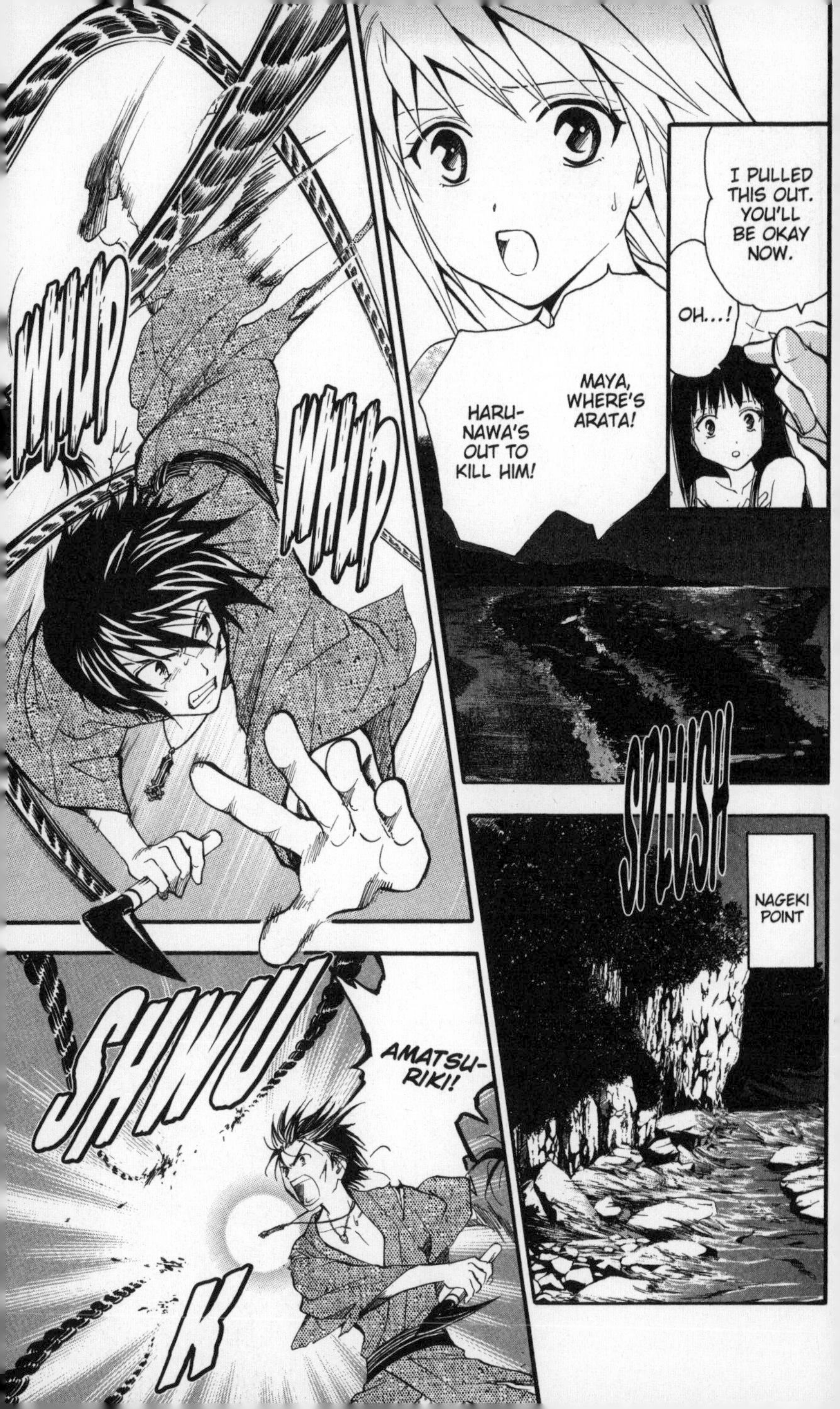

I PULLED THIS OUT. YOU'LL BE OKAY NOW.
OH...!
MAYA, WHERE'S ARATA!
HARU-NAWA'S OUT TO KILL HIM!
SPLUSH
NAGEKI POINT
WHUP
WHUP
SHWU
AMATSU-RIKI!
K

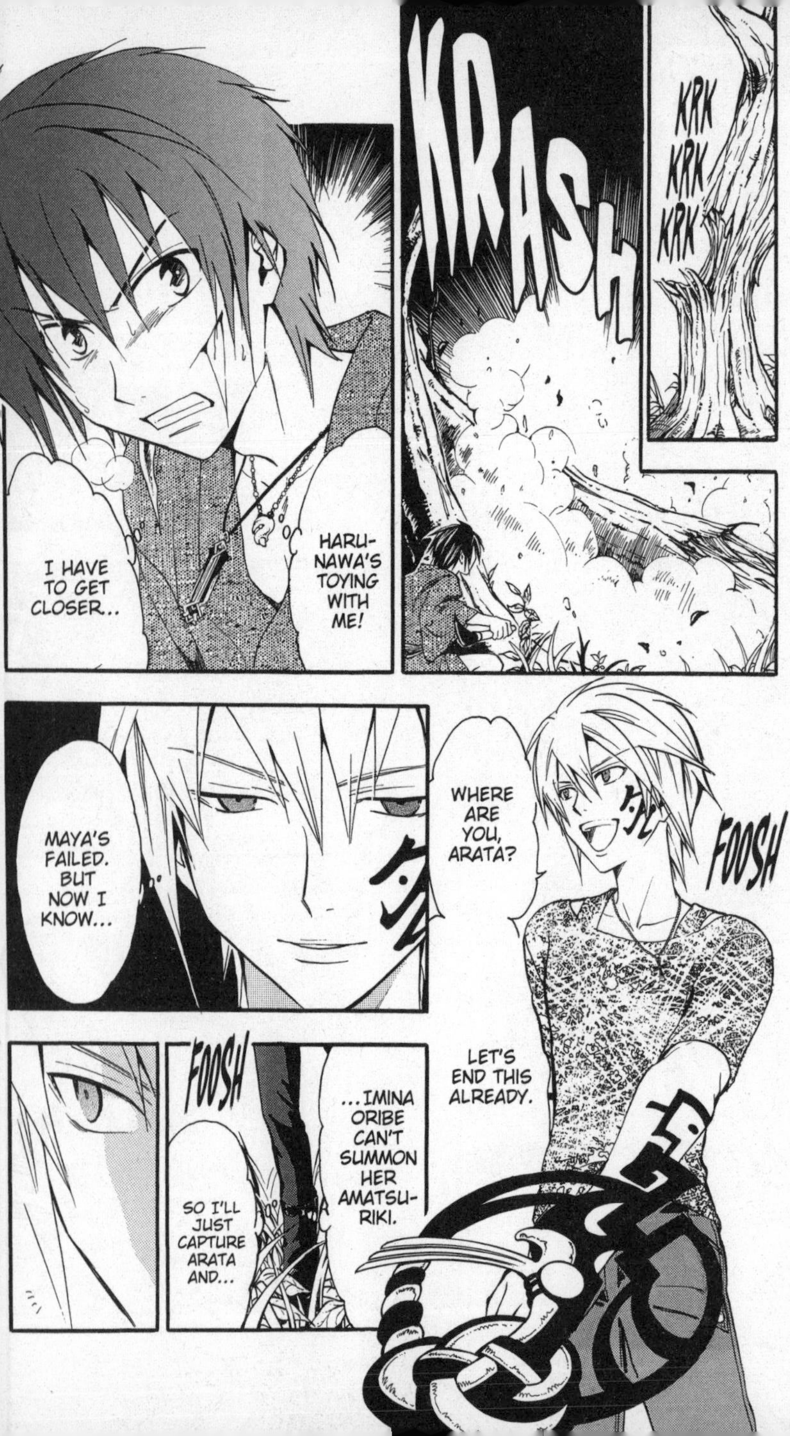
KRK
KRK
KRK
KRASH
HARU-NAWA'S TOYING WITH ME!
I HAVE TO GET CLOSER...
WHERE ARE YOU, ARATA?
FOOSH
LET'S END THIS ALREADY.
MAYA'S FAILED. BUT NOW I KNOW...
FOOSH
...IMINA ORIBE CAN'T SUMMON HER AMATSURIKI.
SO I'LL JUST CAPTURE ARATA AND...

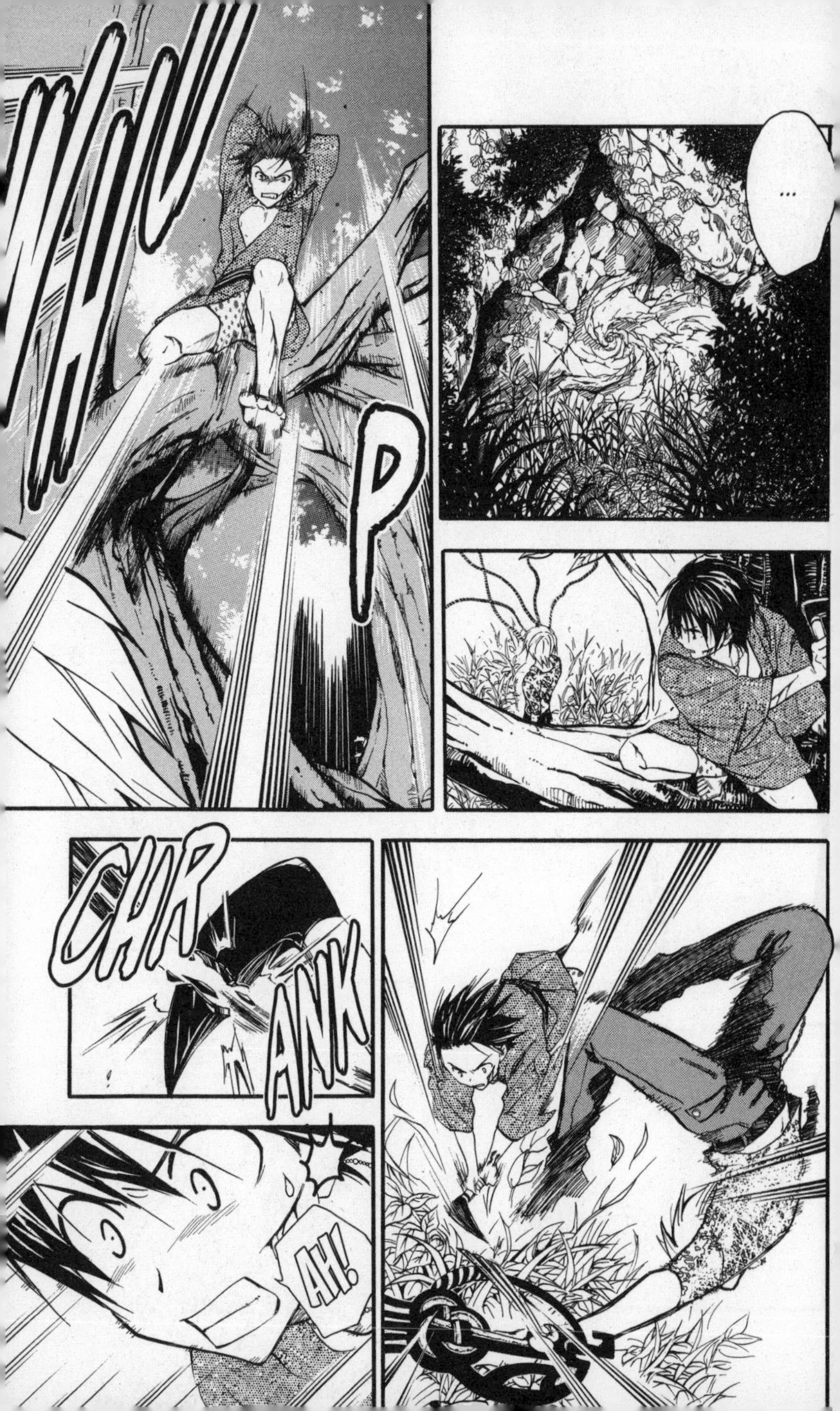
...
WHU
P
CHR
ANK
AH!

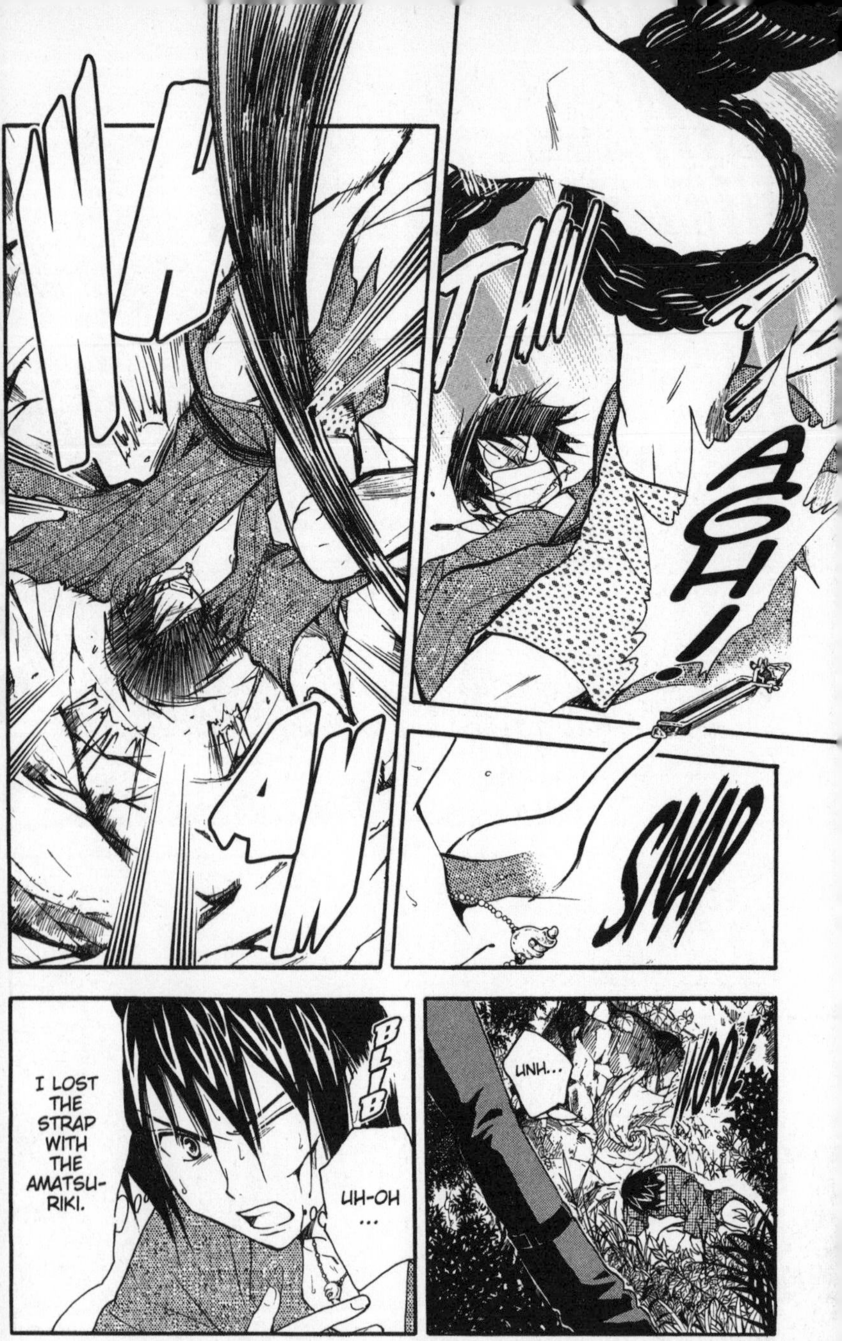
ASH!
SNAP
UNH...
I LOST THE STRAP WITH THE AMATSURIKI.
BLIB
UH-OH ...

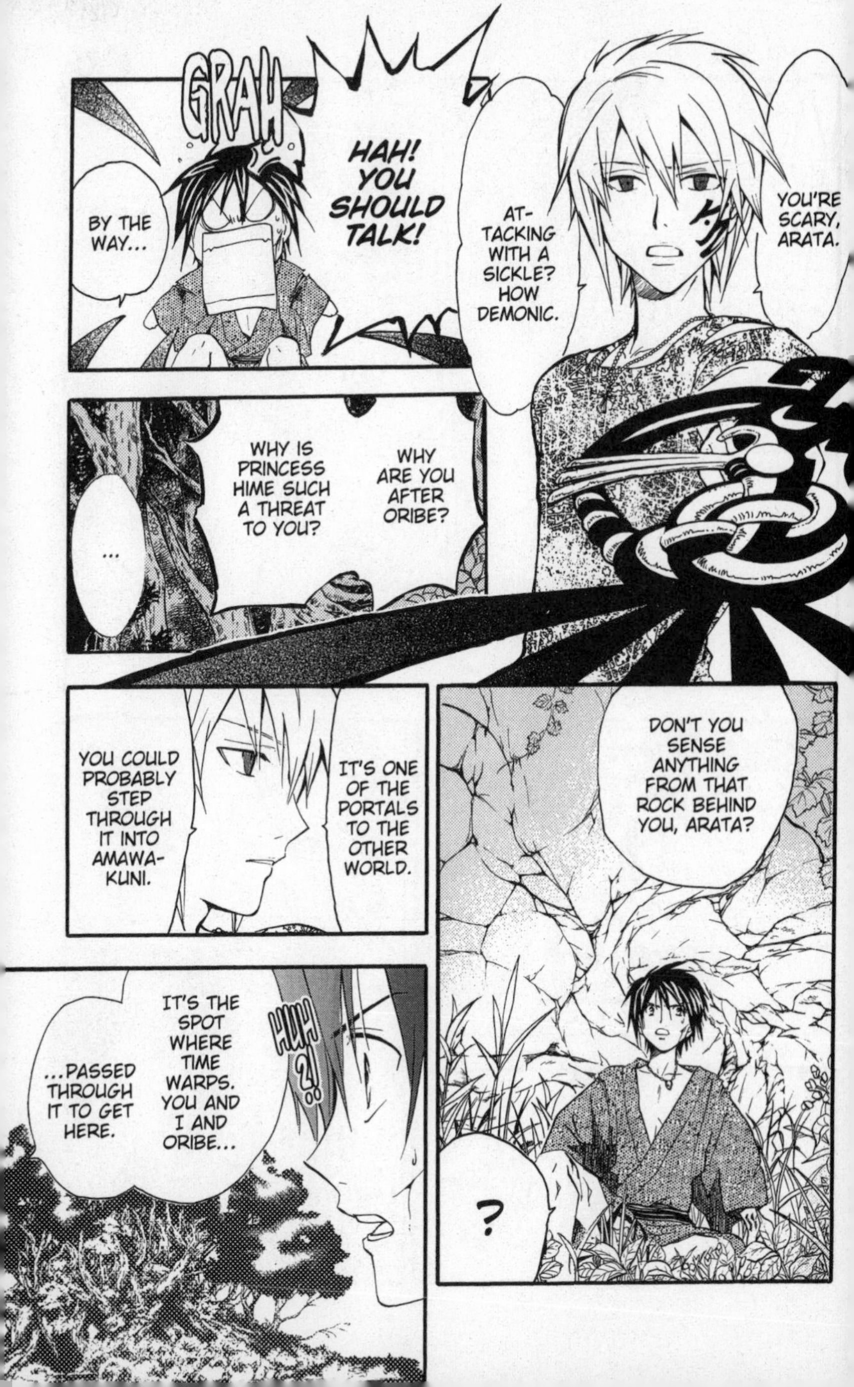
YOU'RE SCARY, ARATA.
AT-TACKING WITH A SICKLE? HOW DEMONIC.
GRAH
HAH! YOU SHOULD TALK!
BY THE WAY...
WHY ARE YOU AFTER ORIBE?
WHY IS PRINCESS HIME SUCH A THREAT TO YOU?
...
DON'T YOU SENSE ANYTHING FROM THAT ROCK BEHIND YOU, ARATA?
?
IT'S ONE OF THE PORTALS TO THE OTHER WORLD.
YOU COULD PROBABLY STEP THROUGH IT INTO AMAWA-KUNI.
HUH?!
IT'S THE SPOT WHERE TIME WARPS. YOU AND I AND ORIBE...
...PASSED THROUGH IT TO GET HERE.

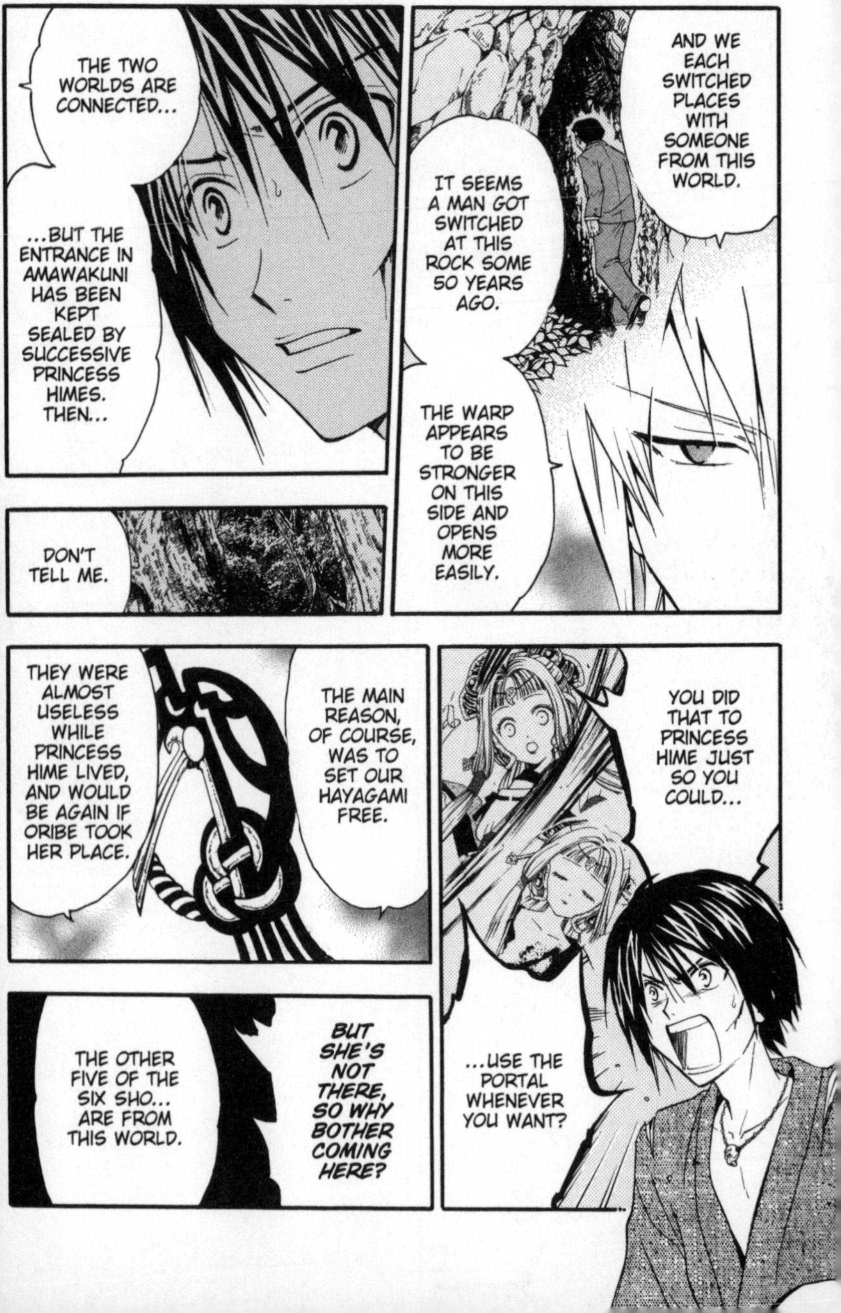
AND WE EACH SWITCHED PLACES WITH SOMEONE FROM THIS WORLD.
IT SEEMS A MAN GOT SWITCHED AT THIS ROCK SOME 50 YEARS AGO.
THE WARP APPEARS TO BE STRONGER ON THIS SIDE AND OPENS MORE EASILY.
THE TWO WORLDS ARE CONNECTED...
...BUT THE ENTRANCE IN AMAWAKUNI HAS BEEN KEPT SEALED BY SUCCESSIVE PRINCESS HIMES. THEN...
DON'T TELL ME.
YOU DID THAT TO PRINCESS HIME JUST SO YOU COULD...
...USE THE PORTAL WHENEVER YOU WANT?
THE MAIN REASON, OF COURSE, WAS TO SET OUR HAYAGAMI FREE.
THEY WERE ALMOST USELESS WHILE PRINCESS HIME LIVED, AND WOULD BE AGAIN IF ORIBE TOOK HER PLACE.
BUT SHE'S NOT THERE, SO WHY BOTHER COMING HERE?
THE OTHER FIVE OF THE SIX SHO... ARE FROM THIS WORLD.

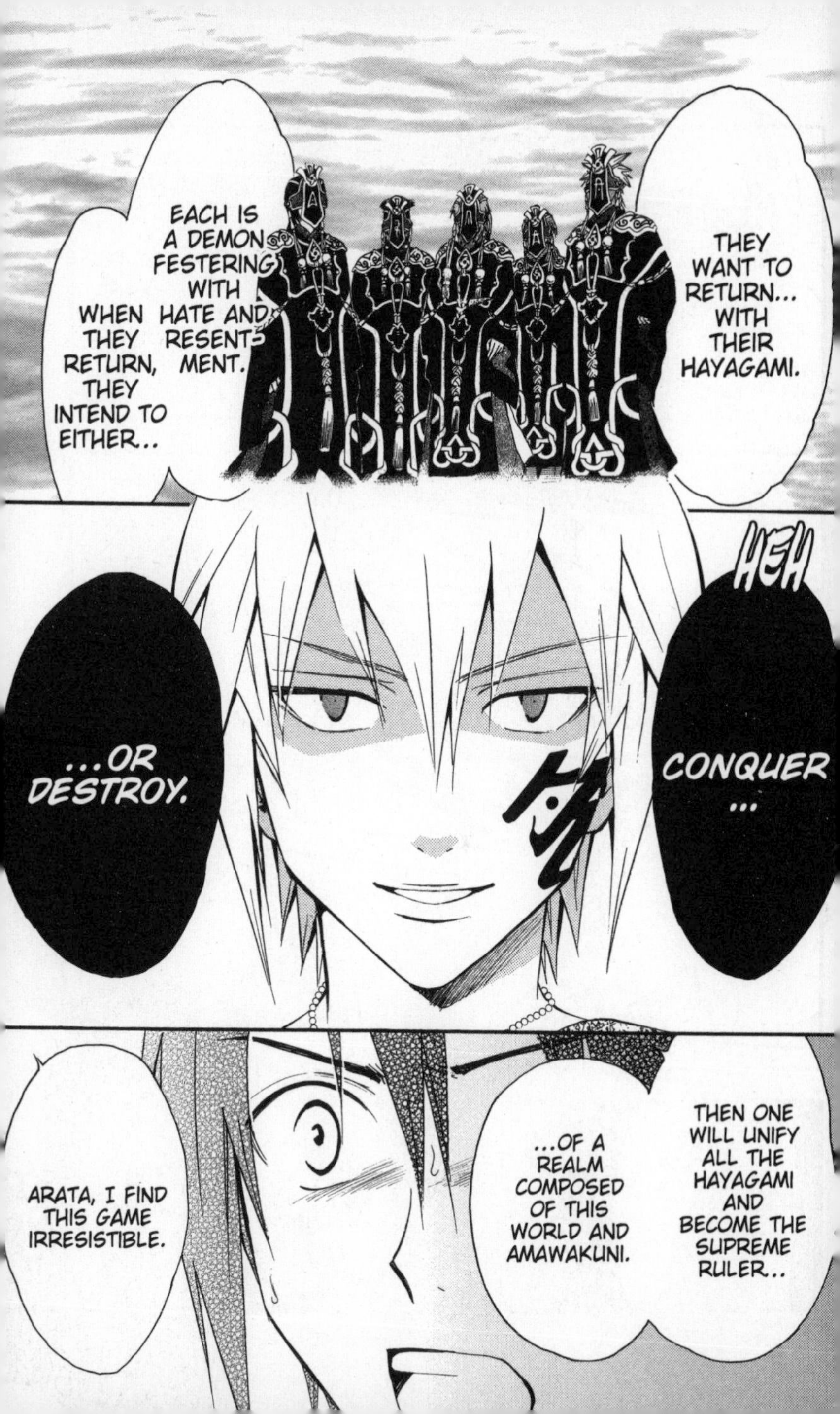
THEY WANT TO RETURN... WITH THEIR HAYAGAMI.
EACH IS A DEMON FESTERING WITH HATE AND RESENT-MENT.
WHEN THEY RETURN, THEY INTEND TO EITHER...
HEH
CONQUER...
...OR DESTROY.
THEN ONE WILL UNIFY ALL THE HAYAGAMI AND BECOME THE SUPREME RULER..
...OF A REALM COMPOSED OF THIS WORLD AND AMAWAKUNI.
ARATA, I FIND THIS GAME IRRESISTIBLE.

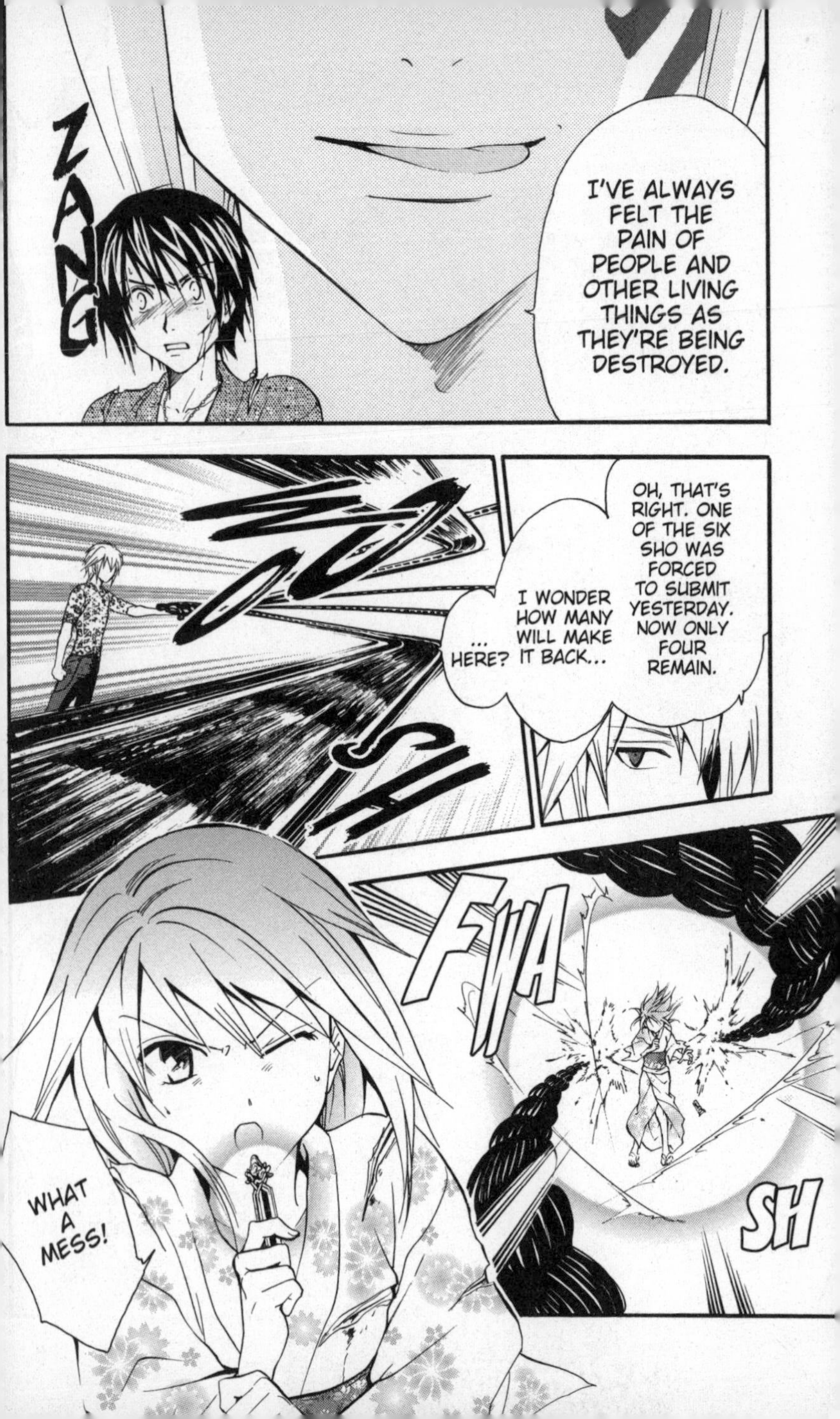
ZANG
I'VE ALWAYS FELT THE PAIN OF PEOPLE AND OTHER LIVING THINGS AS THEY'RE BEING DESTROYED.
OH, THAT'S RIGHT. ONE OF THE SIX SHO WAS FORCED TO SUBMIT YESTERDAY. NOW ONLY FOUR REMAIN.
I WONDER HOW MANY WILL MAKE IT BACK...
... HERE?
FWA
SH
WHAT A MESS!

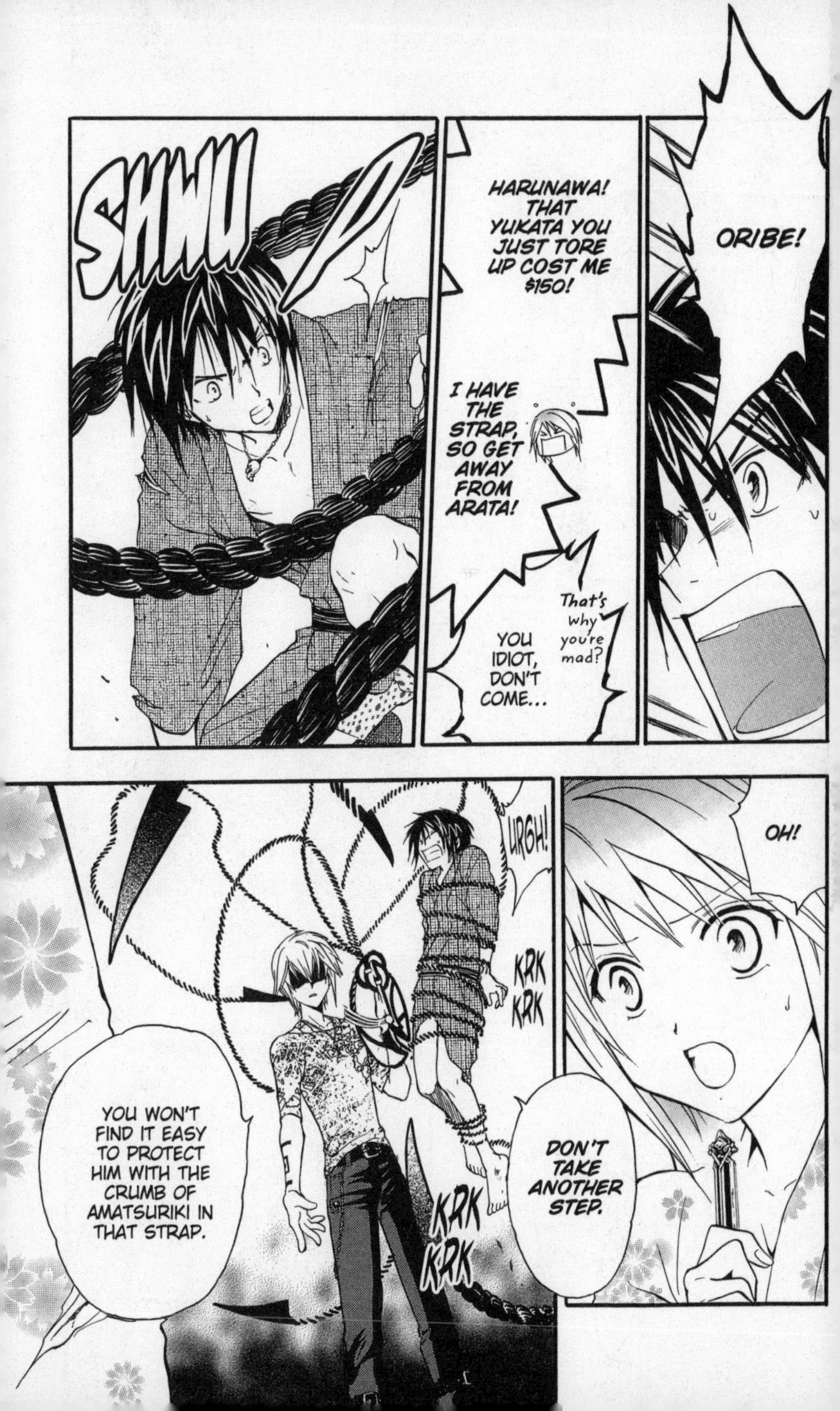
ORIBE!
HARUNAWA! THAT YUKATA YOU JUST TORE UP COST ME $150!
I HAVE THE STRAP, SO GET AWAY FROM ARATA!
That's why you're mad?
YOU IDIOT, DON'T COME...
SHWU
OH!
DON'T TAKE ANOTHER STEP.
URGH!
KRK KRK
YOU WON'T FIND IT EASY TO PROTECT HIM WITH THE CRUMB OF AMATSURIKI IN THAT STRAP.
KRK KRK

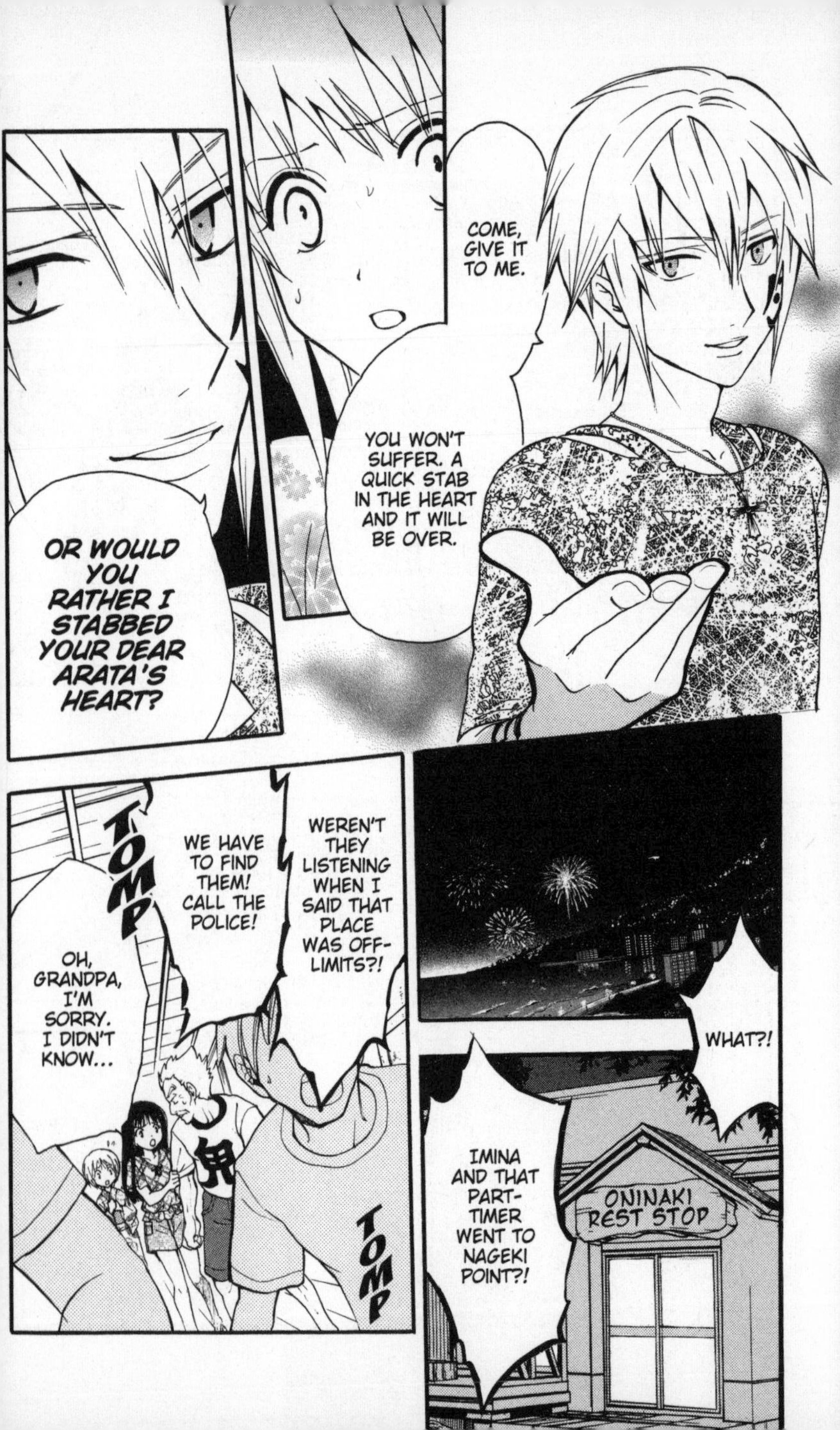
COME, GIVE IT TO ME.
YOU WON'T SUFFER. A QUICK STAB IN THE HEART AND IT WILL BE OVER.
OR WOULD YOU RATHER I STABBED YOUR DEAR ARATA'S HEART?
WHAT?!
ONINAKI REST STOP
IMINA AND THAT PART-TIMER WENT TO NAGEKI POINT?!
WEREN'T THEY LISTENING WHEN I SAID THAT PLACE WAS OFF-LIMITS?!
WE HAVE TO FIND THEM! CALL THE POLICE!
TOMP
OH, GRANDPA, I'M SORRY. I DIDN'T KNOW...
TOMP

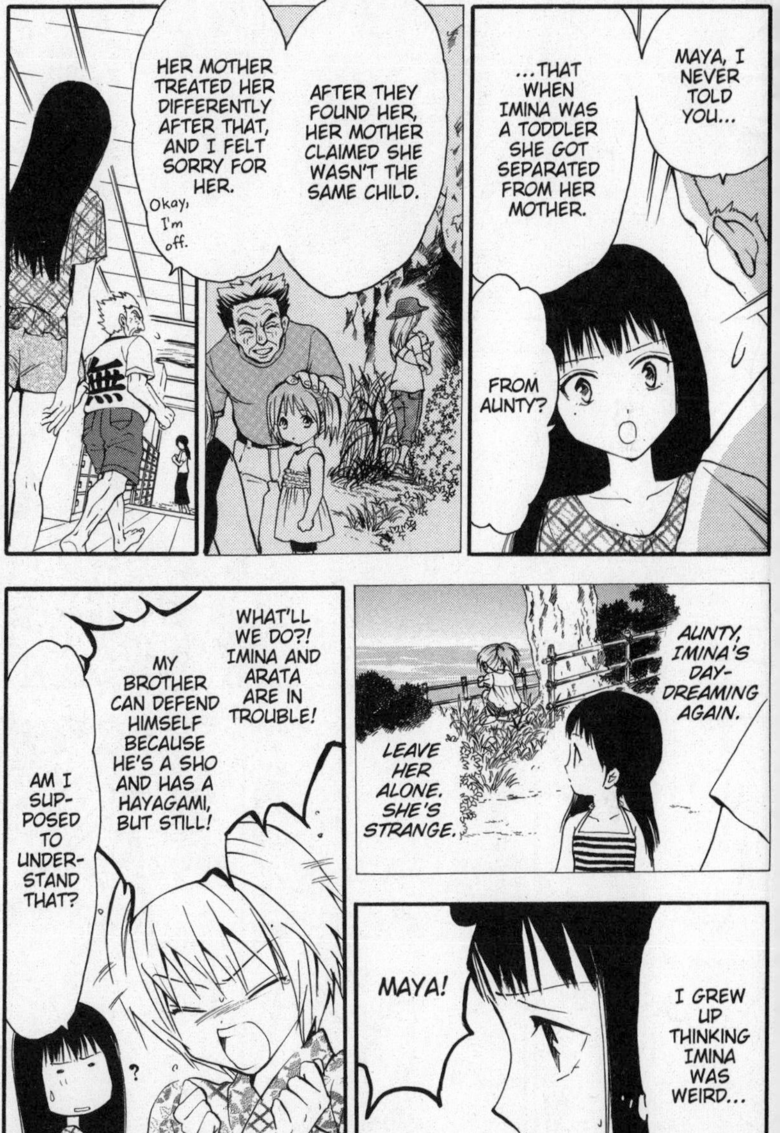
MAYA, I NEVER TOLD YOU...
...THAT WHEN IMINA WAS A TODDLER SHE GOT SEPARATED FROM HER MOTHER.
FROM AUNTY?
AFTER THEY FOUND HER, HER MOTHER CLAIMED SHE WASN'T THE SAME CHILD.
HER MOTHER TREATED HER DIFFERENTLY AFTER THAT, AND I FELT SORRY FOR HER.
Okay, I'm off.
AUNTY, IMINA'S DAY-DREAMING AGAIN.
LEAVE HER ALONE. SHE'S STRANGE.
I GREW UP THINKING IMINA WAS WEIRD...
MAYA!
WHAT'LL WE DO?! IMINA AND ARATA ARE IN TROUBLE!
MY BROTHER CAN DEFEND HIMSELF BECAUSE HE'S A SHO AND HAS A HAYAGAMI, BUT STILL!
AM I SUP-POSED TO UNDER-STAND THAT?
?

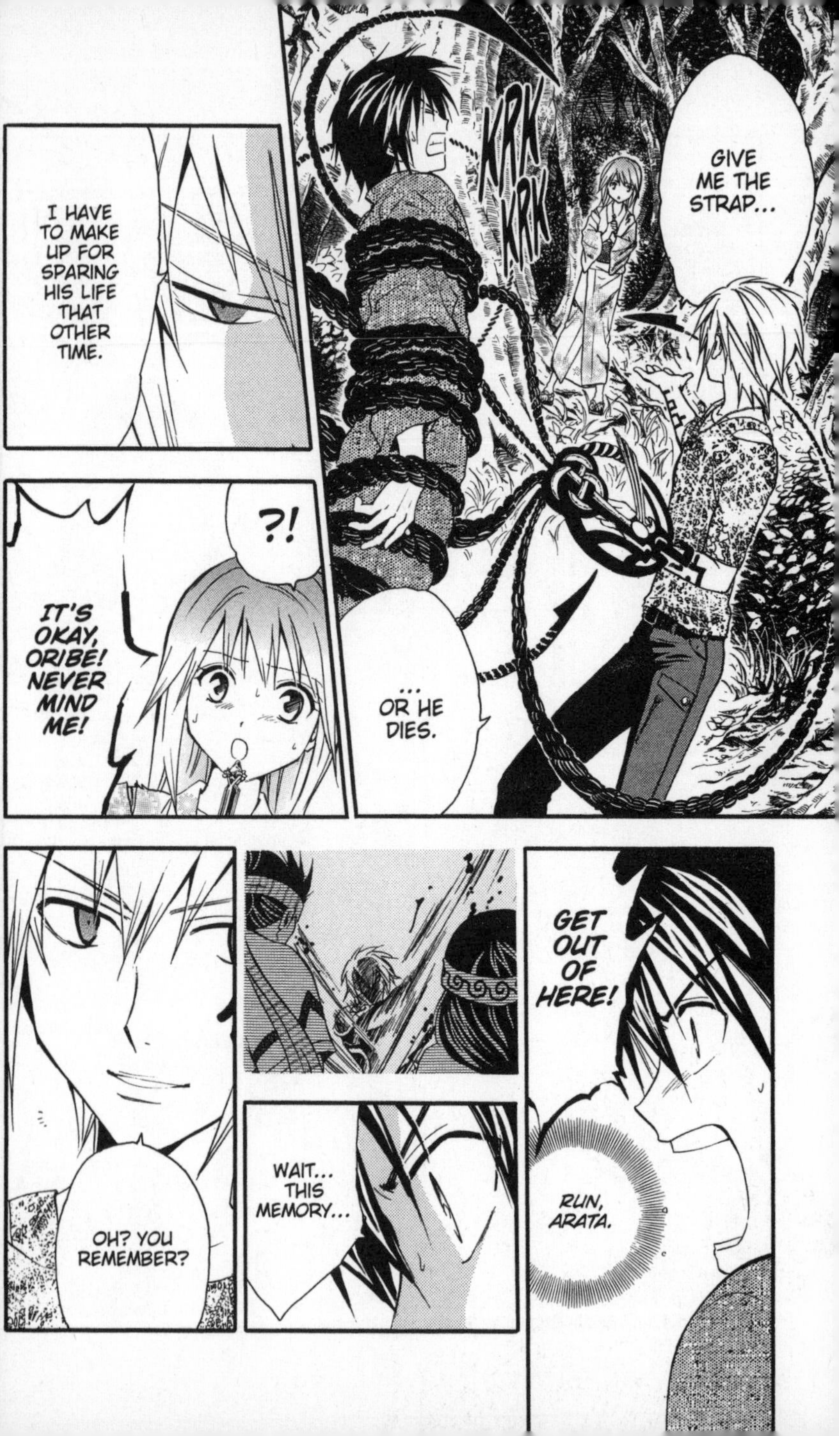
KRK KRK
GIVE ME THE STRAP...
... OR HE DIES.
I HAVE TO MAKE UP FOR SPARING HIS LIFE THAT OTHER TIME.
?!
IT'S OKAY, ORIBE! NEVER MIND ME!
GET OUT OF HERE!
RUN, ARATA.
WAIT... THIS MEMORY...
OH? YOU REMEMBER?

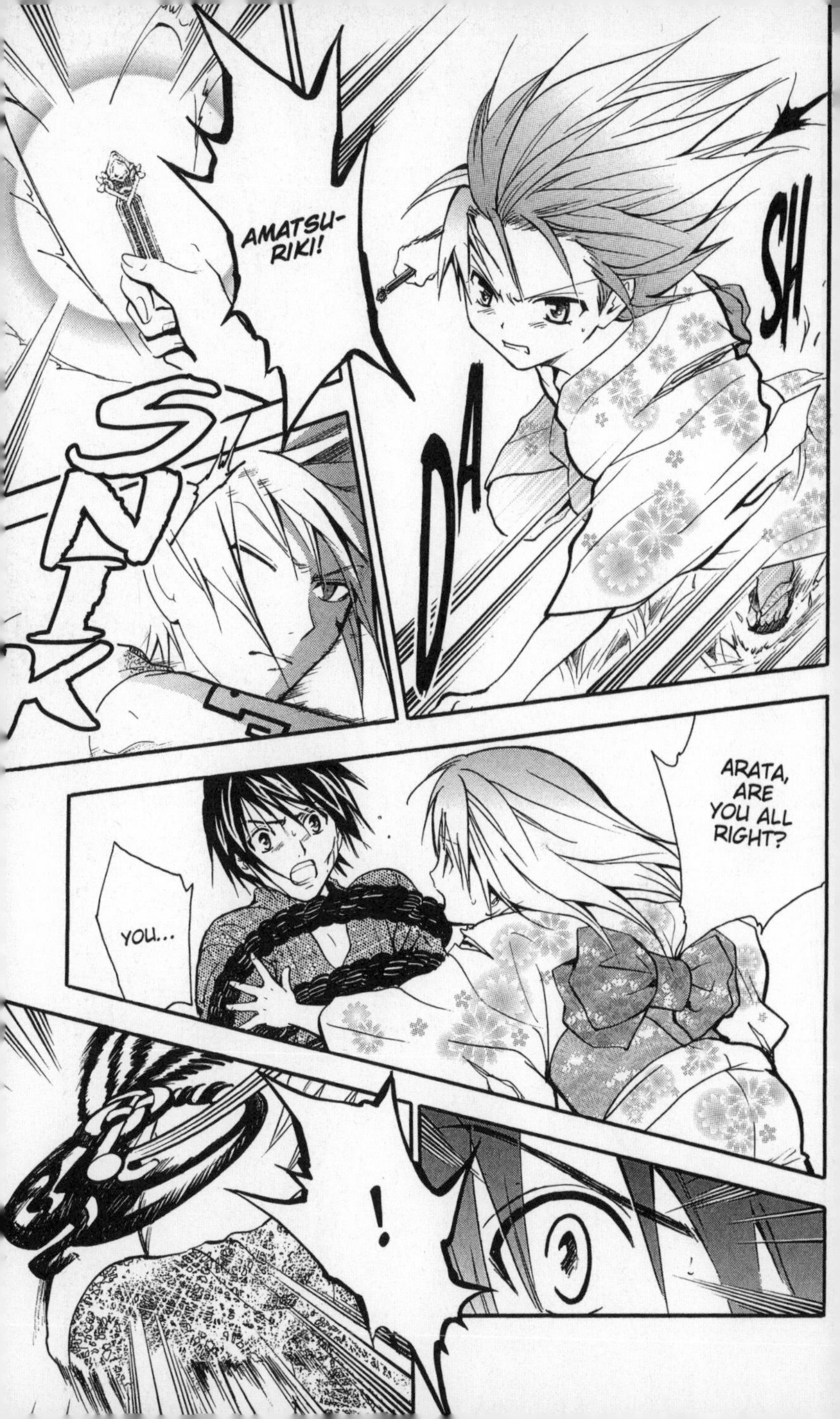
DA
SH
AMATSU-RIKI!
SNIK
ARATA, ARE YOU ALL RIGHT?
YOU...
!

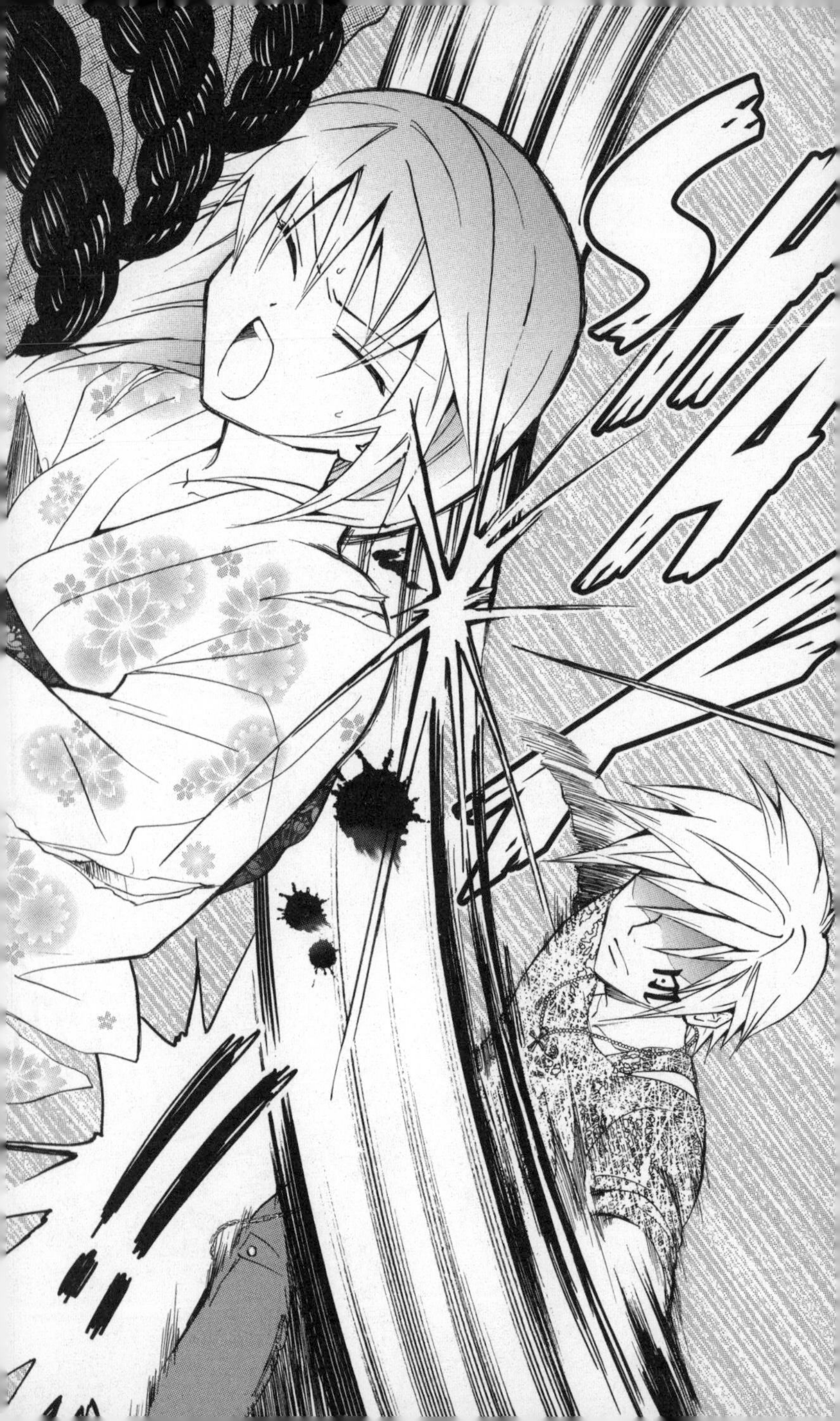

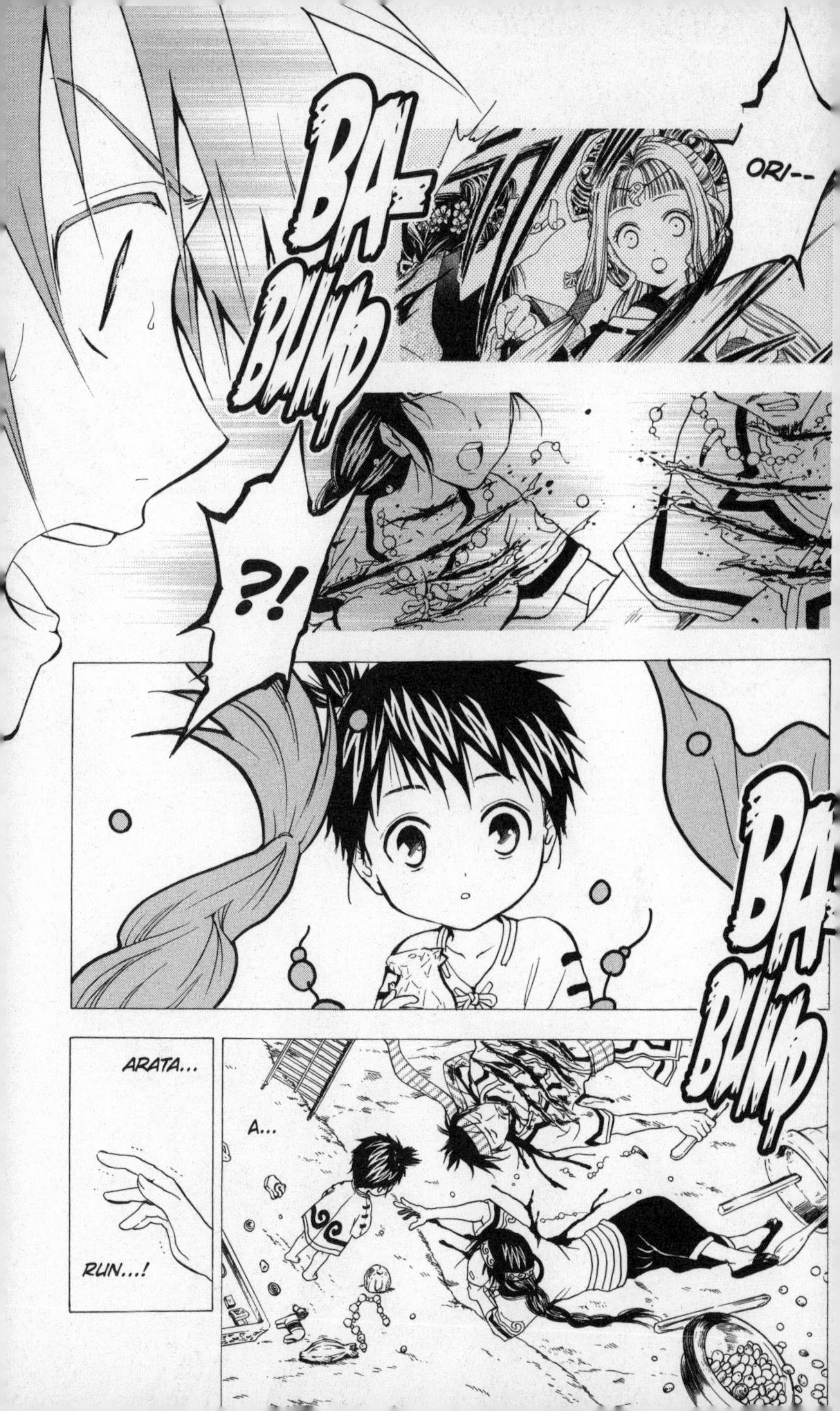
ORI--
BA-BUMP
?!
BA-BUMP
A...
ARATA...
RUN...!

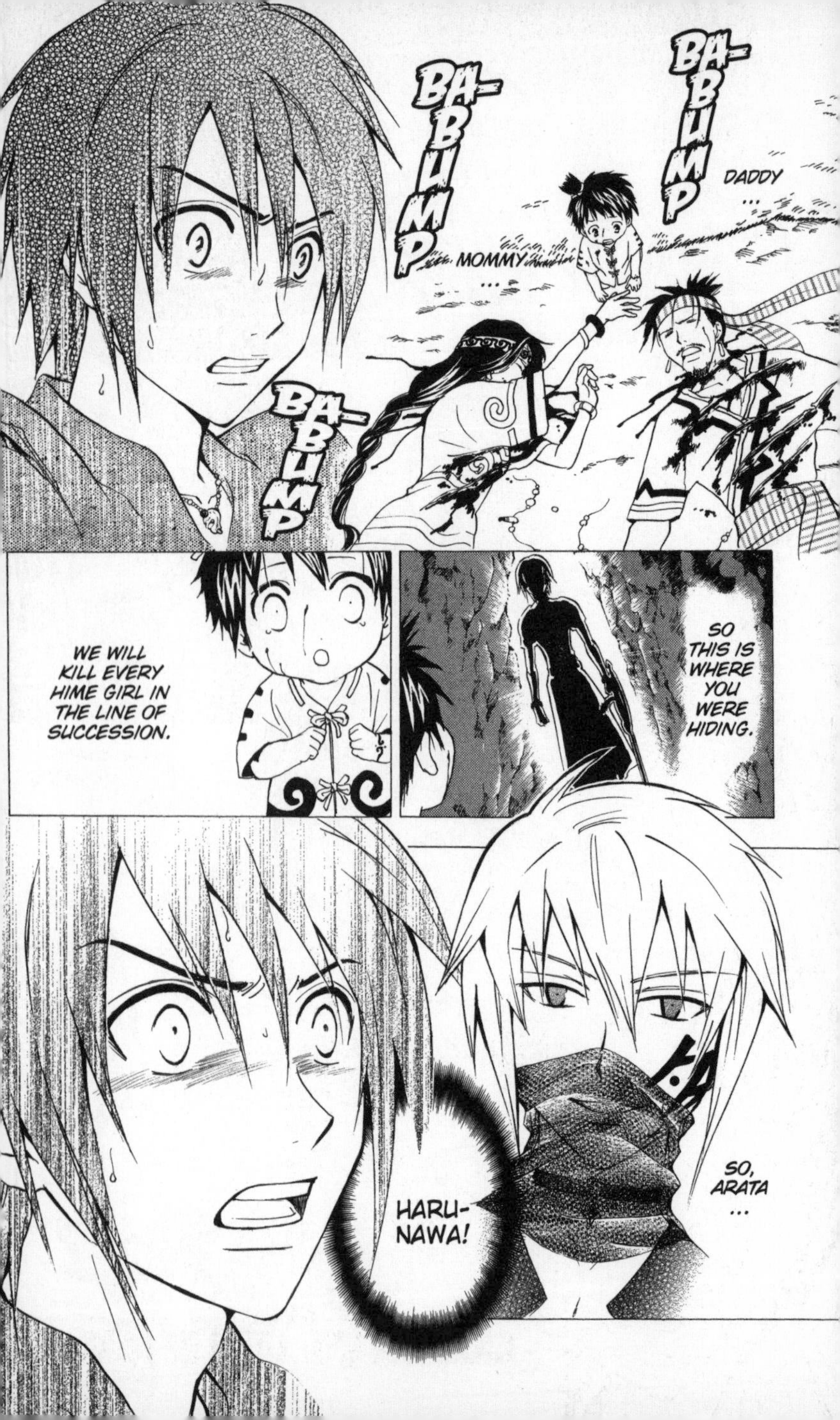
BA-BUMP
DADDY ...
BA-BUMP
MOMMY ...
BA-BUMP
SO THIS IS WHERE YOU WERE HIDING.
WE WILL KILL EVERY HIME GIRL IN THE LINE OF SUCCESSION.
SO, ARATA ...
HARUNAWA!

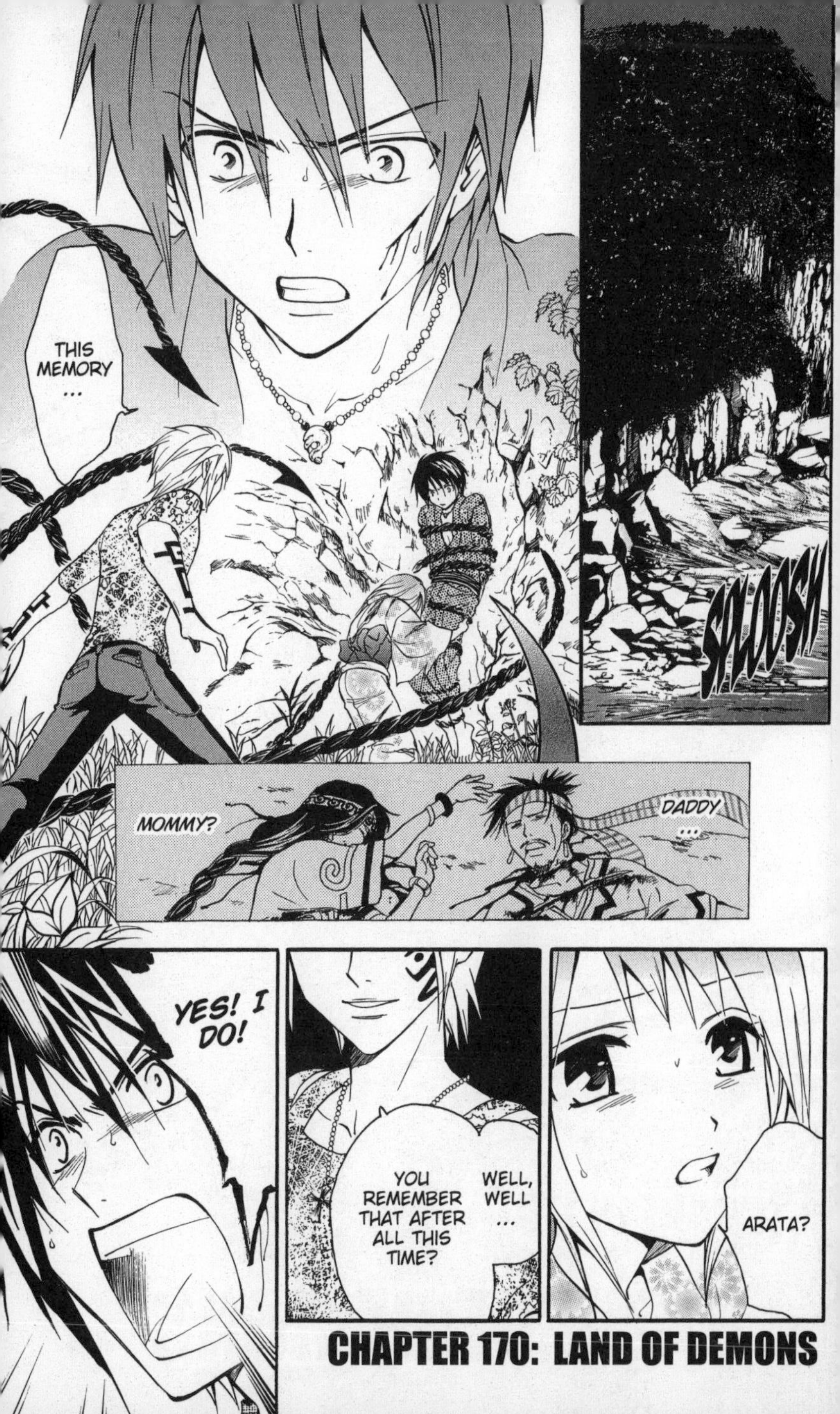
SPLOOSH
THIS MEMORY ...
DADDY ...
MOMMY?
ARATA?
WELL, WELL ...
YOU REMEMBER THAT AFTER ALL THIS TIME?
YES! I DO!

CHAPTER 170: LAND OF DEMONS

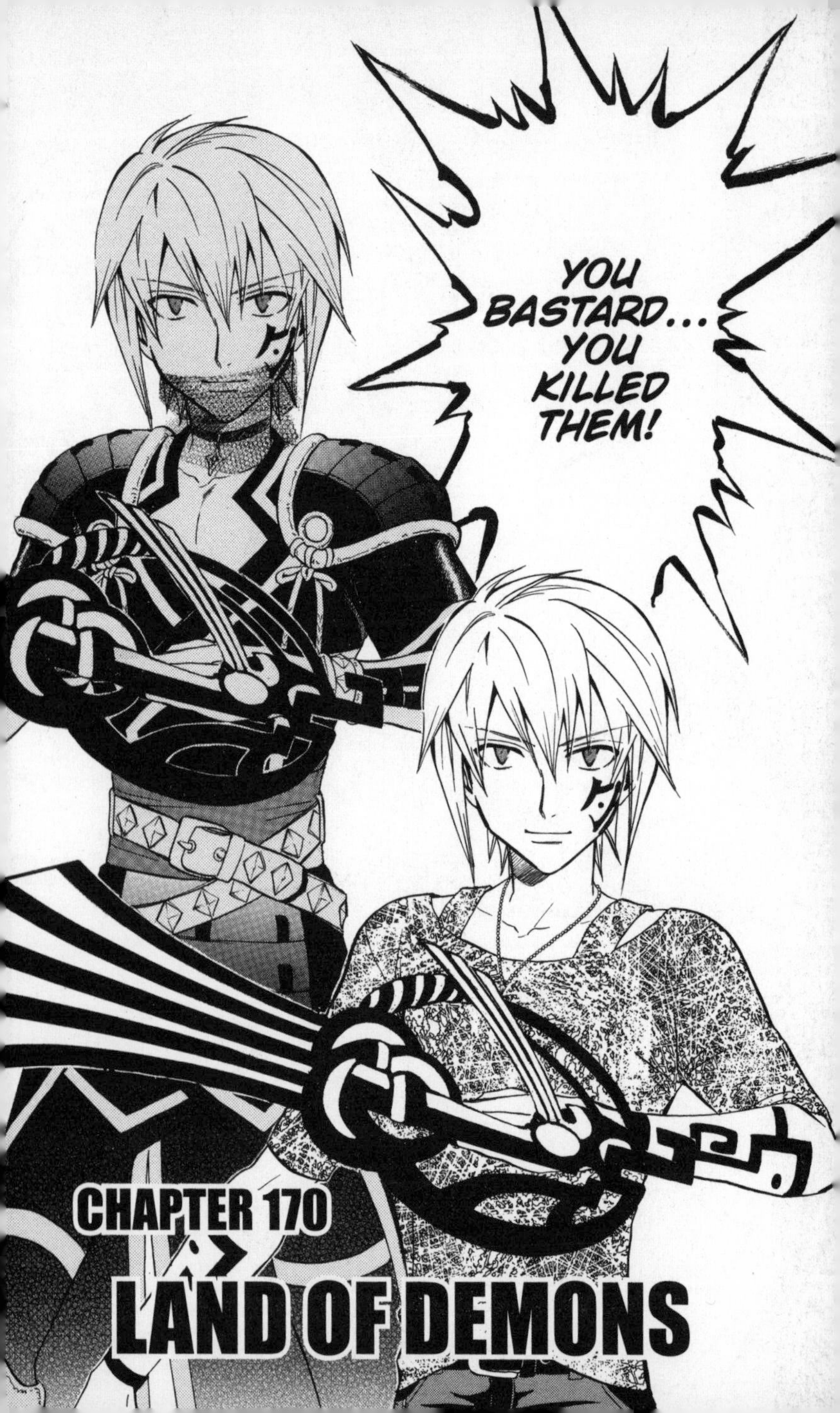
YOU BASTARD... YOU KILLED THEM!
CHAPTER 170
LAND OF DEMONS

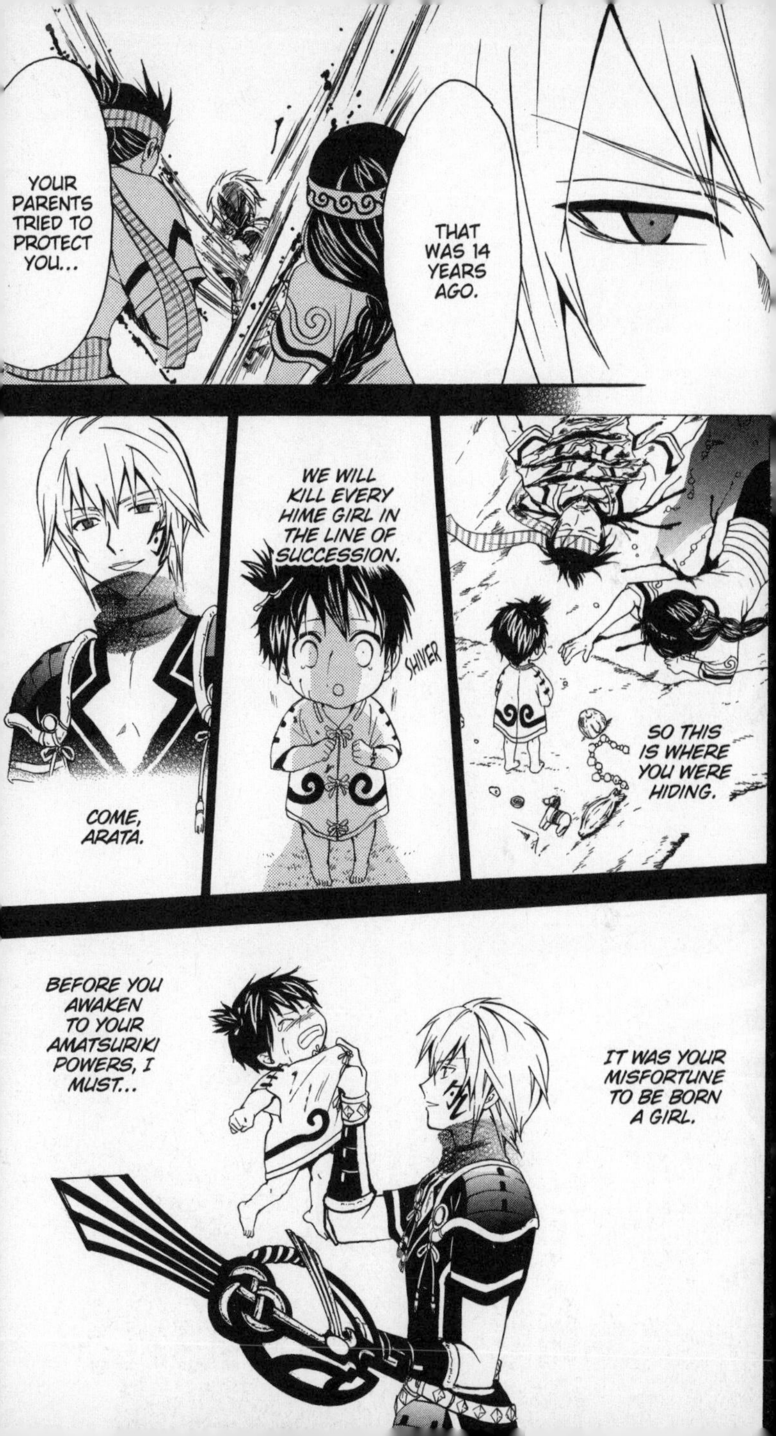
THAT WAS 14 YEARS AGO.
YOUR PARENTS TRIED TO PROTECT YOU...
SO THIS IS WHERE YOU WERE HIDING.
WE WILL KILL EVERY HIME GIRL IN THE LINE OF SUCCESSION.
SHIVER
COME, ARATA.
IT WAS YOUR MISFORTUNE TO BE BORN A GIRL.
BEFORE YOU AWAKEN TO YOUR AMATSURIKI POWERS, I MUST...

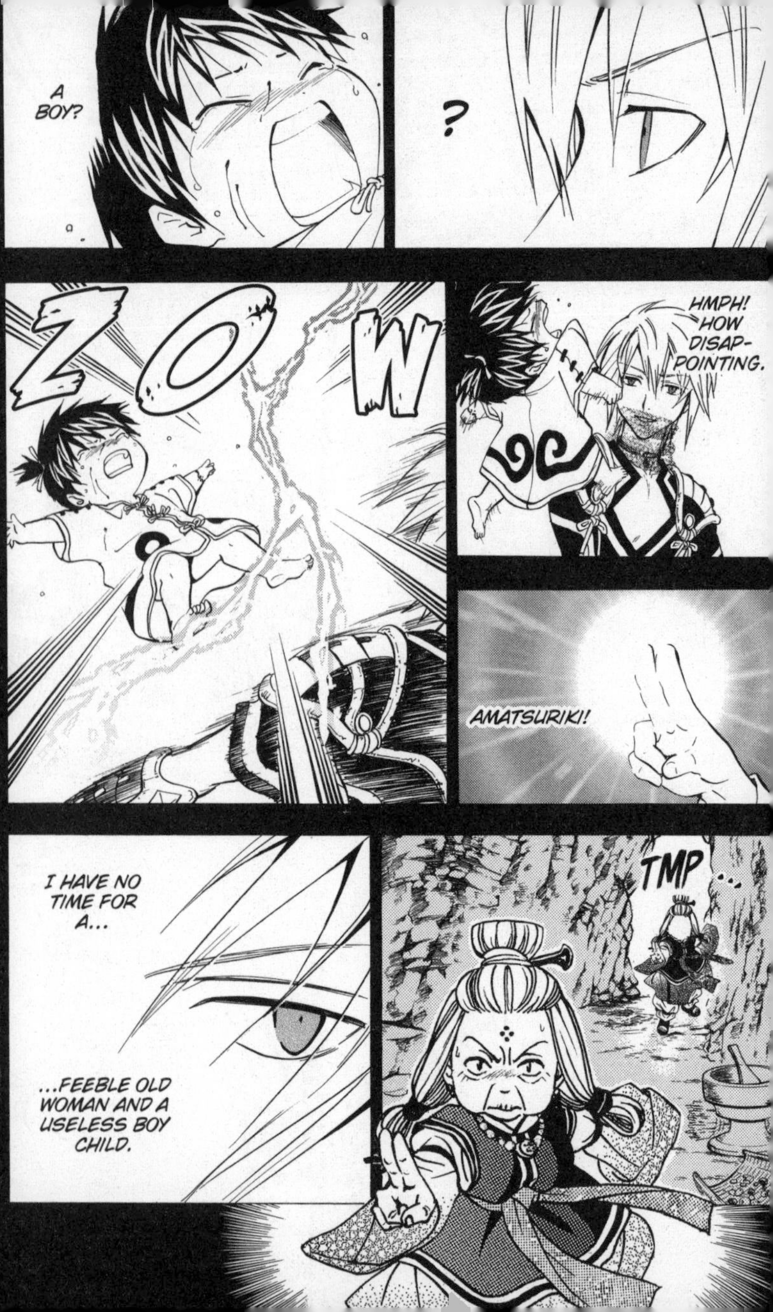
?
A BOY?
HMPH! HOW DISAP-POINTING.
AMATSURIKI!
ZOW
TMP...
I HAVE NO TIME FOR A...
...FEEBLE OLD WOMAN AND A USELESS BOY CHILD.

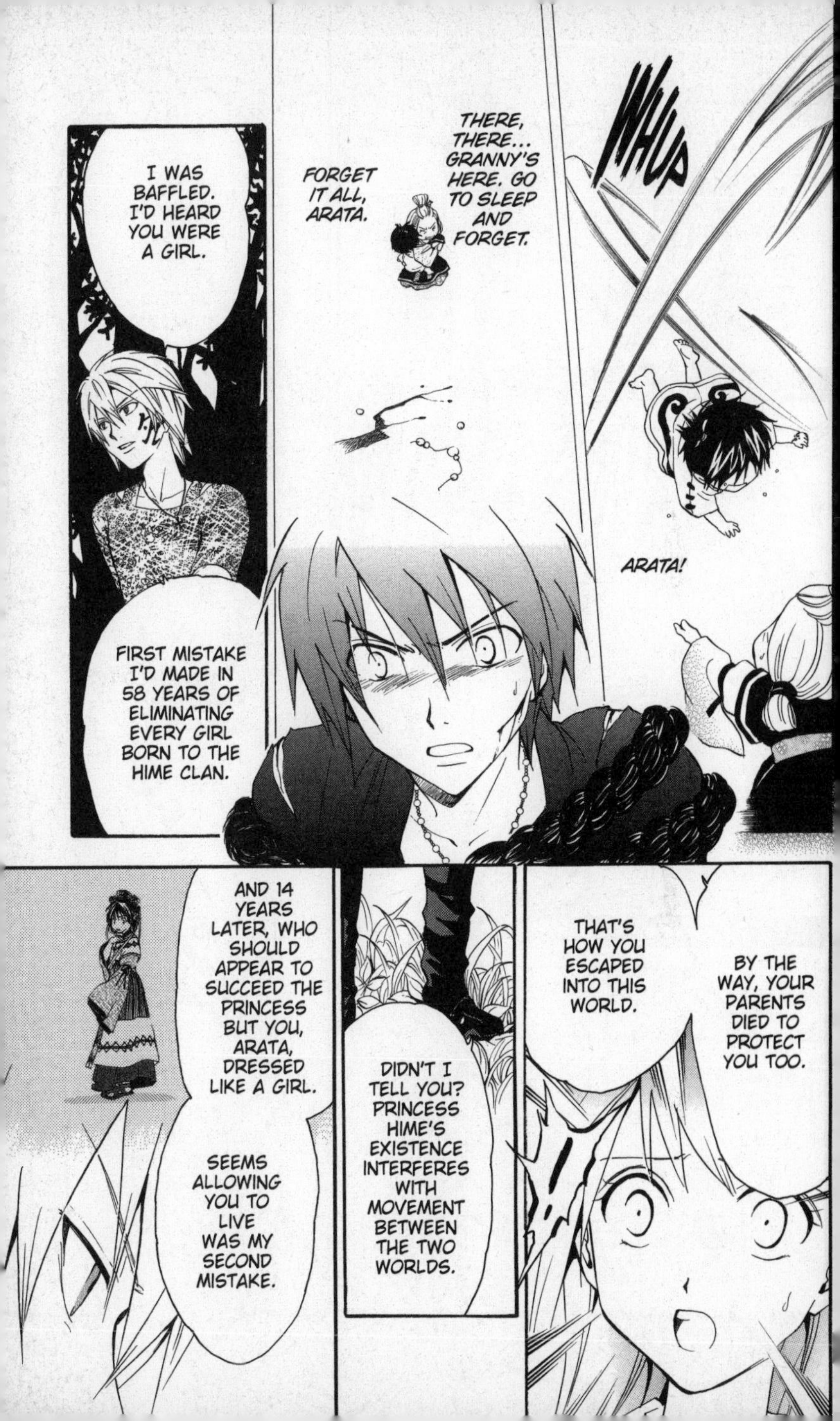
WHUP
ARATA!
THERE, THERE... GRANNY'S HERE. GO TO SLEEP AND FORGET.
FORGET IT ALL, ARATA.
I WAS BAFFLED. I'D HEARD YOU WERE A GIRL.
FIRST MISTAKE I'D MADE IN 58 YEARS OF ELIMINATING EVERY GIRL BORN TO THE HIME CLAN.
THAT'S HOW YOU ESCAPED INTO THIS WORLD.
BY THE WAY, YOUR PARENTS DIED TO PROTECT YOU TOO.
DIDN'T I TELL YOU? PRINCESS HIME'S EXISTENCE INTERFERES WITH MOVEMENT BETWEEN THE TWO WORLDS.
AND 14 YEARS LATER, WHO SHOULD APPEAR TO SUCCEED THE PRINCESS BUT YOU, ARATA, DRESSED LIKE A GIRL.
SEEMS ALLOWING YOU TO LIVE WAS MY SECOND MISTAKE.

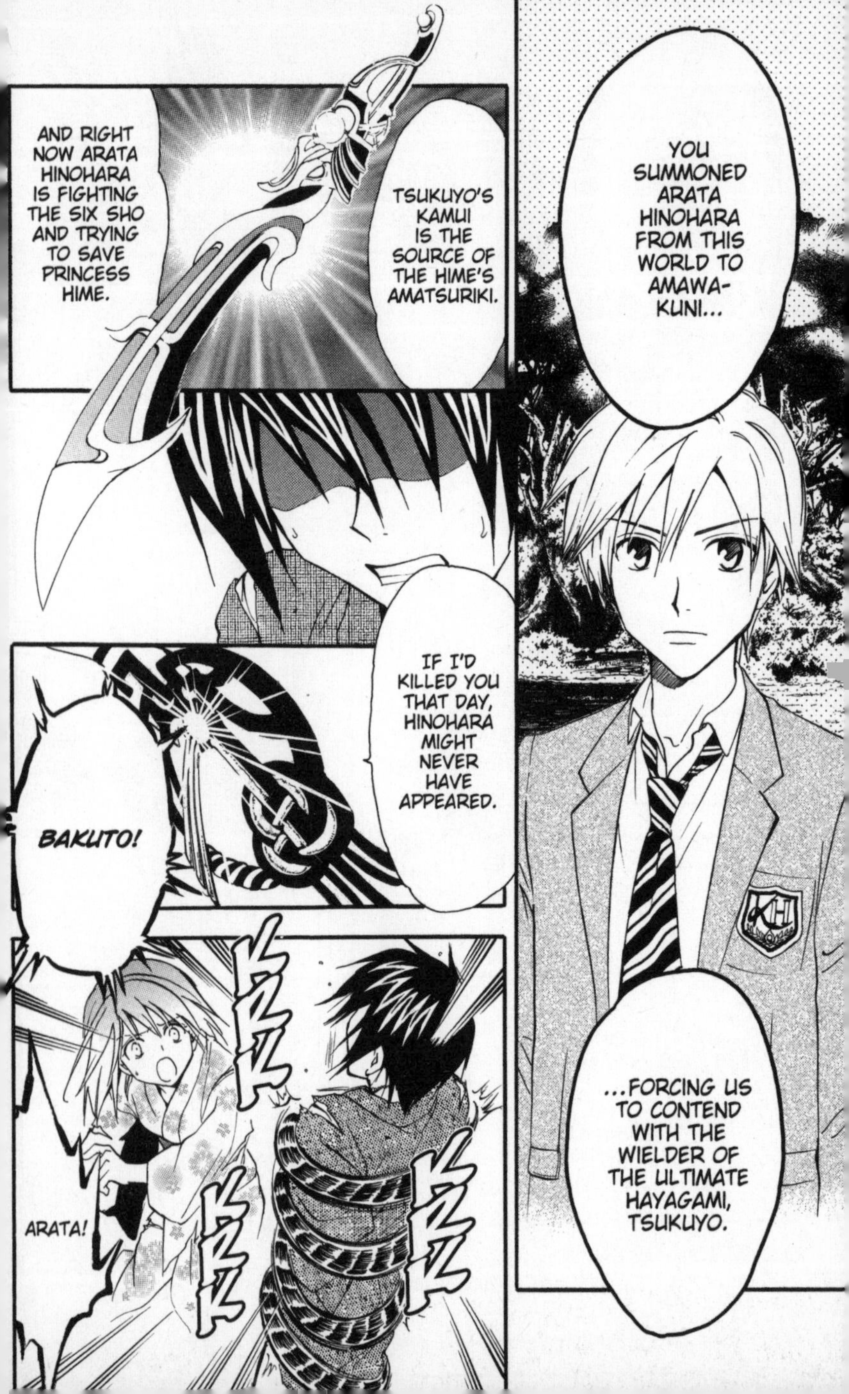
YOU SUMMONED ARATA HINOHARA FROM THIS WORLD TO AMAWA-KUNI...
...FORCING US TO CONTEND WITH THE WIELDER OF THE ULTIMATE HAYAGAMI, TSUKUYO.
TSUKUYO'S KAMUI IS THE SOURCE OF THE HIME'S AMATSURIKI.
AND RIGHT NOW ARATA HINOHARA IS FIGHTING THE SIX SHO AND TRYING TO SAVE PRINCESS HIME.
IF I'D KILLED YOU THAT DAY, HINOHARA MIGHT NEVER HAVE APPEARED.
BAKUTO!
ARATA!

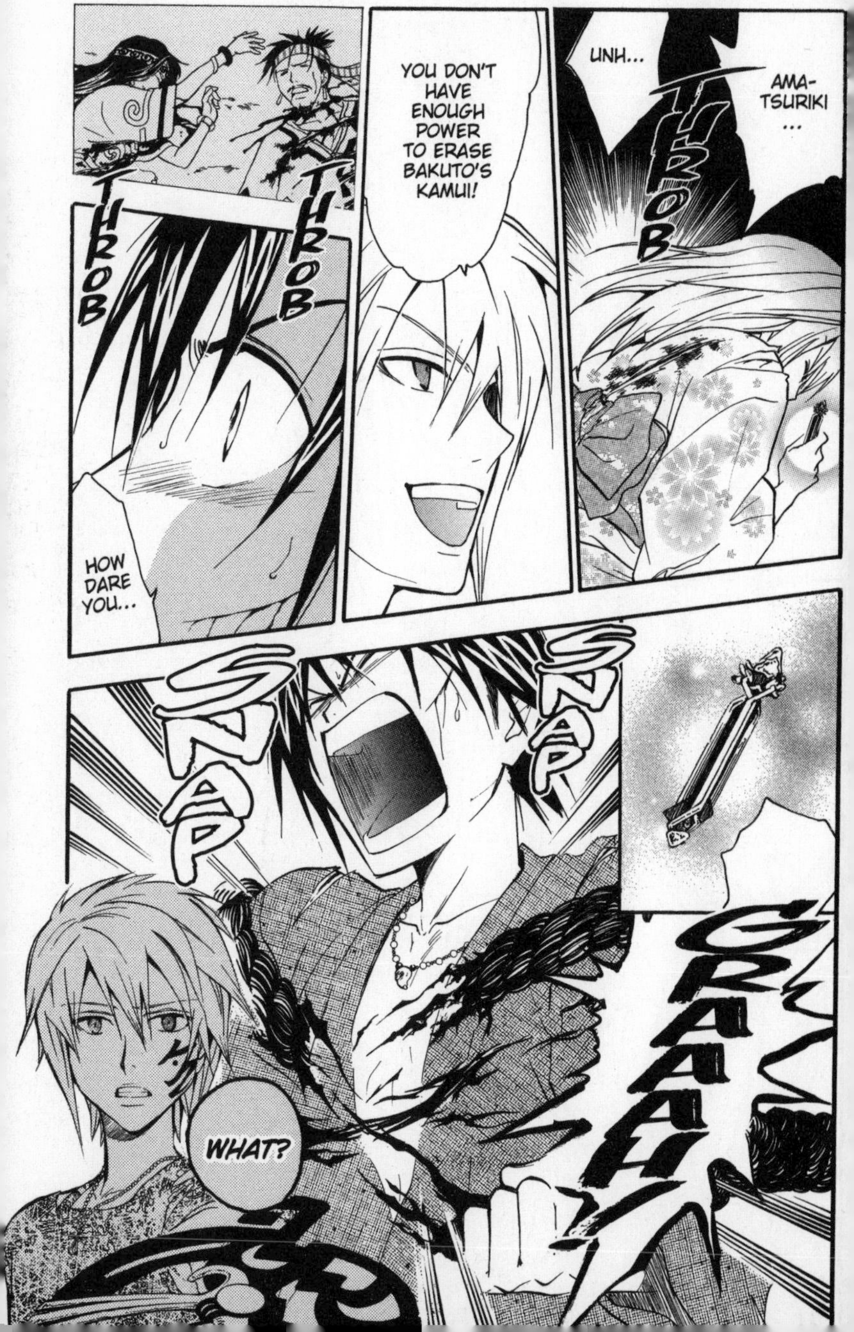
UNH...
THROB
AMA-TSURIKI ...
YOU DON'T HAVE ENOUGH POWER TO ERASE BAKUTO'S KAMUI!
THROB
THROB
HOW DARE YOU...
GRAAAH!
SNAP
SNAP
WHAT?

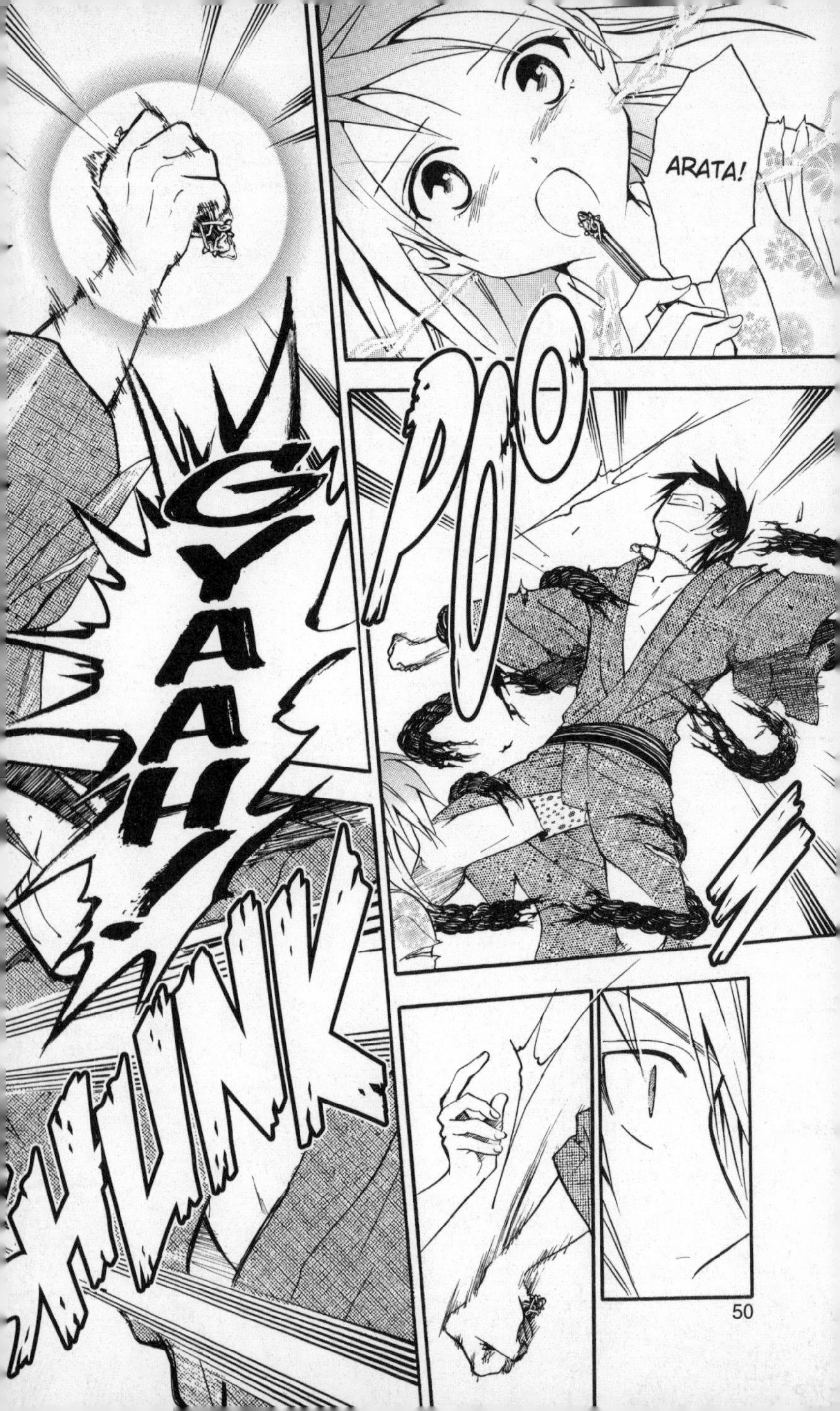

ARATA!
POOO
GYAAAH!
THUNK

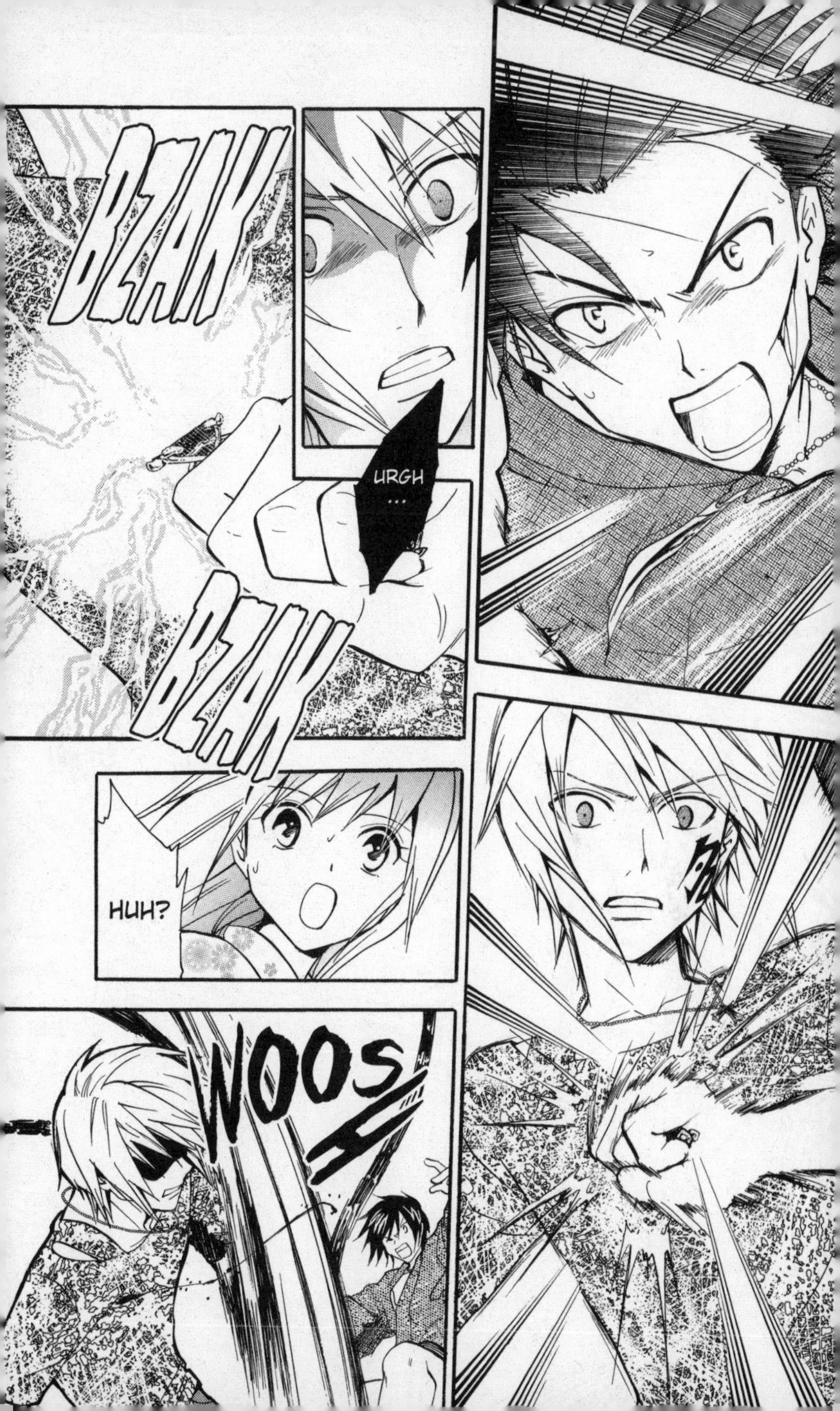
BZAK
URGH ...
BZAK
HUH?
WOOSH

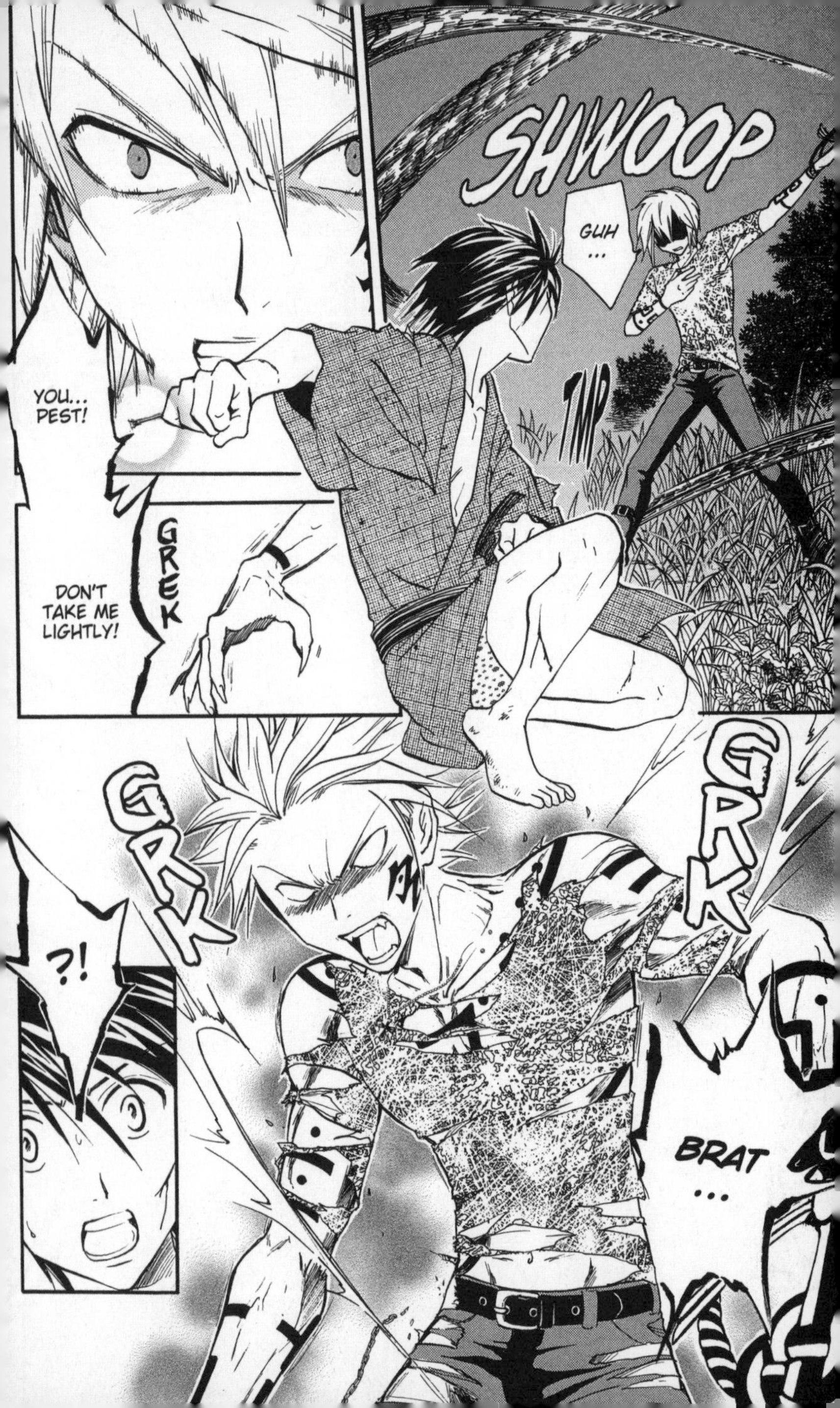

SHWOOP
GUH...
TMP
YOU... PEST!
GREK
DON'T TAKE ME LIGHTLY!
GRK
GRK
BRAT...
?!

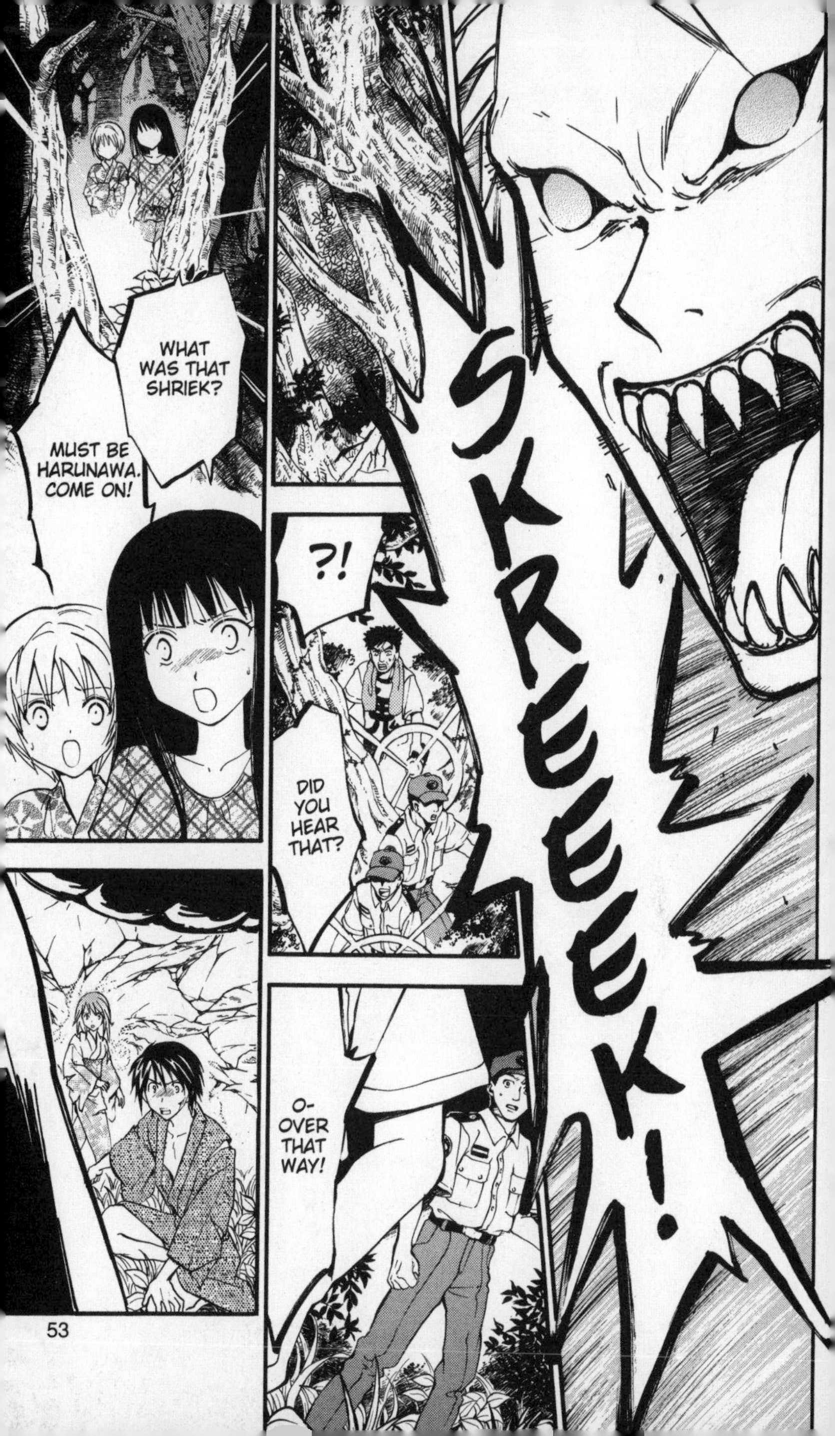
SKREEEEK!
?!
DID YOU HEAR THAT?
O-OVER THAT WAY!
WHAT WAS THAT SHRIEK?
MUST BE HARUNAWA. COME ON!

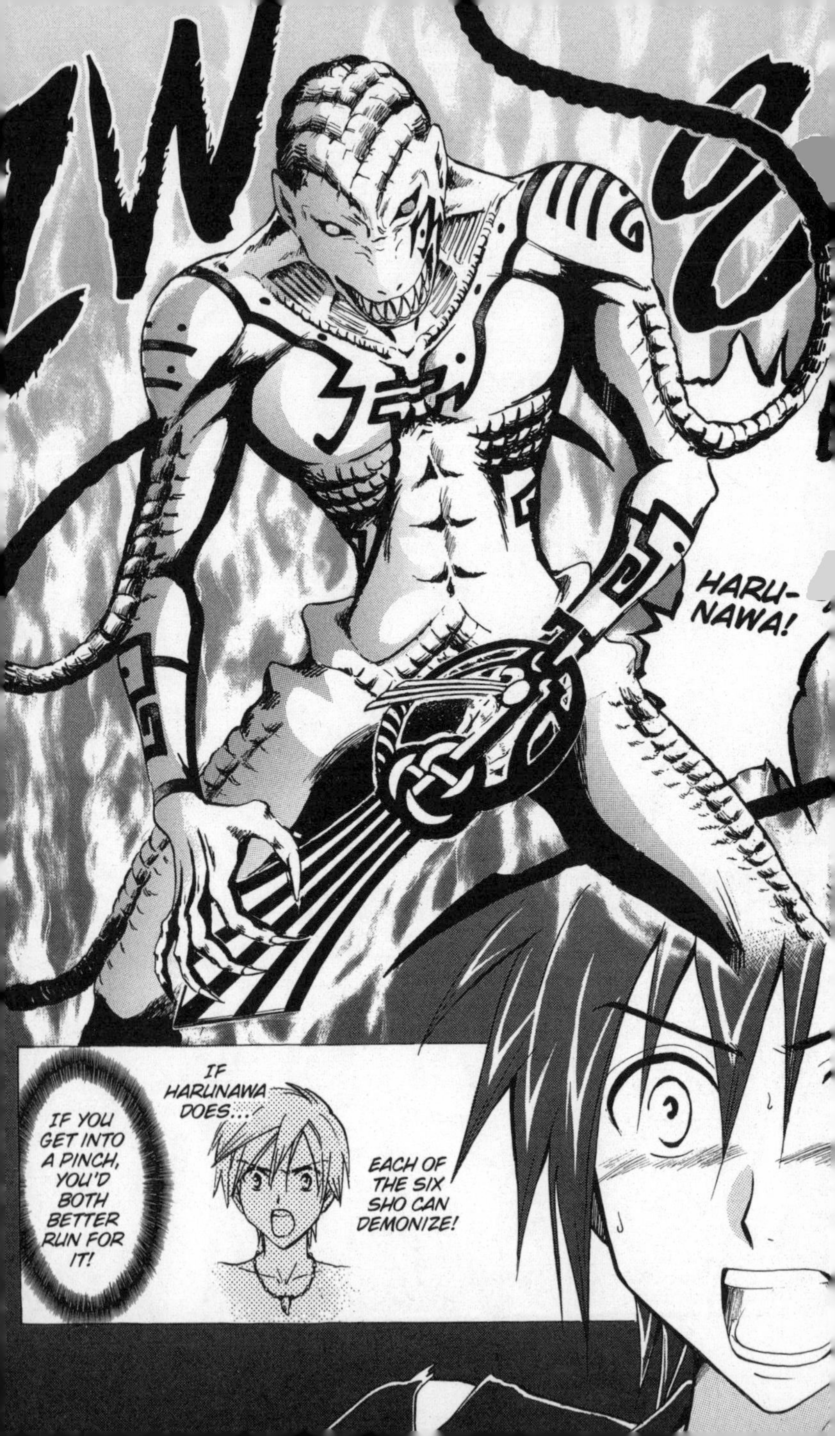
HARU-NAWA!
IF HARUNAWA DOES...
EACH OF THE SIX SHO CAN DEMONIZE!
IF YOU GET INTO A PINCH, YOU'D BOTH BETTER RUN FOR IT!

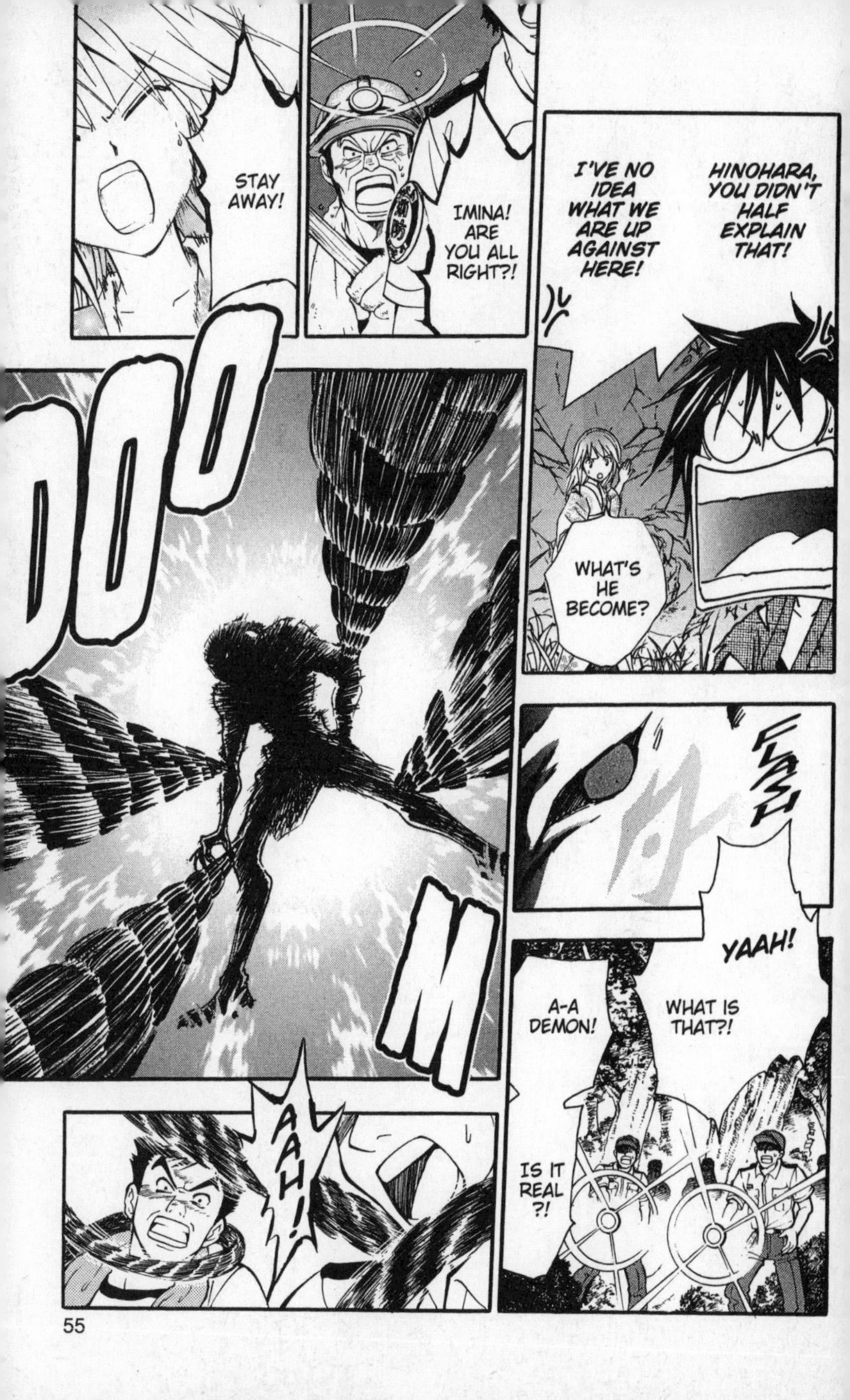
HINOHARA, YOU DIDN'T HALF EXPLAIN THAT!
I'VE NO IDEA WHAT WE ARE UP AGAINST HERE!
WHAT'S HE BECOME?
IMINA! ARE YOU ALL RIGHT?!
STAY AWAY!
FLASH
DOOOM
YAAH!
WHAT IS THAT?!
A-A DEMON!
IS IT REAL?!
AAAH!

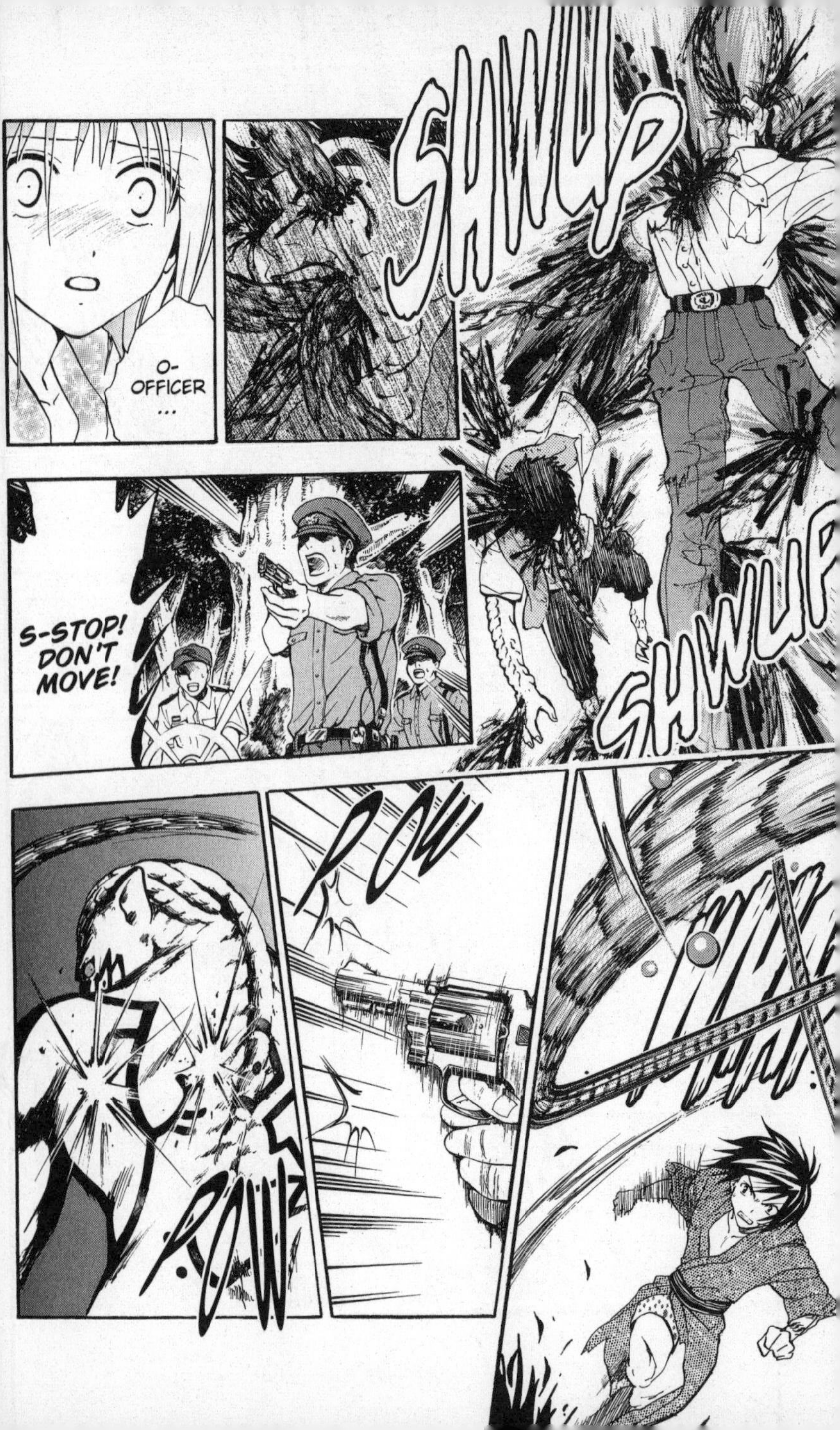
SHWUP
SHWUP
O-OFFICER ...
S-STOP! DON'T MOVE!
POW
POW

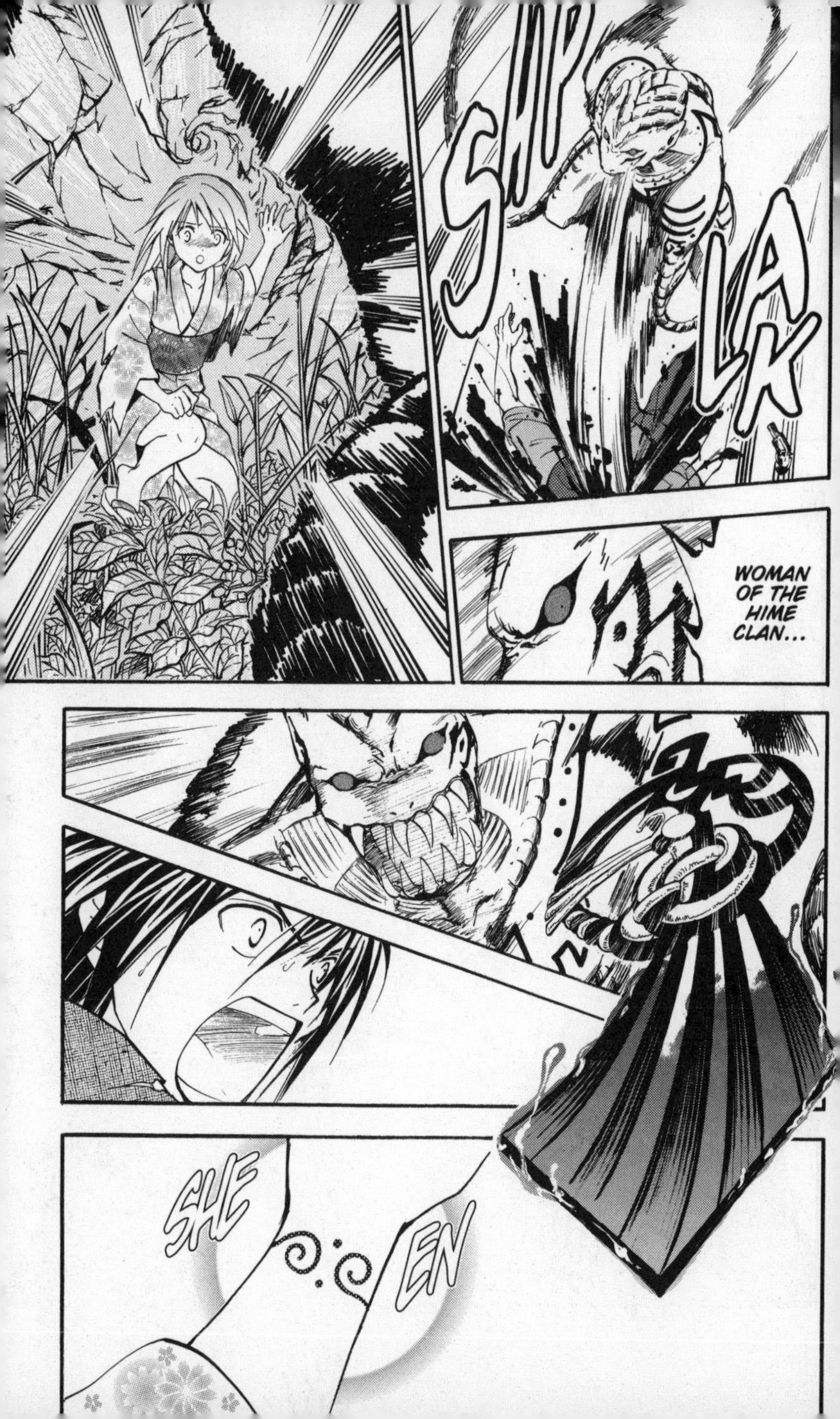
SHPLALK
WOMAN OF THE HIME CLAN...
SHE
EN

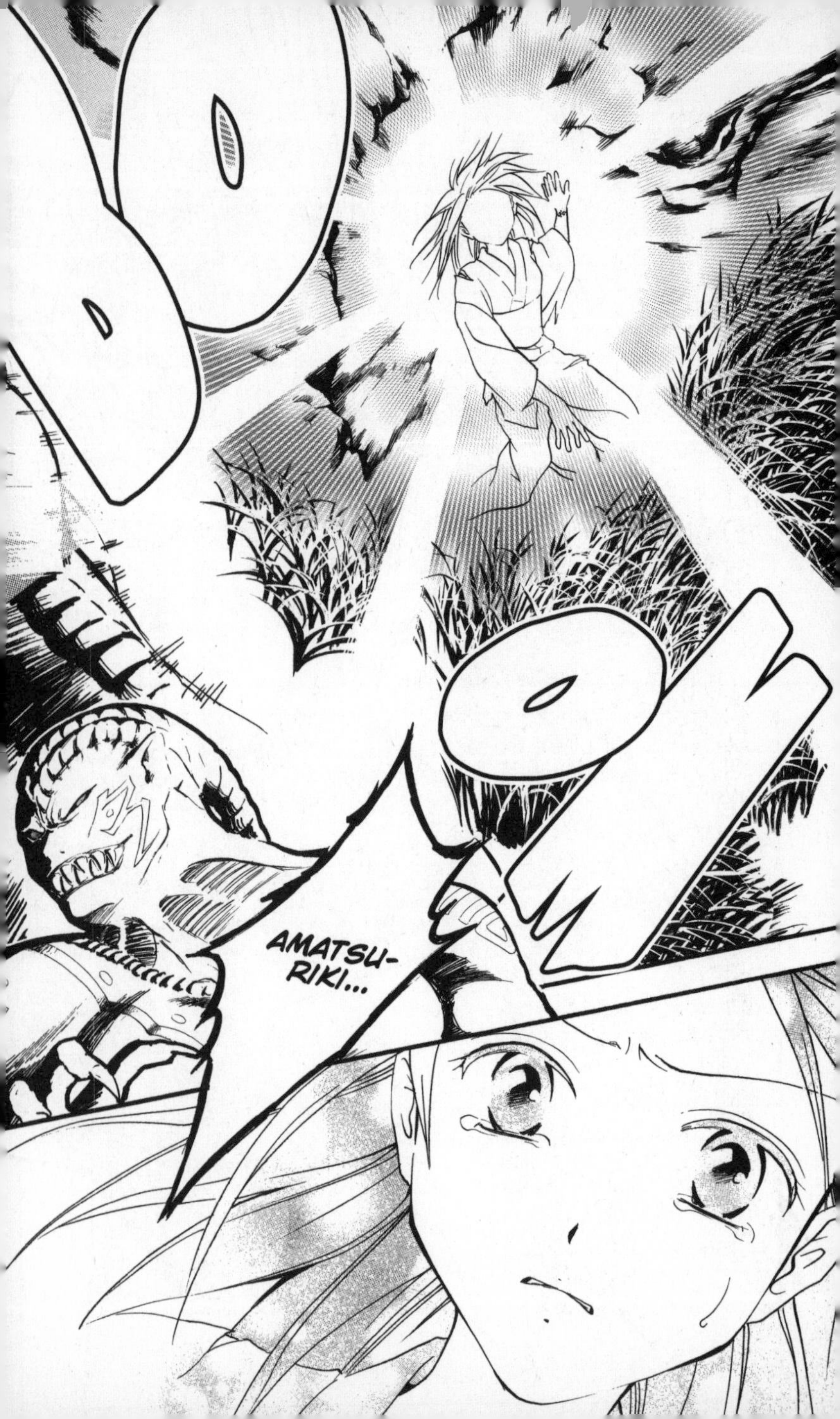
AMATSU-
RIKI...

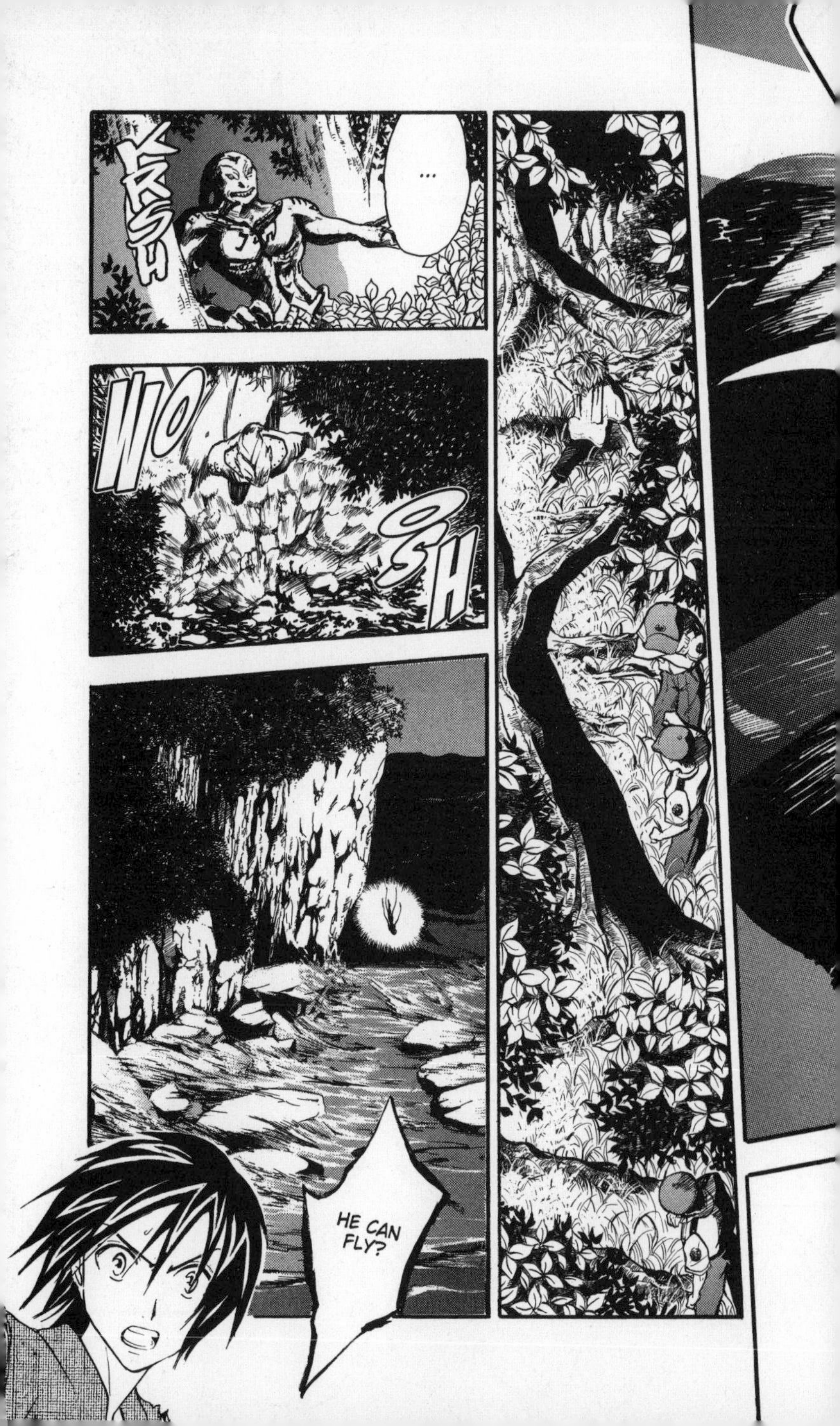
...
KRSH
WOOSH
HE CAN FLY?

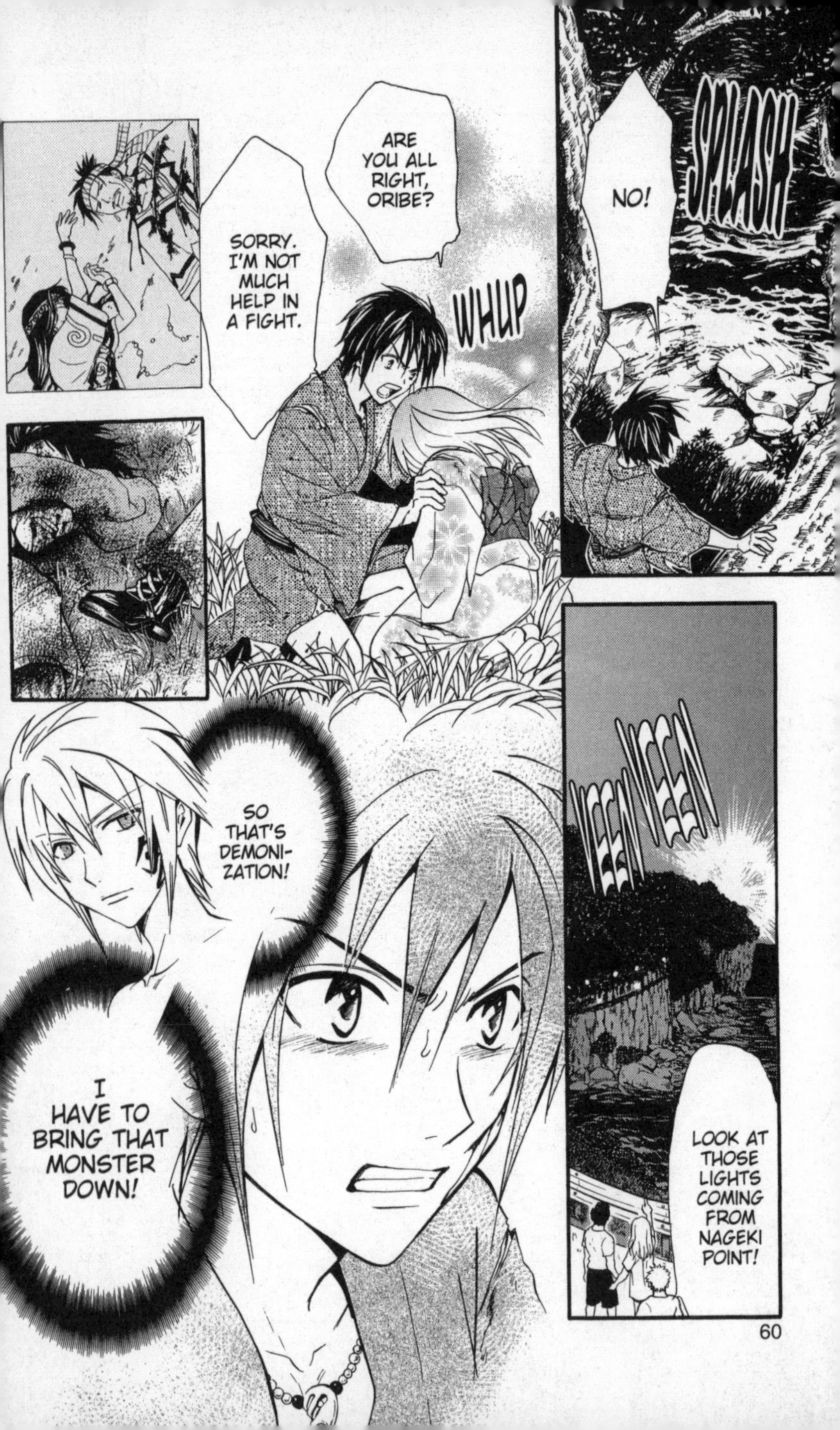
SPLASH
NO!
ARE YOU ALL RIGHT, ORIBE?
SORRY. I'M NOT MUCH HELP IN A FIGHT.
WHUP
VEEN VEEN
LOOK AT THOSE LIGHTS COMING FROM NAGEKI POINT!
SO THAT'S DEMONIZATION!
I HAVE TO BRING THAT MONSTER DOWN!

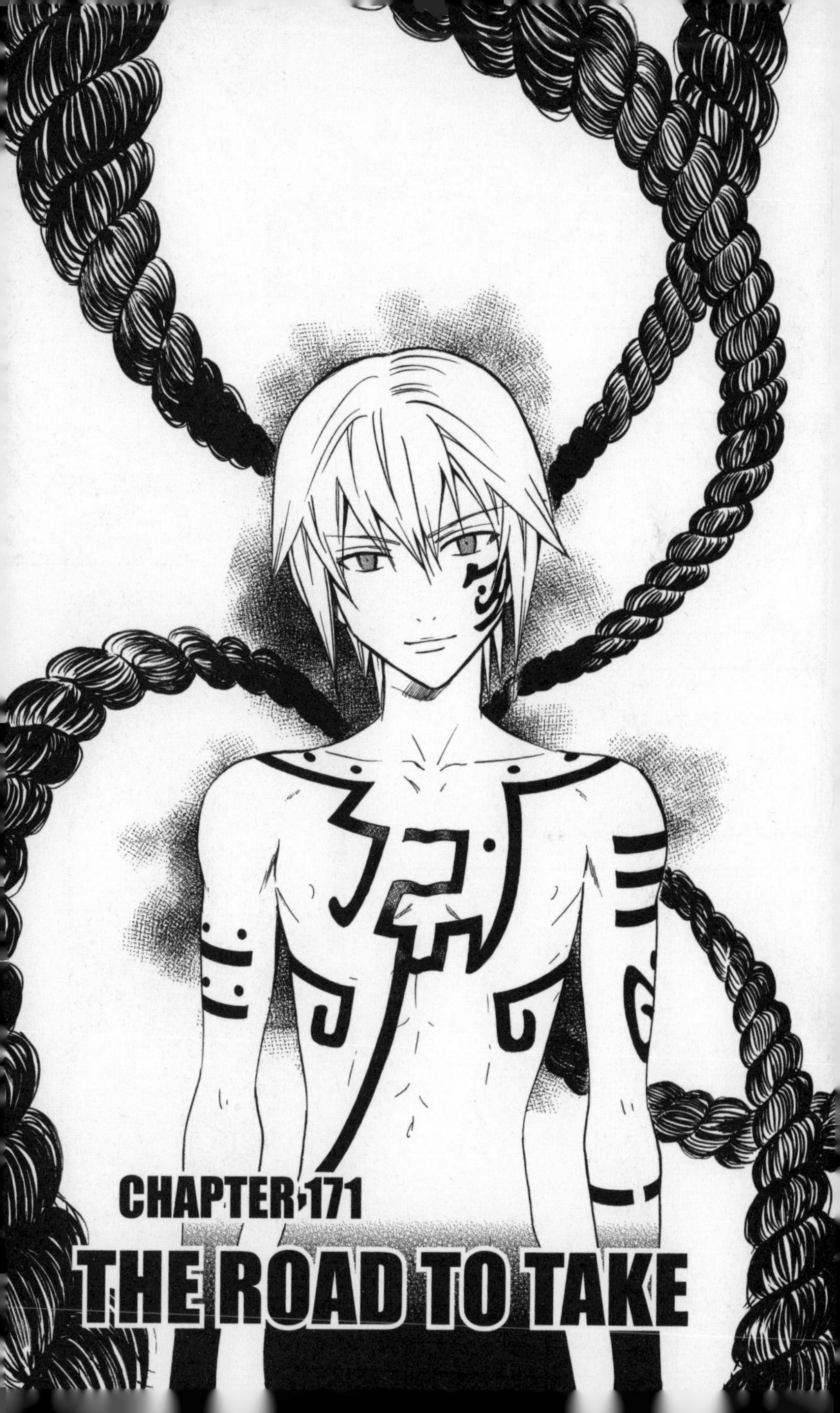
CHAPTER 171
THE ROAD TO TAKE

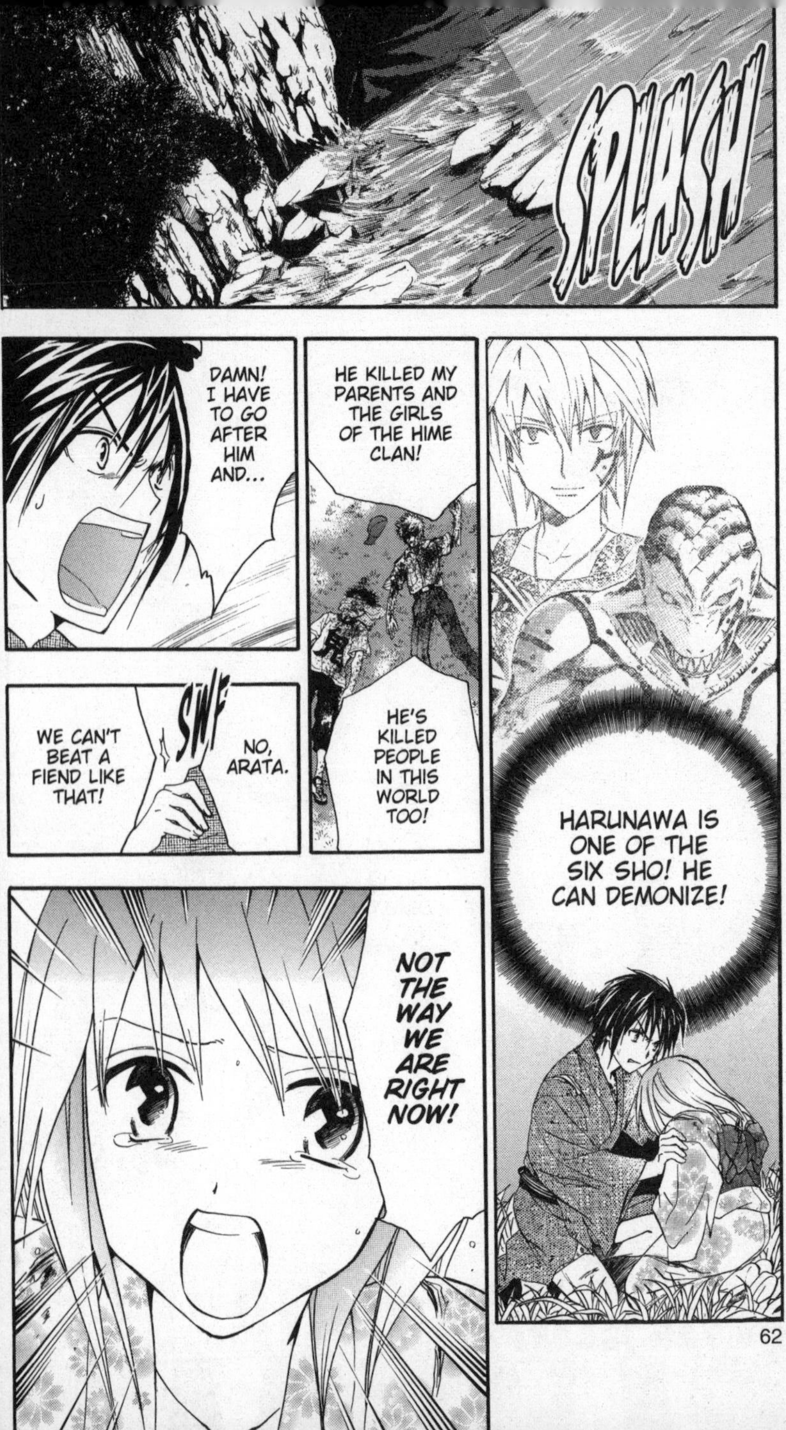
SPLASH
HARUNAWA IS ONE OF THE SIX SHO! HE CAN DEMONIZE!
HE KILLED MY PARENTS AND THE GIRLS OF THE HIME CLAN!
HE'S KILLED PEOPLE IN THIS WORLD TOO!
DAMN! I HAVE TO GO AFTER HIM AND...
SWF
NO, ARATA.
WE CAN'T BEAT A FIEND LIKE THAT!
NOT THE WAY WE ARE RIGHT NOW!

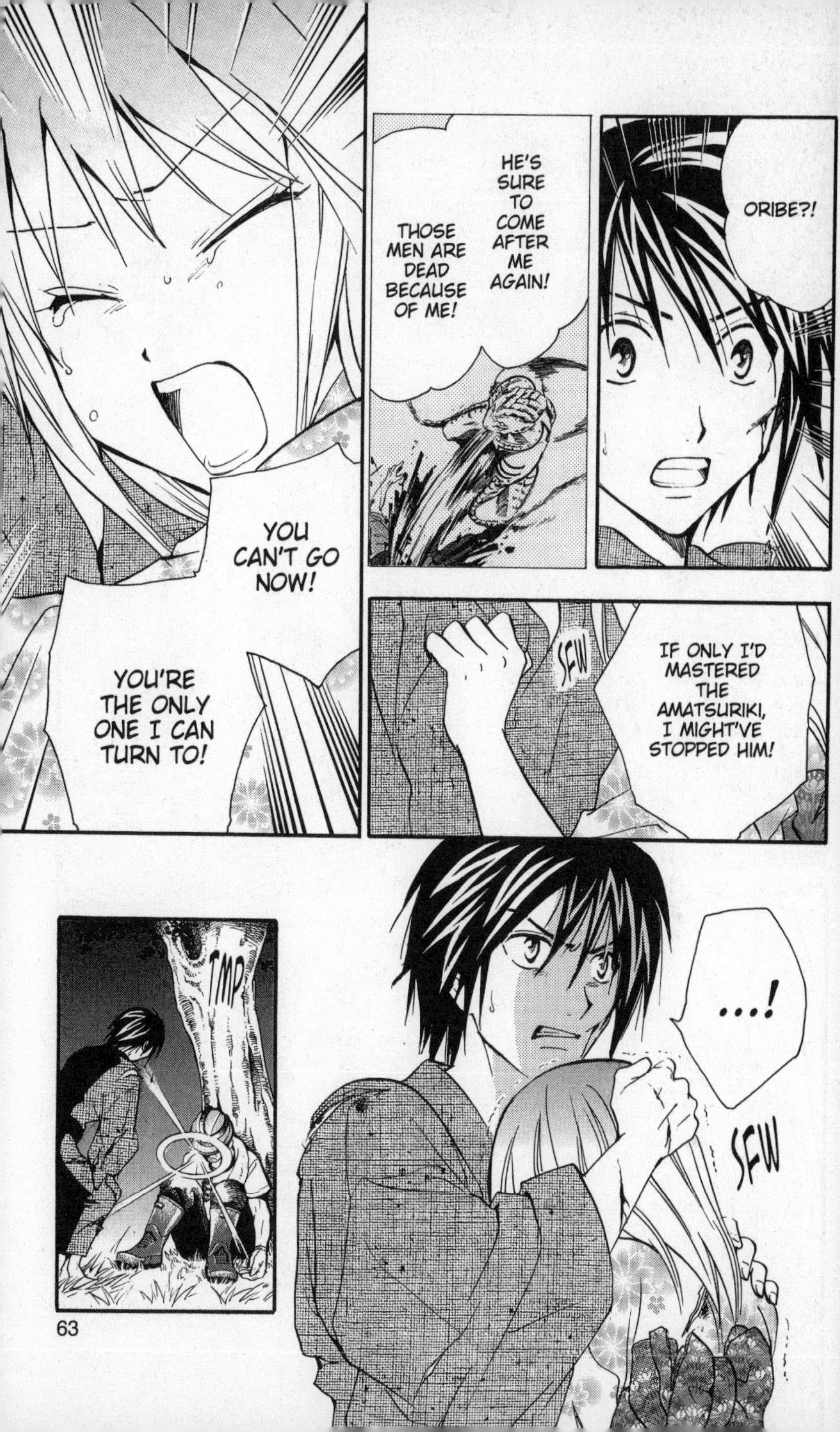
ORIBE?!
HE'S SURE TO COME AFTER ME AGAIN!
THOSE MEN ARE DEAD BECAUSE OF ME!
IF ONLY I'D MASTERED THE AMATSURIKI, I MIGHT'VE STOPPED HIM!
SFW
YOU CAN'T GO NOW!
YOU'RE THE ONLY ONE I CAN TURN TO!
...!
SFW
TMP

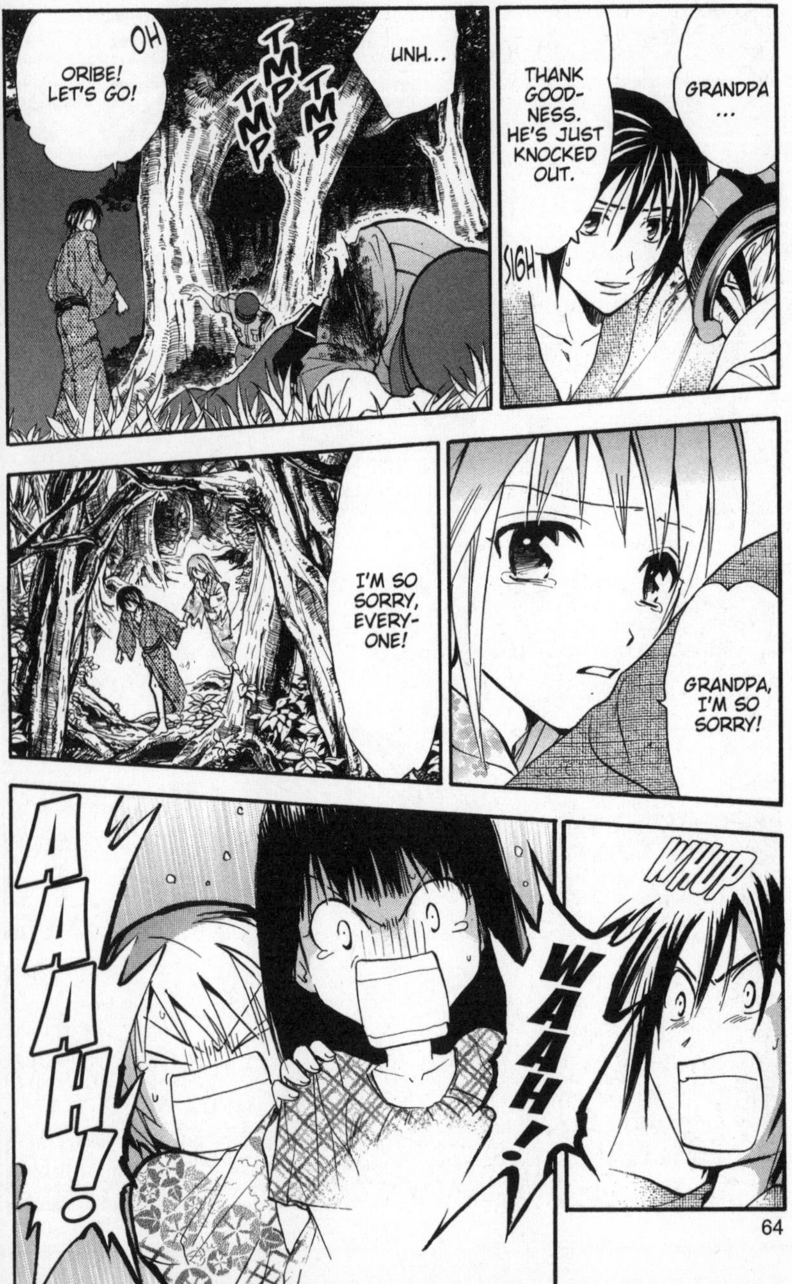
GRANDPA ...
THANK GOOD-NESS. HE'S JUST KNOCKED OUT.
SIGH
UNH...
TMP TMP TMP
OH
ORIBE! LET'S GO!
GRANDPA, I'M SO SORRY!
I'M SO SORRY, EVERY-ONE!
WHUP
WAAH!
AAAAH!

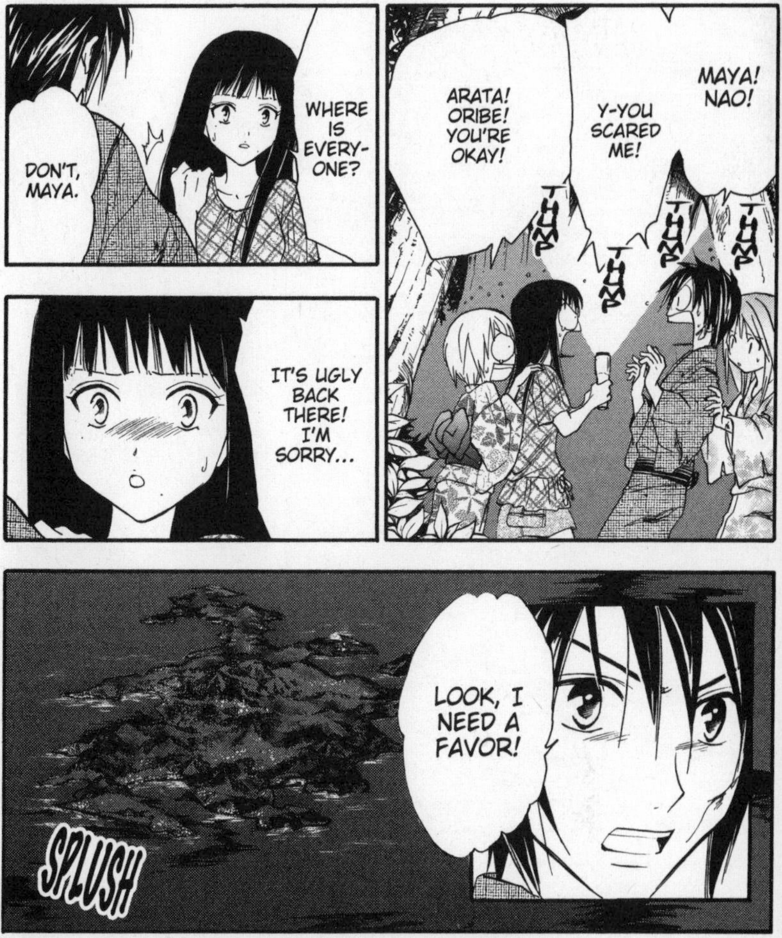
MAYA! NAO!
THUMP
THUMP
Y-YOU SCARED ME!
THUMP
ARATA! ORIBE! YOU'RE OKAY!
THUMP
WHERE IS EVERYONE?
DON'T, MAYA.
IT'S UGLY BACK THERE! I'M SORRY...
LOOK, I NEED A FAVOR!
SPLUSH
SPLOOSH

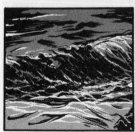

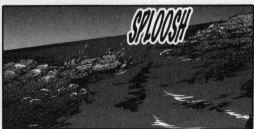

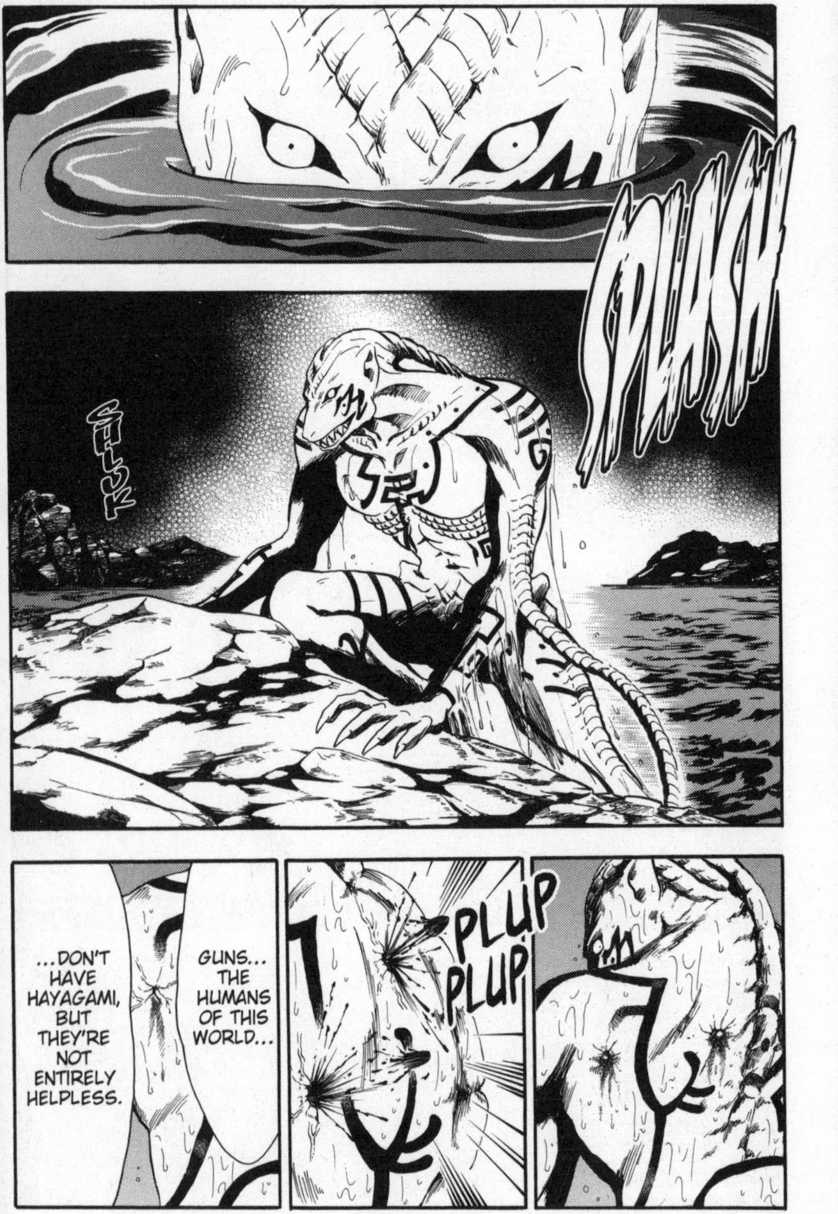
SPLASH
SHLUK
PLUP
PLUP
GUNS... THE HUMANS OF THIS WORLD...
...DON'T HAVE HAYAGAMI, BUT THEY'RE NOT ENTIRELY HELPLESS.

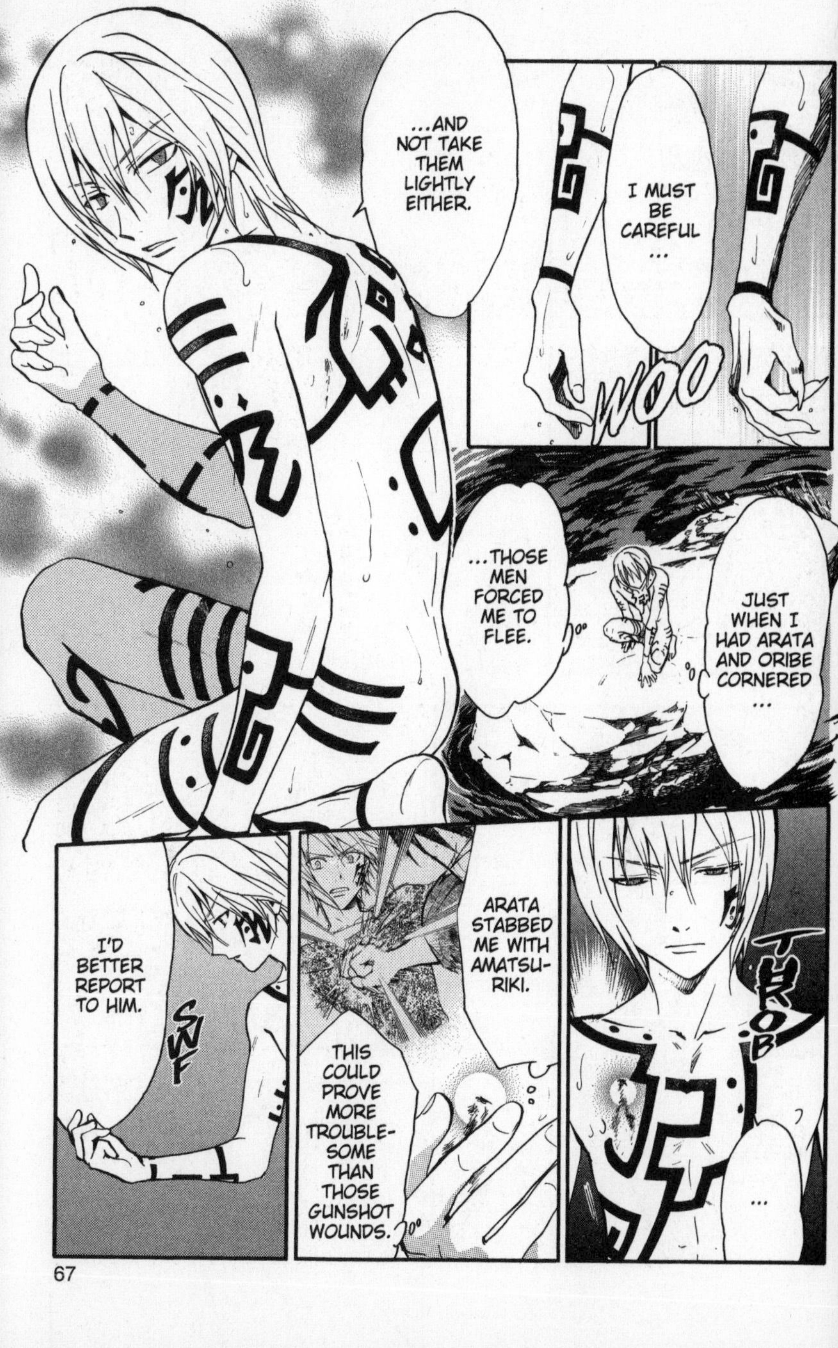
I MUST BE CAREFUL ...
WOO
JUST WHEN I HAD ARATA AND ORIBE CORNERED ...
...THOSE MEN FORCED ME TO FLEE.
...AND NOT TAKE THEM LIGHTLY EITHER.
THROB
...
ARATA STABBED ME WITH AMATSU-RIKI.
THIS COULD PROVE MORE TROUBLE-SOME THAN THOSE GUNSHOT WOUNDS.
I'D BETTER REPORT TO HIM.
SWF

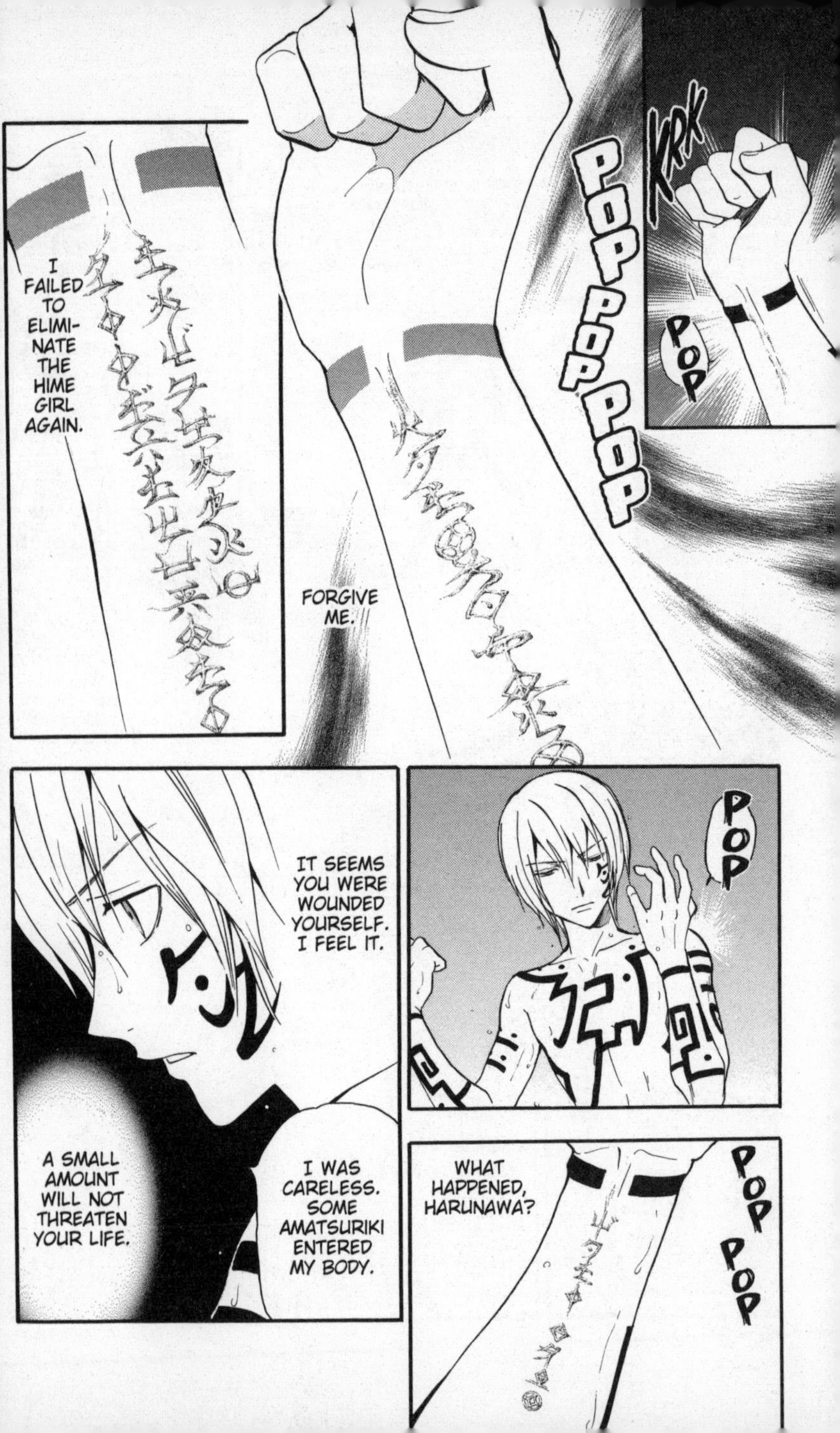
KRK
POP POP
POP POP POP POP POP
FORGIVE ME.
I FAILED TO ELIMI-NATE THE HIME GIRL AGAIN.
POP POP
POP POP POP
WHAT HAPPENED, HARUNAWA?
IT SEEMS YOU WERE WOUNDED YOURSELF. I FEEL IT.
I WAS CARELESS. SOME AMATSURIKI ENTERED MY BODY.
A SMALL AMOUNT WILL NOT THREATEN YOUR LIFE.

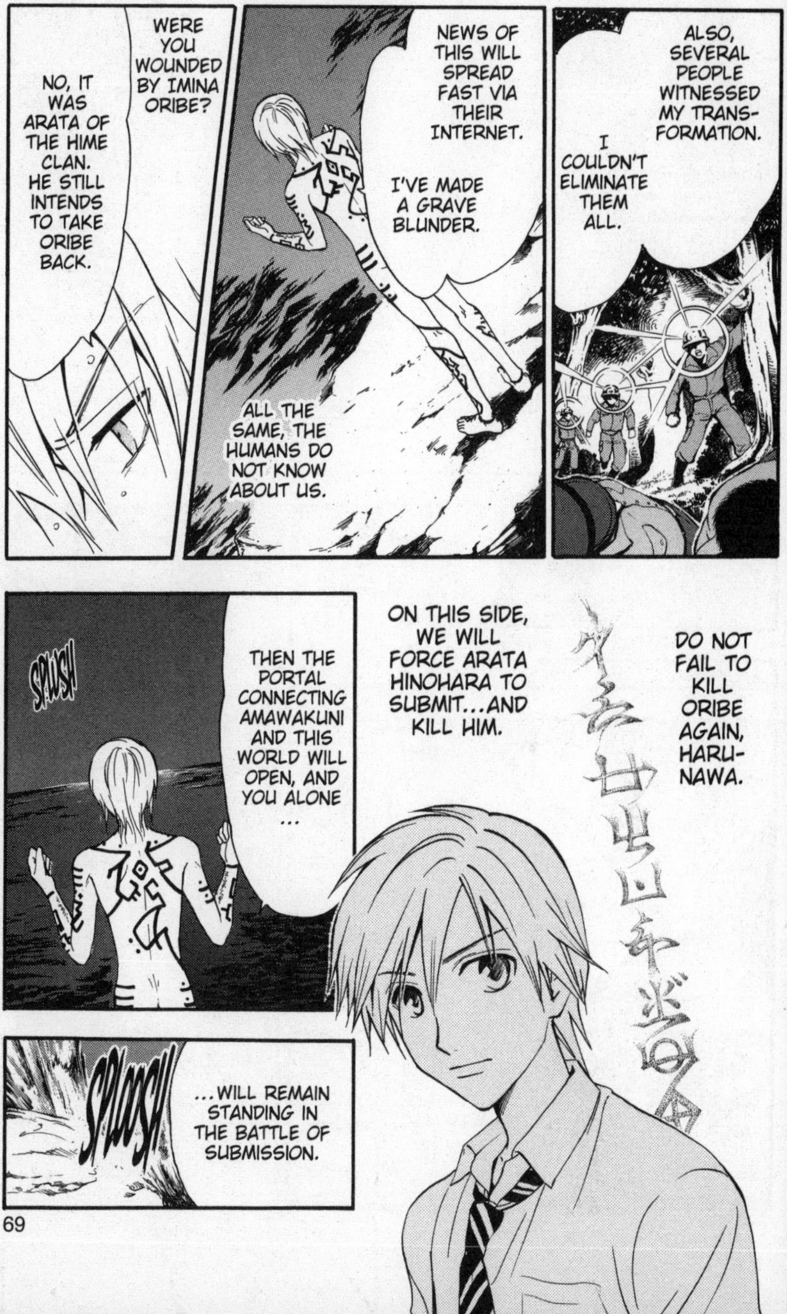
ALSO, SEVERAL PEOPLE WITNESSED MY TRANS-FORMATION.
I COULDN'T ELIMINATE THEM ALL.
NEWS OF THIS WILL SPREAD FAST VIA THEIR INTERNET.
I'VE MADE A GRAVE BLUNDER.
ALL THE SAME, THE HUMANS DO NOT KNOW ABOUT US.
WERE YOU WOUNDED BY IMINA ORIBE?
NO, IT WAS ARATA OF THE HIME CLAN. HE STILL INTENDS TO TAKE ORIBE BACK.
DO NOT FAIL TO KILL ORIBE AGAIN, HARU-NAWA.
ON THIS SIDE, WE WILL FORCE ARATA HINOHARA TO SUBMIT...AND KILL HIM.
THEN THE PORTAL CONNECTING AMAWAKUNI AND THIS WORLD WILL OPEN, AND YOU ALONE ...
SPLUSH
SPLOOSH
...WILL REMAIN STANDING IN THE BATTLE OF SUBMISSION.

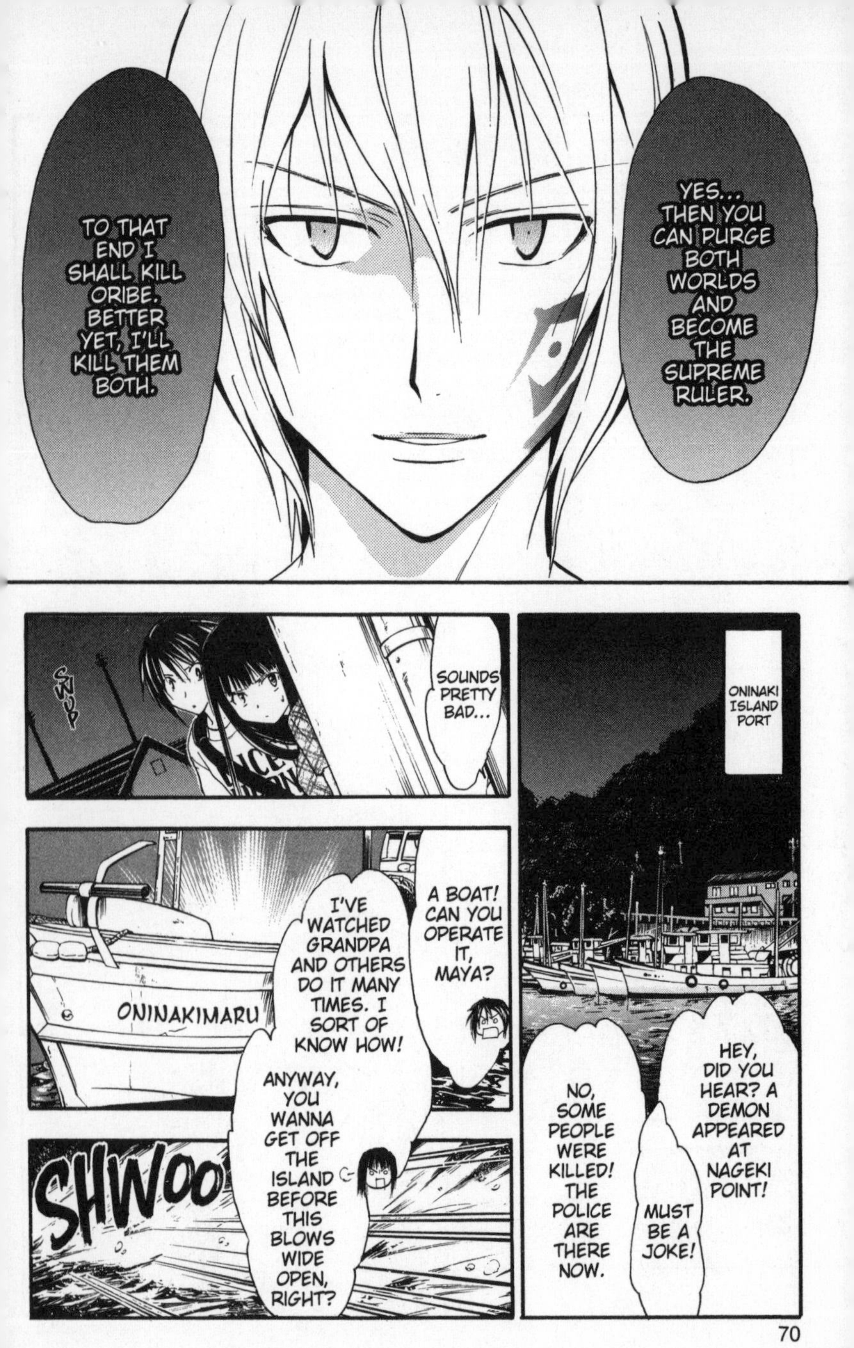
YES... THEN YOU CAN PURGE BOTH WORLDS AND BECOME THE SUPREME RULER.
TO THAT END I SHALL KILL ORIBE. BETTER YET, I'LL KILL THEM BOTH.
ONINAKI ISLAND PORT
HEY, DID YOU HEAR? A DEMON APPEARED AT NAGEKI POINT!
MUST BE A JOKE!
NO, SOME PEOPLE WERE KILLED! THE POLICE ARE THERE NOW.
SOUNDS PRETTY BAD...
SWUP
A BOAT! CAN YOU OPERATE IT, MAYA?
I'VE WATCHED GRANDPA AND OTHERS DO IT MANY TIMES. I SORT OF KNOW HOW!
ONINAKIMARU
ANYWAY, YOU WANNA GET OFF THE ISLAND BEFORE THIS BLOWS WIDE OPEN, RIGHT?
SHWOO

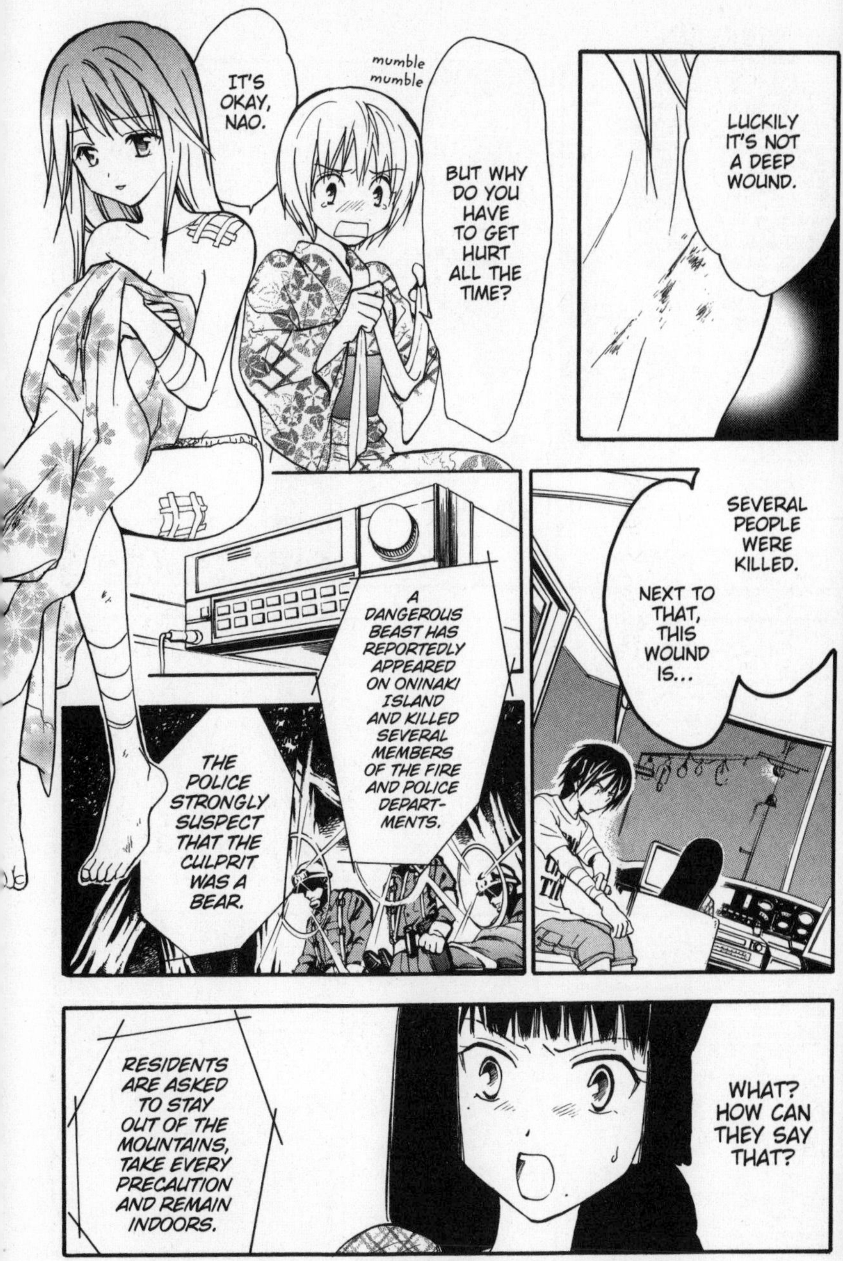
LUCKILY IT'S NOT A DEEP WOUND.
mumble mumble
BUT WHY DO YOU HAVE TO GET HURT ALL THE TIME?
IT'S OKAY, NAO.
SEVERAL PEOPLE WERE KILLED.
NEXT TO THAT, THIS WOUND IS...
A DANGEROUS BEAST HAS REPORTEDLY APPEARED ON ONINAKI ISLAND AND KILLED SEVERAL MEMBERS OF THE FIRE AND POLICE DEPART-MENTS.
THE POLICE STRONGLY SUSPECT THAT THE CULPRIT WAS A BEAR.
WHAT? HOW CAN THEY SAY THAT?
RESIDENTS ARE ASKED TO STAY OUT OF THE MOUNTAINS, TAKE EVERY PRECAUTION AND REMAIN INDOORS.

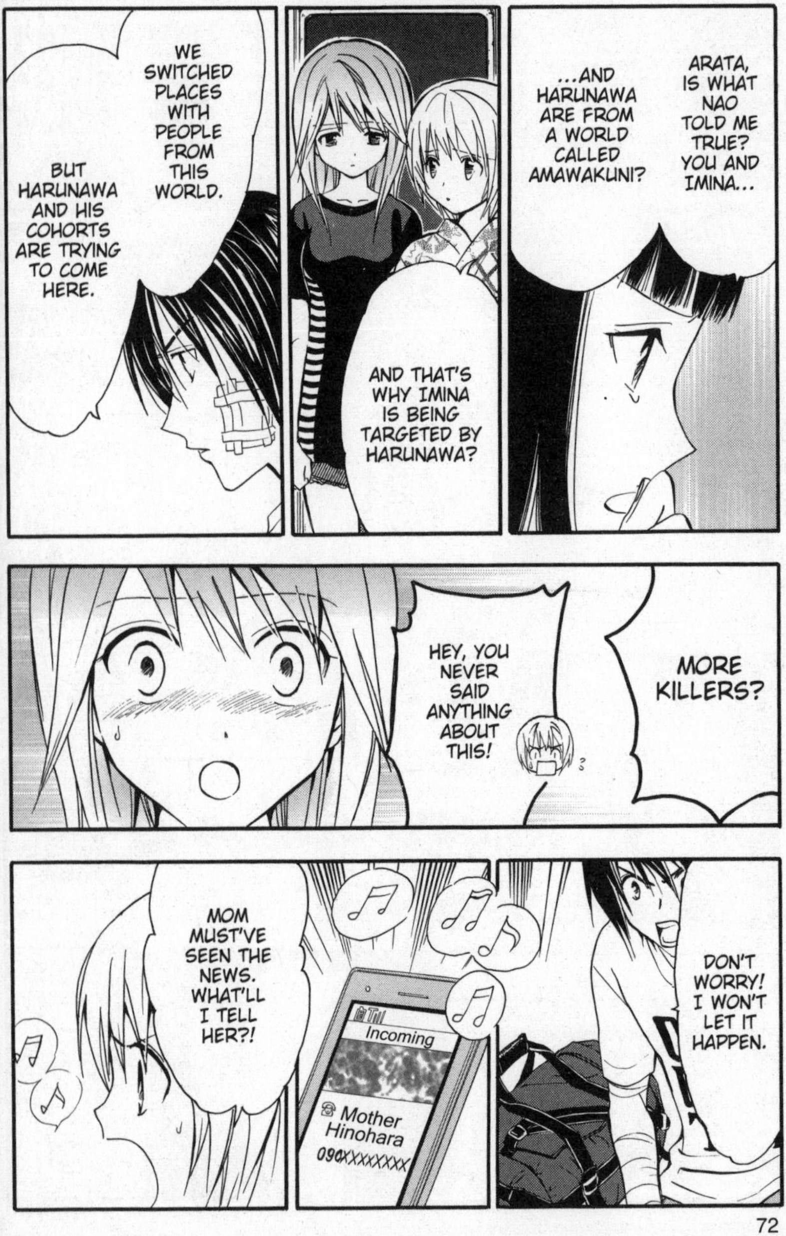
ARATA, IS WHAT NAO TOLD ME TRUE? YOU AND IMINA...
...AND HARUNAWA ARE FROM A WORLD CALLED AMAWAKUNI?
AND THAT'S WHY IMINA IS BEING TARGETED BY HARUNAWA?
WE SWITCHED PLACES WITH PEOPLE FROM THIS WORLD.
BUT HARUNAWA AND HIS COHORTS ARE TRYING TO COME HERE.
MORE KILLERS?
HEY, YOU NEVER SAID ANYTHING ABOUT THIS!
DON'T WORRY! I WON'T LET IT HAPPEN.
Incoming
Mother Hinohara
090XXXXXXXX
MOM MUST'VE SEEN THE NEWS. WHAT'LL I TELL HER?!

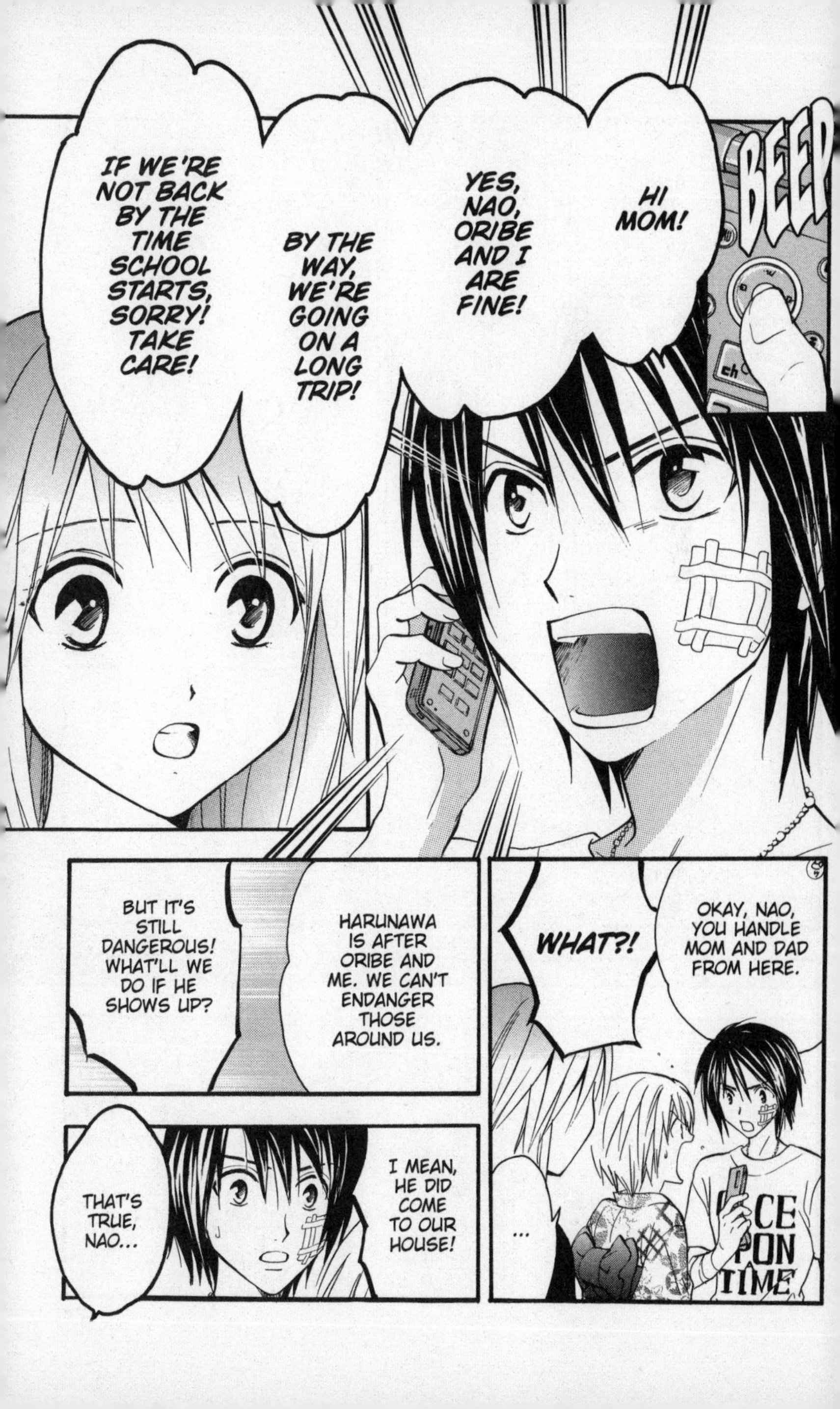
BEEP
HI MOM!
YES, NAO, ORIBE AND I ARE FINE!
BY THE WAY, WE'RE GOING ON A LONG TRIP!
IF WE'RE NOT BACK BY THE TIME SCHOOL STARTS, SORRY! TAKE CARE!
OKAY, NAO, YOU HANDLE MOM AND DAD FROM HERE.
WHAT?!
...
HARUNAWA IS AFTER ORIBE AND ME. WE CAN'T ENDANGER THOSE AROUND US.
BUT IT'S STILL DANGEROUS! WHAT'LL WE DO IF HE SHOWS UP?
I MEAN, HE DID COME TO OUR HOUSE!
THAT'S TRUE, NAO...

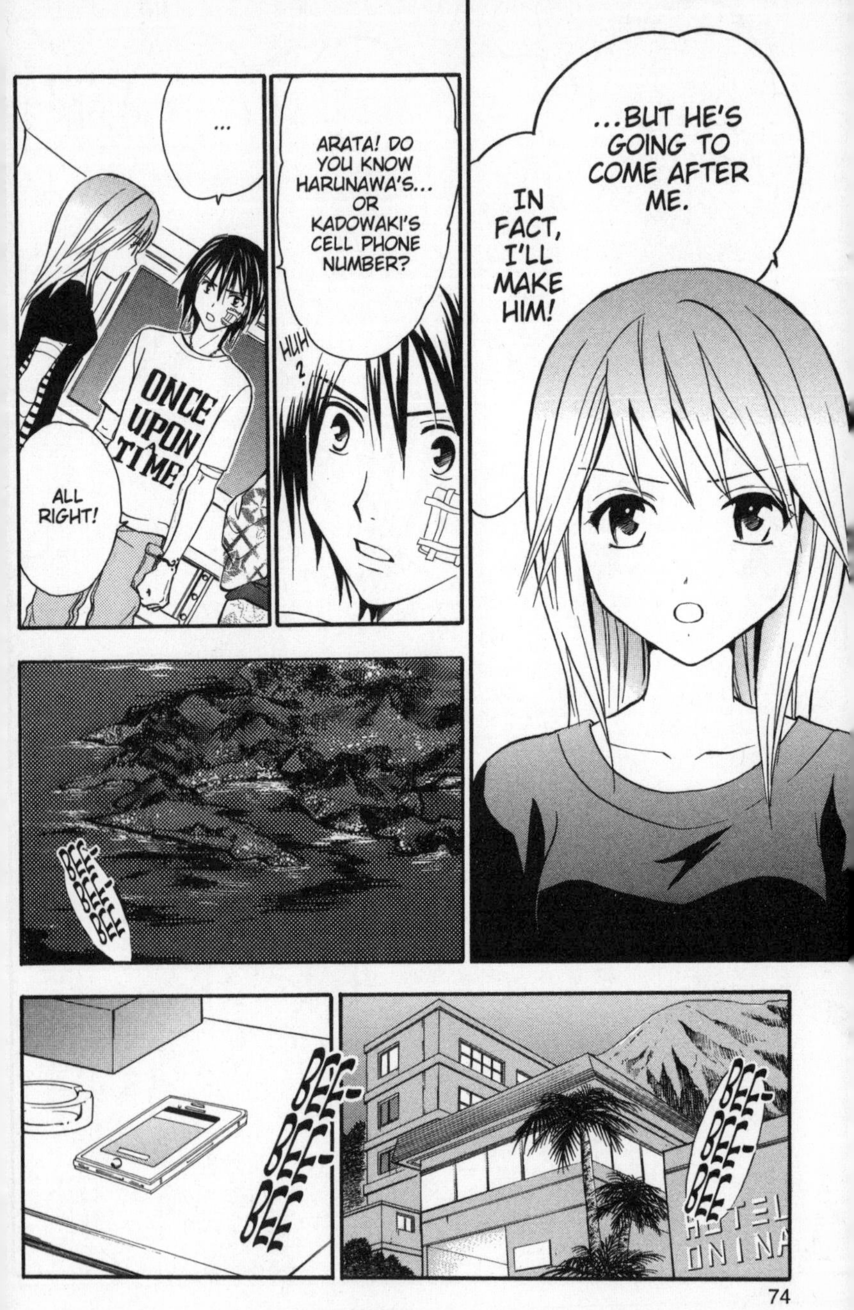
...BUT HE'S GOING TO COME AFTER ME.
IN FACT, I'LL MAKE HIM!
ARATA! DO YOU KNOW HARUNAWA'S... OR KADOWAKI'S CELL PHONE NUMBER?
HUH?
...
ALL RIGHT!
BEE-BEE-BEE
BEE-BEE-BEE
HOTEL
ONINA
BEE-BEE-BEE

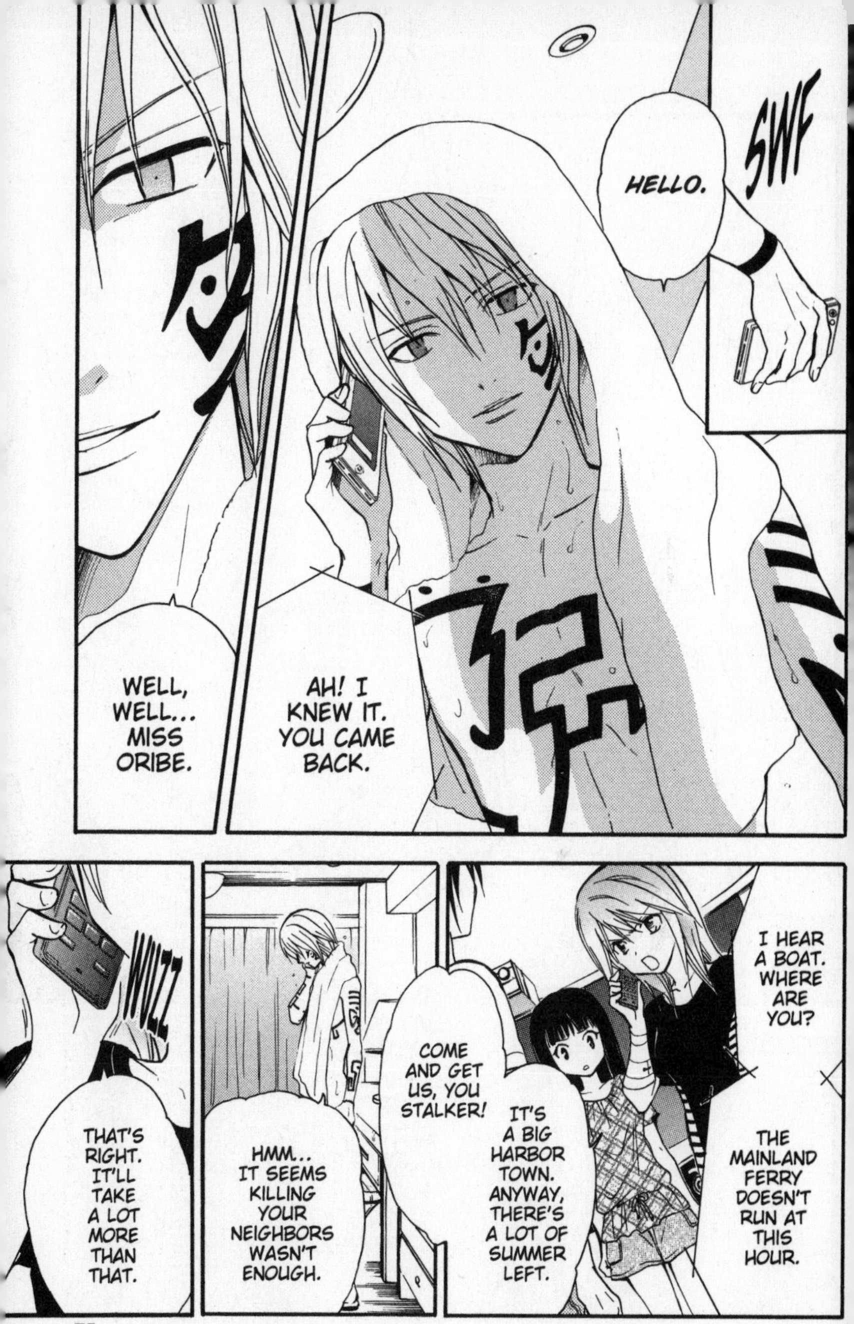
SWF
HELLO.
AH! I KNEW IT. YOU CAME BACK.
WELL, WELL... MISS ORIBE.
I HEAR A BOAT. WHERE ARE YOU?
THE MAINLAND FERRY DOESN'T RUN AT THIS HOUR.
IT'S A BIG HARBOR TOWN. ANYWAY, THERE'S A LOT OF SUMMER LEFT.
COME AND GET US, YOU STALKER!
HMM... IT SEEMS KILLING YOUR NEIGHBORS WASN'T ENOUGH.
WUZZ
THAT'S RIGHT. IT'LL TAKE A LOT MORE THAN THAT.

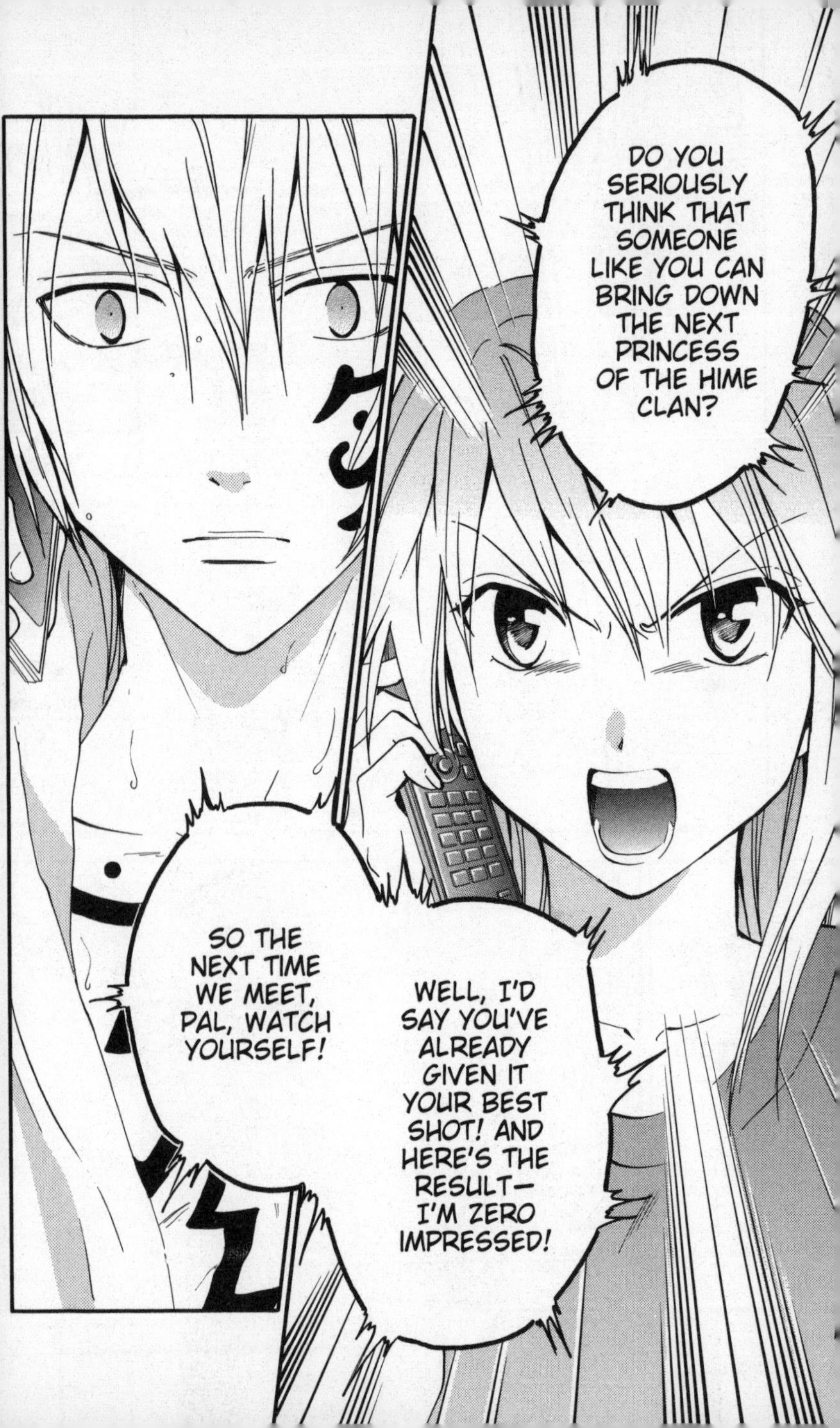
DO YOU SERIOUSLY THINK THAT SOMEONE LIKE YOU CAN BRING DOWN THE NEXT PRINCESS OF THE HIME CLAN?
WELL, I'D SAY YOU'VE ALREADY GIVEN IT YOUR BEST SHOT! AND HERE'S THE RESULT— I'M ZERO IMPRESSED!
SO THE NEXT TIME WE MEET, PAL, WATCH YOURSELF!

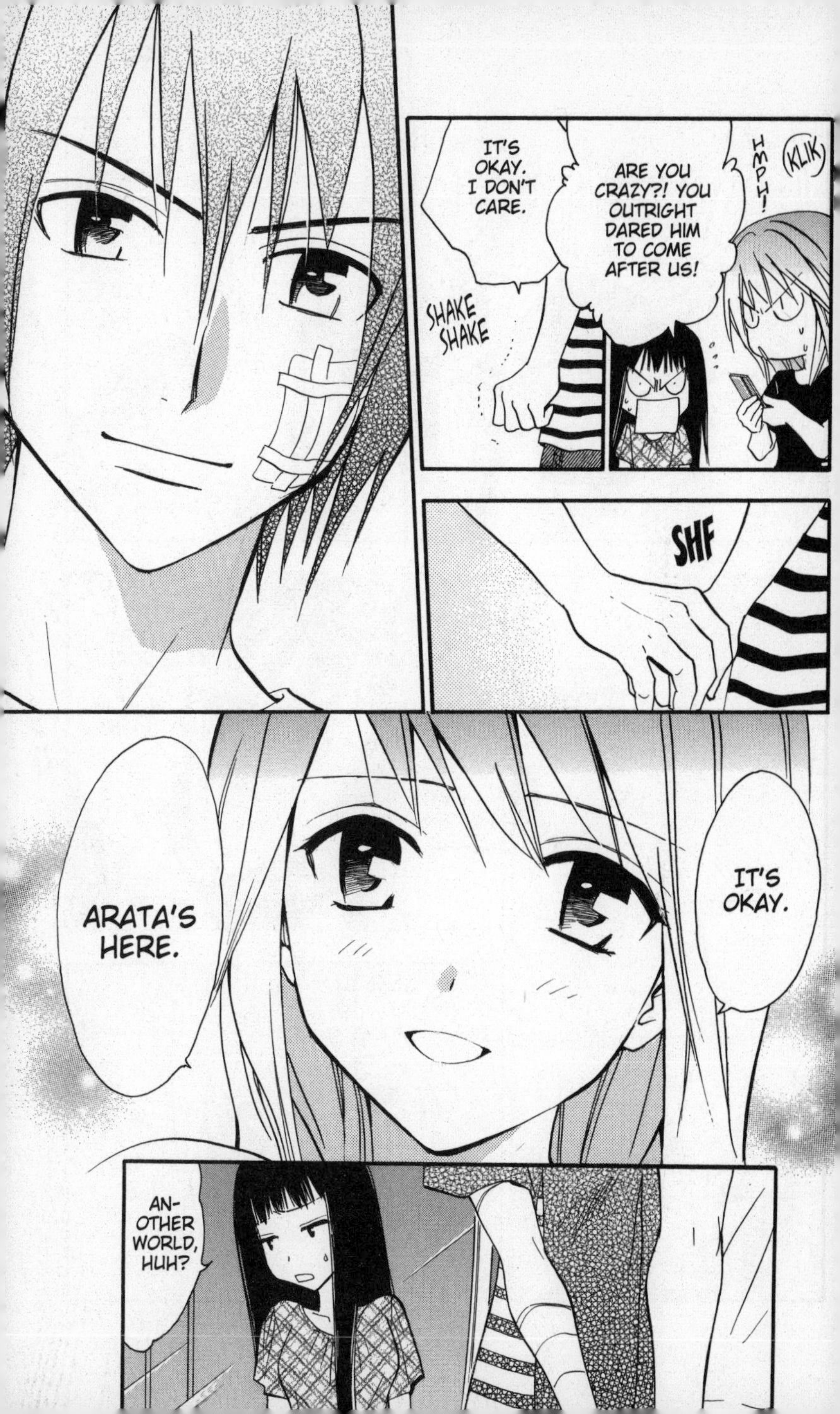
KLIK
HMPH!
ARE YOU CRAZY?! YOU OUTRIGHT DARED HIM TO COME AFTER US!
IT'S OKAY. I DON'T CARE.
SHAKE SHAKE
SHF
IT'S OKAY.
ARATA'S HERE.
AN-OTHER WORLD, HUH?

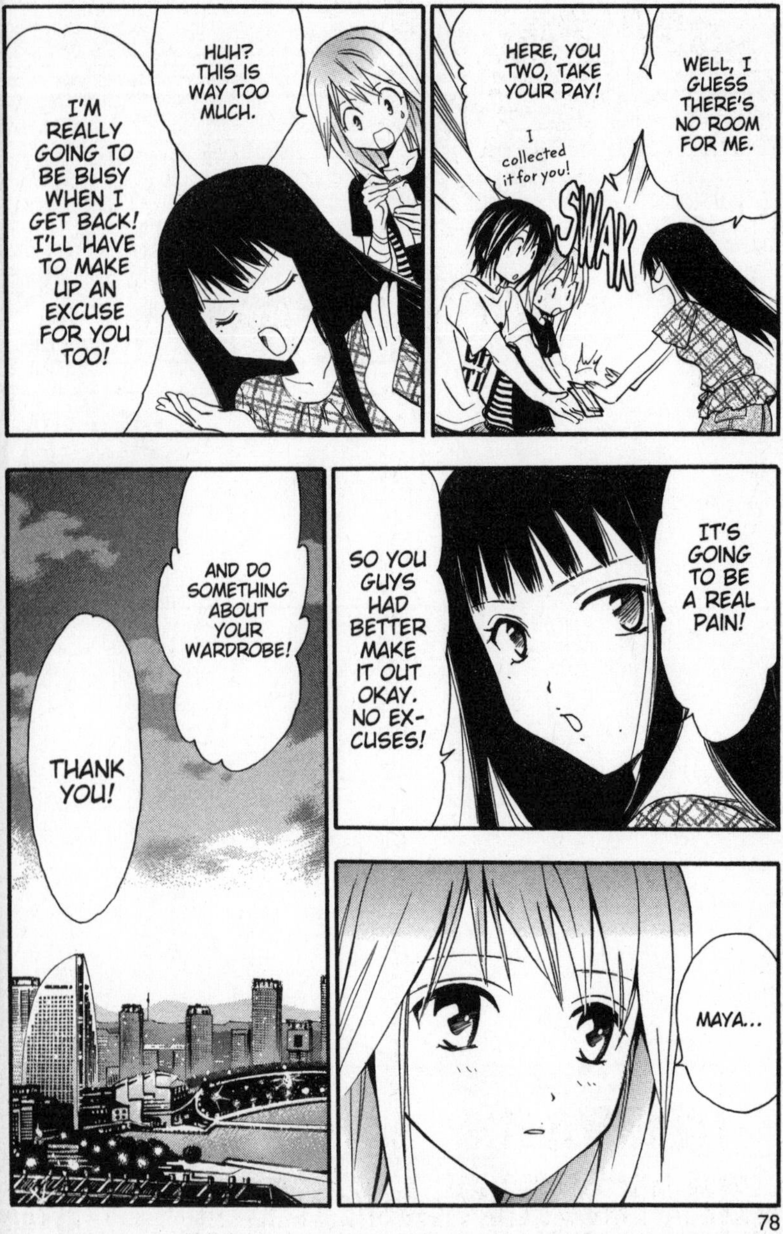
WELL, I GUESS THERE'S NO ROOM FOR ME.
HERE, YOU TWO, TAKE YOUR PAY!
I collected it for you!
SWAK
HUH? THIS IS WAY TOO MUCH.
I'M REALLY GOING TO BE BUSY WHEN I GET BACK! I'LL HAVE TO MAKE UP AN EXCUSE FOR YOU TOO!
IT'S GOING TO BE A REAL PAIN!
SO YOU GUYS HAD BETTER MAKE IT OUT OKAY. NO EX-CUSES!
MAYA...
AND DO SOMETHING ABOUT YOUR WARDROBE!
THANK YOU!

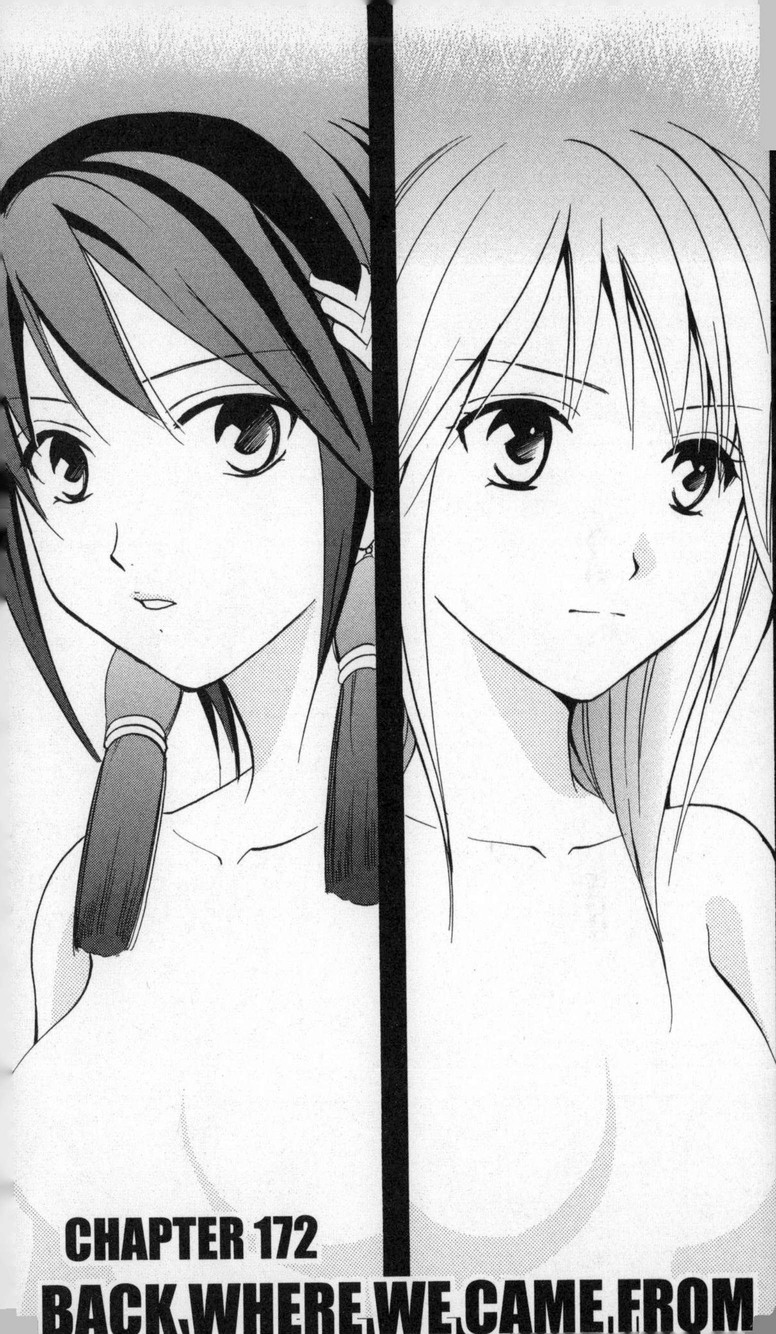
CHAPTER 172
BACK.WHERE.WE.CAME.FROM

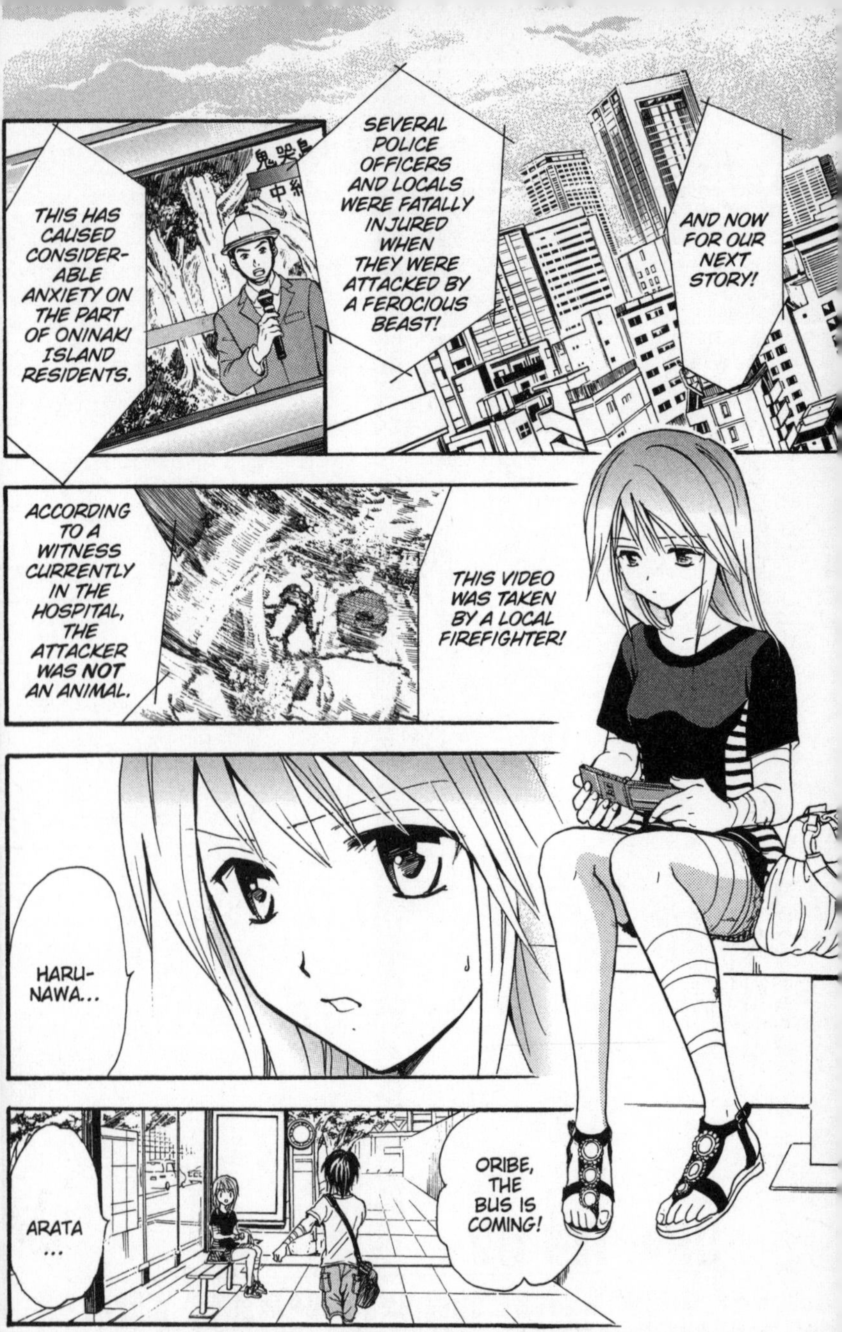
AND NOW FOR OUR NEXT STORY!
SEVERAL POLICE OFFICERS AND LOCALS WERE FATALLY INJURED WHEN THEY WERE ATTACKED BY A FEROCIOUS BEAST!
THIS HAS CAUSED CONSIDER-ABLE ANXIETY ON THE PART OF ONINAKI ISLAND RESIDENTS.
THIS VIDEO WAS TAKEN BY A LOCAL FIREFIGHTER!
ACCORDING TO A WITNESS CURRENTLY IN THE HOSPITAL, THE ATTACKER WAS NOT AN ANIMAL.
HARU-NAWA...
ORIBE, THE BUS IS COMING!
ARATA ...

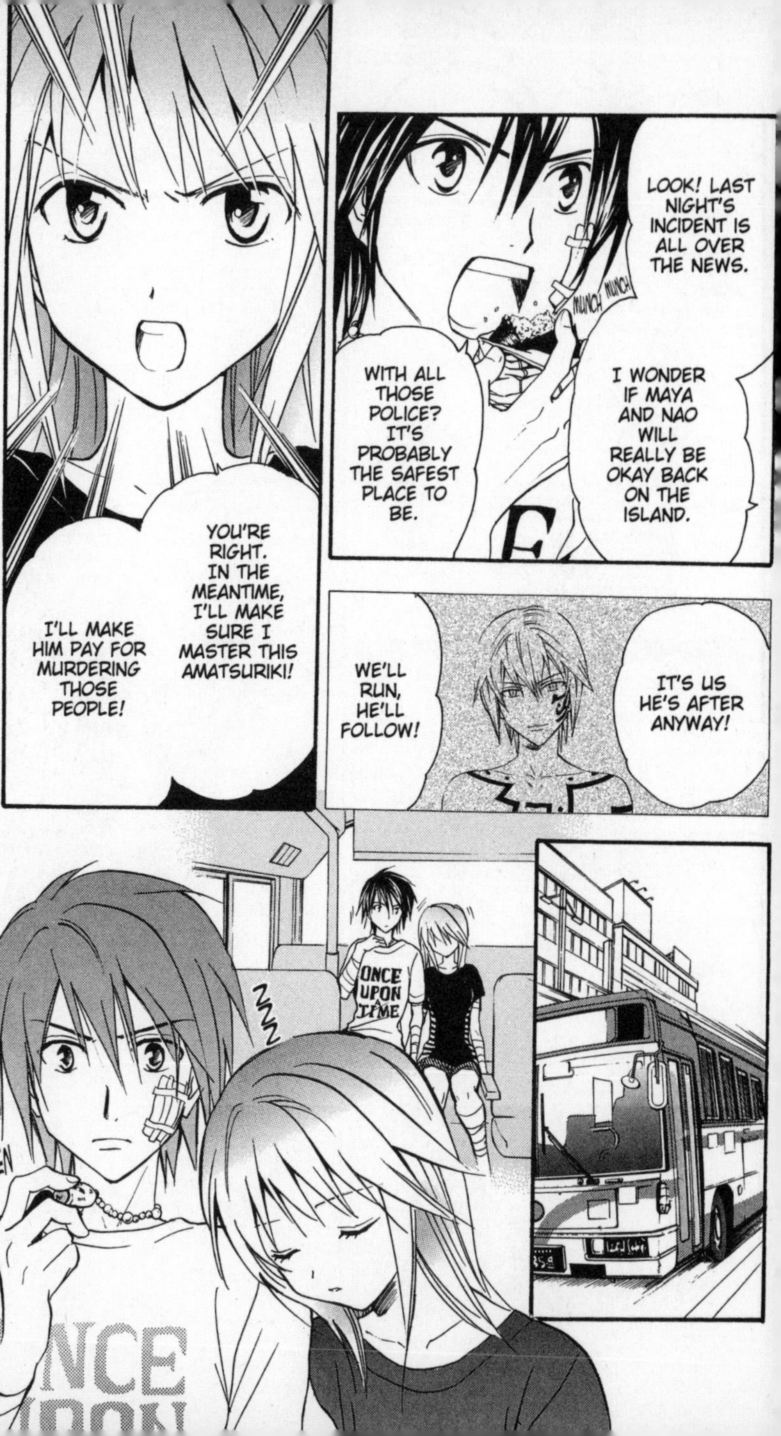
LOOK! LAST NIGHT'S INCIDENT IS ALL OVER THE NEWS.
MUNCH MUNCH
I WONDER IF MAYA AND NAO WILL REALLY BE OKAY BACK ON THE ISLAND.
WITH ALL THOSE POLICE? IT'S PROBABLY THE SAFEST PLACE TO BE.
IT'S US HE'S AFTER ANYWAY!
WE'LL RUN, HE'LL FOLLOW!
YOU'RE RIGHT. IN THE MEANTIME, I'LL MAKE SURE I MASTER THIS AMATSURIKI!
I'LL MAKE HIM PAY FOR MURDERING THOSE PEOPLE!
ONCE UPON A TIME
ZZZ
SHEEN

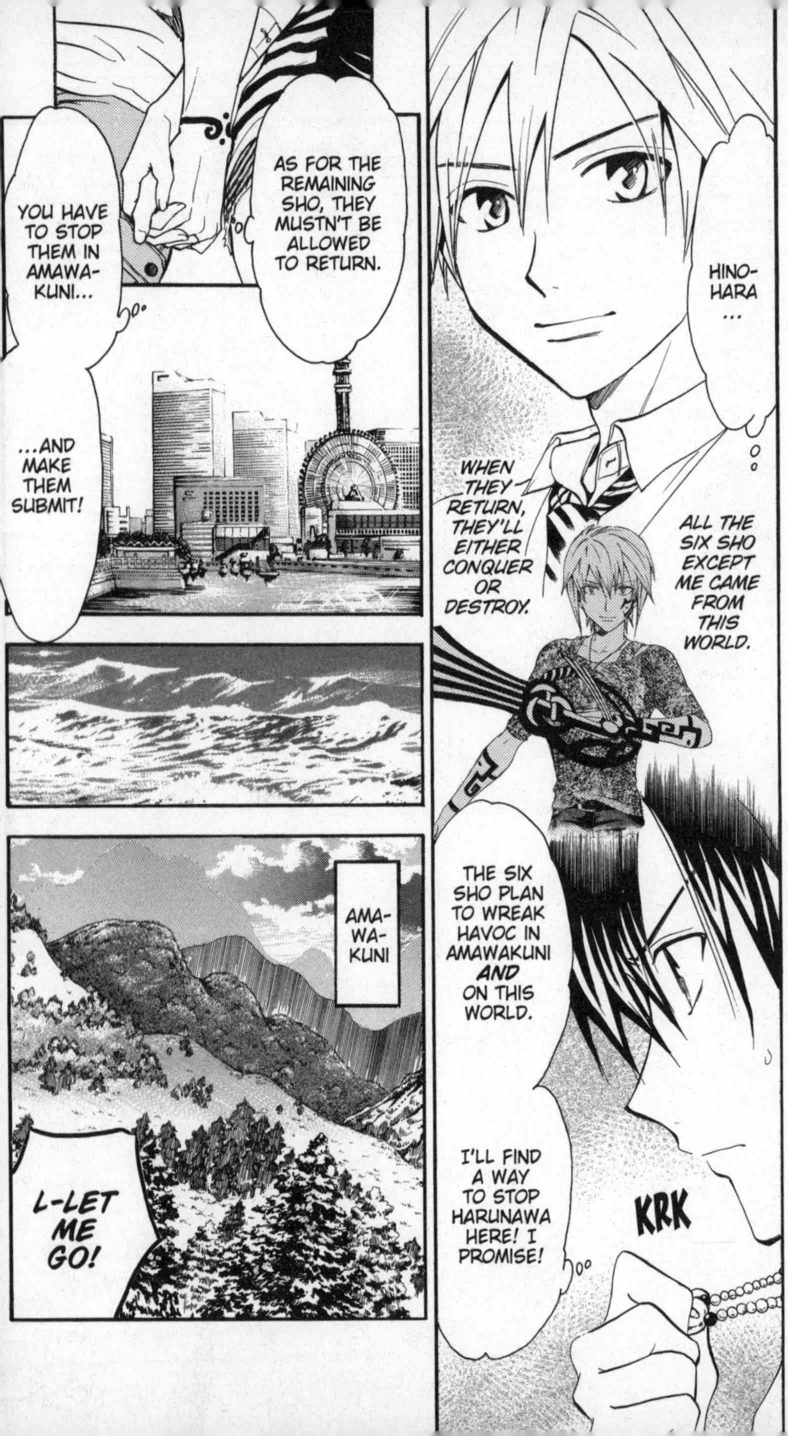
HINO-HARA...
ALL THE SIX SHO EXCEPT ME CAME FROM THIS WORLD.
WHEN THEY RETURN, THEY'LL EITHER CONQUER OR DESTROY.
THE SIX SHO PLAN TO WREAK HAVOC IN AMAWAKUNI AND ON THIS WORLD.
I'LL FIND A WAY TO STOP HARUNAWA HERE! I PROMISE!
KRK
AS FOR THE REMAINING SHO, THEY MUSTN'T BE ALLOWED TO RETURN.
YOU HAVE TO STOP THEM IN AMAWA-KUNI...
...AND MAKE THEM SUBMIT!
AMA-WA-KUNI
L-LET ME GO!

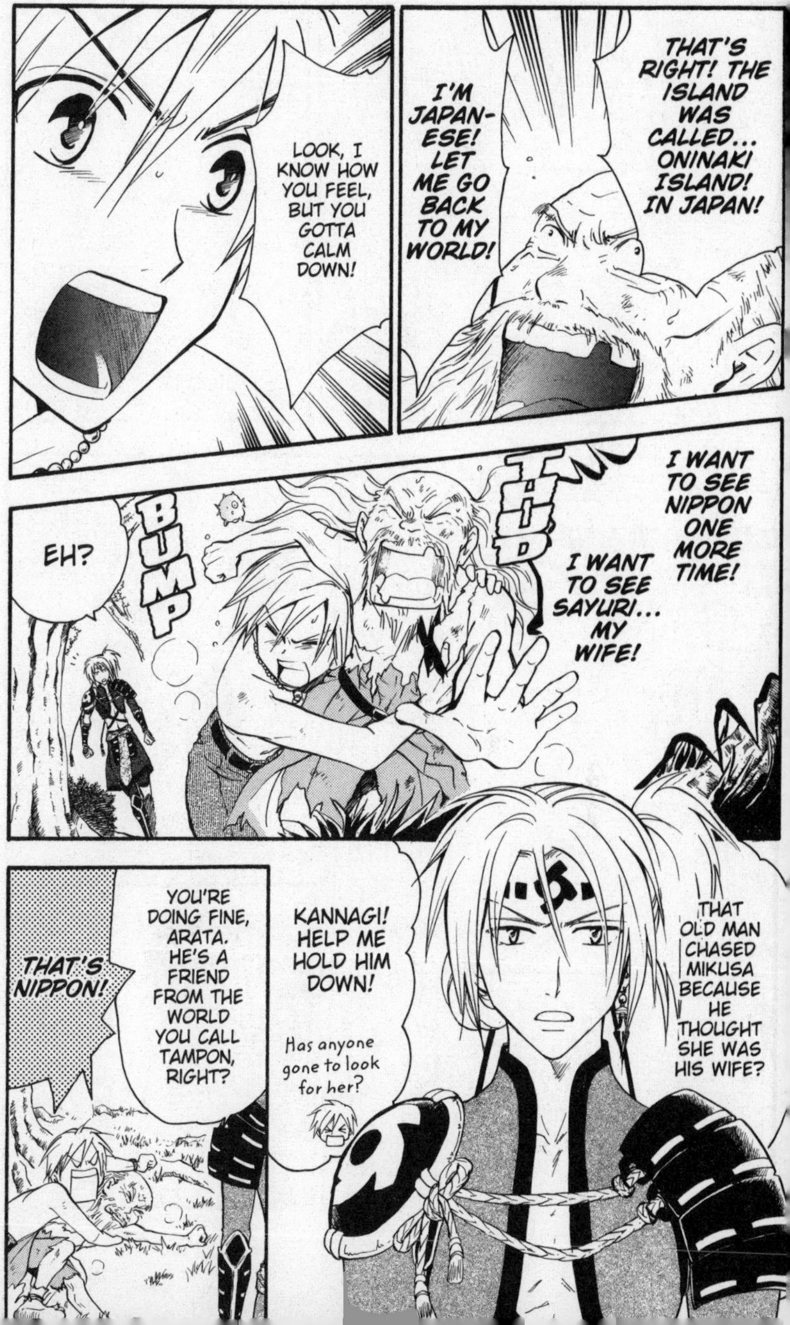
THAT'S RIGHT! THE ISLAND WAS CALLED... ONINAKI ISLAND! IN JAPAN!
I'M JAPAN-ESE! LET ME GO BACK TO MY WORLD!
LOOK, I KNOW HOW YOU FEEL, BUT YOU GOTTA CALM DOWN!
I WANT TO SEE NIPPON ONE MORE TIME!
THUD
I WANT TO SEE SAYURI... MY WIFE!
BUMP
EH?
THAT OLD MAN CHASED MIKUSA BECAUSE HE THOUGHT SHE WAS HIS WIFE?
KANNAGI! HELP ME HOLD HIM DOWN!
Has anyone gone to look for her?
YOU'RE DOING FINE, ARATA. HE'S A FRIEND FROM THE WORLD YOU CALL TAMPON, RIGHT?
THAT'S NIPPON!

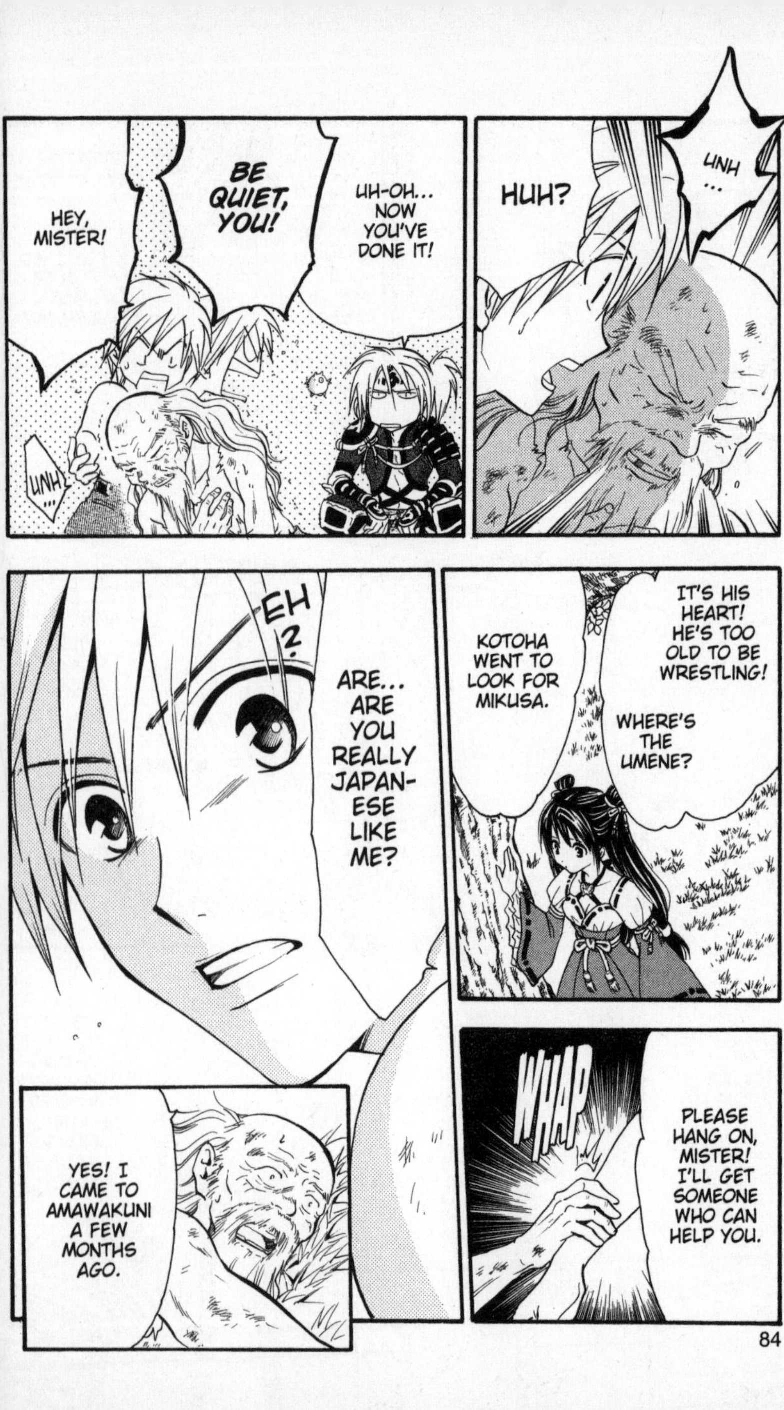
UNH ...
HUH?
UH-OH... NOW YOU'VE DONE IT!
BE QUIET, YOU!
HEY, MISTER!
UNH ...
IT'S HIS HEART! HE'S TOO OLD TO BE WRESTLING!
WHERE'S THE UMENE?
KOTOHA WENT TO LOOK FOR MIKUSA.
WHAP
PLEASE HANG ON, MISTER! I'LL GET SOMEONE WHO CAN HELP YOU.
EH?
ARE... ARE YOU REALLY JAPANESE LIKE ME?
YES! I CAME TO AMAWAKUNI A FEW MONTHS AGO.

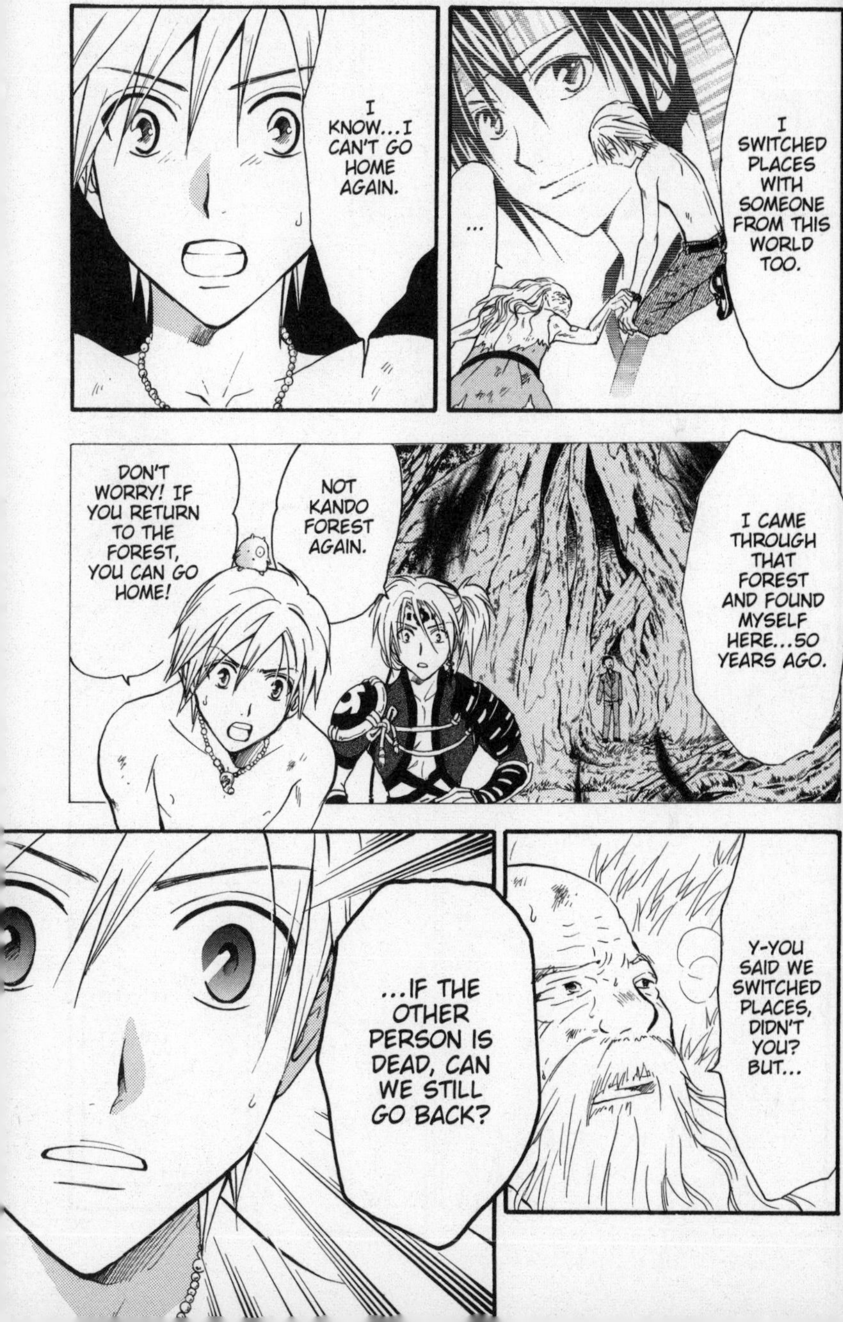
I SWITCHED PLACES WITH SOMEONE FROM THIS WORLD TOO.
...
I KNOW...I CAN'T GO HOME AGAIN.
I CAME THROUGH THAT FOREST AND FOUND MYSELF HERE...50 YEARS AGO.
NOT KANDO FOREST AGAIN.
DON'T WORRY! IF YOU RETURN TO THE FOREST, YOU CAN GO HOME!
Y-YOU SAID WE SWITCHED PLACES, DIDN'T YOU? BUT...
...IF THE OTHER PERSON IS DEAD, CAN WE STILL GO BACK?

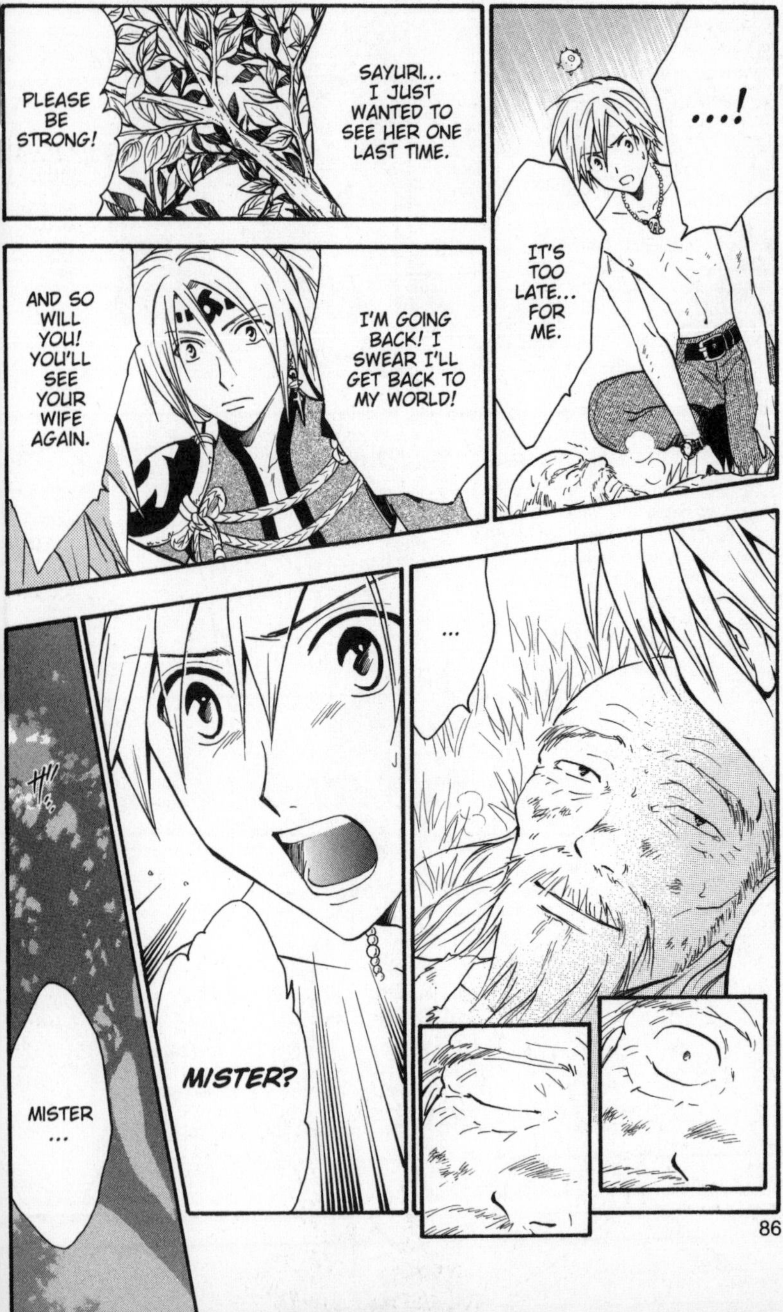
...!
IT'S TOO LATE... FOR ME.
SAYURI... I JUST WANTED TO SEE HER ONE LAST TIME.
PLEASE BE STRONG!
I'M GOING BACK! I SWEAR I'LL GET BACK TO MY WORLD!
AND SO WILL YOU! YOU'LL SEE YOUR WIFE AGAIN.
...
MISTER?
MISTER ...

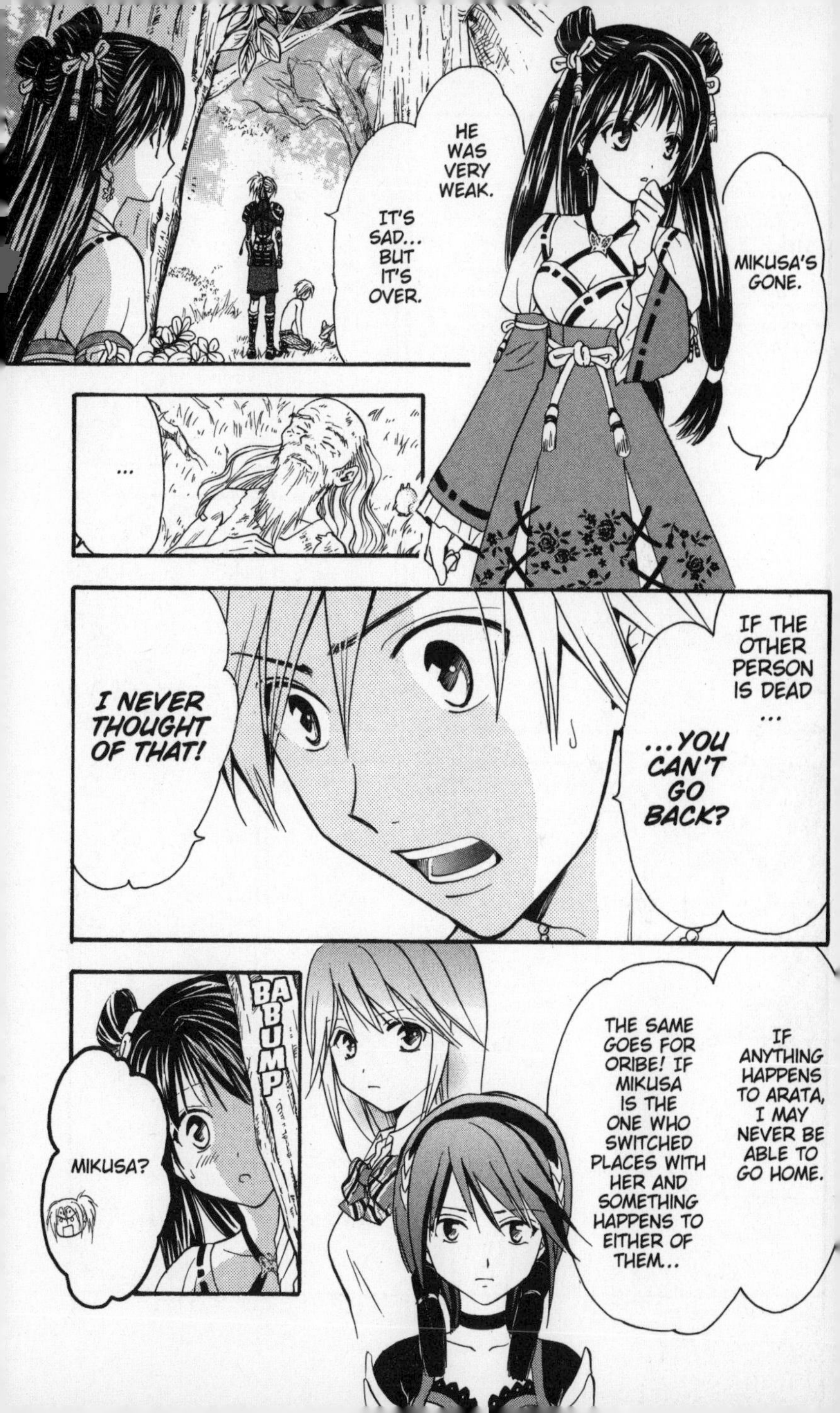
MIKUSA'S GONE.
HE WAS VERY WEAK.
IT'S SAD... BUT IT'S OVER.
...
IF THE OTHER PERSON IS DEAD...
...YOU CAN'T GO BACK?
I NEVER THOUGHT OF THAT!
IF ANYTHING HAPPENS TO ARATA, I MAY NEVER BE ABLE TO GO HOME.
THE SAME GOES FOR ORIBE! IF MIKUSA IS THE ONE WHO SWITCHED PLACES WITH HER AND SOMETHING HAPPENS TO EITHER OF THEM..
BABUMP
MIKUSA?

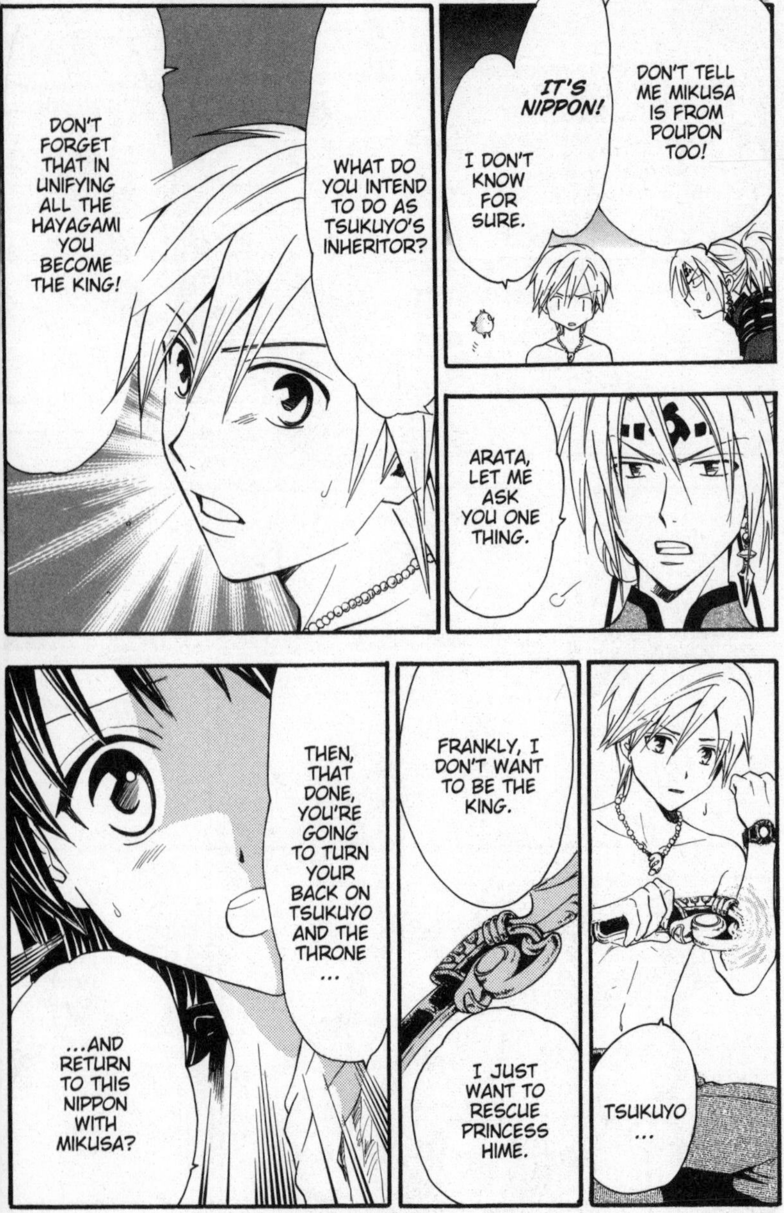
DON'T TELL ME MIKUSA IS FROM POUPON TOO!
IT'S NIPPON!
I DON'T KNOW FOR SURE.
ARATA, LET ME ASK YOU ONE THING.
WHAT DO YOU INTEND TO DO AS TSUKUYO'S INHERITOR?
DON'T FORGET THAT IN UNIFYING ALL THE HAYAGAMI YOU BECOME THE KING!
TSUKUYO...
FRANKLY, I DON'T WANT TO BE THE KING.
I JUST WANT TO RESCUE PRINCESS HIME.
THEN, THAT DONE, YOU'RE GOING TO TURN YOUR BACK ON TSUKUYO AND THE THRONE...
...AND RETURN TO THIS NIPPON WITH MIKUSA?

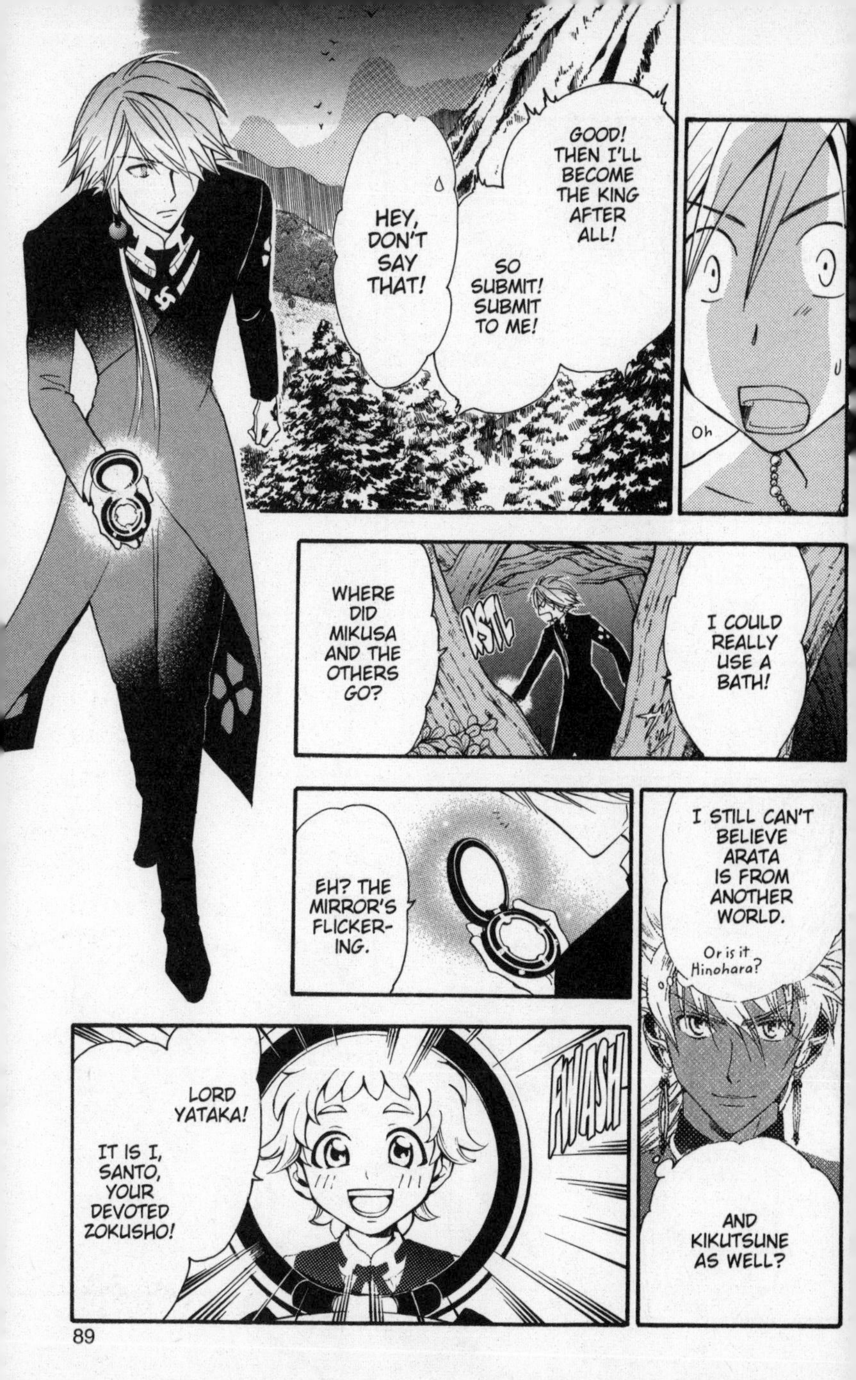
Oh
GOOD! THEN I'LL BECOME THE KING AFTER ALL!
SO SUBMIT! SUBMIT TO ME!
HEY, DON'T SAY THAT!
I COULD REALLY USE A BATH!
RSTL
WHERE DID MIKUSA AND THE OTHERS GO?
I STILL CAN'T BELIEVE ARATA IS FROM ANOTHER WORLD.
Or is it Hinohara?
AND KIKUTSUNE AS WELL?
EH? THE MIRROR'S FLICKER-ING.
FWASH
LORD YATAKA!
IT IS I, SANTO, YOUR DEVOTED ZOKUSHO!

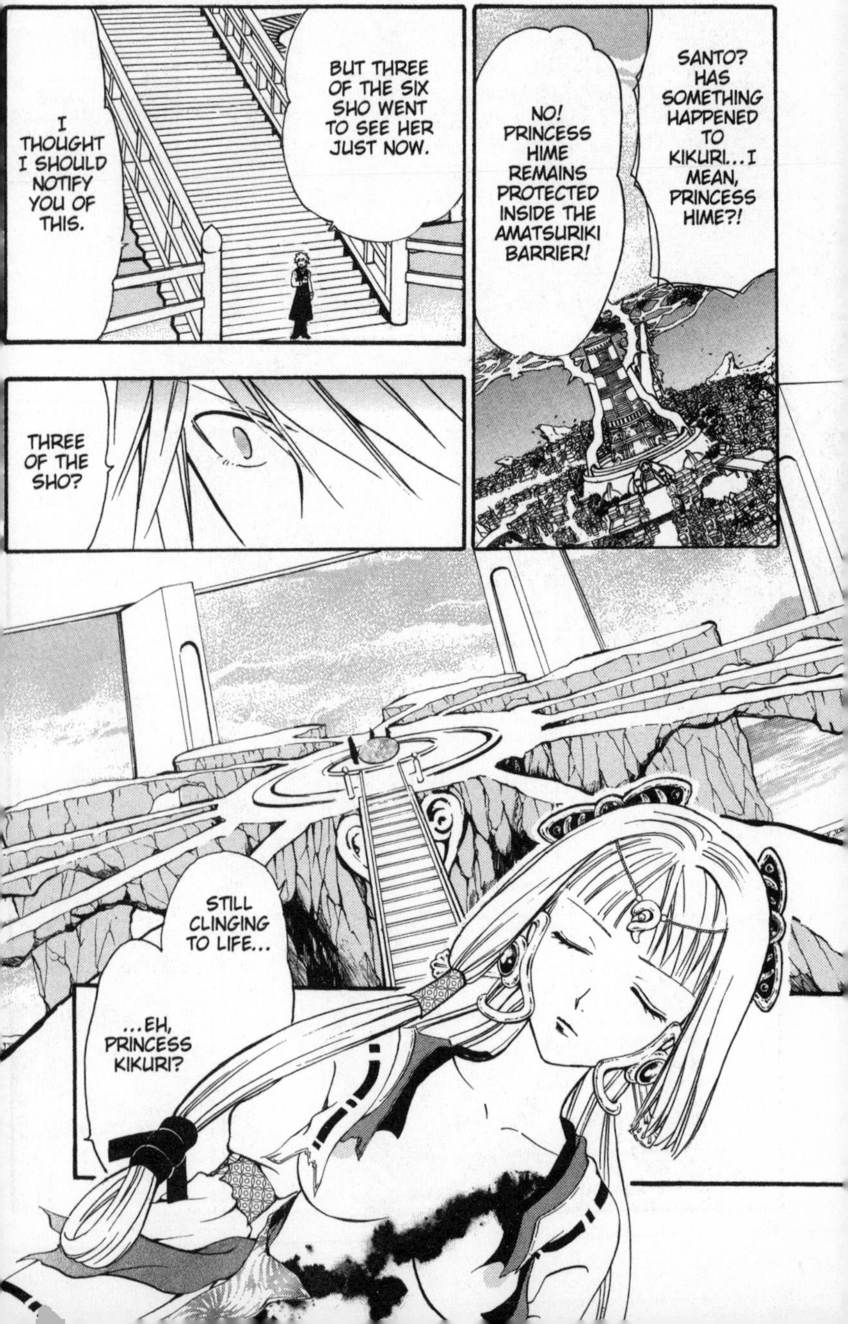
SANTO? HAS SOMETHING HAPPENED TO KIKURI...I MEAN, PRINCESS HIME?!
NO! PRINCESS HIME REMAINS PROTECTED INSIDE THE AMATSURIKI BARRIER!
BUT THREE OF THE SIX SHO WENT TO SEE HER JUST NOW.
I THOUGHT I SHOULD NOTIFY YOU OF THIS.
THREE OF THE SHO?
STILL CLINGING TO LIFE...
...EH, PRINCESS KIKURI?

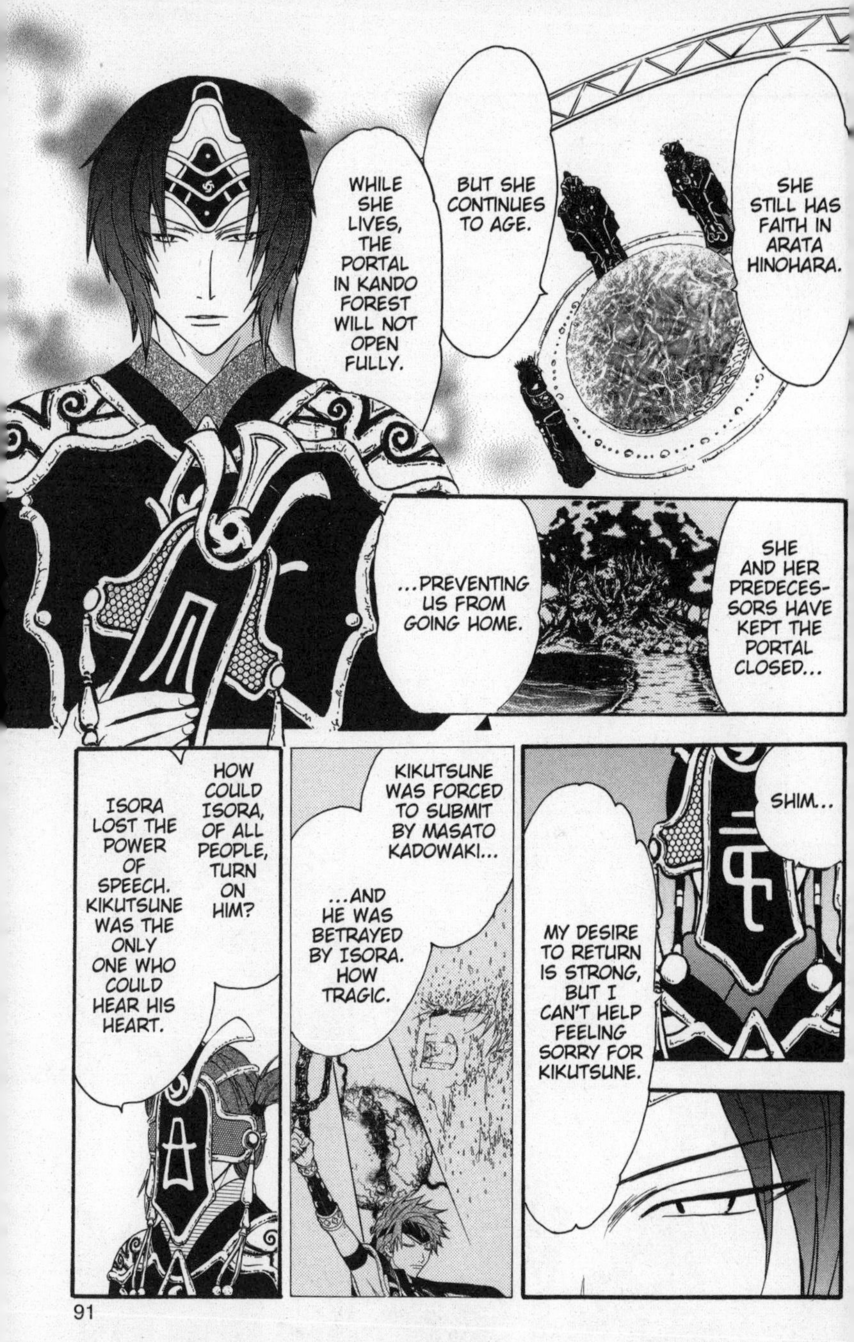
SHE STILL HAS FAITH IN ARATA HINOHARA.
BUT SHE CONTINUES TO AGE.
WHILE SHE LIVES, THE PORTAL IN KANDO FOREST WILL NOT OPEN FULLY.
SHE AND HER PREDECES-SORS HAVE KEPT THE PORTAL CLOSED...
...PREVENTING US FROM GOING HOME.
SHIM...
MY DESIRE TO RETURN IS STRONG, BUT I CAN'T HELP FEELING SORRY FOR KIKUTSUNE.
KIKUTSUNE WAS FORCED TO SUBMIT BY MASATO KADOWAKI...
...AND HE WAS BETRAYED BY ISORA. HOW TRAGIC.
HOW COULD ISORA, OF ALL PEOPLE, TURN ON HIM?
ISORA LOST THE POWER OF SPEECH. KIKUTSUNE WAS THE ONLY ONE WHO COULD HEAR HIS HEART.

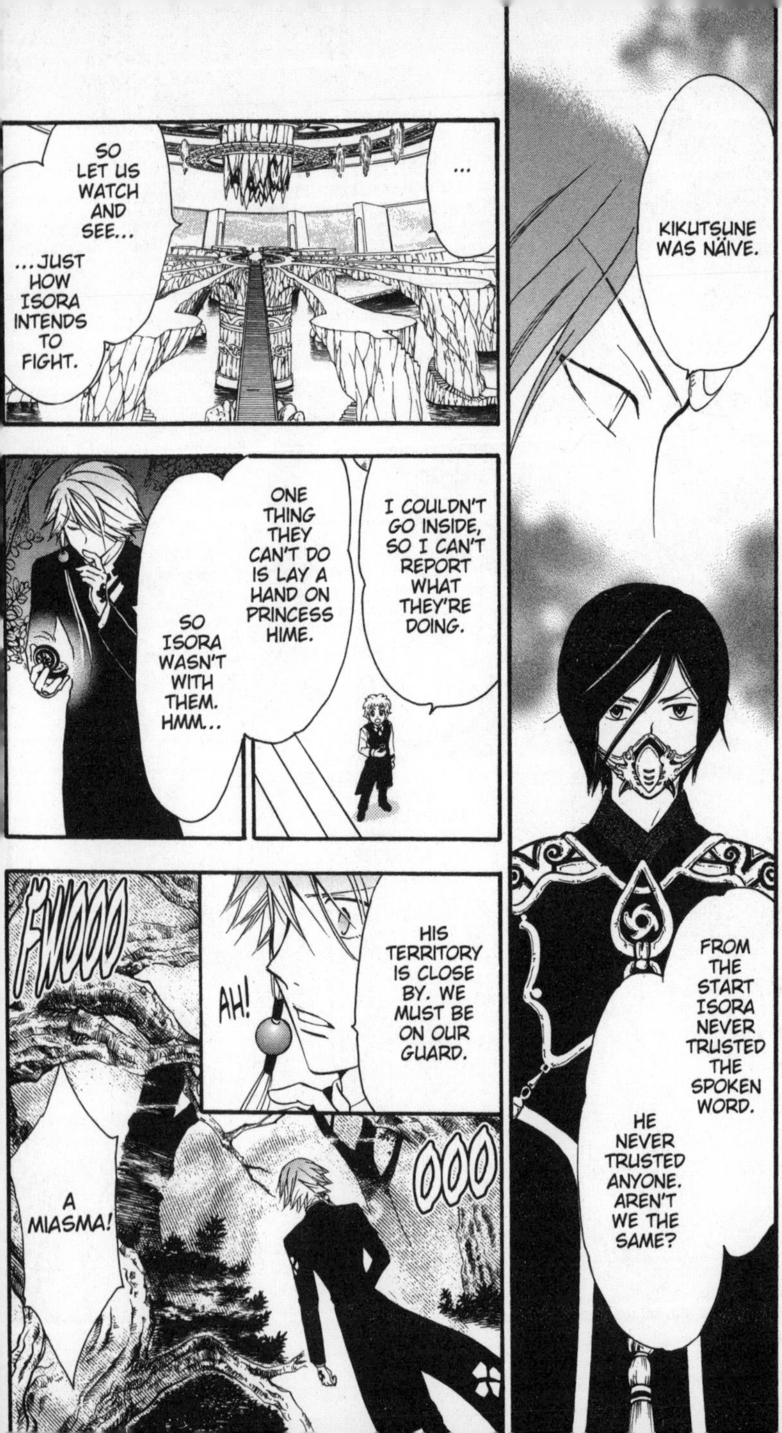
KIKUTSUNE WAS NÄIVE.
FROM THE START ISORA NEVER TRUSTED THE SPOKEN WORD.
HE NEVER TRUSTED ANYONE. AREN'T WE THE SAME?
...
SO LET US WATCH AND SEE...
...JUST HOW ISORA INTENDS TO FIGHT.
I COULDN'T GO INSIDE, SO I CAN'T REPORT WHAT THEY'RE DOING.
ONE THING THEY CAN'T DO IS LAY A HAND ON PRINCESS HIME.
SO ISORA WASN'T WITH THEM. HMM...
HIS TERRITORY IS CLOSE BY. WE MUST BE ON OUR GUARD.
AH!
FWOOOOOO
A MIASMA!

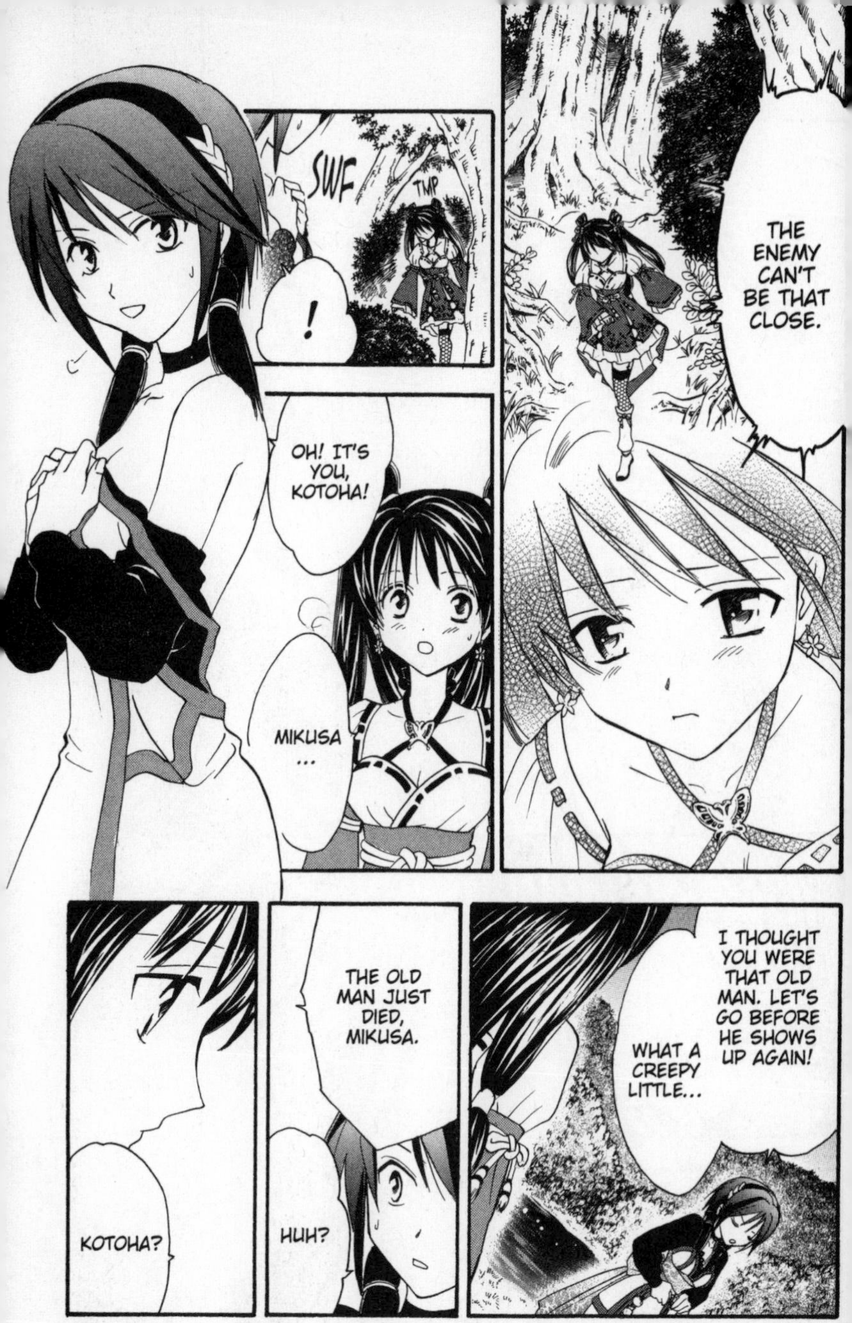
THE ENEMY CAN'T BE THAT CLOSE.
SWF
TMP
!
OH! IT'S YOU, KOTOHA!
MIKUSA ...
I THOUGHT YOU WERE THAT OLD MAN. LET'S GO BEFORE HE SHOWS UP AGAIN!
WHAT A CREEPY LITTLE...
THE OLD MAN JUST DIED, MIKUSA.
HUH?
KOTOHA?

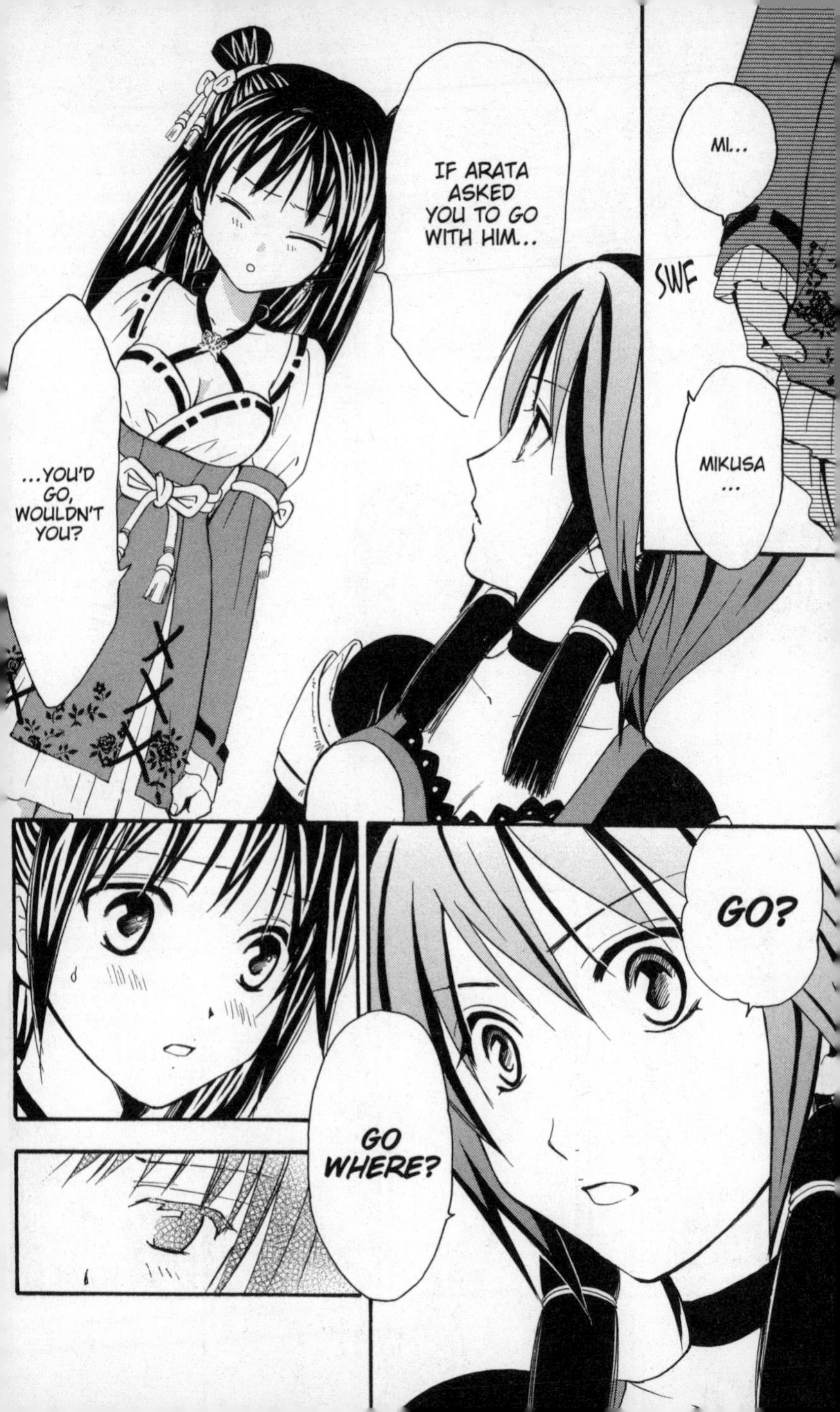
MI...
SWF
MIKUSA...
IF ARATA ASKED YOU TO GO WITH HIM...
...YOU'D GO, WOULDN'T YOU?
GO?
GO WHERE?

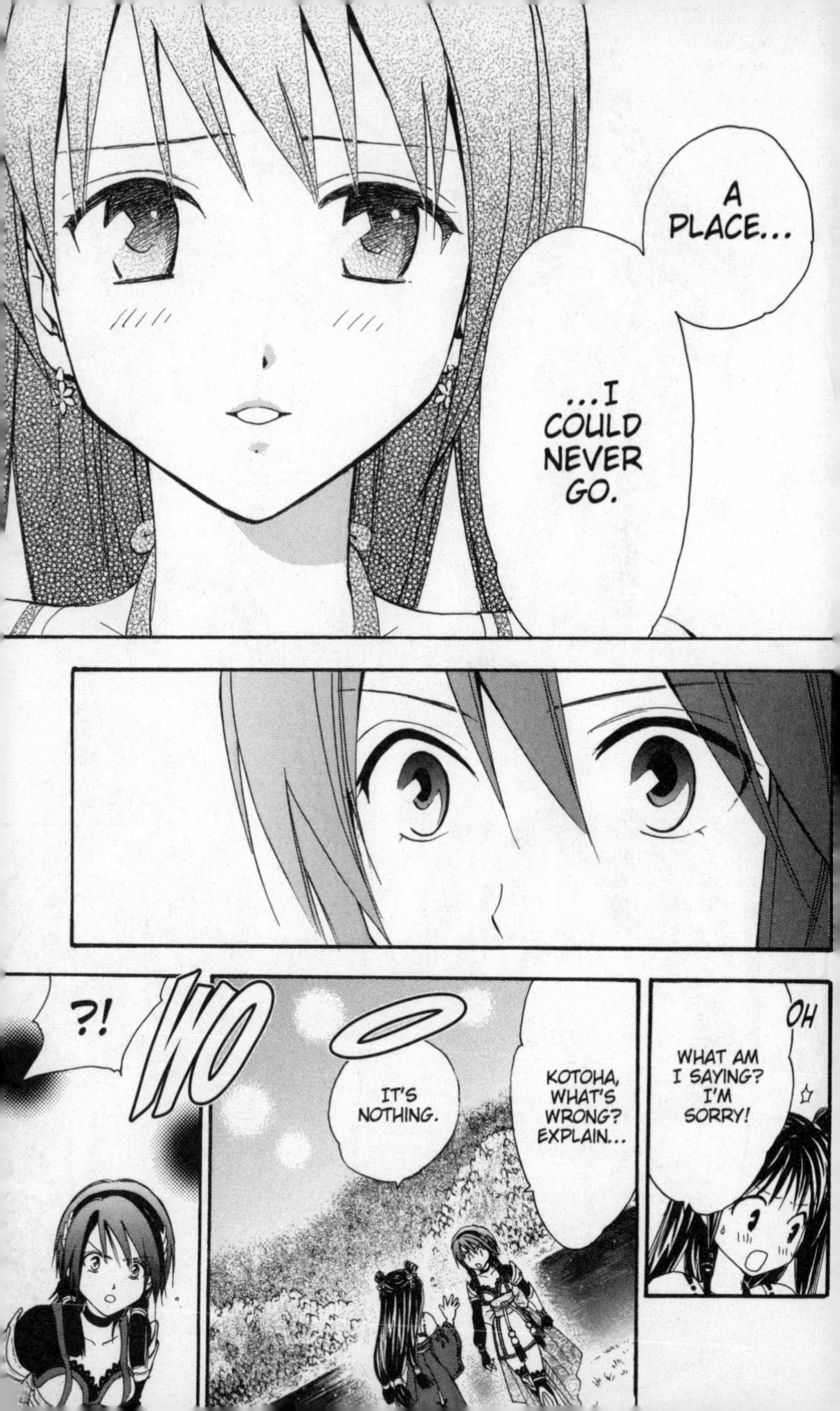
A PLACE...
...I COULD NEVER GO.
OH
WHAT AM I SAYING? I'M SORRY!
KOTOHA, WHAT'S WRONG? EXPLAIN...
IT'S NOTHING.
WO
?!

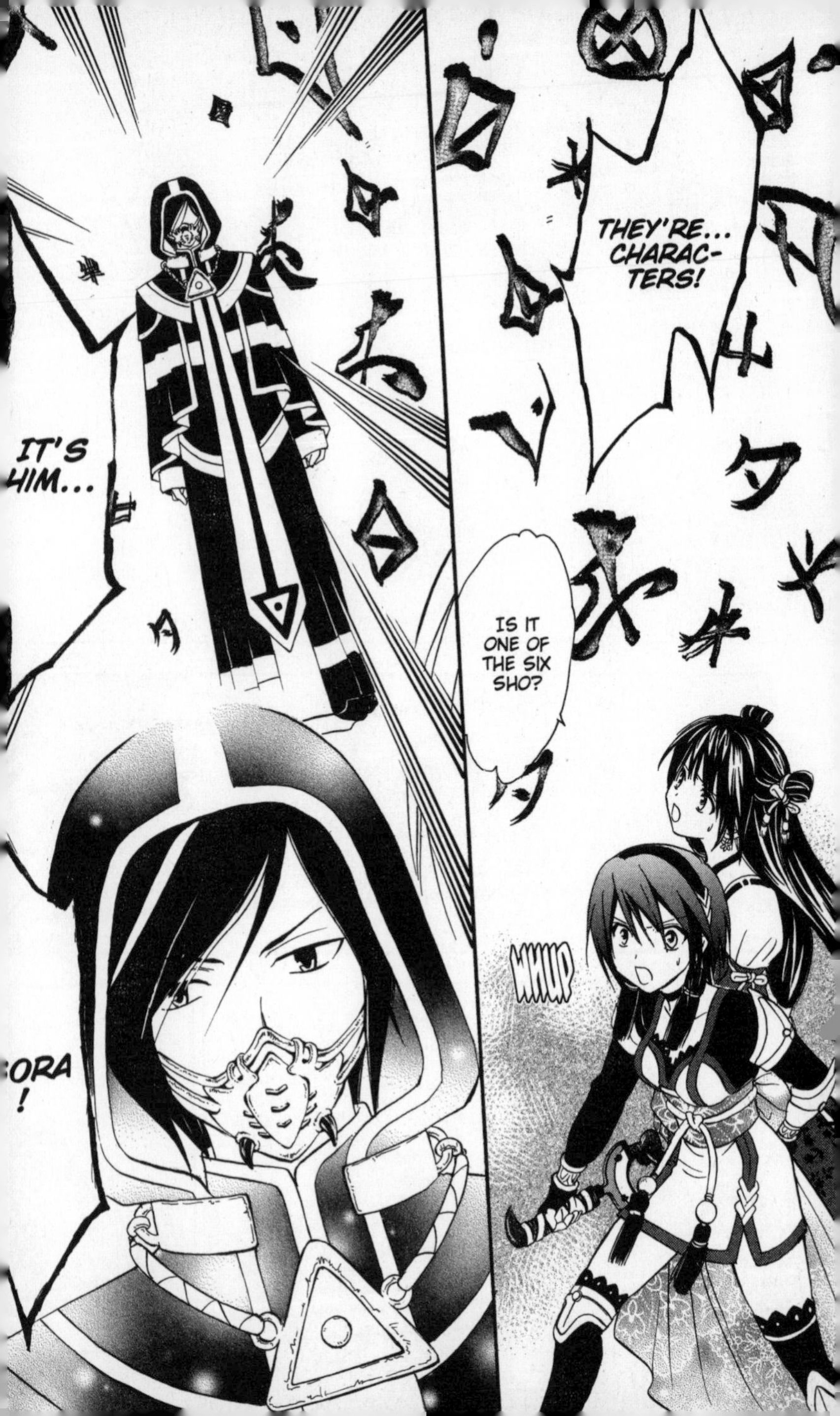

THEY'RE... CHARACTERS!
IS IT ONE OF THE SIX SHO?
WHUP
IT'S HIM...
ORA!

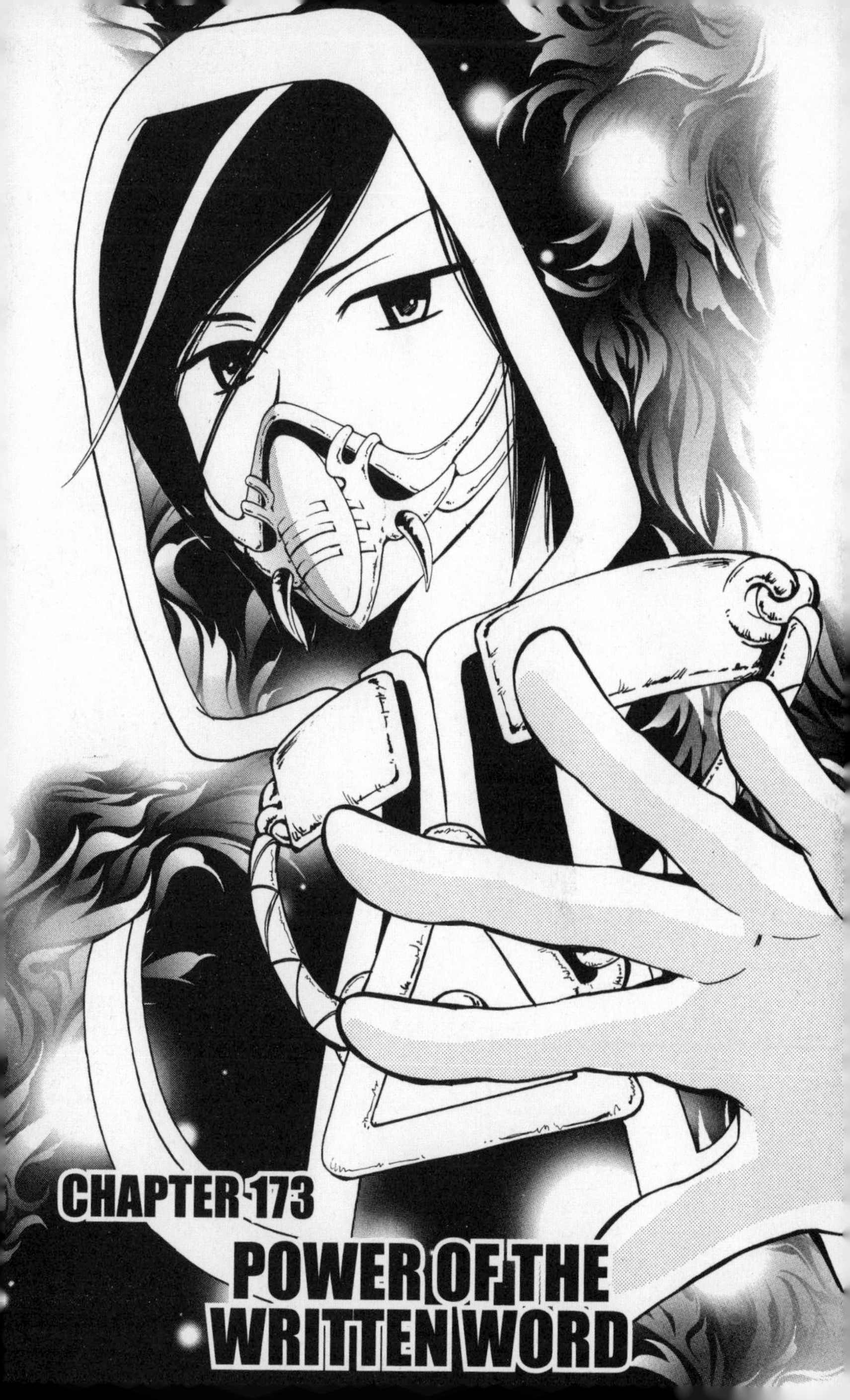
CHAPTER 173
POWER OF THE WRITTEN WORD

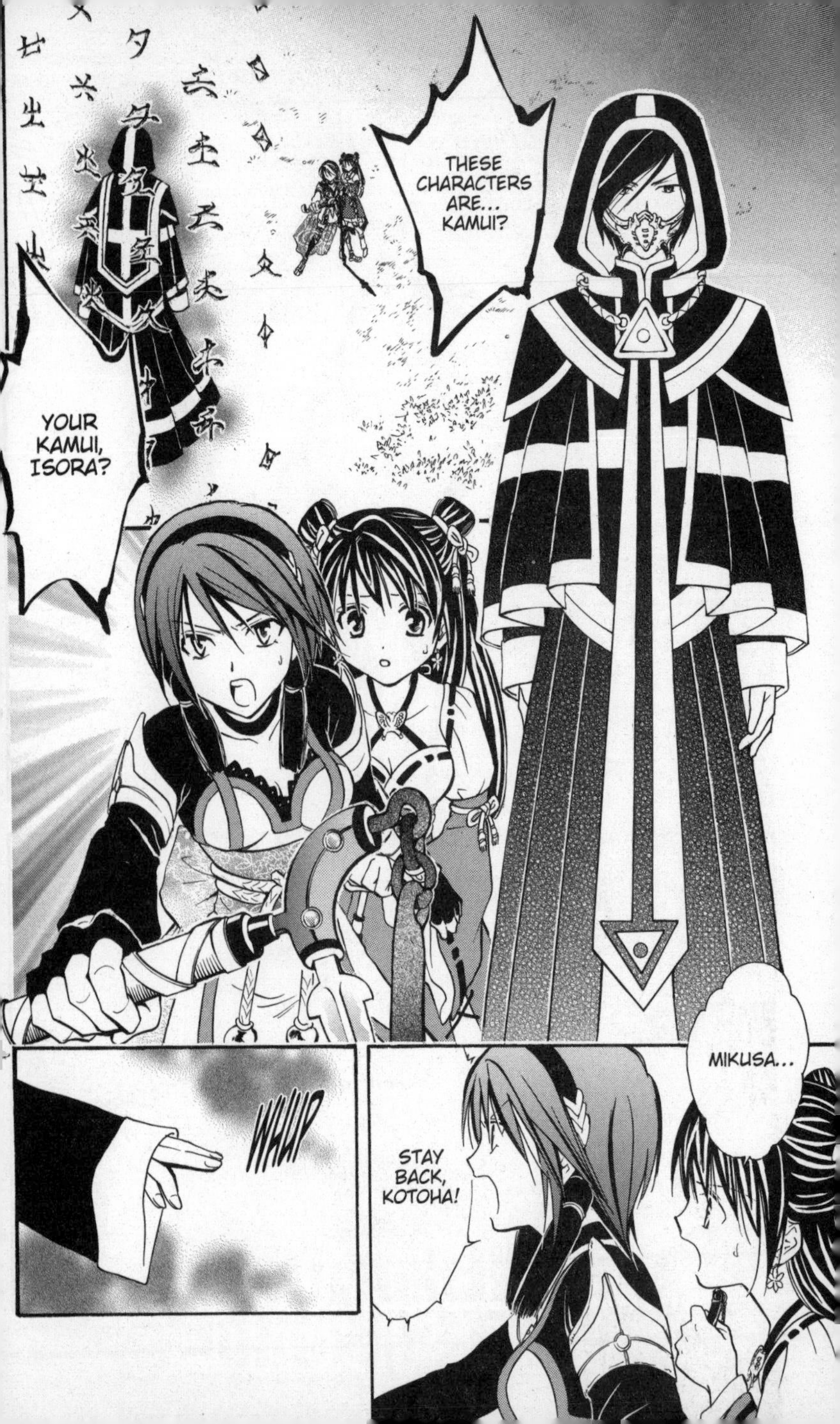
THESE CHARACTERS ARE... KAMUI?
YOUR KAMUI, ISORA?
MIKUSA...
STAY BACK, KOTOHA!
WHIP

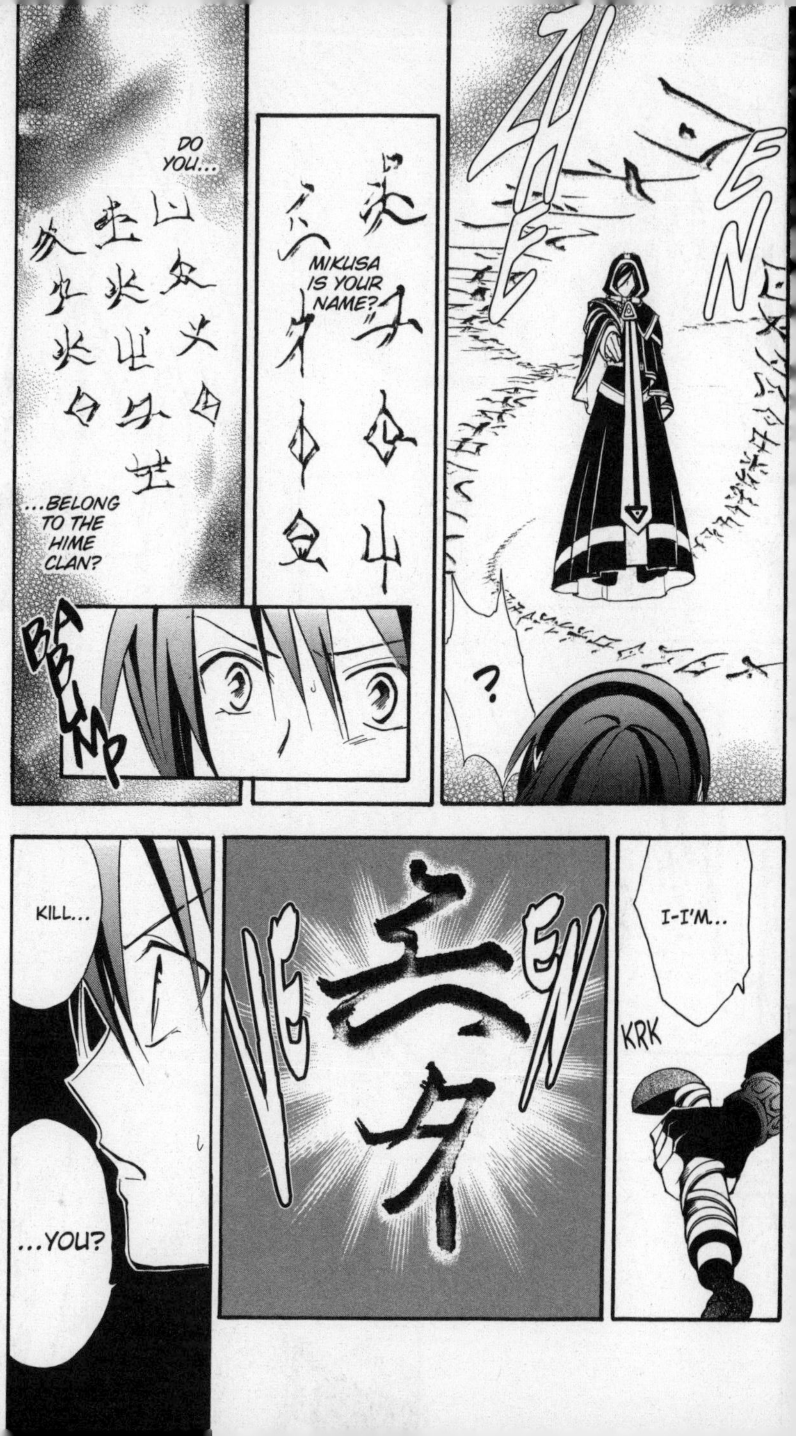
?
MIKUSA IS YOUR NAME?
BABUMP
DO YOU...
...BELONG TO THE HIME CLAN?
I-I'M...
KRK
KILL...
...YOU?

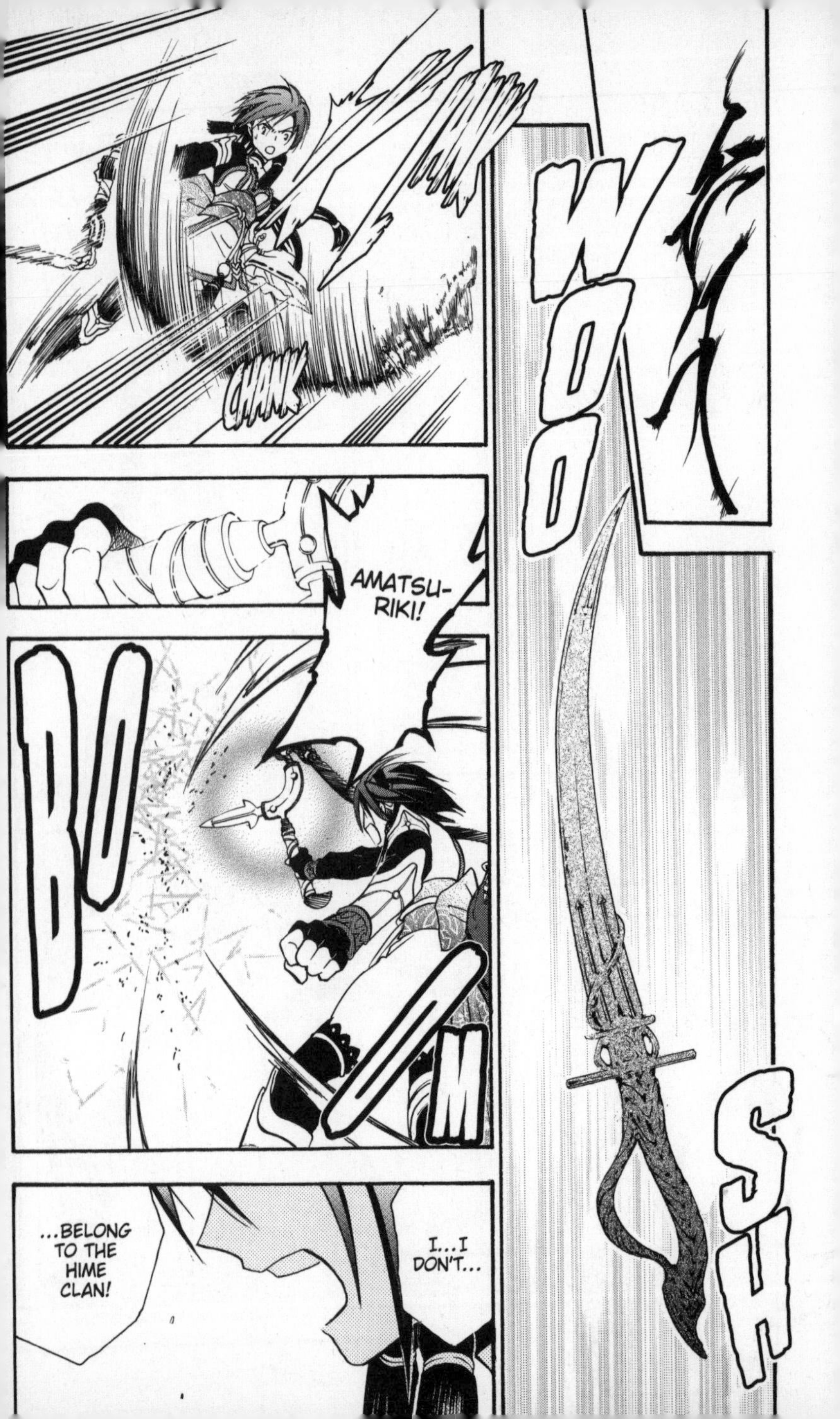

WOOO
SH
CHANK
AMATSU-RIKI!
BOOM
I...I DON'T...
...BELONG TO THE HIME CLAN!

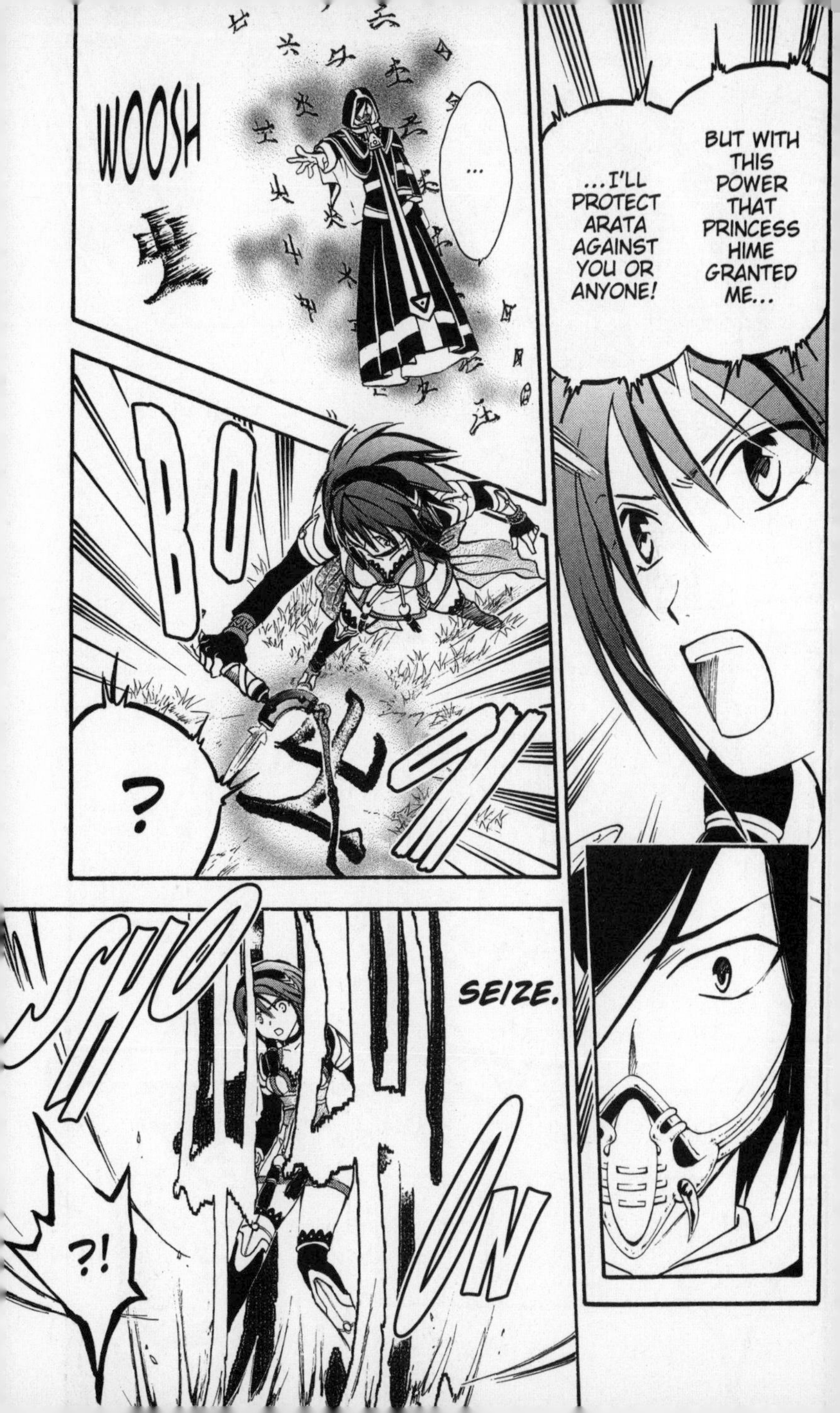
BUT WITH THIS POWER THAT PRINCESS HIME GRANTED ME...
...I'LL PROTECT ARATA AGAINST YOU OR ANYONE!
...
WOOSH
BO
?
SEIZE.
SHO
ON
?!

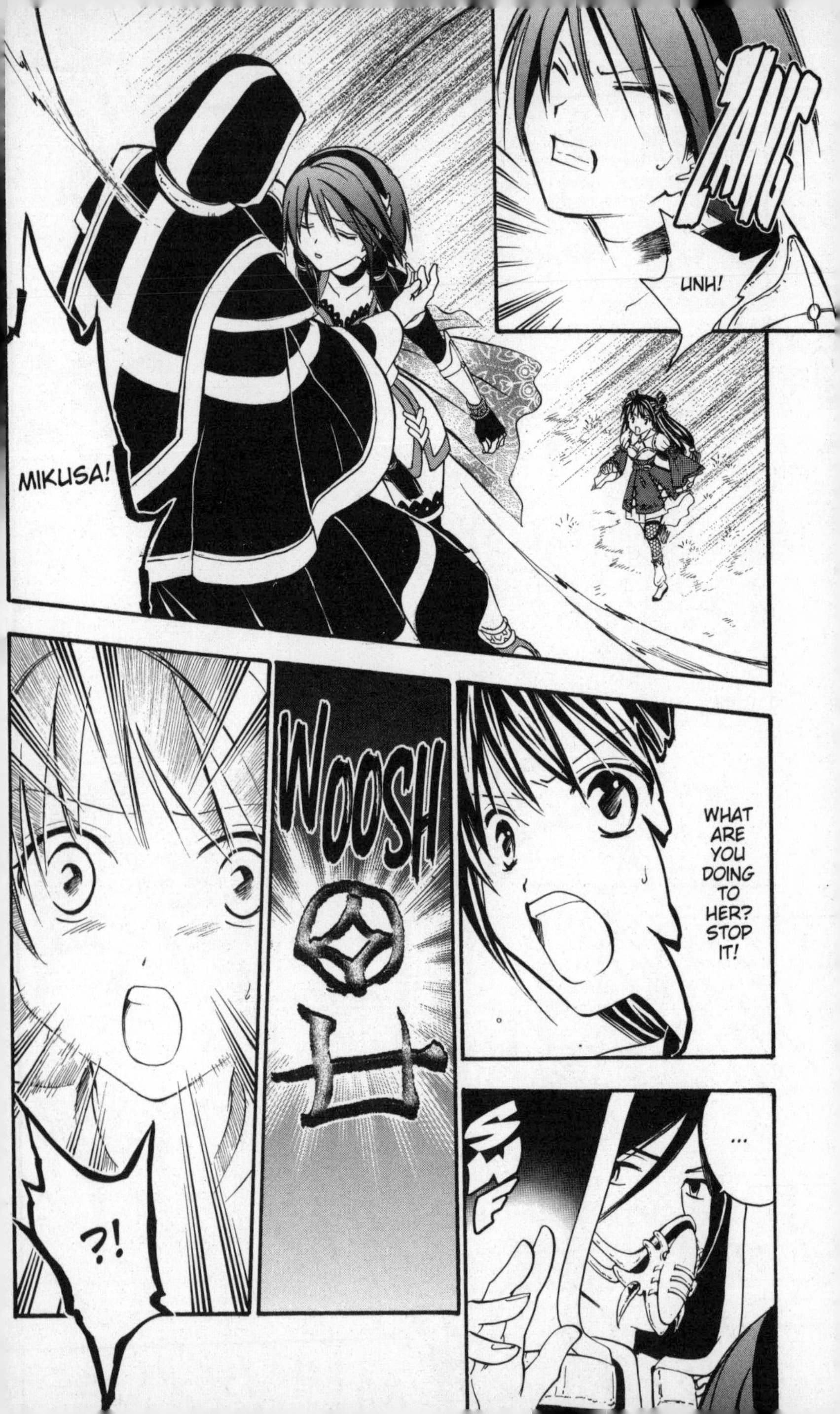
TANG
UNH!
MIKUSA!
WHAT ARE YOU DOING TO HER? STOP IT!
SWF
...
WOOSH
?!

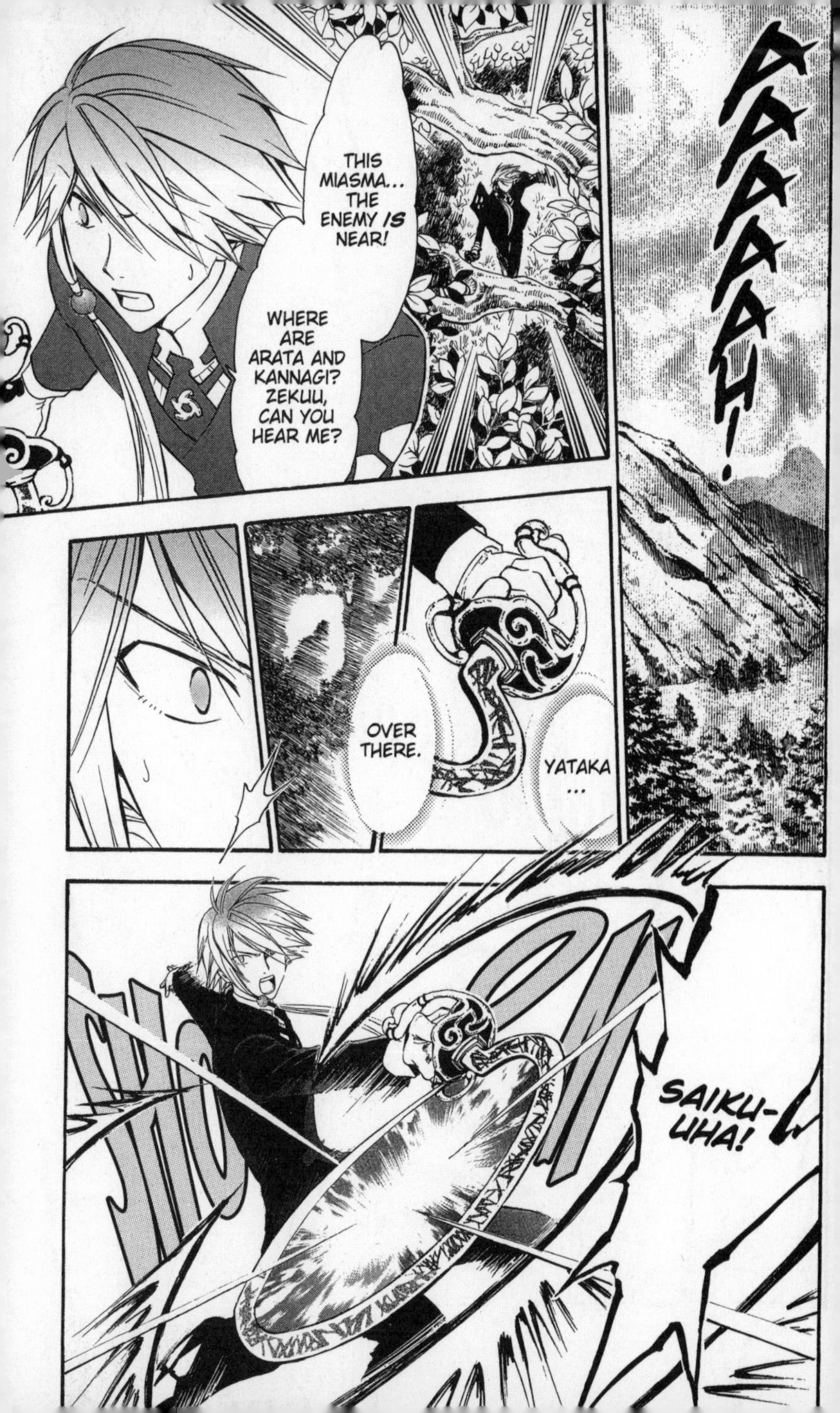
AAAAAH!
THIS MIASMA... THE ENEMY *IS* NEAR!
WHERE ARE ARATA AND KANNAGI? ZEKUU, CAN YOU HEAR ME?
YATAKA...
OVER THERE.
SAIKU-UHA!

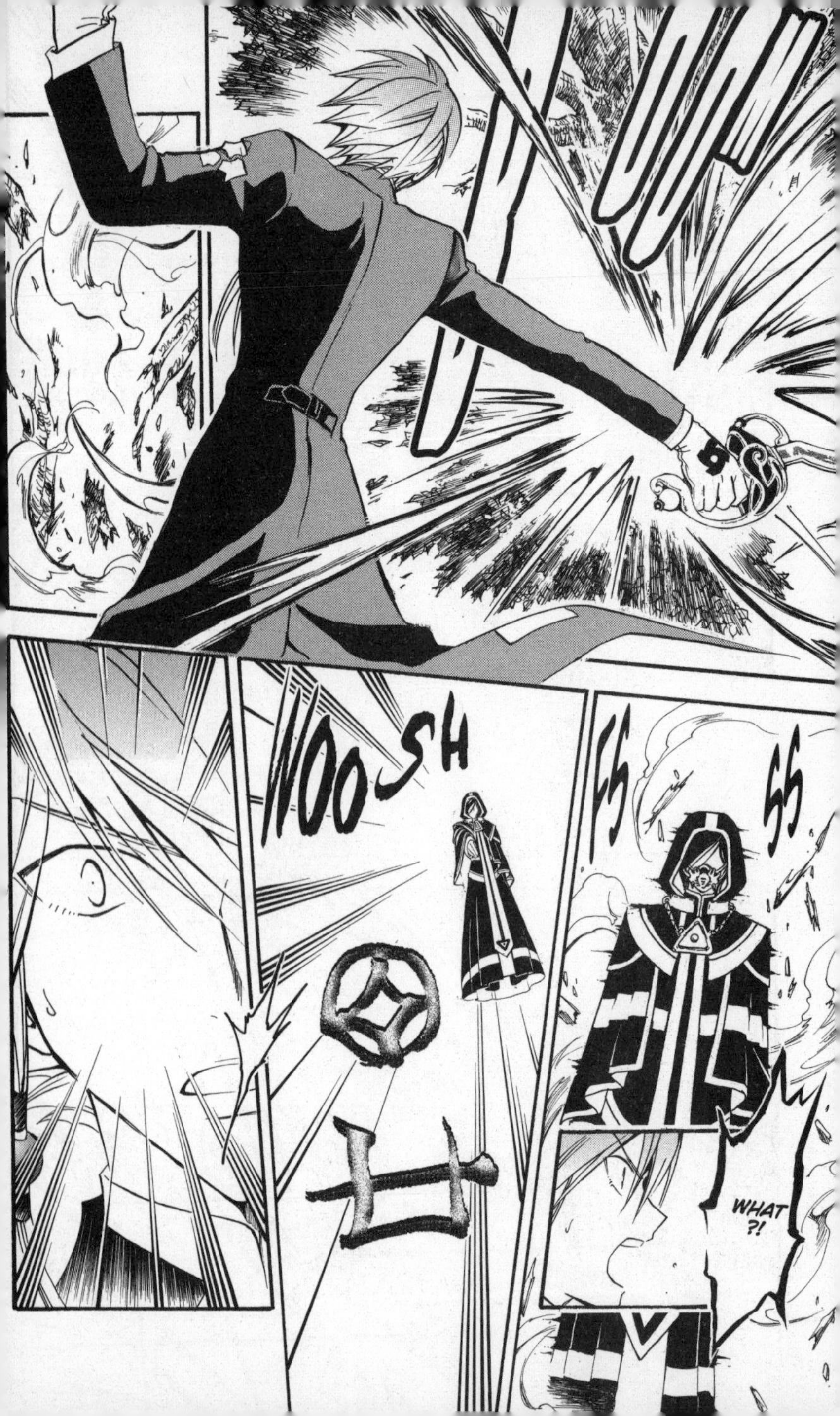
FSSS
WHAT ?!
WOOSH

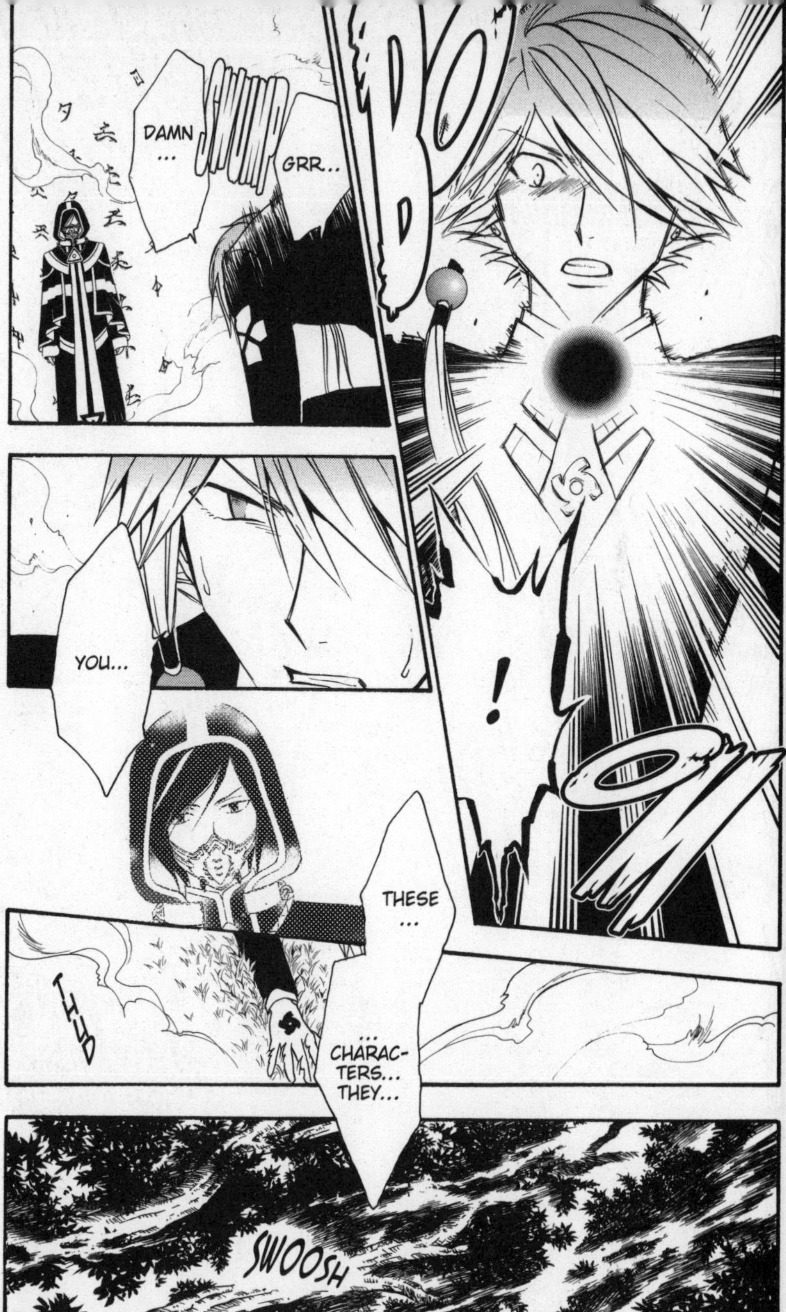
!
GRR...
DAMN ...
YOU...
THESE ...
... CHARAC-TERS... THEY...
THUD
SWOOSH

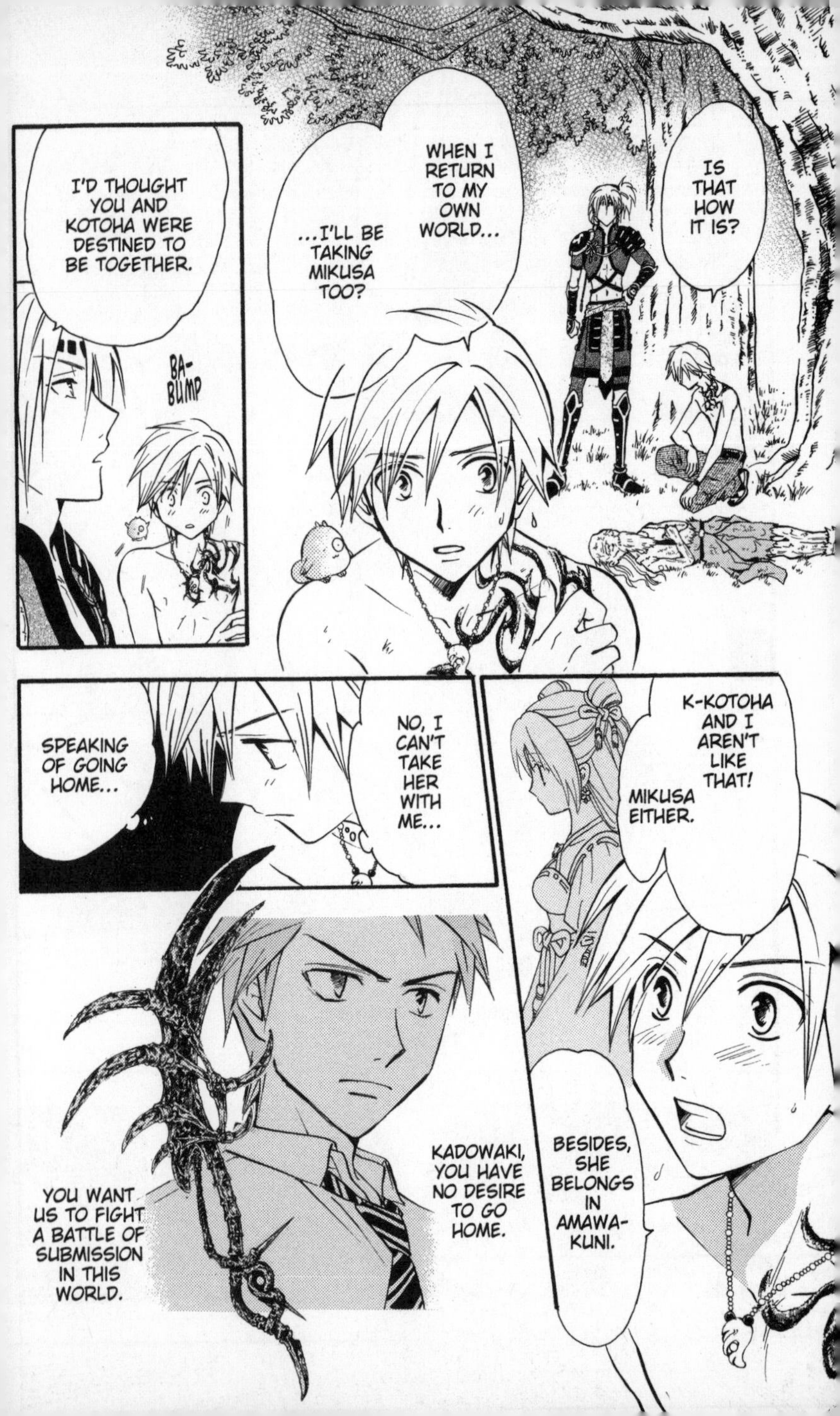
IS THAT HOW IT IS?
WHEN I RETURN TO MY OWN WORLD...
...I'LL BE TAKING MIKUSA TOO?
I'D THOUGHT YOU AND KOTOHA WERE DESTINED TO BE TOGETHER.
BA-BUMP
K-KOTOHA AND I AREN'T LIKE THAT!
MIKUSA EITHER.
BESIDES, SHE BELONGS IN AMAWA-KUNI.
NO, I CAN'T TAKE HER WITH ME...
SPEAKING OF GOING HOME...
KADOWAKI, YOU HAVE NO DESIRE TO GO HOME.
YOU WANT US TO FIGHT A BATTLE OF SUBMISSION IN THIS WORLD.

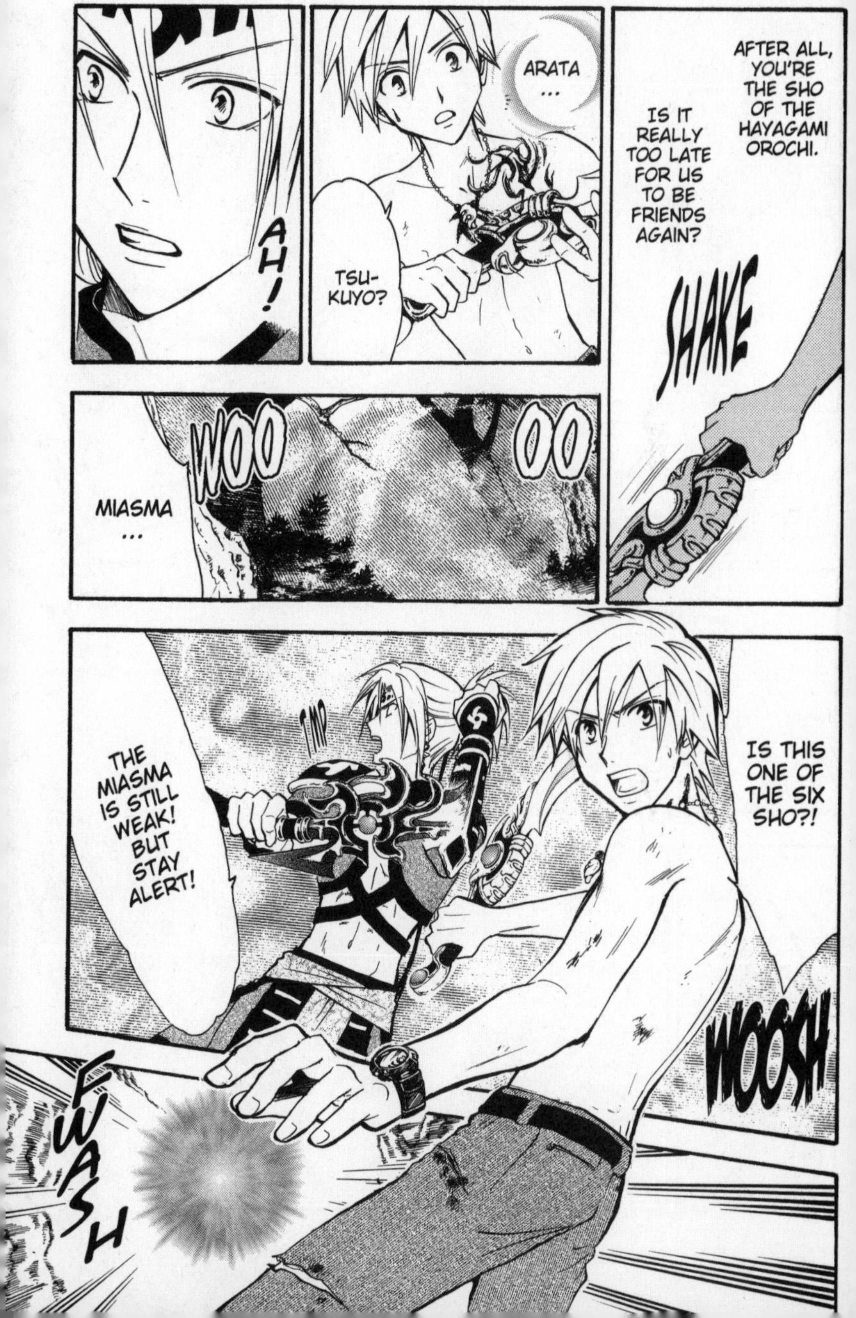

AFTER ALL, YOU'RE THE SHO OF THE HAYAGAMI OROCHI.
IS IT REALLY TOO LATE FOR US TO BE FRIENDS AGAIN?
SHAKE
ARATA ...
TSU-KUYO?
AH!
WOO OO
MIASMA ...
IS THIS ONE OF THE SIX SHO?!
THE MIASMA IS STILL WEAK! BUT STAY ALERT!
WOOSH
FWASH

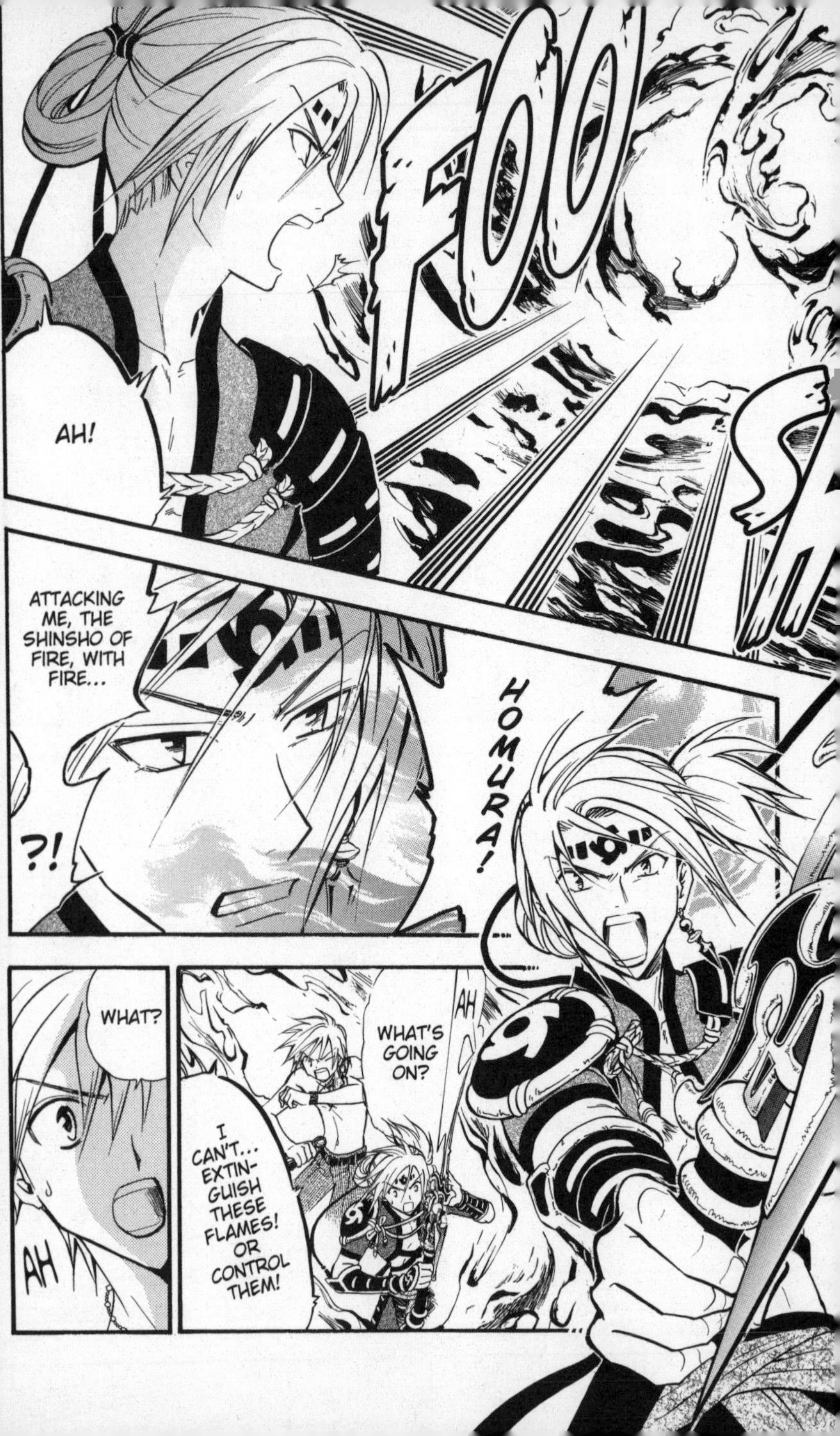
FOOO
AH!
HOMURA!
ATTACKING ME, THE SHINSHO OF FIRE, WITH FIRE...
?!
WHAT'S GOING ON?
AH
I CAN'T... EXTINGUISH THESE FLAMES! OR CONTROL THEM!
WHAT?
AH

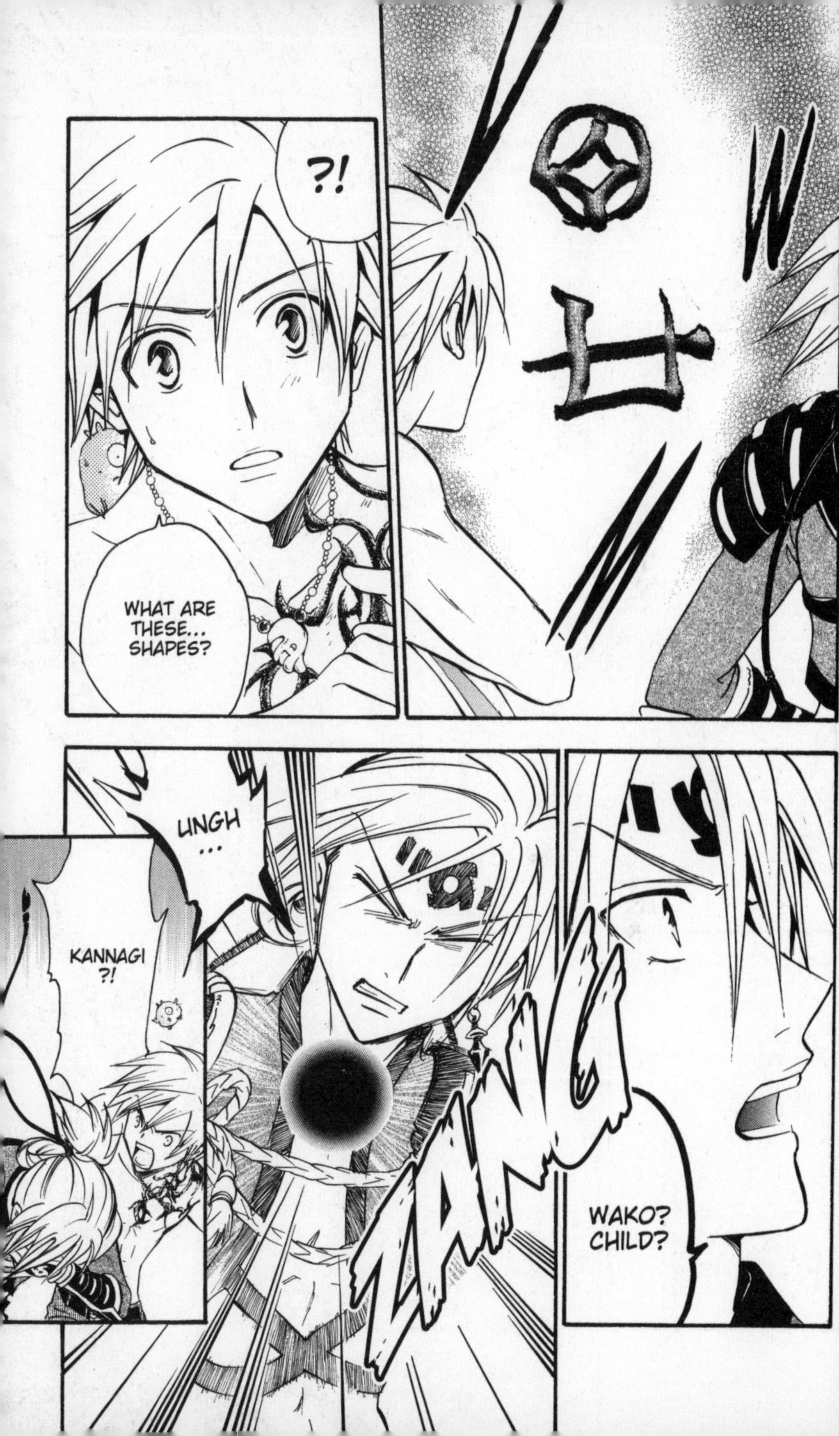
?!
WHAT ARE THESE... SHAPES?
WAKO? CHILD?
UNGH ...
KANNAGI ?!

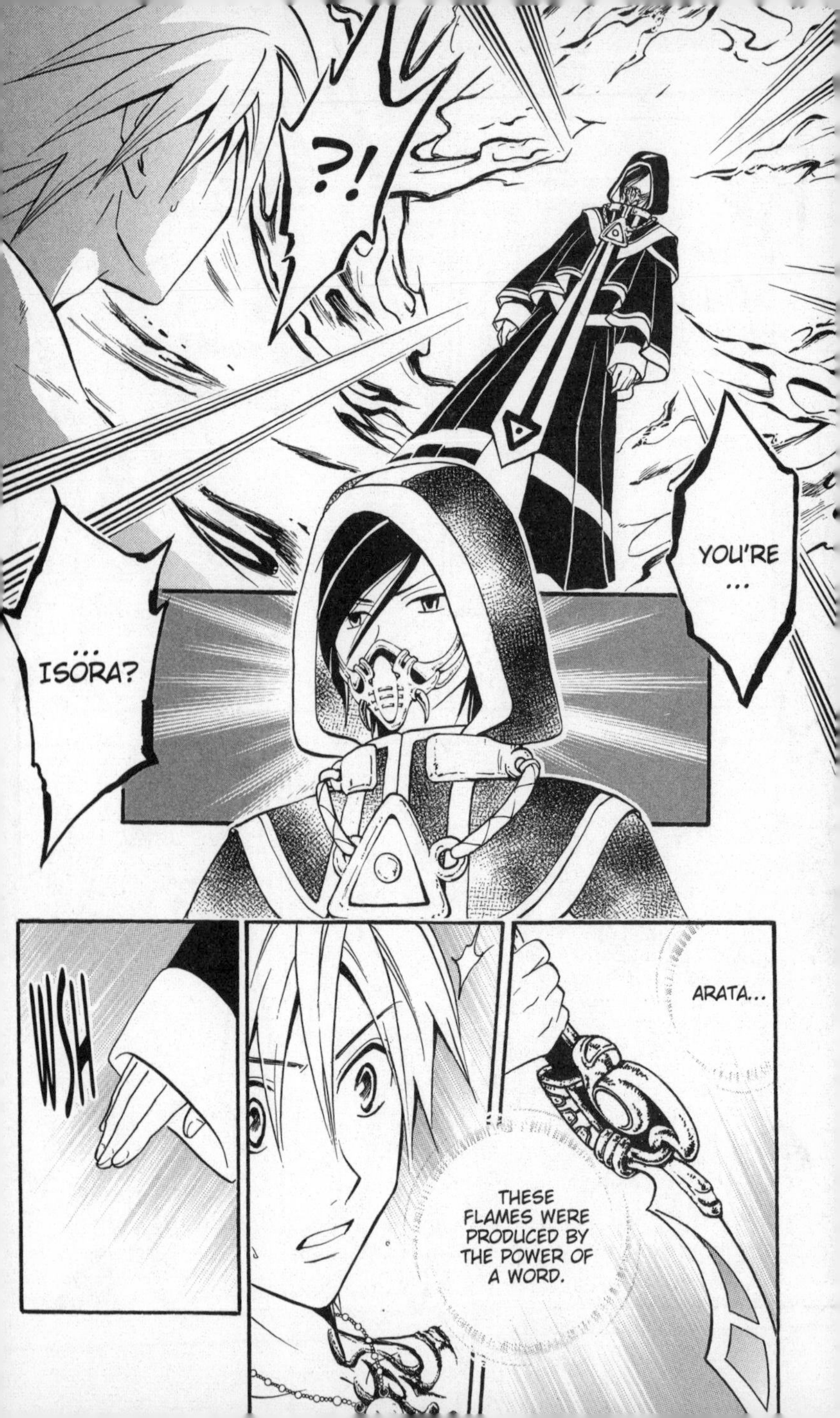
?!
YOU'RE ...
... ISORA?
ARATA...
THESE FLAMES WERE PRODUCED BY THE POWER OF A WORD.
WSH

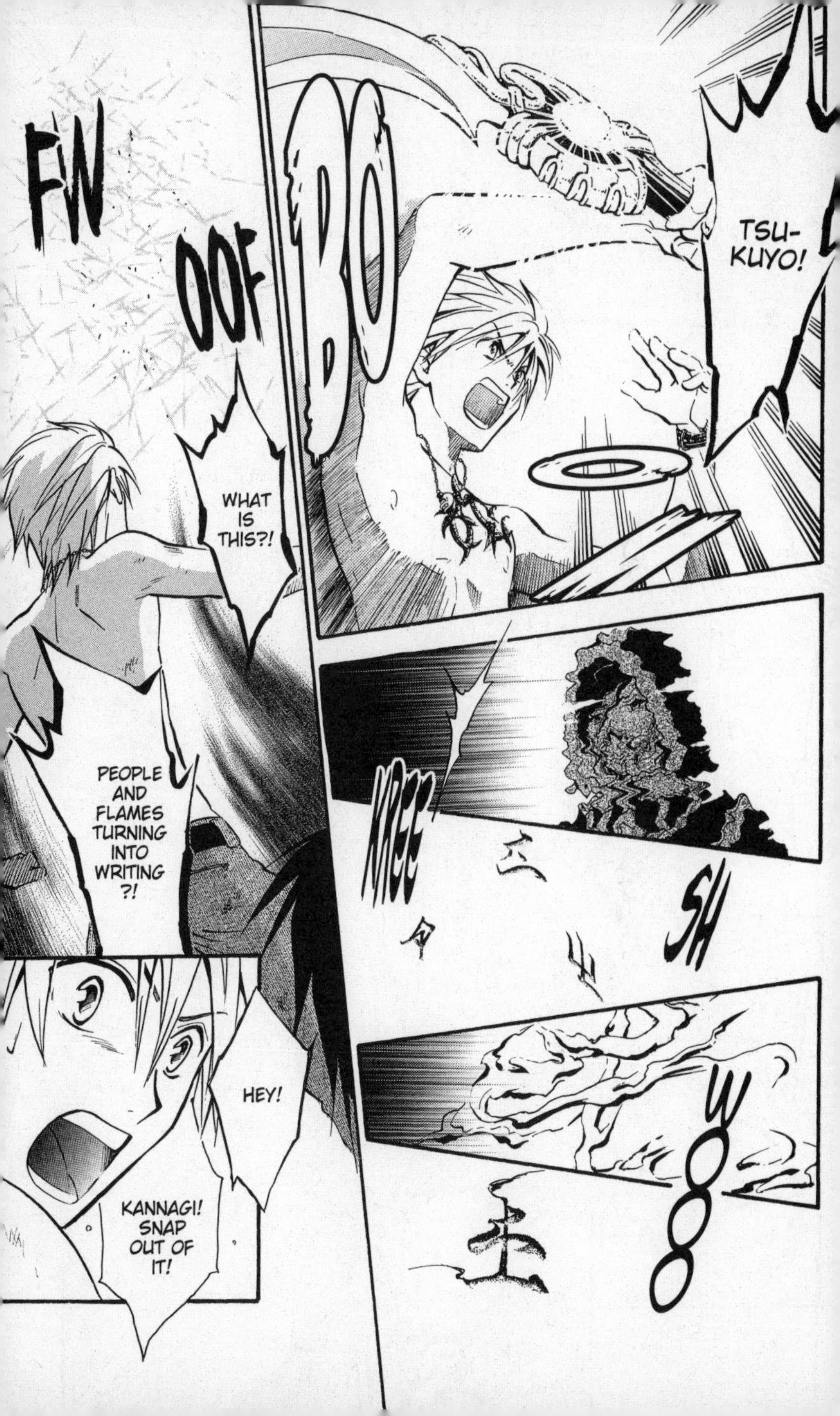

TSU-KUYO!
BO
KREE
SH
YOOOO
FWOOF
WHAT IS THIS?!
PEOPLE AND FLAMES TURNING INTO WRITING?!
HEY!
KANNAGI! SNAP OUT OF IT!

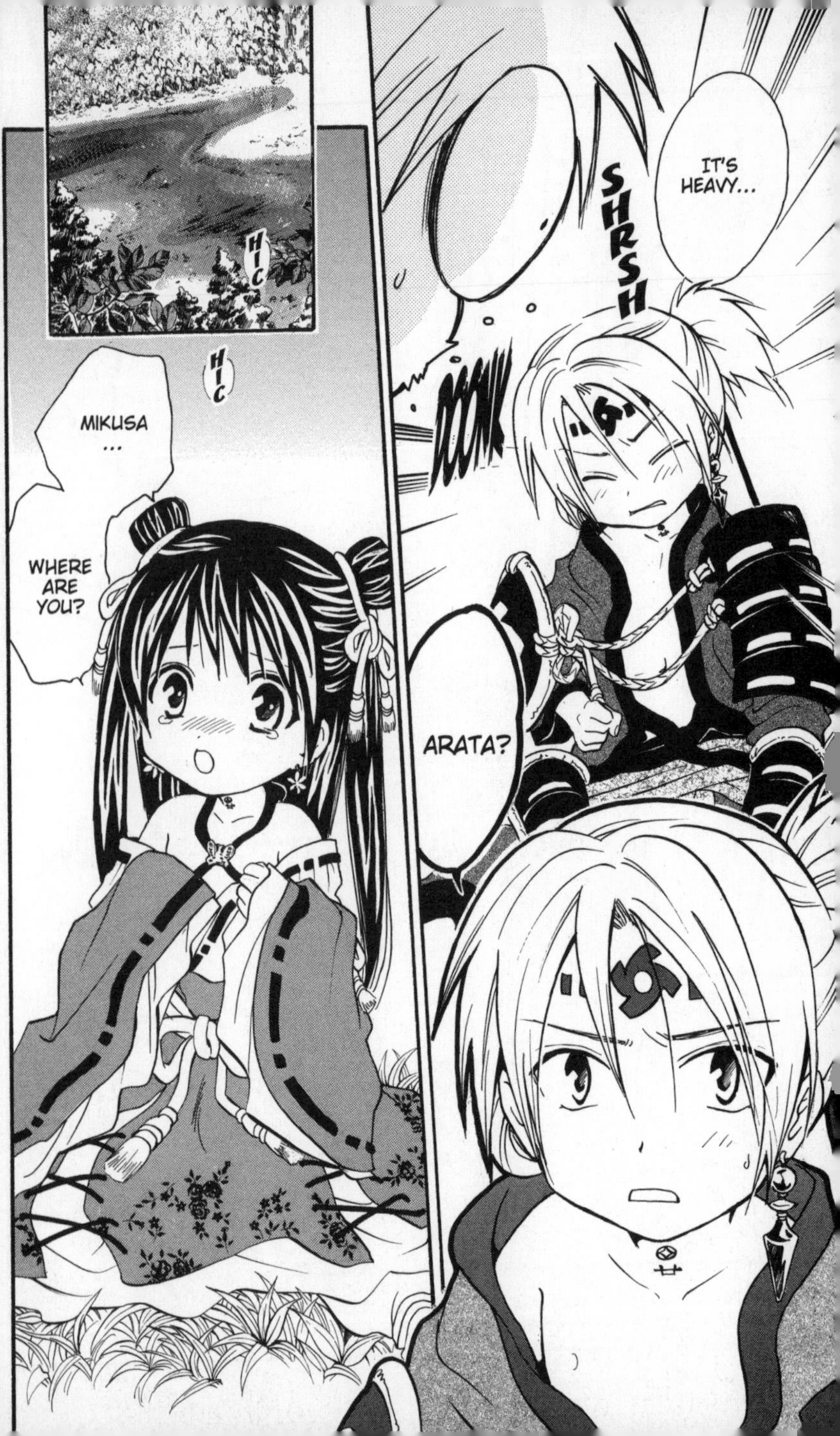
IT'S HEAVY...
SHRSH
DOINK
ARATA?
HIC
HIC
MIKUSA ...
WHERE ARE YOU?

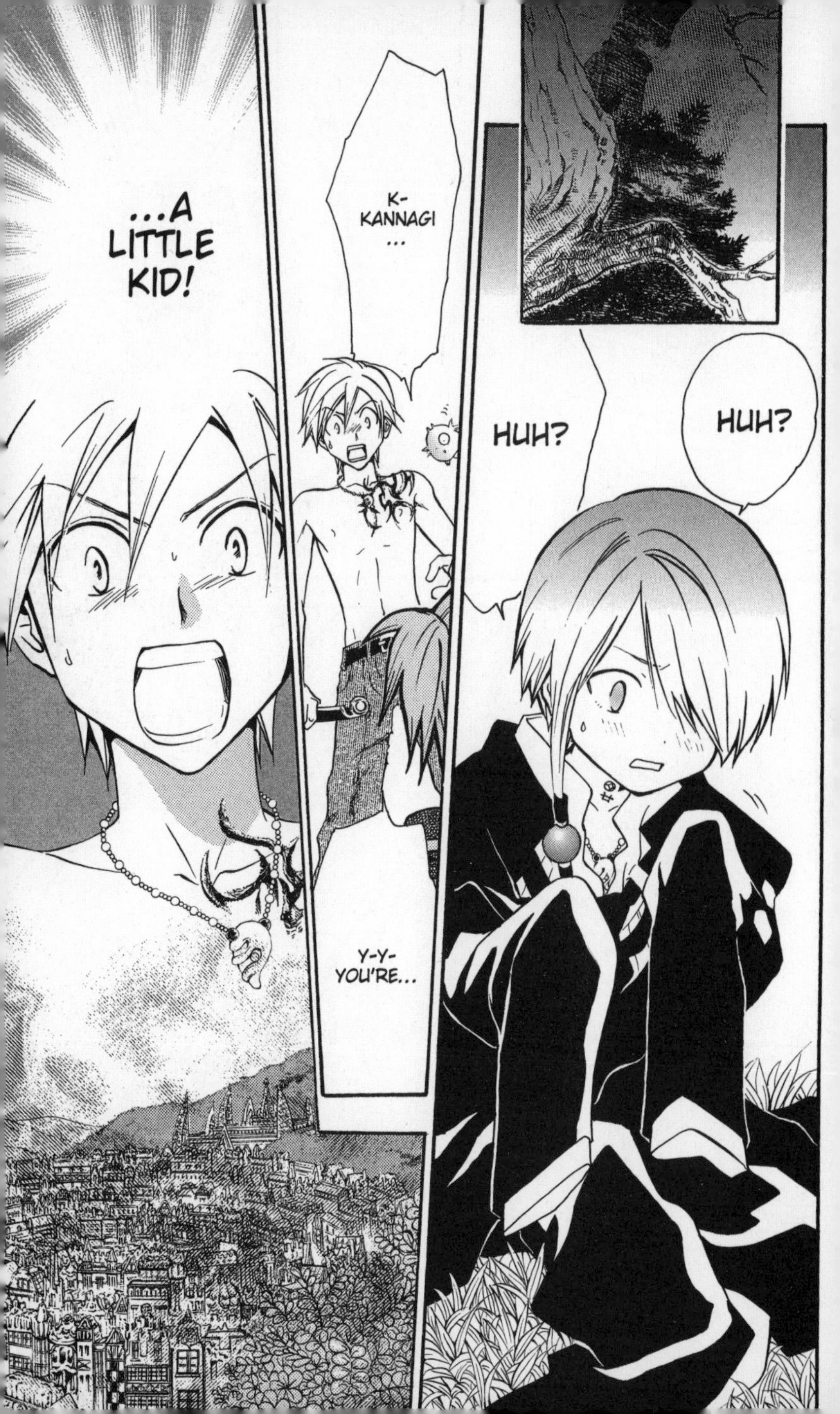
HUH?
HUH?
K-KANNAGI...
Y-Y-YOU'RE...
...A LITTLE KID!

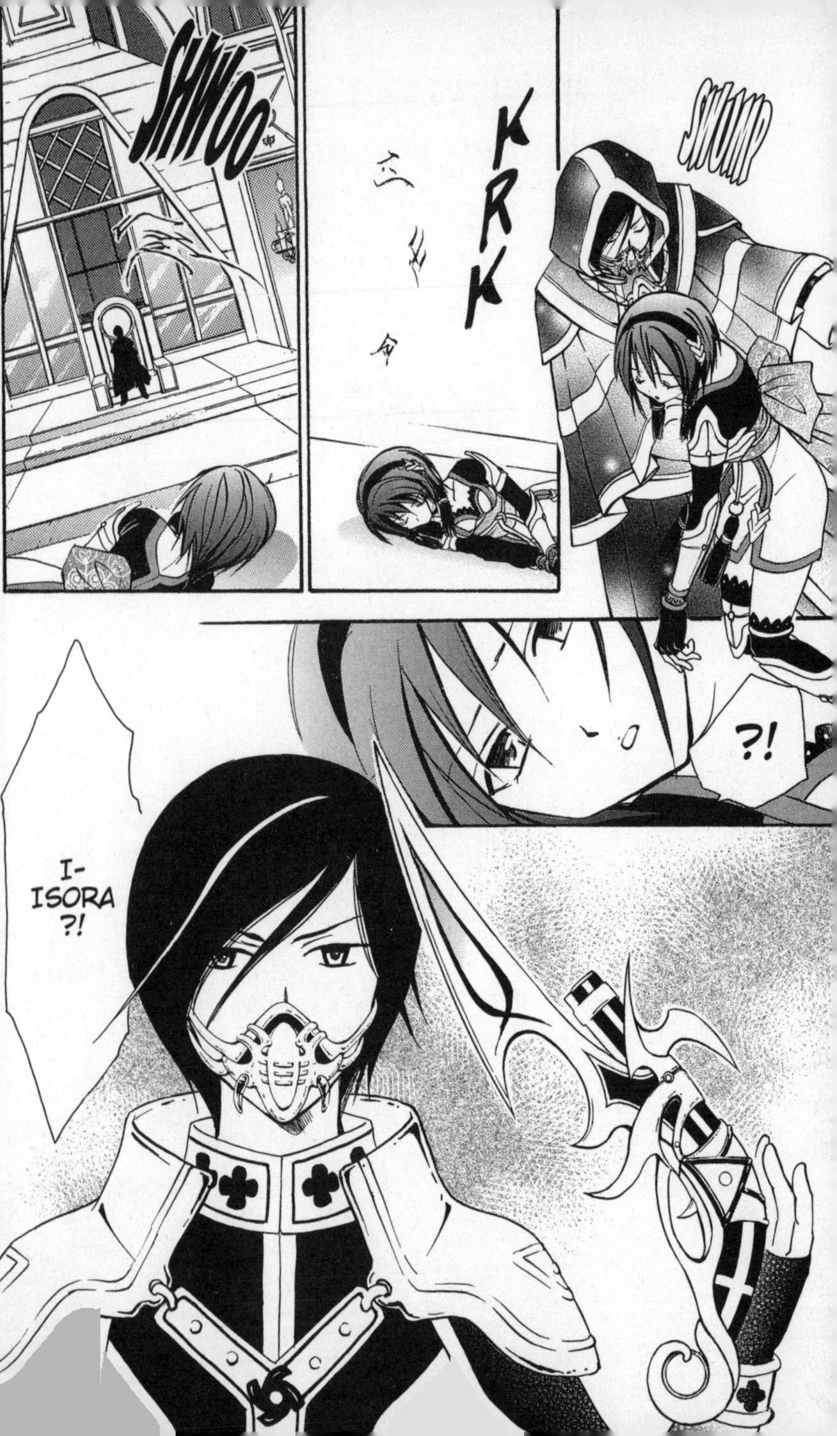
SWUMP
KRK
SHWOO
?!
I-
ISORA
?!

CHAPTER 174

THE LANGUAGE OF SOUND

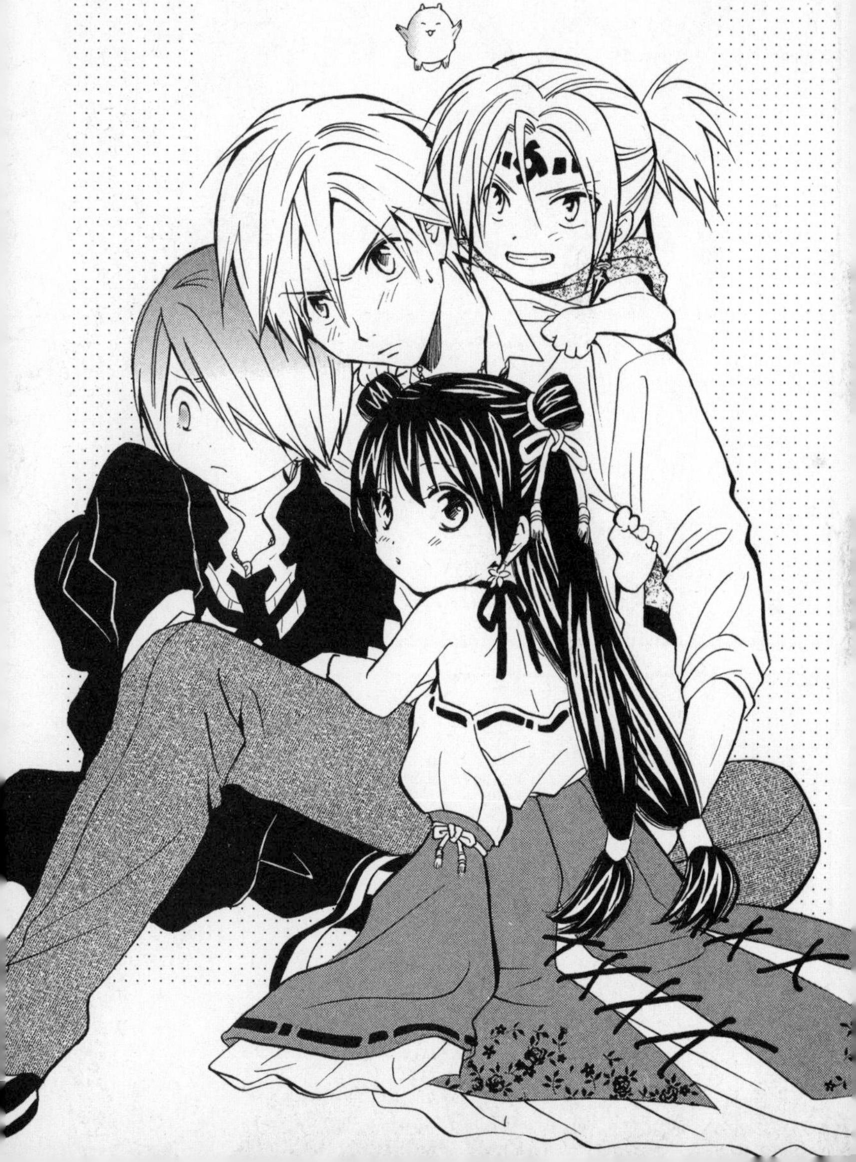

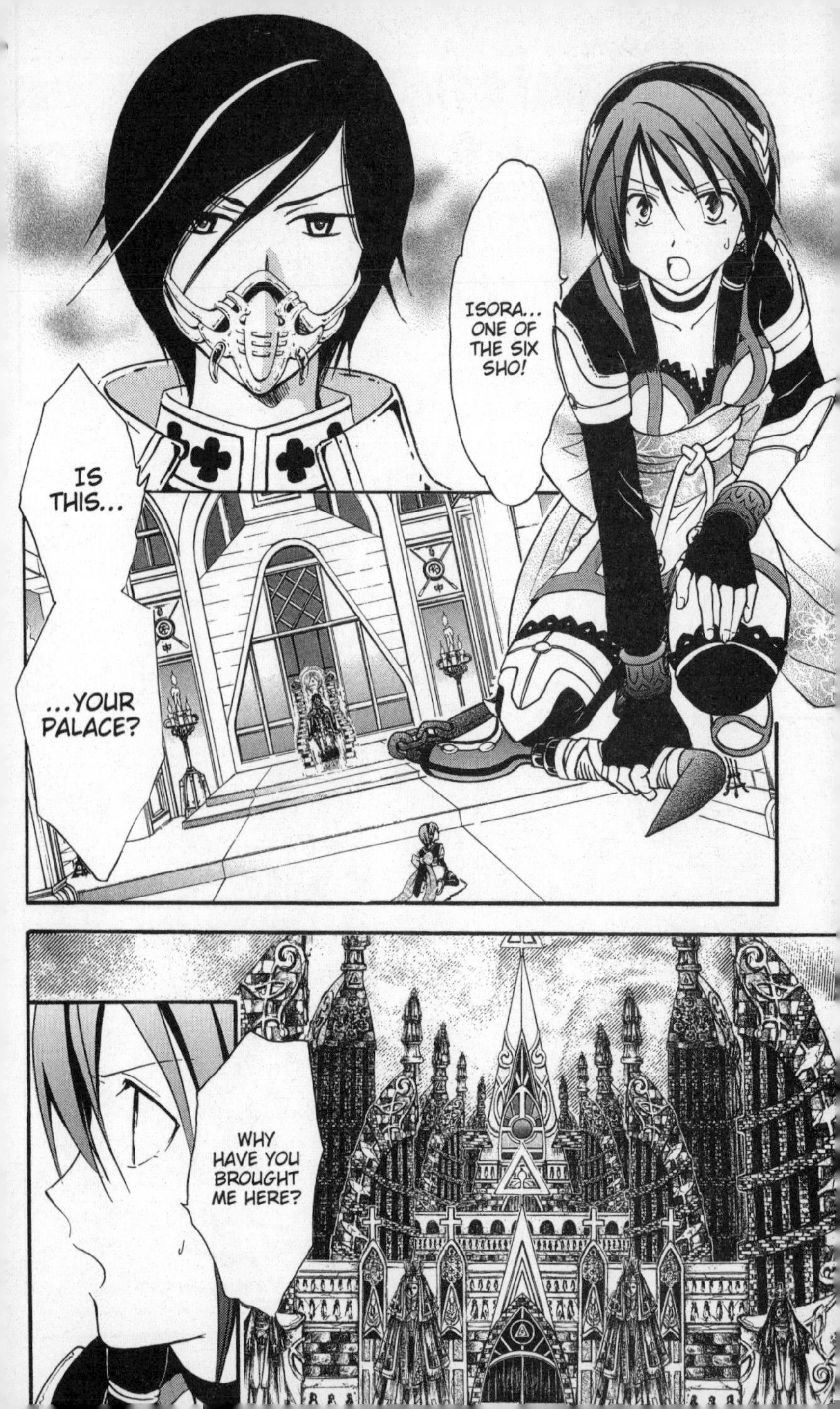
ISORA... ONE OF THE SIX SHO!
IS THIS...
...YOUR PALACE?
WHY HAVE YOU BROUGHT ME HERE?

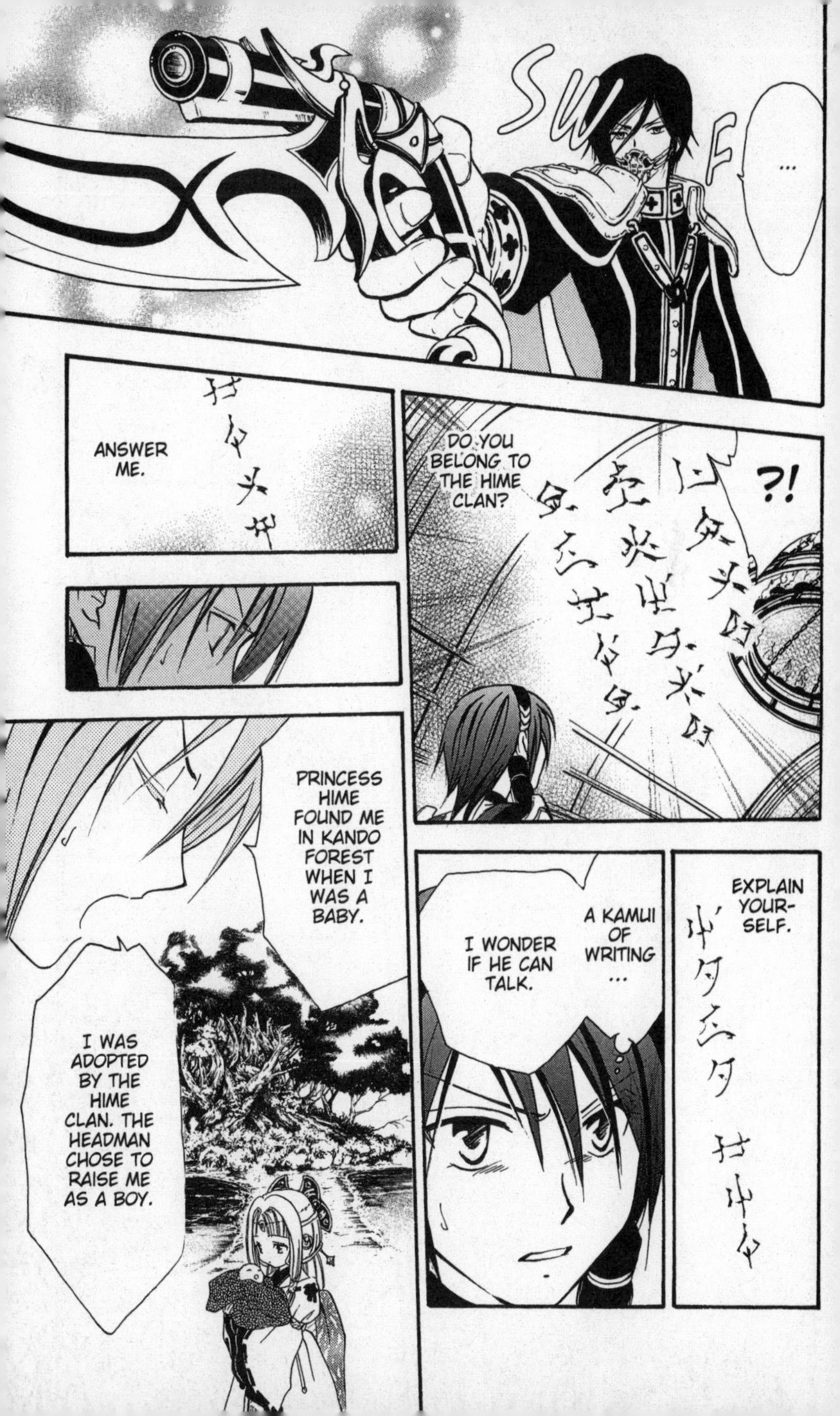
SW
F
...
?!
DO YOU BELONG TO THE HIME CLAN?
ANSWER ME.
EXPLAIN YOUR-SELF.
A KAMUI OF WRITING ...
I WONDER IF HE CAN TALK.
PRINCESS HIME FOUND ME IN KANDO FOREST WHEN I WAS A BABY.
I WAS ADOPTED BY THE HIME CLAN. THE HEADMAN CHOSE TO RAISE ME AS A BOY.

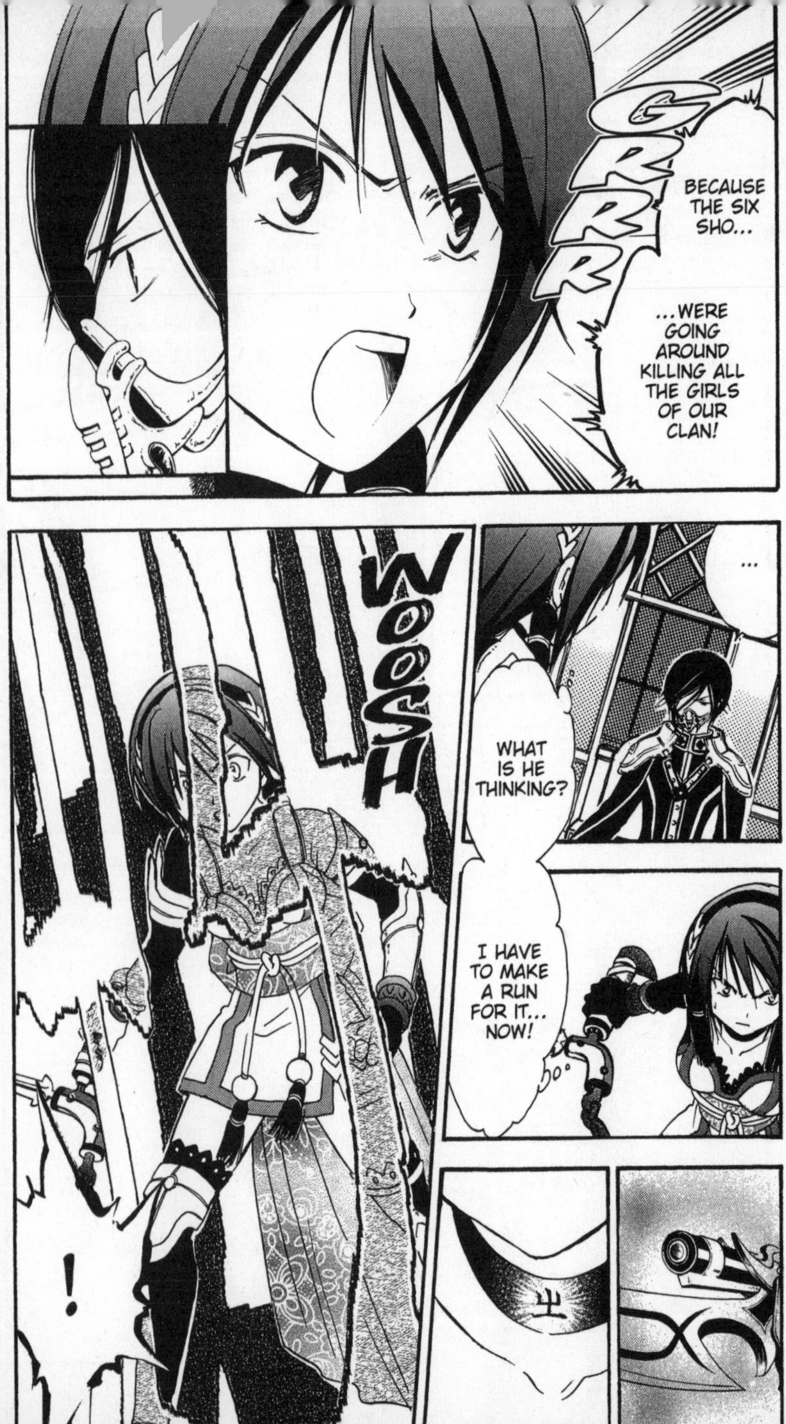
GRRR
BECAUSE THE SIX SHO...
...WERE GOING AROUND KILLING ALL THE GIRLS OF OUR CLAN!
...
WHAT IS HE THINKING?
I HAVE TO MAKE A RUN FOR IT... NOW!
WOOSH
!

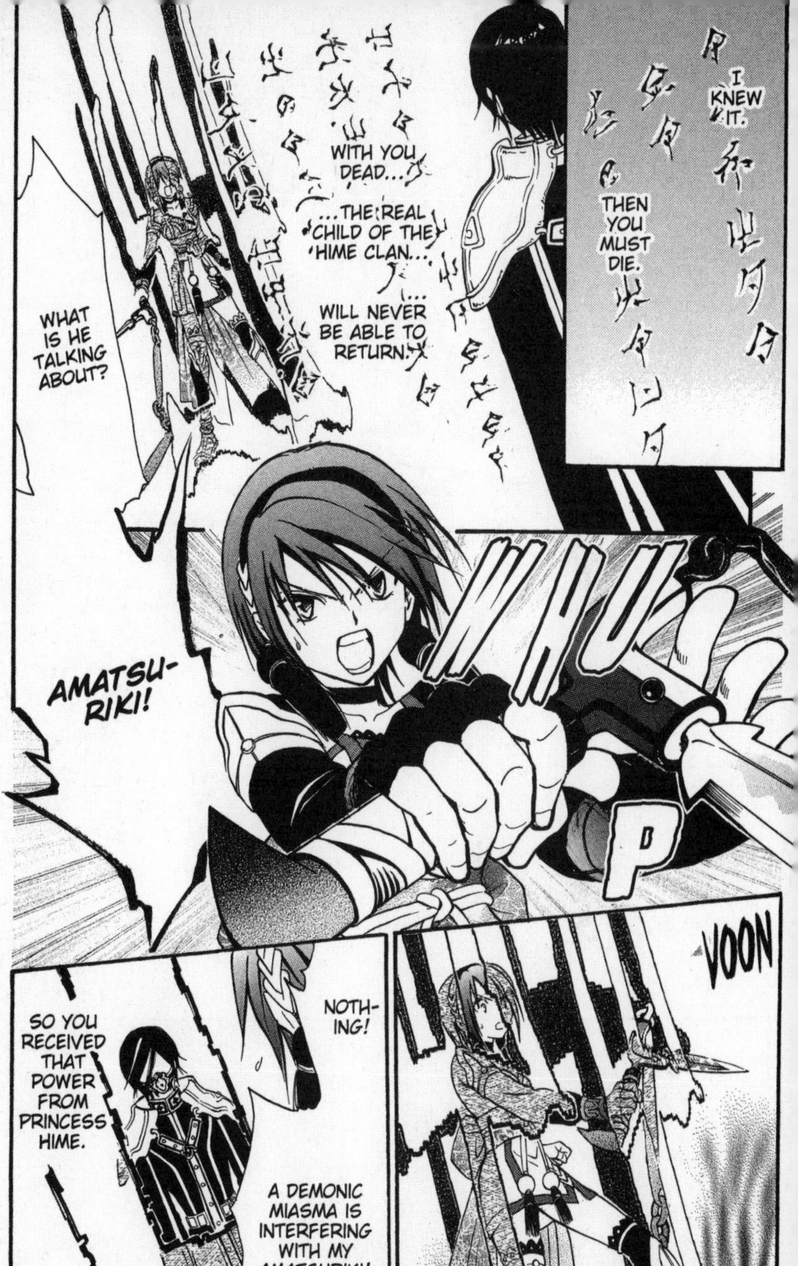
I KNEW IT.
THEN YOU MUST DIE.
WITH YOU DEAD...
...THE REAL CHILD OF THE HIME CLAN...
...WILL NEVER BE ABLE TO RETURN.
WHAT IS HE TALKING ABOUT?
AMATSURIKI!
WHUP
VOON
NOTH-ING!
SO YOU RECEIVED THAT POWER FROM PRINCESS HIME.
A DEMONIC MIASMA IS INTERFERING WITH MY AMATSURIKI!

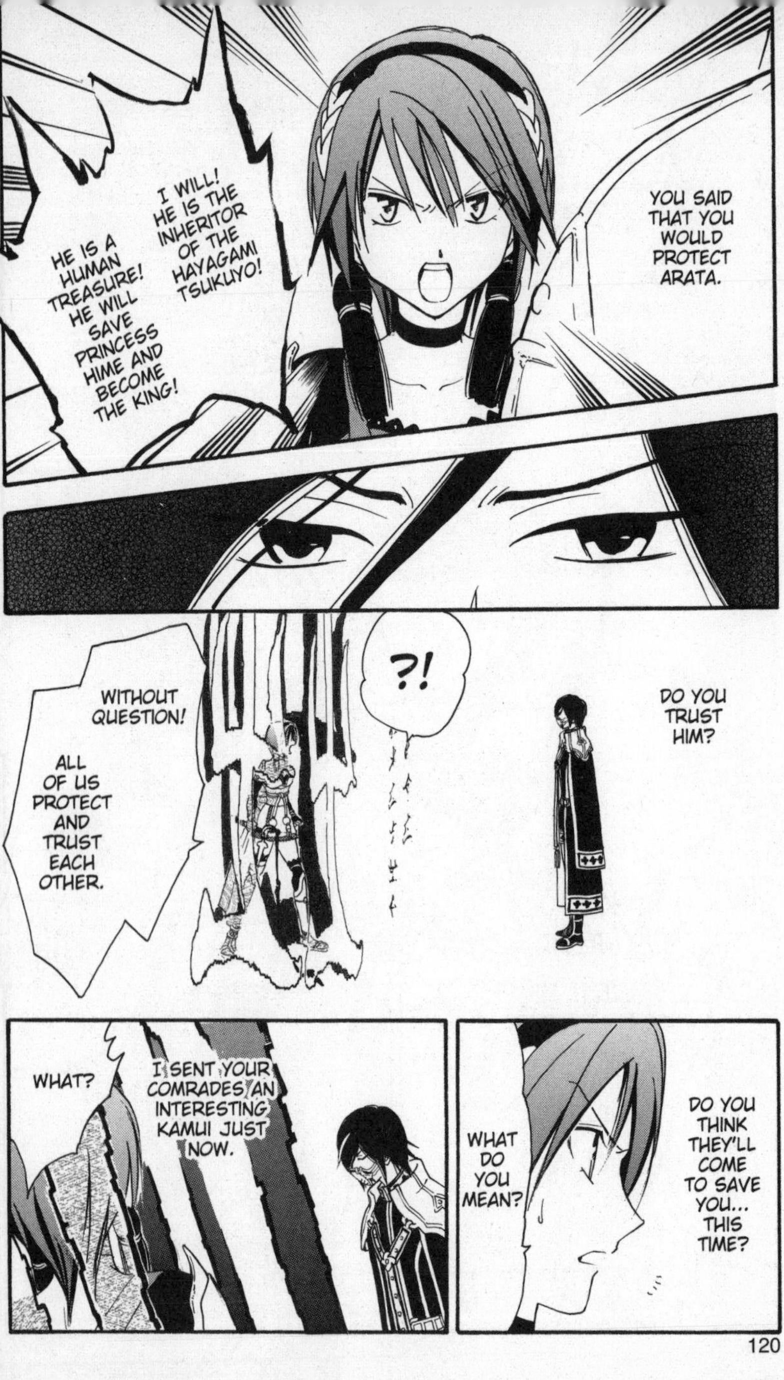
YOU SAID THAT YOU WOULD PROTECT ARATA.
I WILL! HE IS THE INHERITOR OF THE HAYAGAMI TSUKUYO!
HE IS A HUMAN TREASURE! HE WILL SAVE PRINCESS HIME AND BECOME THE KING!
DO YOU TRUST HIM?
?!
WITHOUT QUESTION!
ALL OF US PROTECT AND TRUST EACH OTHER.
DO YOU THINK THEY'LL COME TO SAVE YOU... THIS TIME?
WHAT DO YOU MEAN?
I SENT YOUR COMRADES AN INTERESTING KAMUI JUST NOW.
WHAT?

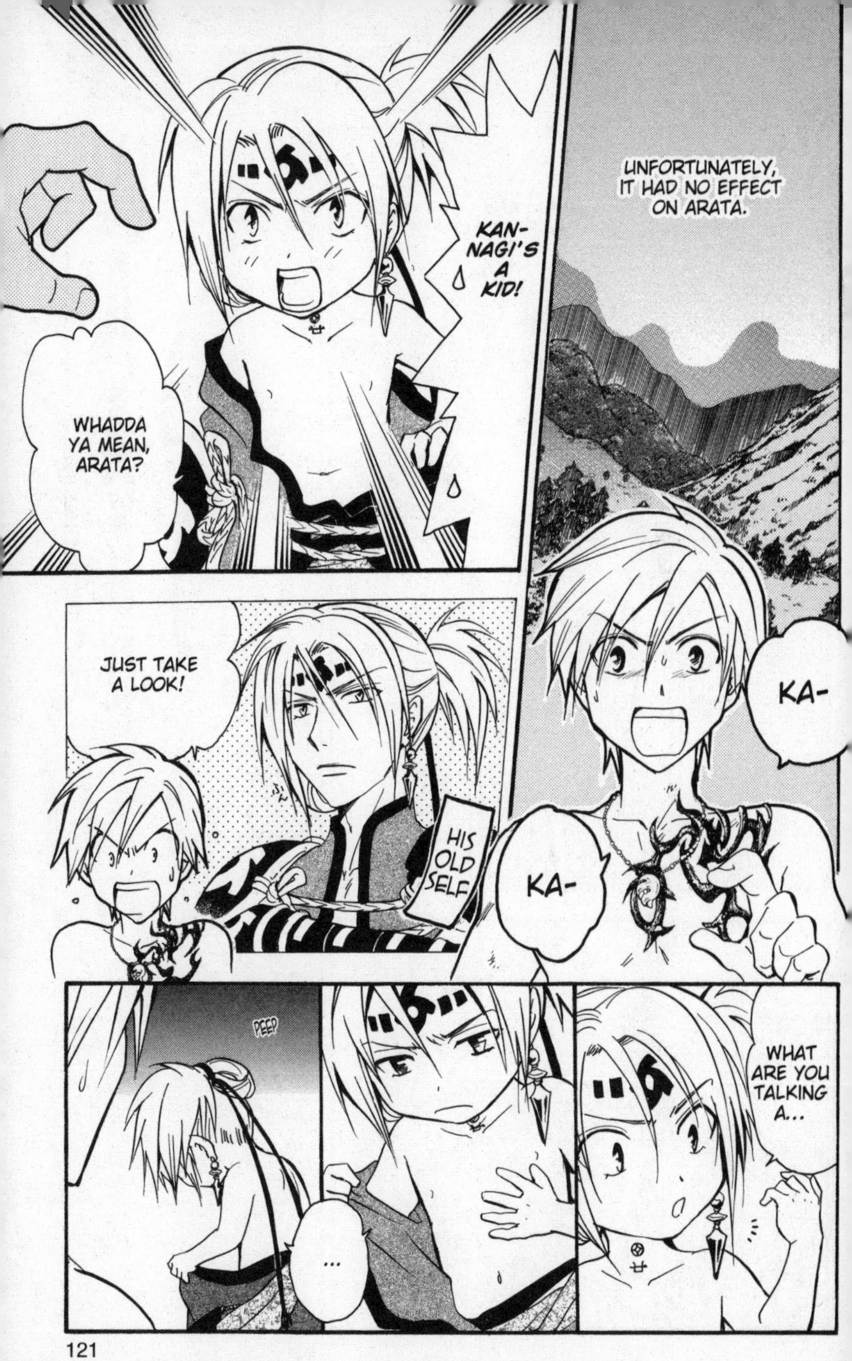
UNFORTUNATELY, IT HAD NO EFFECT ON ARATA.
KA-
KA-
KAN-NAGI'S A KID!
WHADDA YA MEAN, ARATA?
JUST TAKE A LOOK!
HIS OLD SELF
WHAT ARE YOU TALKING A...
...
PEEP

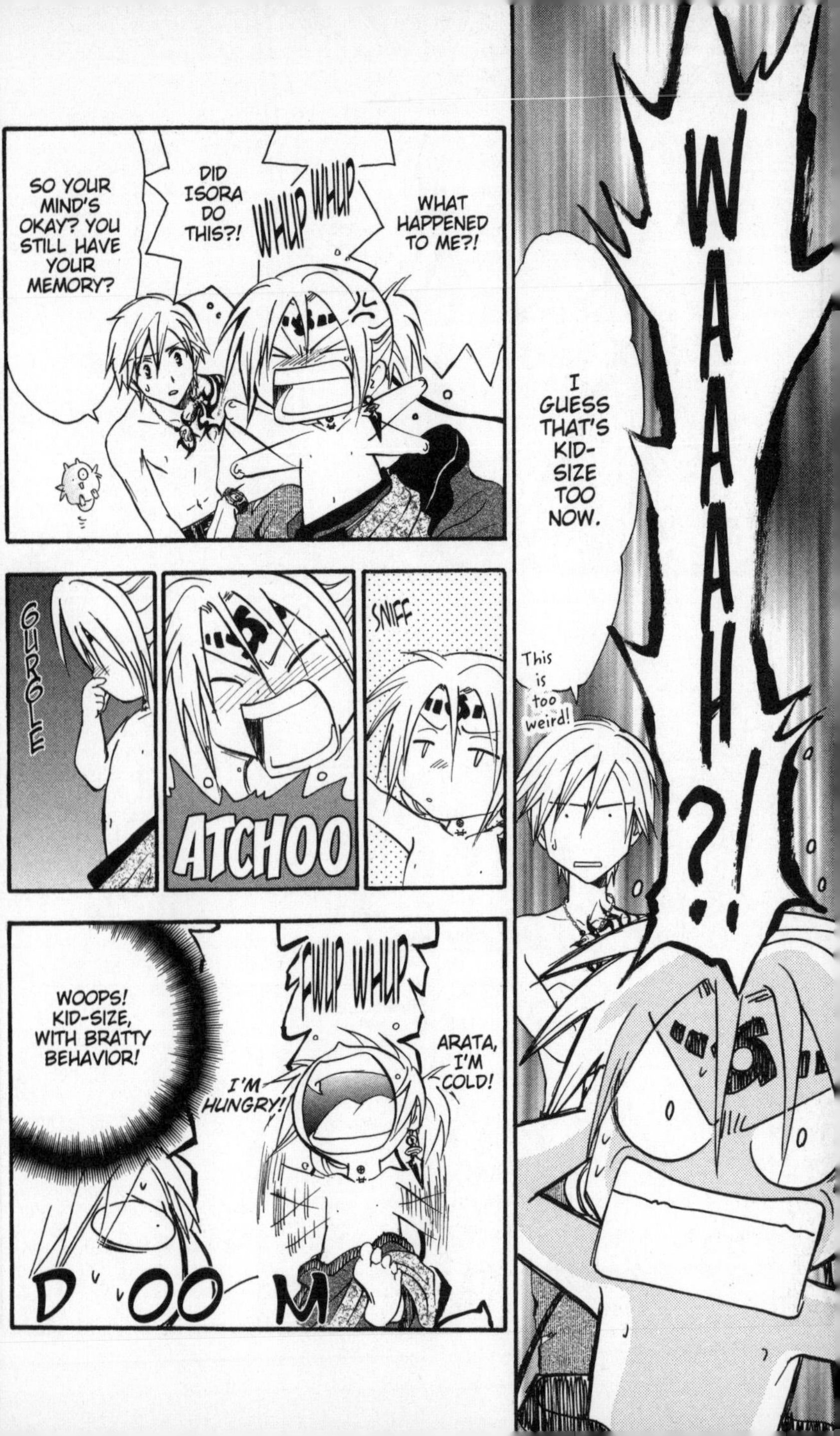
WAAAH?!
I GUESS THAT'S KID-SIZE TOO NOW.
This is too weird!
WHAT HAPPENED TO ME?!
WHUP WHUP
DID ISORA DO THIS?!
SO YOUR MIND'S OKAY? YOU STILL HAVE YOUR MEMORY?
SNIFF
ATCHOO
GURGLE
FWUP WHUP
ARATA, I'M COLD!
I'M HUNGRY!
WOOPS! KID-SIZE, WITH BRATTY BEHAVIOR!
DOOM

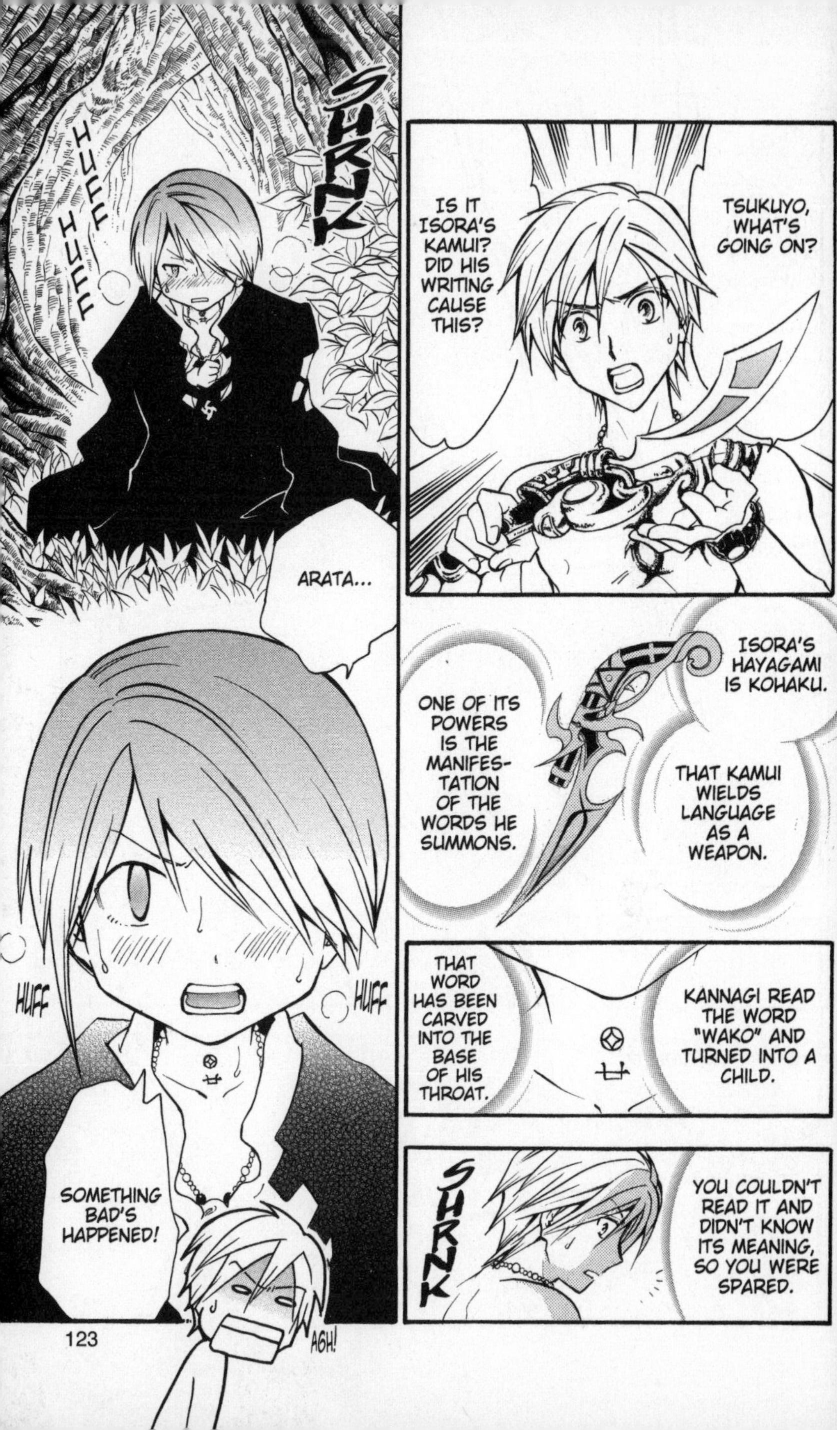
TSUKUYO, WHAT'S GOING ON?
IS IT ISORA'S KAMUI? DID HIS WRITING CAUSE THIS?
ISORA'S HAYAGAMI IS KOHAKU.
THAT KAMUI WIELDS LANGUAGE AS A WEAPON.
ONE OF ITS POWERS IS THE MANIFES-TATION OF THE WORDS HE SUMMONS.
KANNAGI READ THE WORD "WAKO" AND TURNED INTO A CHILD.
THAT WORD HAS BEEN CARVED INTO THE BASE OF HIS THROAT.
YOU COULDN'T READ IT AND DIDN'T KNOW ITS MEANING, SO YOU WERE SPARED.
SHRNK
SHRNK
HUFF HUFF
ARATA...
HUFF
HUFF
SOMETHING BAD'S HAPPENED!
AGH!

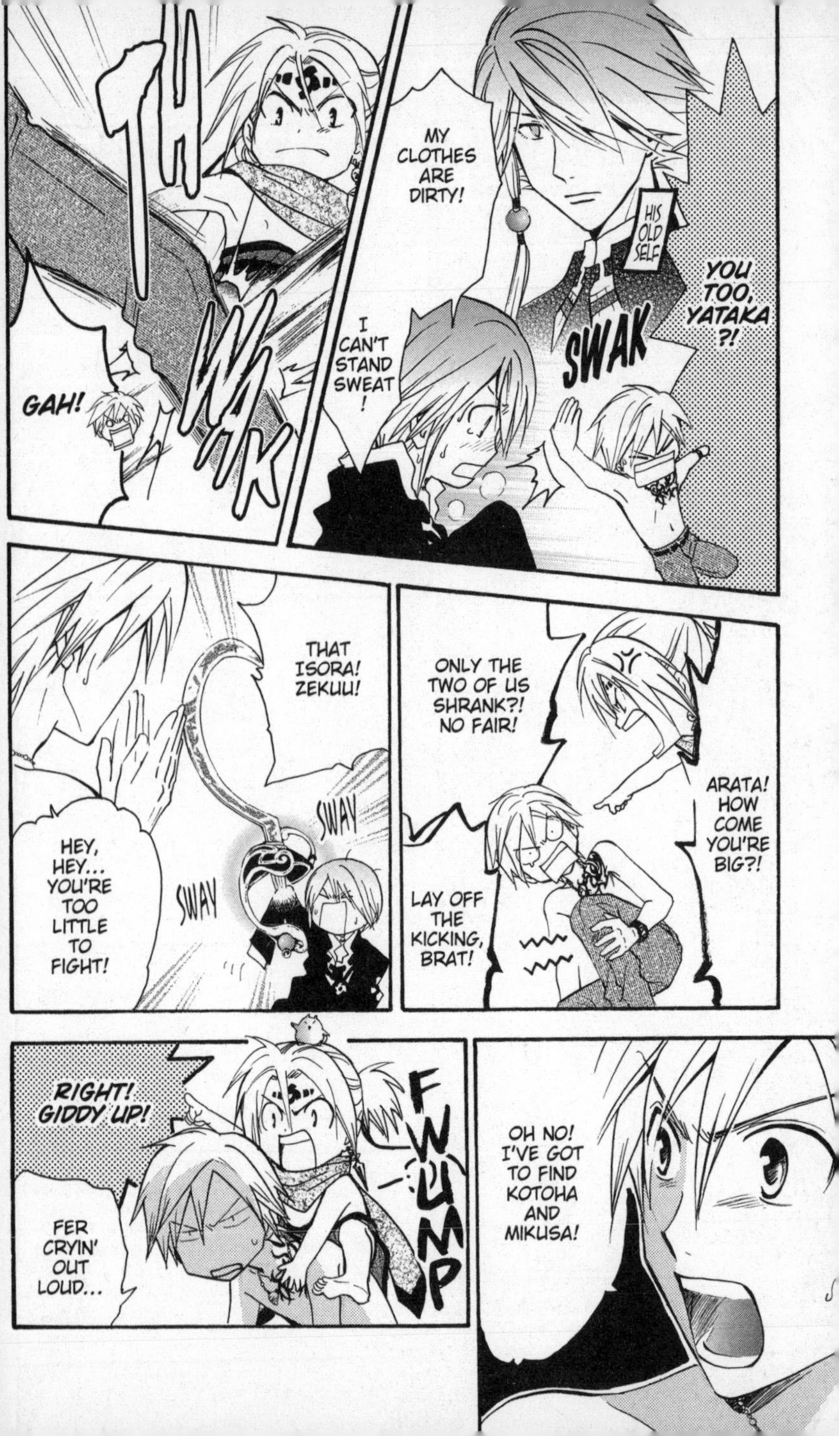
YOU TOO, YATAKA?!
HIS OLD SELF
MY CLOTHES ARE DIRTY!
SWAK
I CAN'T STAND SWEAT!
THWAK
GAH!
ARATA! HOW COME YOU'RE BIG?!
ONLY THE TWO OF US SHRANK?! NO FAIR!
LAY OFF THE KICKING, BRAT!
THAT ISORA! ZEKUU!
SWAY
SWAY
HEY, HEY... YOU'RE TOO LITTLE TO FIGHT!
OH NO! I'VE GOT TO FIND KOTOHA AND MIKUSA!
FWUMP
RIGHT! GIDDY UP!
FER CRYIN' OUT LOUD...

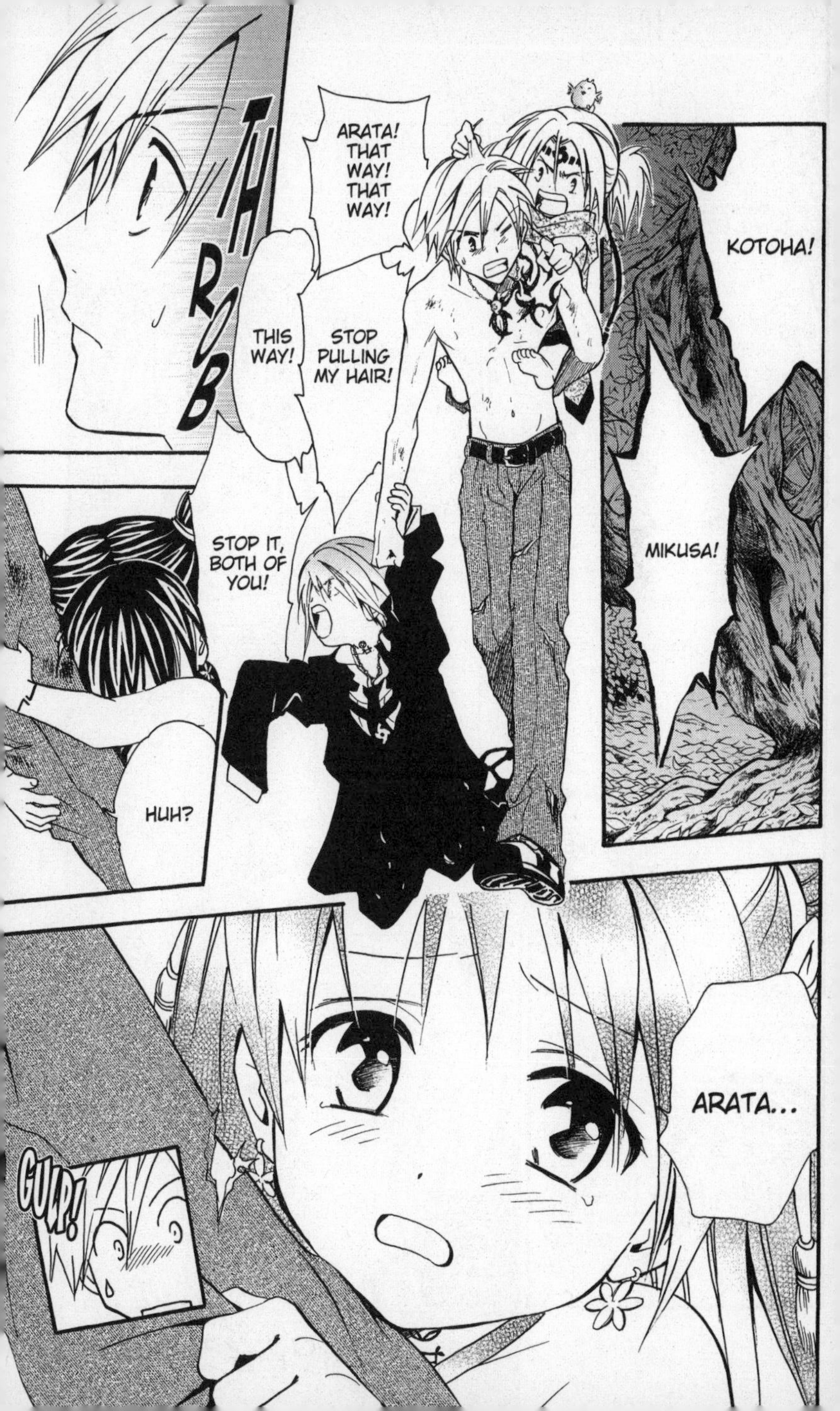
KOTOHA!
MIKUSA!
ARATA! THAT WAY! THAT WAY!
STOP PULLING MY HAIR!
THIS WAY!
STOP IT, BOTH OF YOU!
THROB
HUH?
ARATA...
GULP!

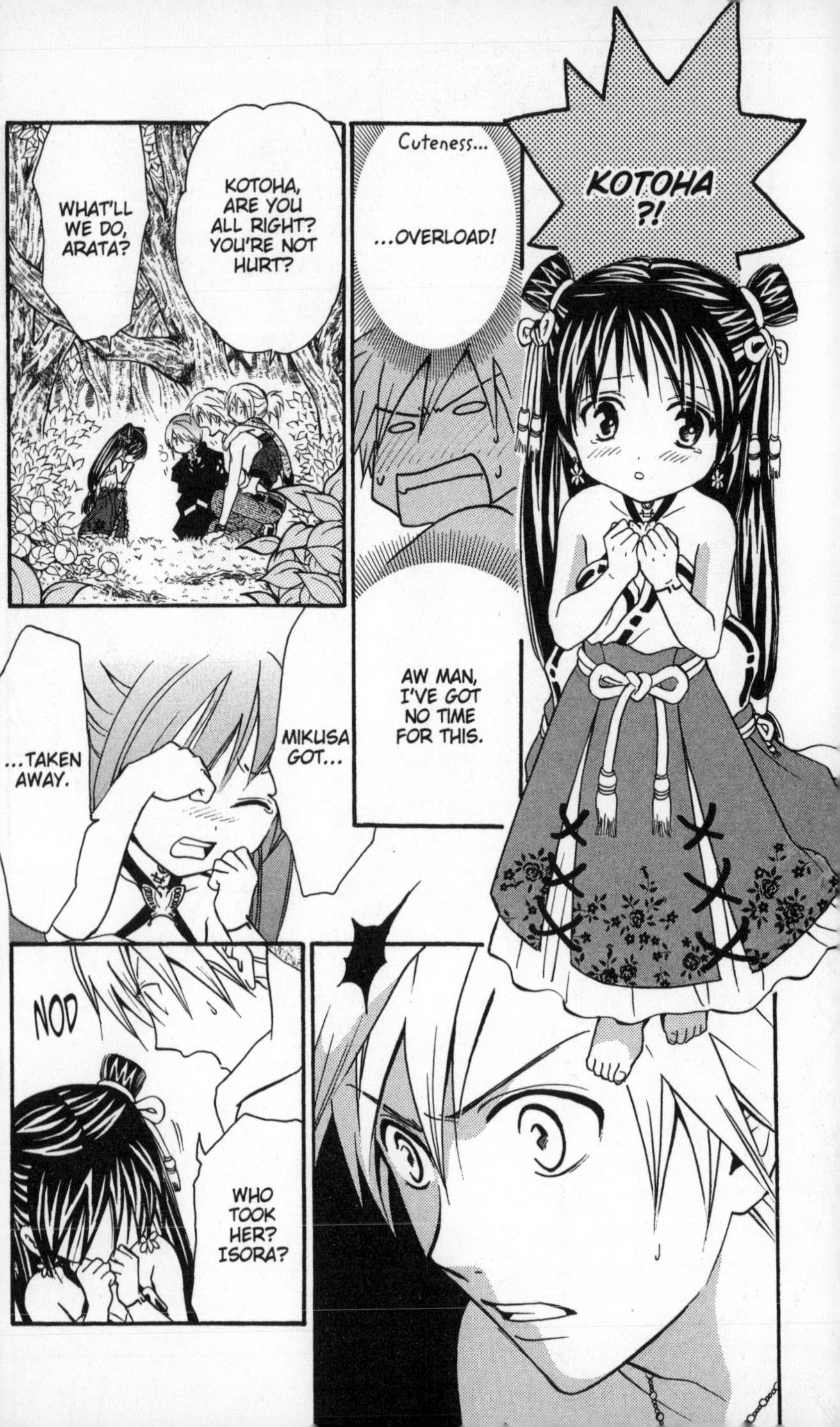
KOTOHA ?!
Cuteness...
...OVERLOAD!
AW MAN, I'VE GOT NO TIME FOR THIS.
KOTOHA, ARE YOU ALL RIGHT? YOU'RE NOT HURT?
WHAT'LL WE DO, ARATA?
MIKUSA GOT...
...TAKEN AWAY.
NOD
WHO TOOK HER? ISORA?

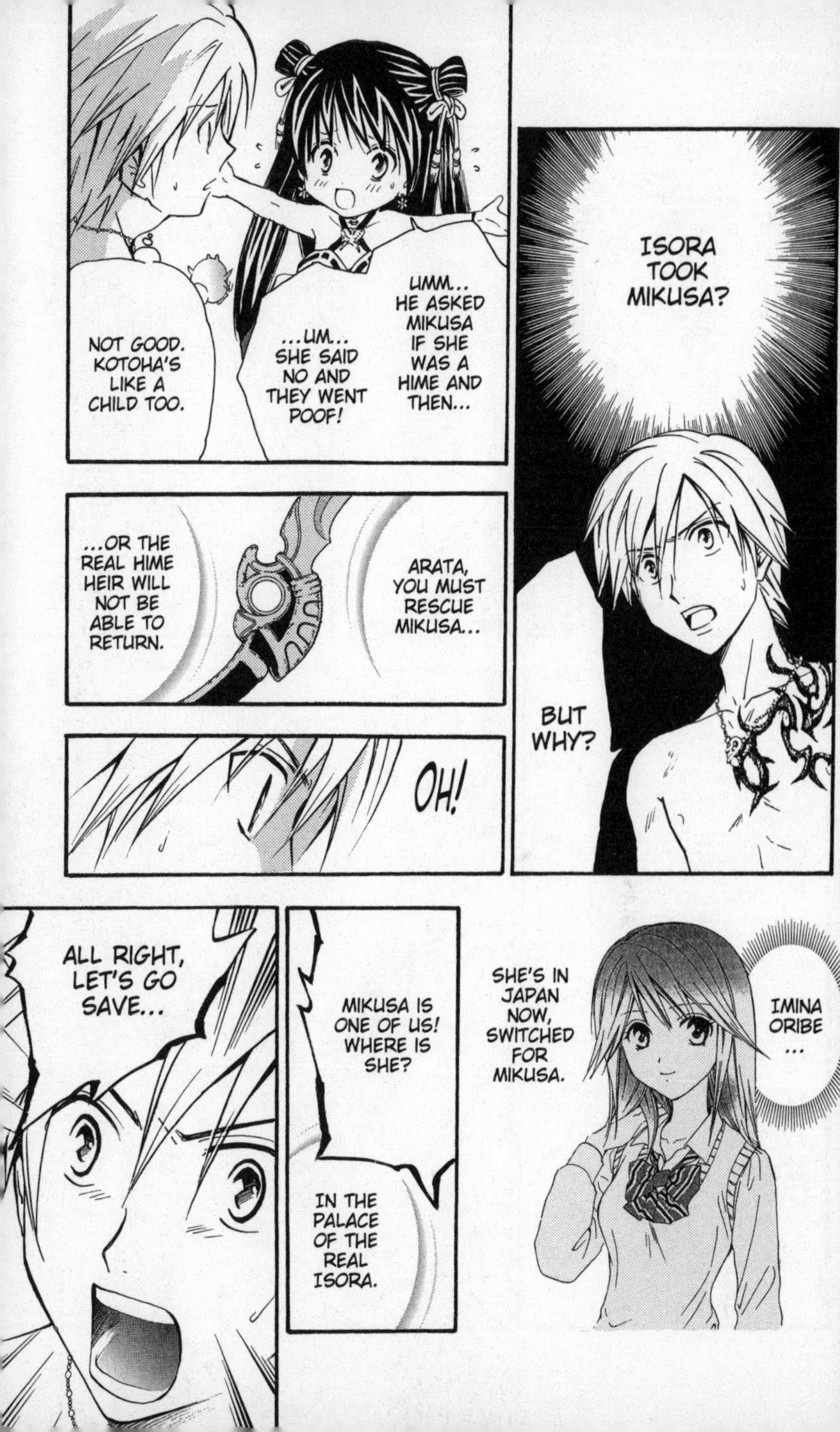
ISORA TOOK MIKUSA?
BUT WHY?
UMM... HE ASKED MIKUSA IF SHE WAS A HIME AND THEN...
...UM... SHE SAID NO AND THEY WENT POOF!
NOT GOOD. KOTOHA'S LIKE A CHILD TOO.
ARATA, YOU MUST RESCUE MIKUSA...
...OR THE REAL HIME HEIR WILL NOT BE ABLE TO RETURN.
OH!
IMINA ORIBE ...
SHE'S IN JAPAN NOW, SWITCHED FOR MIKUSA.
MIKUSA IS ONE OF US! WHERE IS SHE?
IN THE PALACE OF THE REAL ISORA.
ALL RIGHT, LET'S GO SAVE...

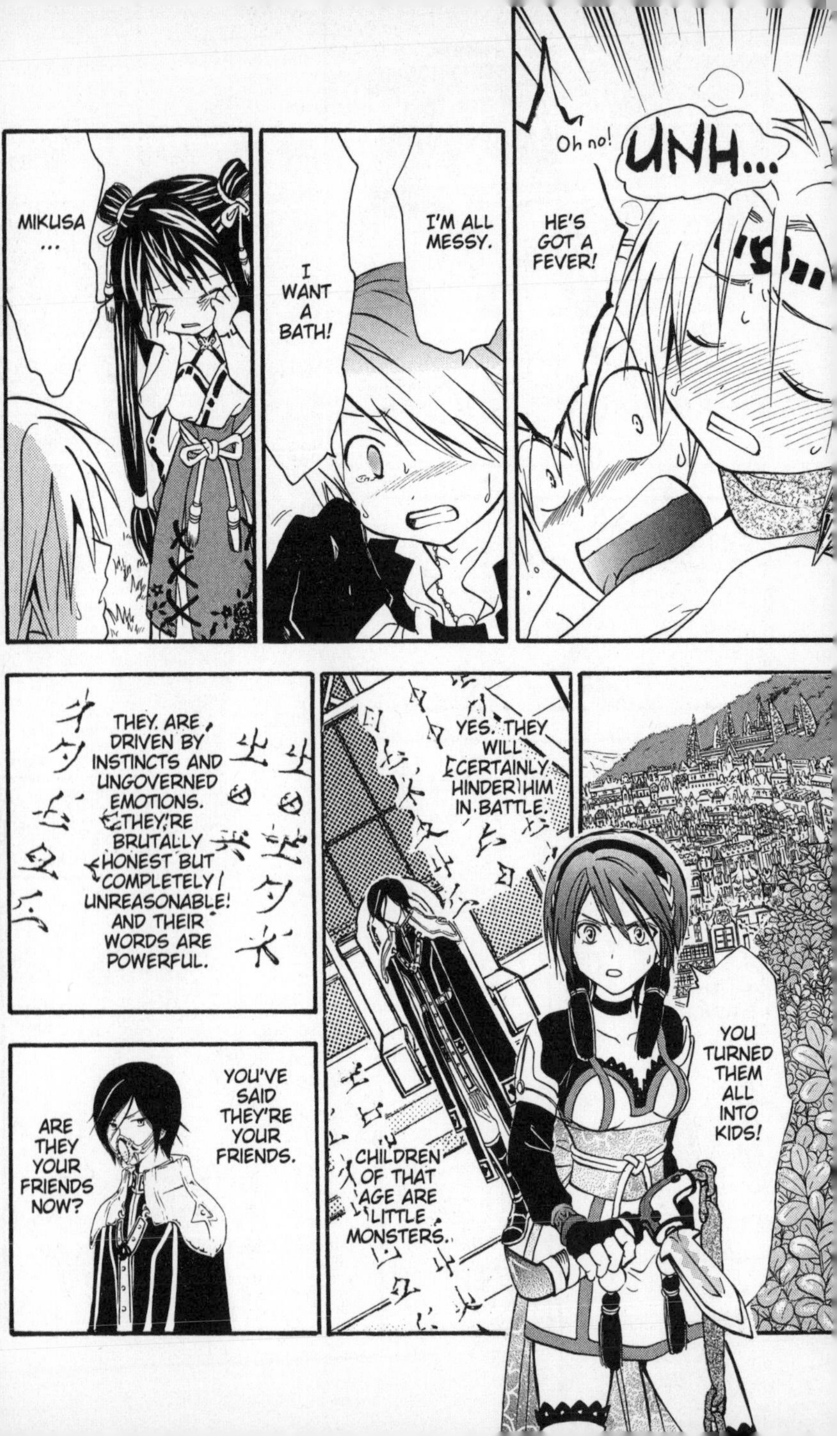
UNH...
Oh no!
HE'S GOT A FEVER!
I'M ALL MESSY.
I WANT A BATH!
MIKUSA ...
YOU TURNED THEM ALL INTO KIDS!
YES. THEY WILL CERTAINLY HINDER HIM IN BATTLE.
CHILDREN OF THAT AGE ARE LITTLE MONSTERS.
THEY ARE DRIVEN BY INSTINCTS AND UNGOVERNED EMOTIONS. THEY'RE BRUTALLY HONEST BUT COMPLETELY UNREASONABLE! AND THEIR WORDS ARE POWERFUL.
YOU'VE SAID THEY'RE YOUR FRIENDS.
ARE THEY YOUR FRIENDS NOW?

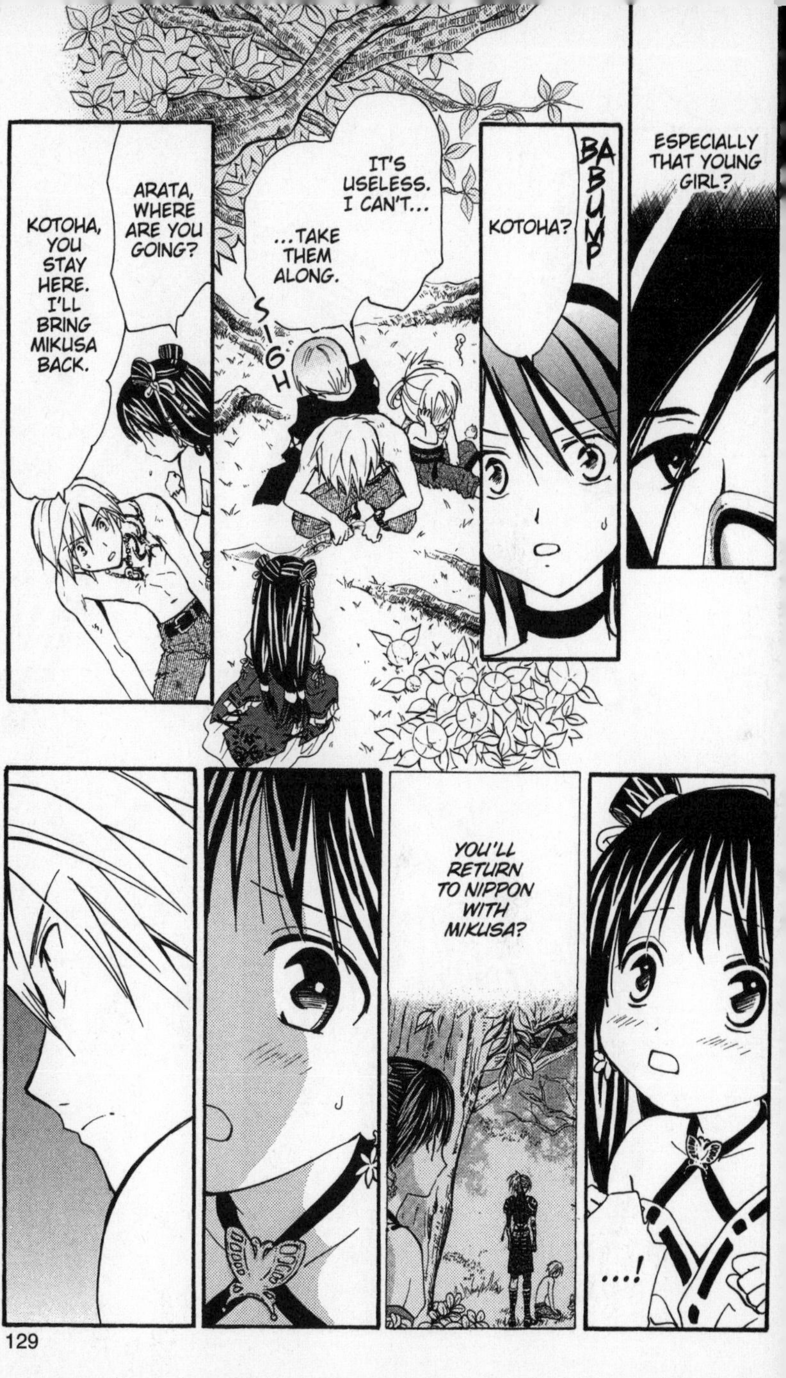
ESPECIALLY THAT YOUNG GIRL?
KOTOHA?
BA BUMP
IT'S USELESS. I CAN'T...
...TAKE THEM ALONG.
SIGH
ARATA, WHERE ARE YOU GOING?
KOTOHA, YOU STAY HERE. I'LL BRING MIKUSA BACK.
...!
YOU'LL RETURN TO NIPPON WITH MIKUSA?

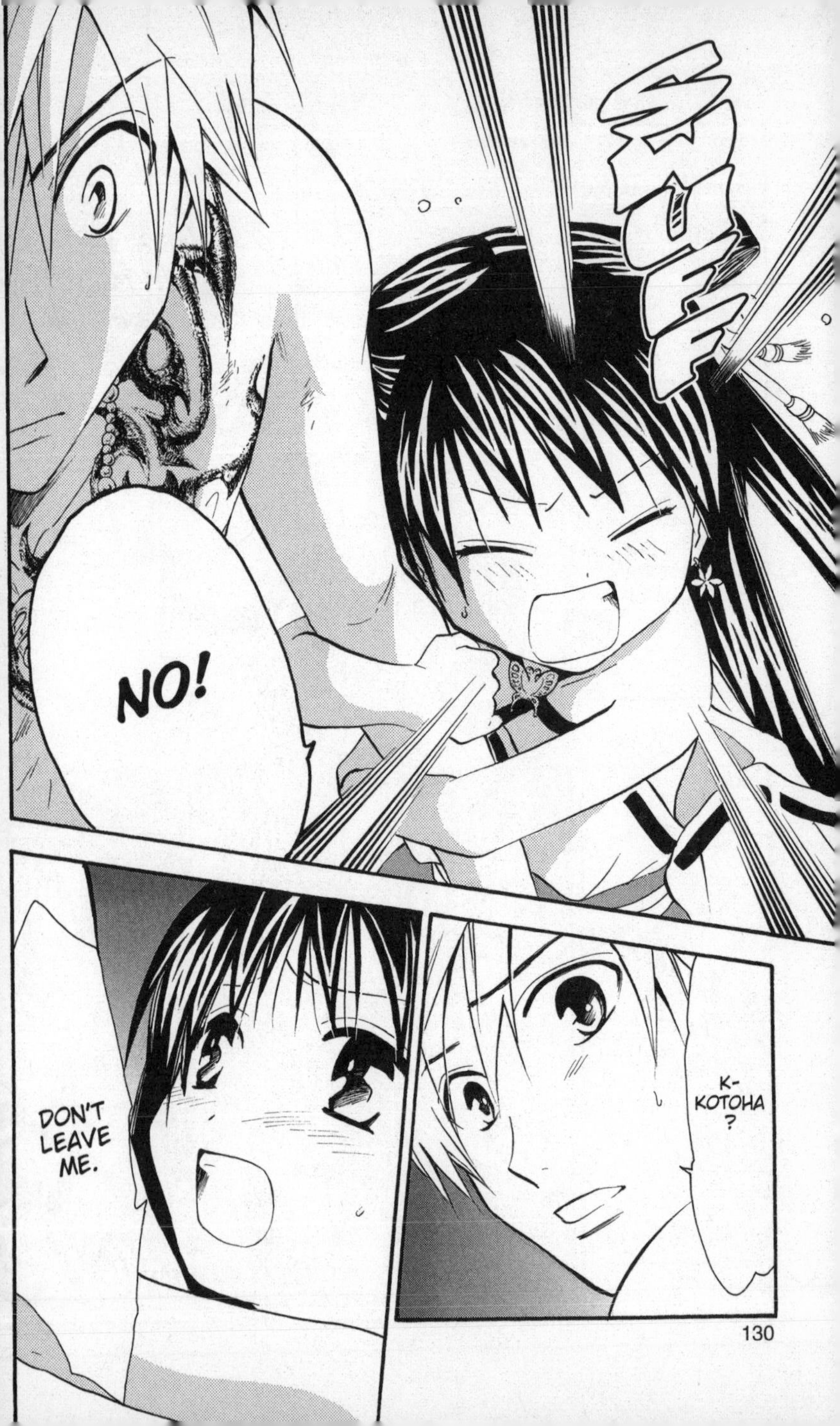
NO!
K-KOTOHA?
DON'T LEAVE ME.

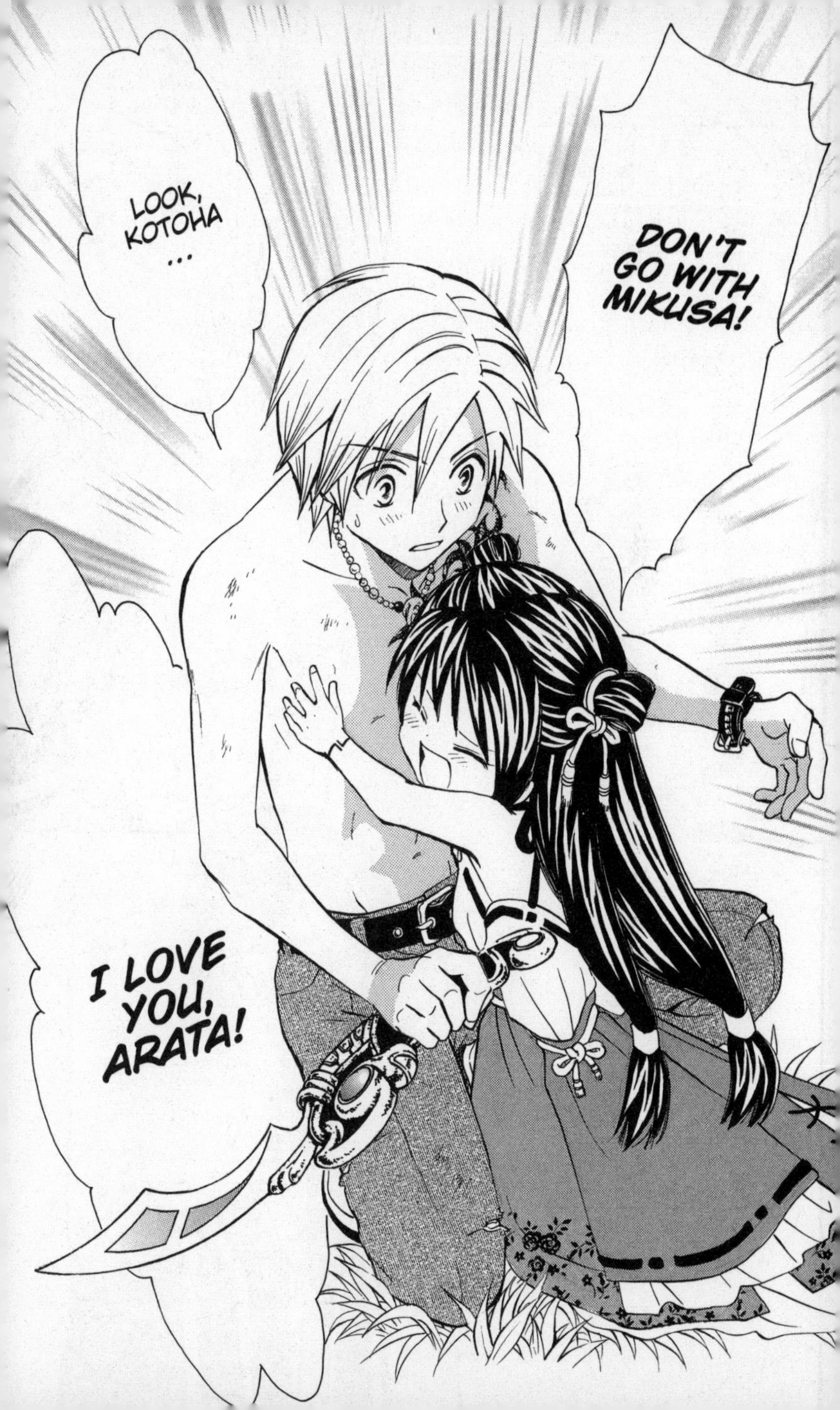
DON'T GO WITH MIKUSA!
LOOK, KOTOHA ...
I LOVE YOU, ARATA!

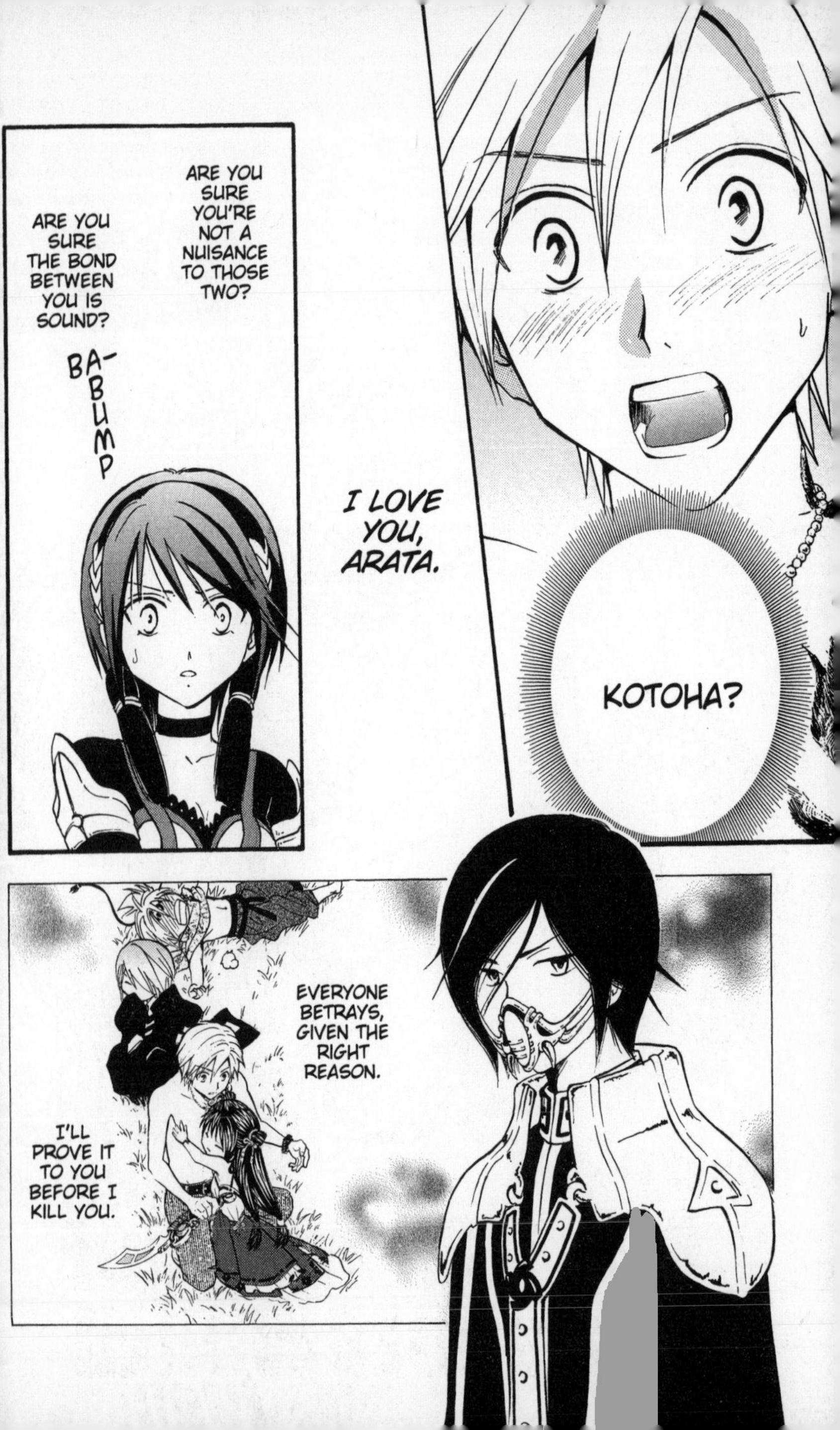
I LOVE YOU, ARATA.
KOTOHA?
ARE YOU SURE YOU'RE NOT A NUISANCE TO THOSE TWO?
ARE YOU SURE THE BOND BETWEEN YOU IS SOUND?
BA-BUMP
EVERYONE BETRAYS, GIVEN THE RIGHT REASON.
I'LL PROVE IT TO YOU BEFORE I KILL YOU.

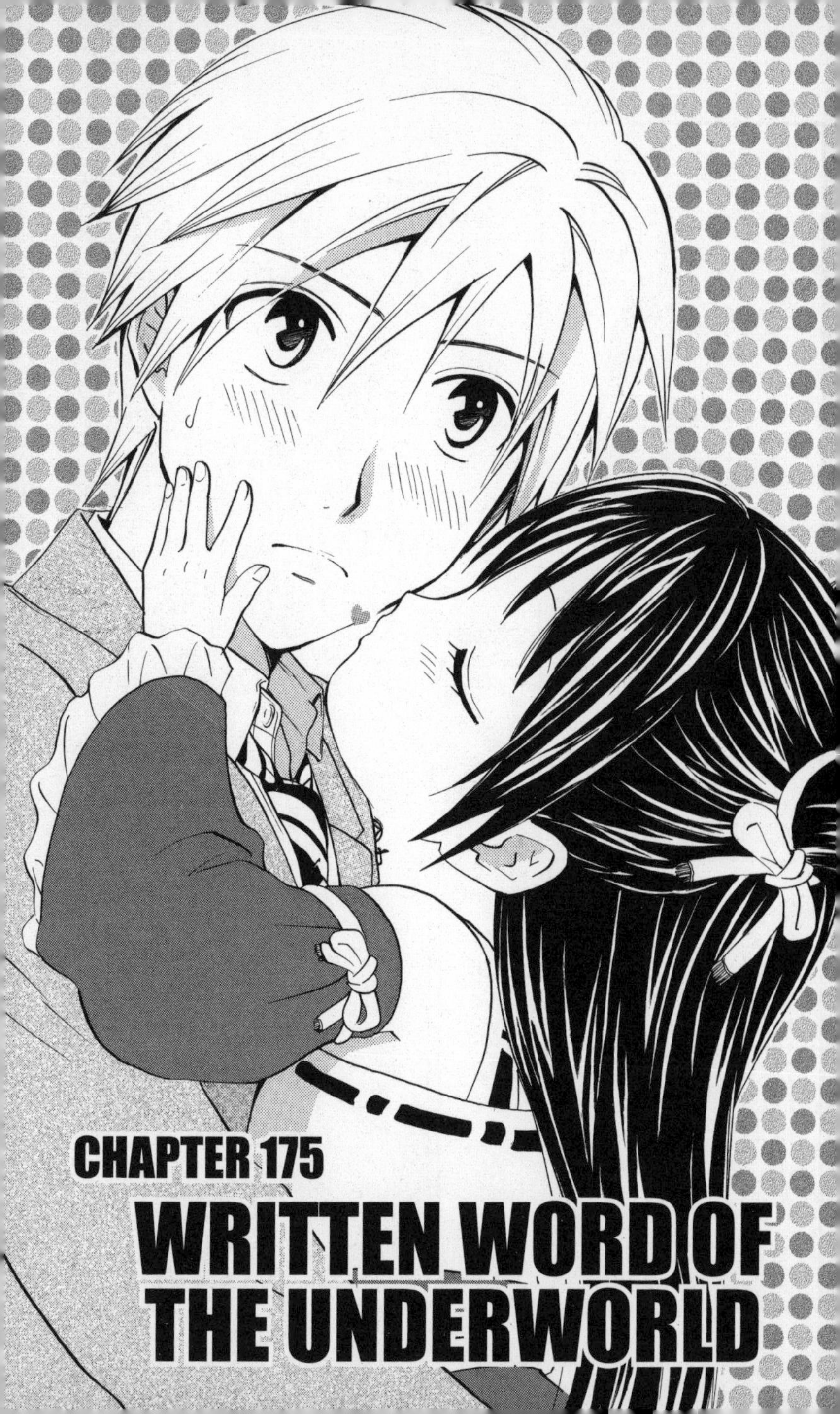
CHAPTER 175
WRITTEN WORD OF THE UNDERWORLD

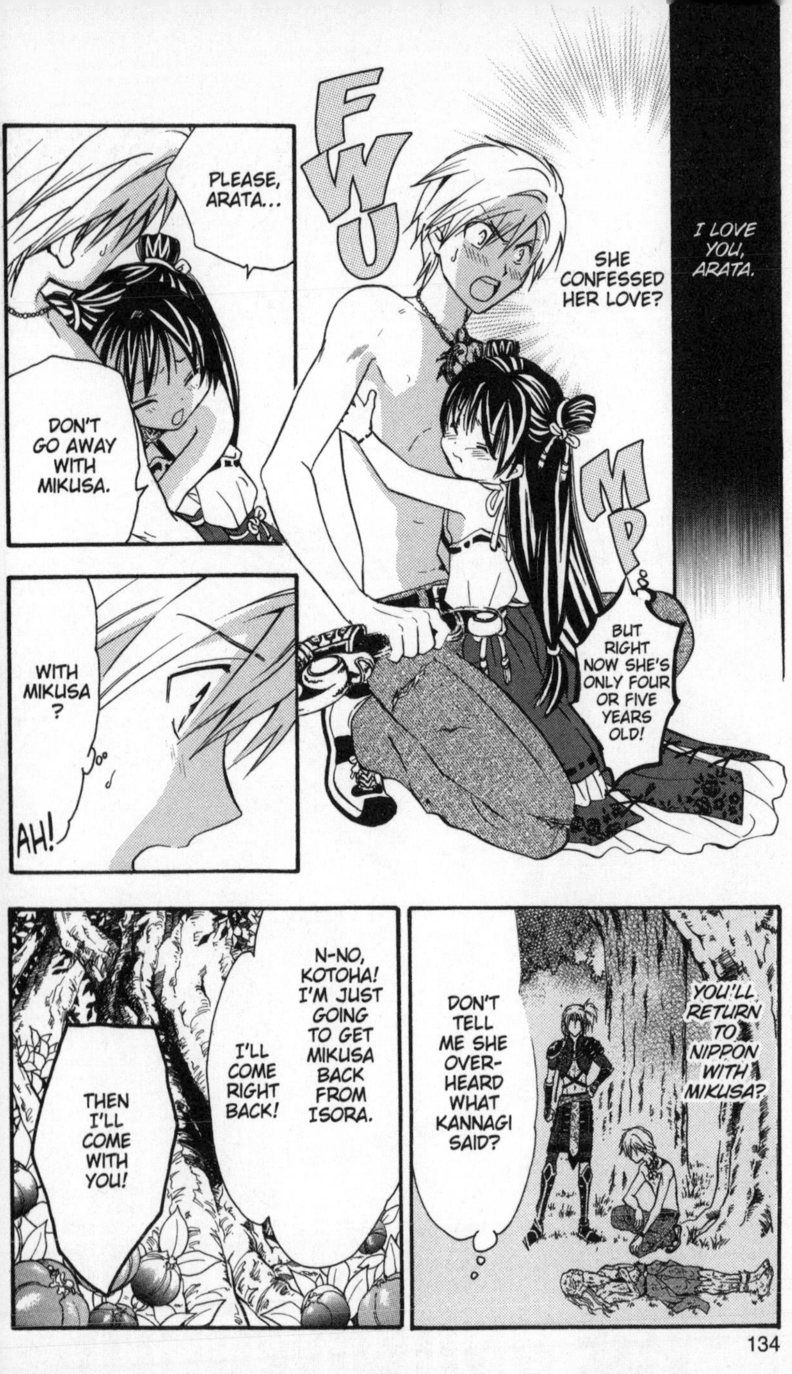
I LOVE YOU, ARATA.
FWU
SHE CONFESSED HER LOVE?
MMP
BUT RIGHT NOW SHE'S ONLY FOUR OR FIVE YEARS OLD!
PLEASE, ARATA...
DON'T GO AWAY WITH MIKUSA.
WITH MIKUSA?
AH!
YOU'LL RETURN TO NIPPON WITH MIKUSA?
DON'T TELL ME SHE OVERHEARD WHAT KANNAGI SAID?
N-NO, KOTOHA! I'M JUST GOING TO GET MIKUSA BACK FROM ISORA.
I'LL COME RIGHT BACK!
THEN I'LL COME WITH YOU!

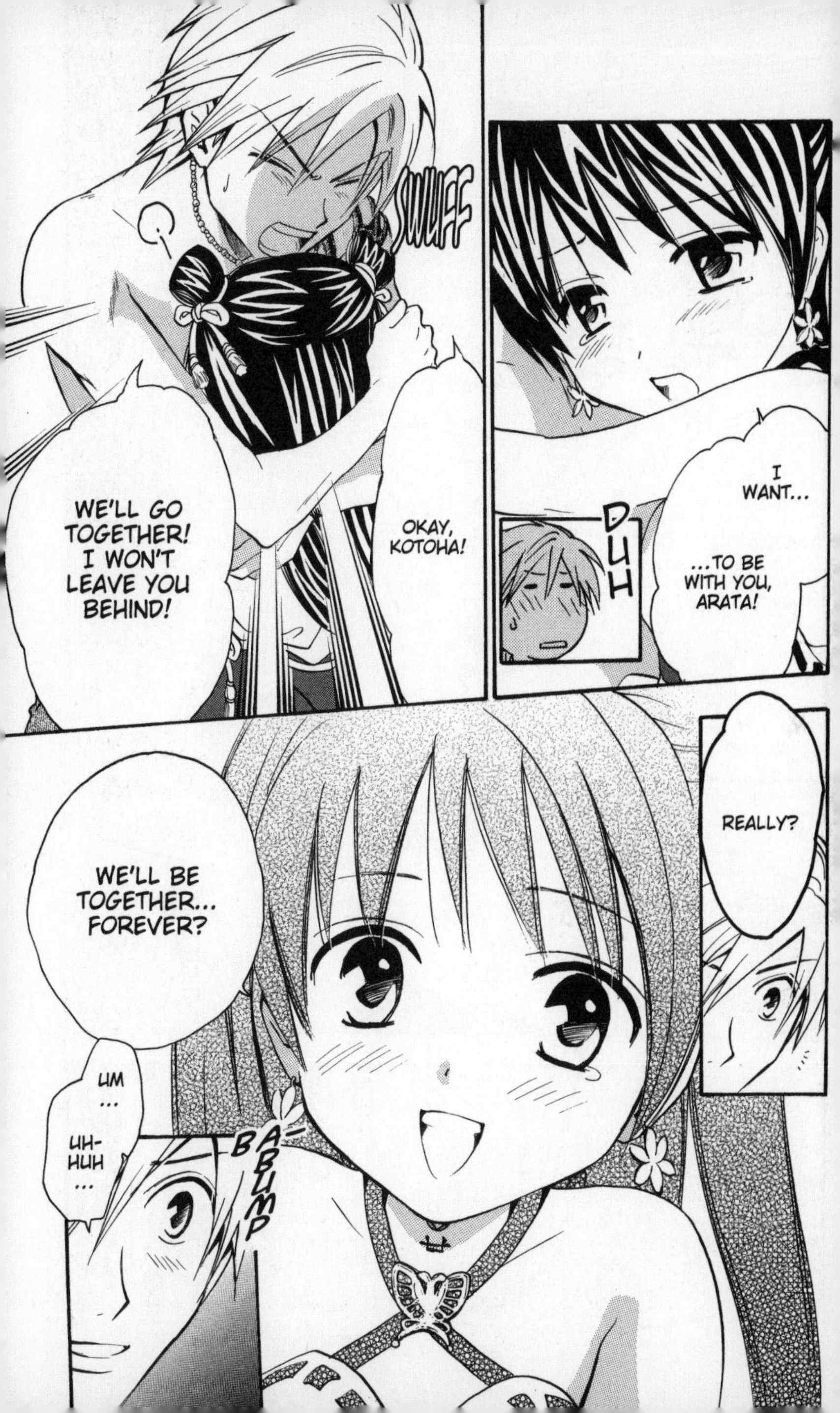
I WANT...
...TO BE WITH YOU, ARATA!
DUH
SWUFF
OKAY, KOTOHA!
WE'LL GO TOGETHER! I WON'T LEAVE YOU BEHIND!
REALLY?
WE'LL BE TOGETHER... FOREVER?
BA-BUMP
UM... UH-HUH...

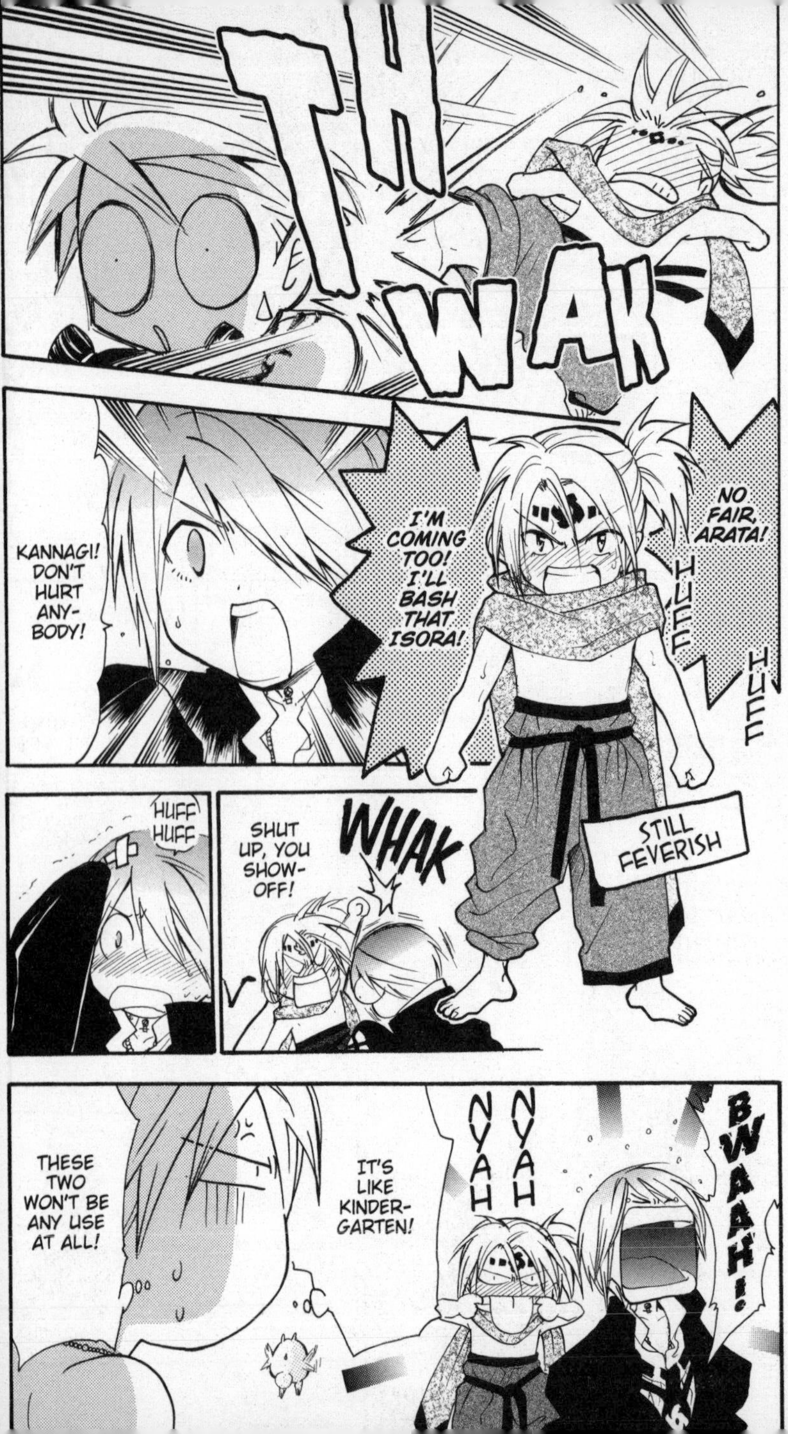
THWAK
NO FAIR, ARATA!
HUFF HUFF
I'M COMING TOO! I'LL BASH THAT ISORA!
KANNAGI! DON'T HURT ANYBODY!
STILL FEVERISH
WHAK
SHUT UP, YOU SHOW-OFF!
HUFF HUFF
BWAAH!!
NYAH NYAH
IT'S LIKE KINDER-GARTEN!
THESE TWO WON'T BE ANY USE AT ALL!

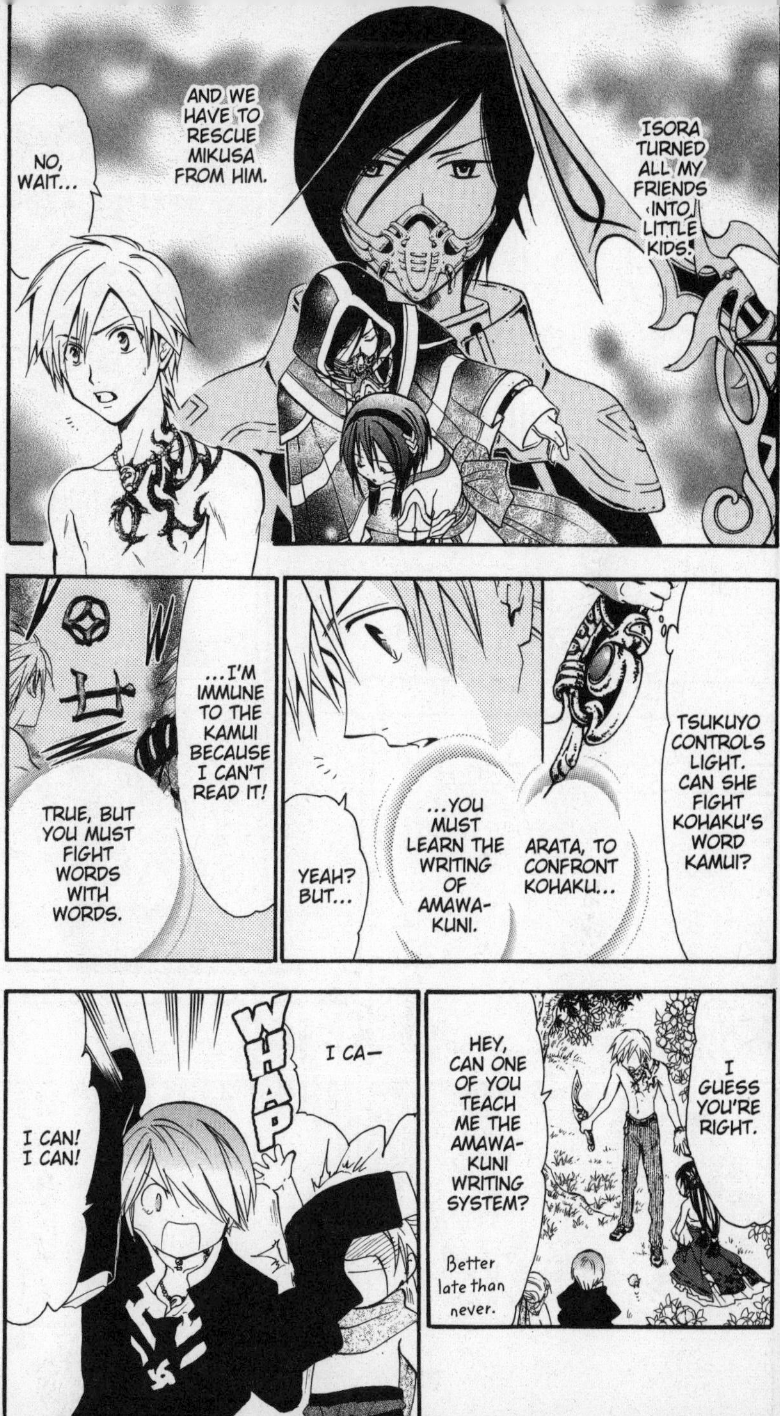
ISORA TURNED ALL MY FRIENDS INTO LITTLE KIDS!
AND WE HAVE TO RESCUE MIKUSA FROM HIM.
NO, WAIT...
TSUKUYO CONTROLS LIGHT. CAN SHE FIGHT KOHAKU'S WORD KAMUI?
ARATA, TO CONFRONT KOHAKU...
...YOU MUST LEARN THE WRITING OF AMAWA-KUNI.
YEAH? BUT...
...I'M IMMUNE TO THE KAMUI BECAUSE I CAN'T READ IT!
TRUE, BUT YOU MUST FIGHT WORDS WITH WORDS.
I GUESS YOU'RE RIGHT.
HEY, CAN ONE OF YOU TEACH ME THE AMAWA-KUNI WRITING SYSTEM?
Better late than never.
I CA—
WHAP
I CAN! I CAN!

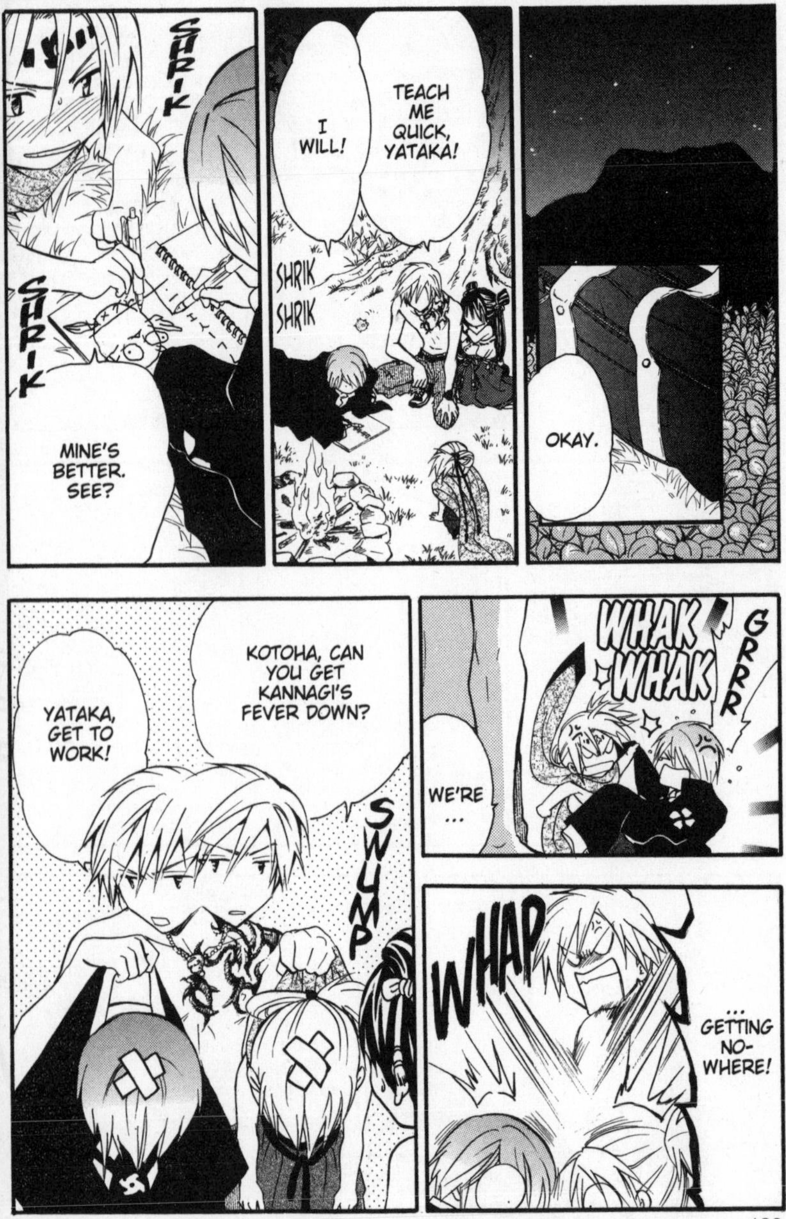
OKAY.
TEACH ME QUICK, YATAKA!
I WILL!
SHRIK SHRIK
SHRIK
SHRIK
MINE'S BETTER. SEE?
WHAK WHAK
GRRR
WE'RE ...
WHAP
... GETTING NO-WHERE!
KOTOHA, CAN YOU GET KANNAGI'S FEVER DOWN?
YATAKA, GET TO WORK!
SWUMP

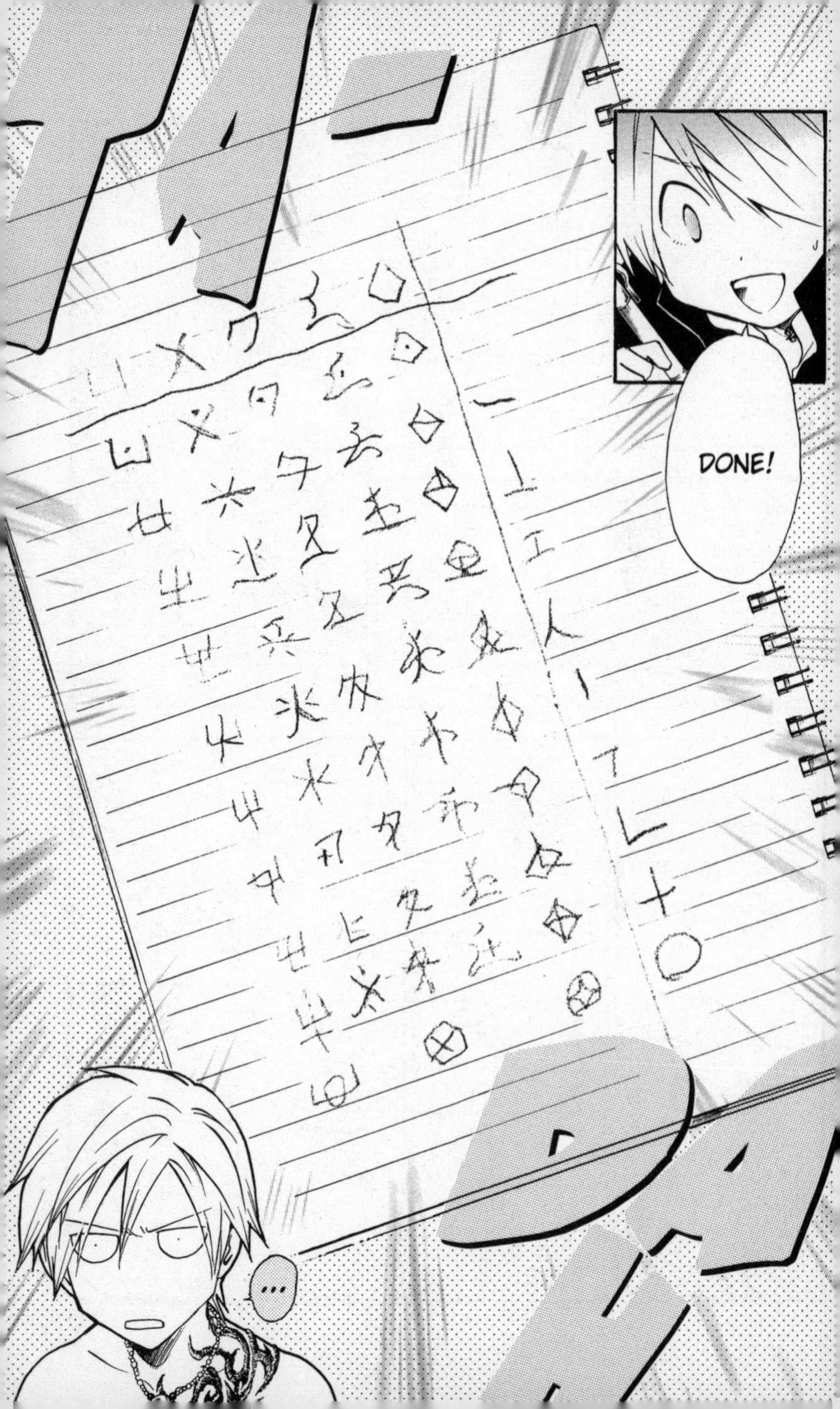
DONE!
...

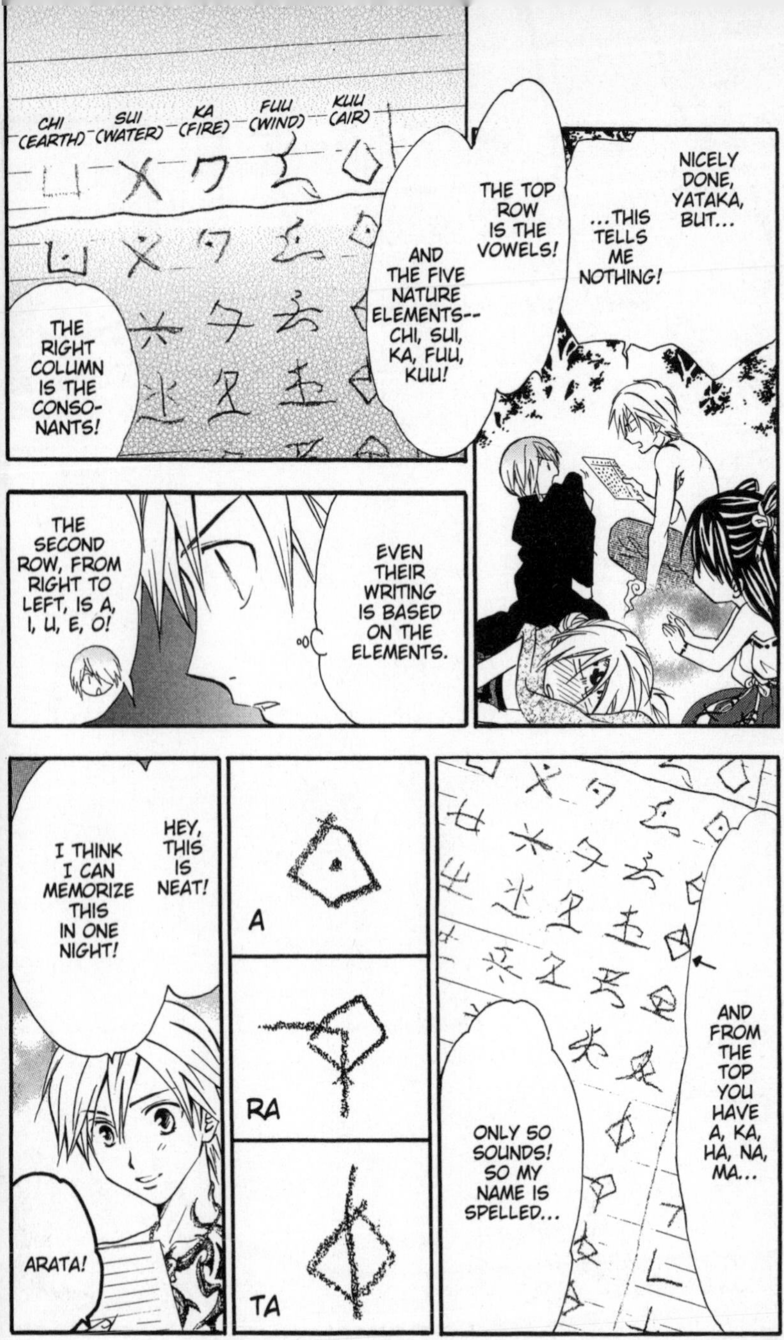

NICELY DONE, YATAKA, BUT...
...THIS TELLS ME NOTHING!
THE TOP ROW IS THE VOWELS!
AND THE FIVE NATURE ELEMENTS--CHI, SUI, KA, FUU, KUU!
KUU (AIR)
FUU (WIND)
KA (FIRE)
SUI (WATER)
CHI (EARTH)
THE RIGHT COLUMN IS THE CONSONANTS!
EVEN THEIR WRITING IS BASED ON THE ELEMENTS.
THE SECOND ROW, FROM RIGHT TO LEFT, IS A, I, U, E, O!
AND FROM THE TOP YOU HAVE A, KA, HA, NA, MA...
ONLY 50 SOUNDS! SO MY NAME IS SPELLED...
A
RA
TA
HEY, THIS IS NEAT!
I THINK I CAN MEMORIZE THIS IN ONE NIGHT!
ARATA!

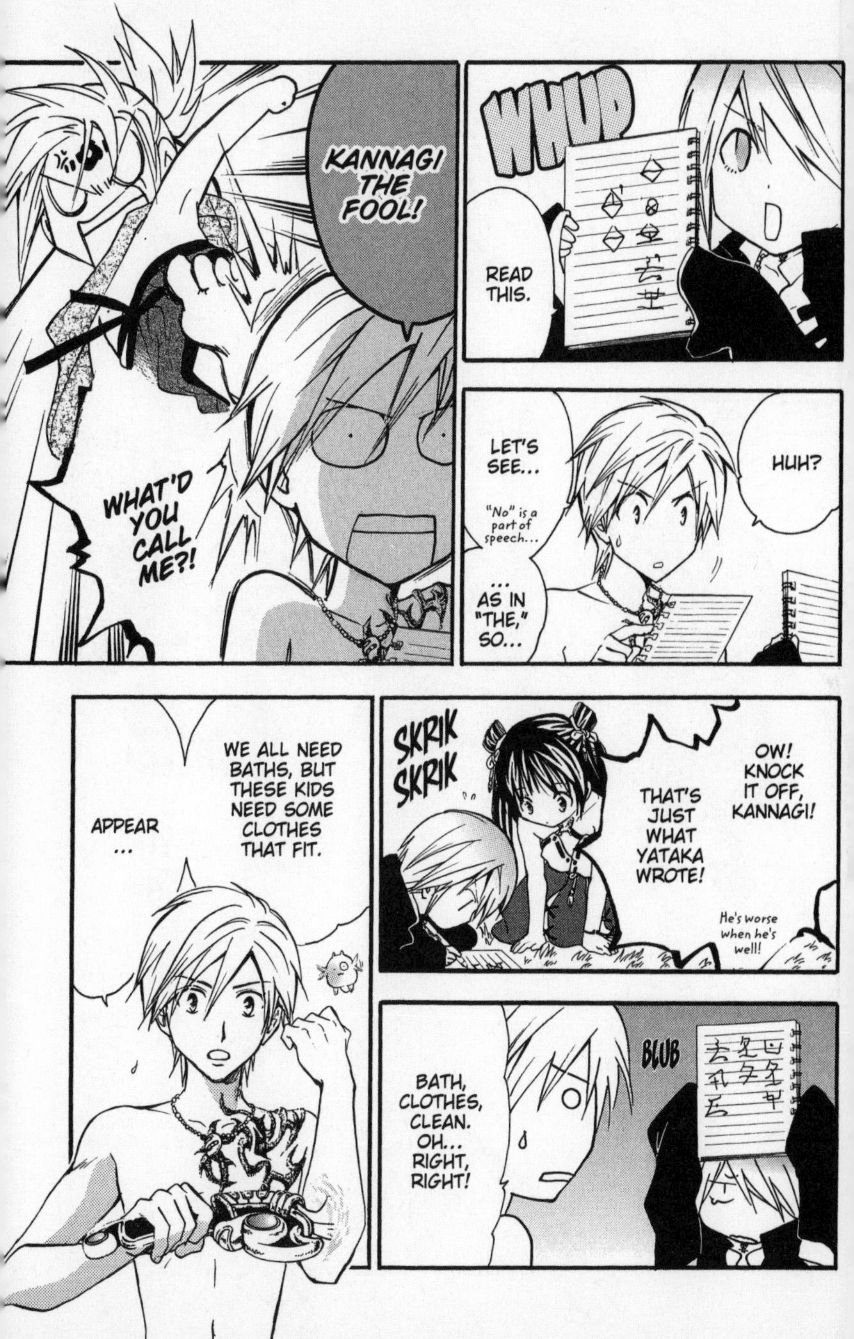
WHUP
READ THIS.
HUH?
LET'S SEE...
"No" is a part of speech...
... AS IN "THE," SO...
KANNAGI THE FOOL!
WHAT'D YOU CALL ME?!
OW! KNOCK IT OFF, KANNAGI!
THAT'S JUST WHAT YATAKA WROTE!
SKRIK SKRIK
He's worse when he's well!
BLUB
BATH, CLOTHES, CLEAN. OH... RIGHT, RIGHT!
WE ALL NEED BATHS, BUT THESE KIDS NEED SOME CLOTHES THAT FIT.
APPEAR ...

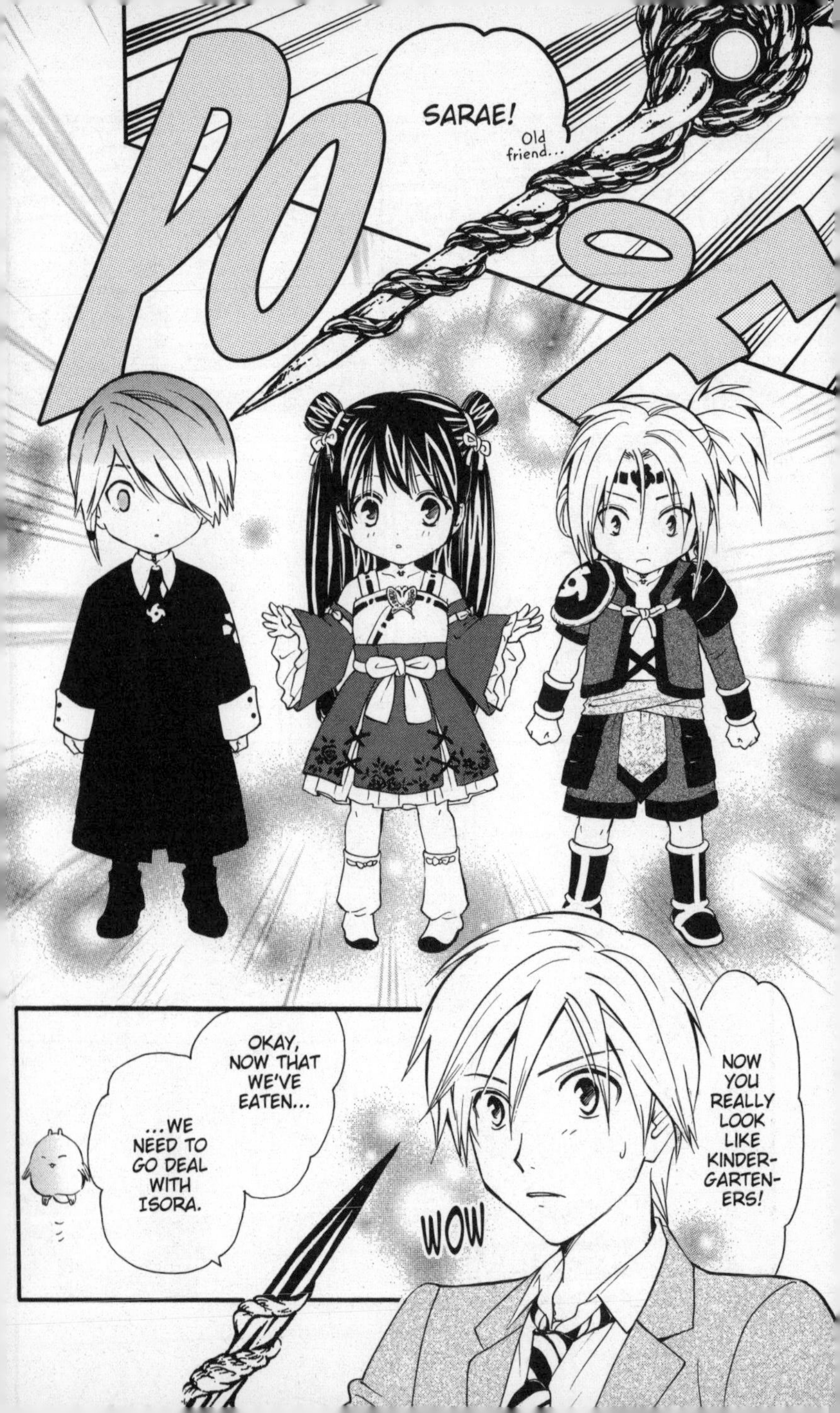
POOF
SARAE!
Old friend...
NOW YOU REALLY LOOK LIKE KINDER-GARTEN-ERS!
WOW
OKAY, NOW THAT WE'VE EATEN...
...WE NEED TO GO DEAL WITH ISORA.

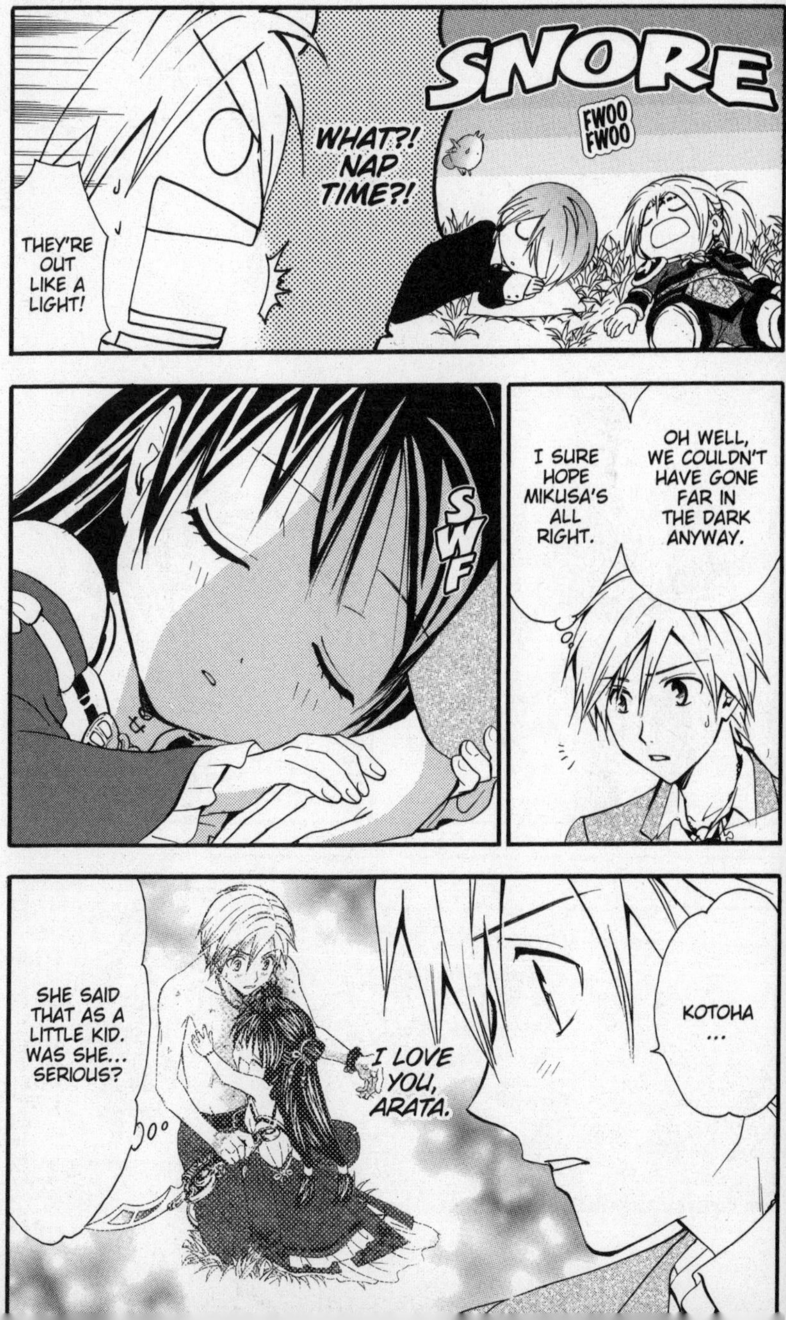
SNORE
FWOO FWOO
WHAT?! NAP TIME?!
THEY'RE OUT LIKE A LIGHT!
OH WELL, WE COULDN'T HAVE GONE FAR IN THE DARK ANYWAY.
I SURE HOPE MIKUSA'S ALL RIGHT.
SWF
KOTOHA...
I LOVE YOU, ARATA.
SHE SAID THAT AS A LITTLE KID. WAS SHE... SERIOUS?

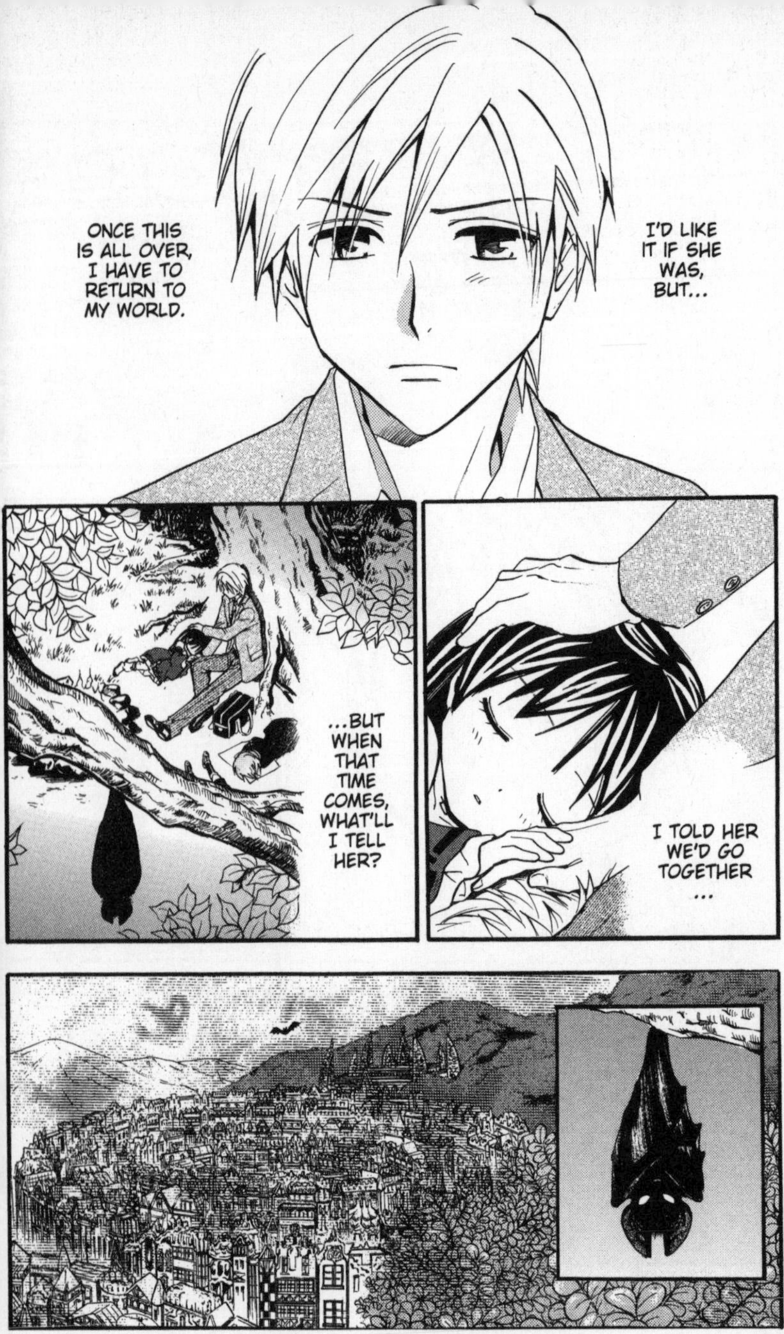
I'D LIKE IT IF SHE WAS, BUT...
ONCE THIS IS ALL OVER, I HAVE TO RETURN TO MY WORLD.
I TOLD HER WE'D GO TOGETHER ...
...BUT WHEN THAT TIME COMES, WHAT'LL I TELL HER?

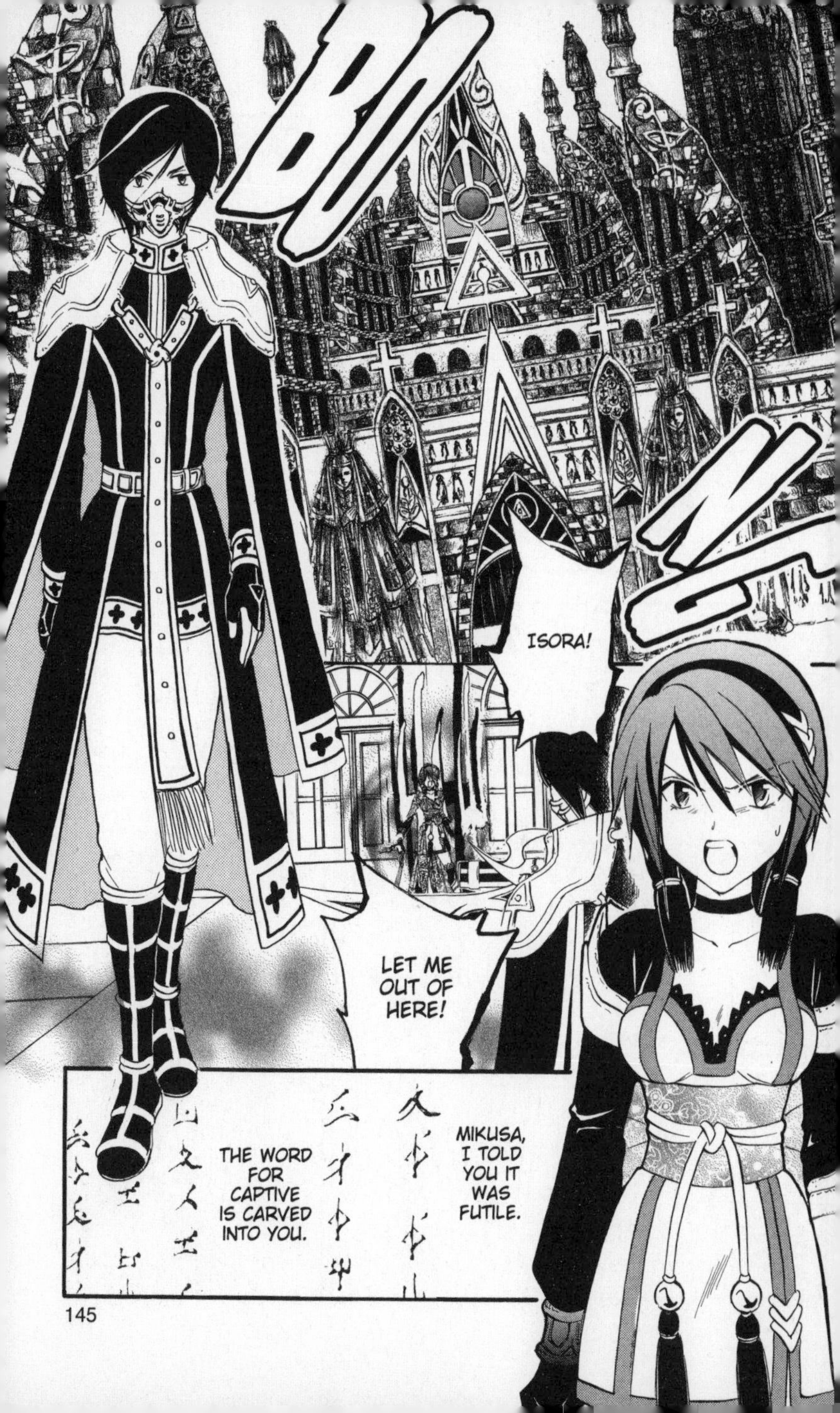

ISORA!
LET ME OUT OF HERE!
MIKUSA, I TOLD YOU IT WAS FUTILE.
THE WORD FOR CAPTIVE IS CARVED INTO YOU.

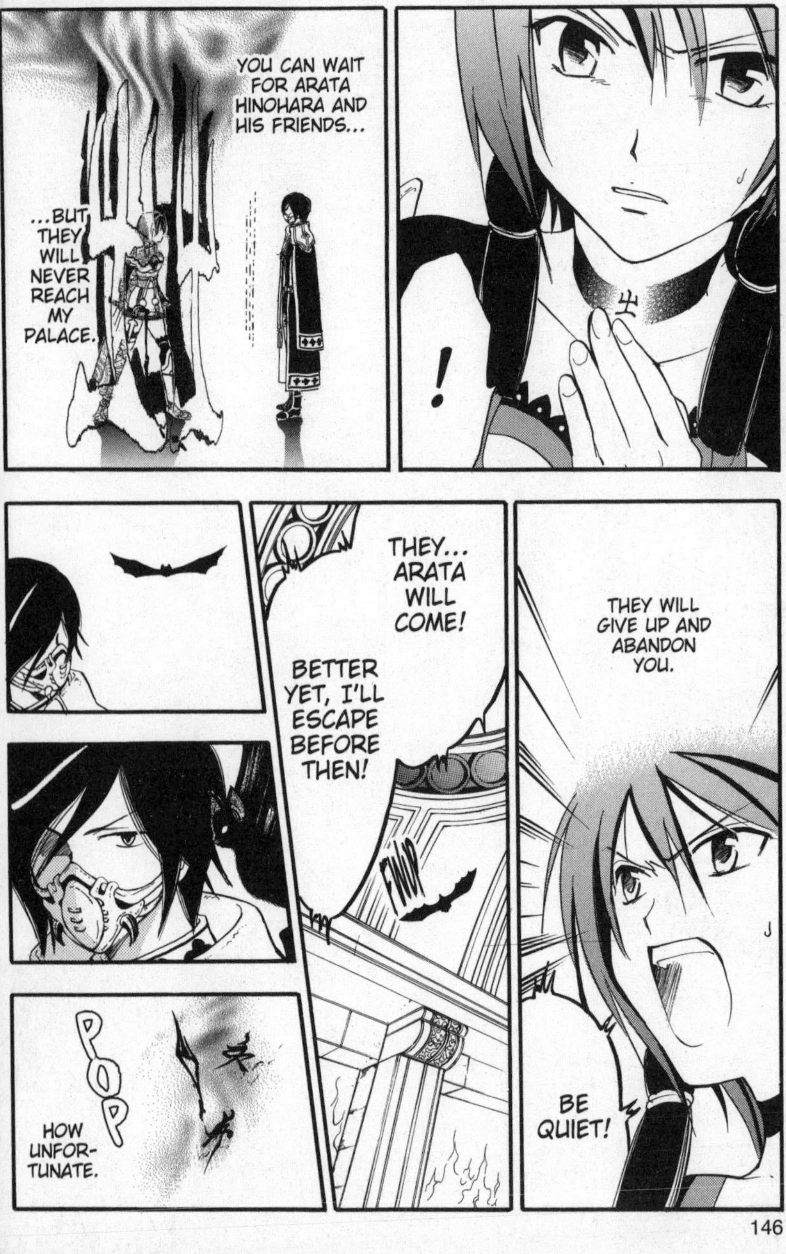
!
YOU CAN WAIT FOR ARATA HINOHARA AND HIS FRIENDS...
...BUT THEY WILL NEVER REACH MY PALACE.
THEY WILL GIVE UP AND ABANDON YOU.
BE QUIET!
THEY... ARATA WILL COME!
BETTER YET, I'LL ESCAPE BEFORE THEN!
FWOP
POP
HOW UNFOR-TUNATE.

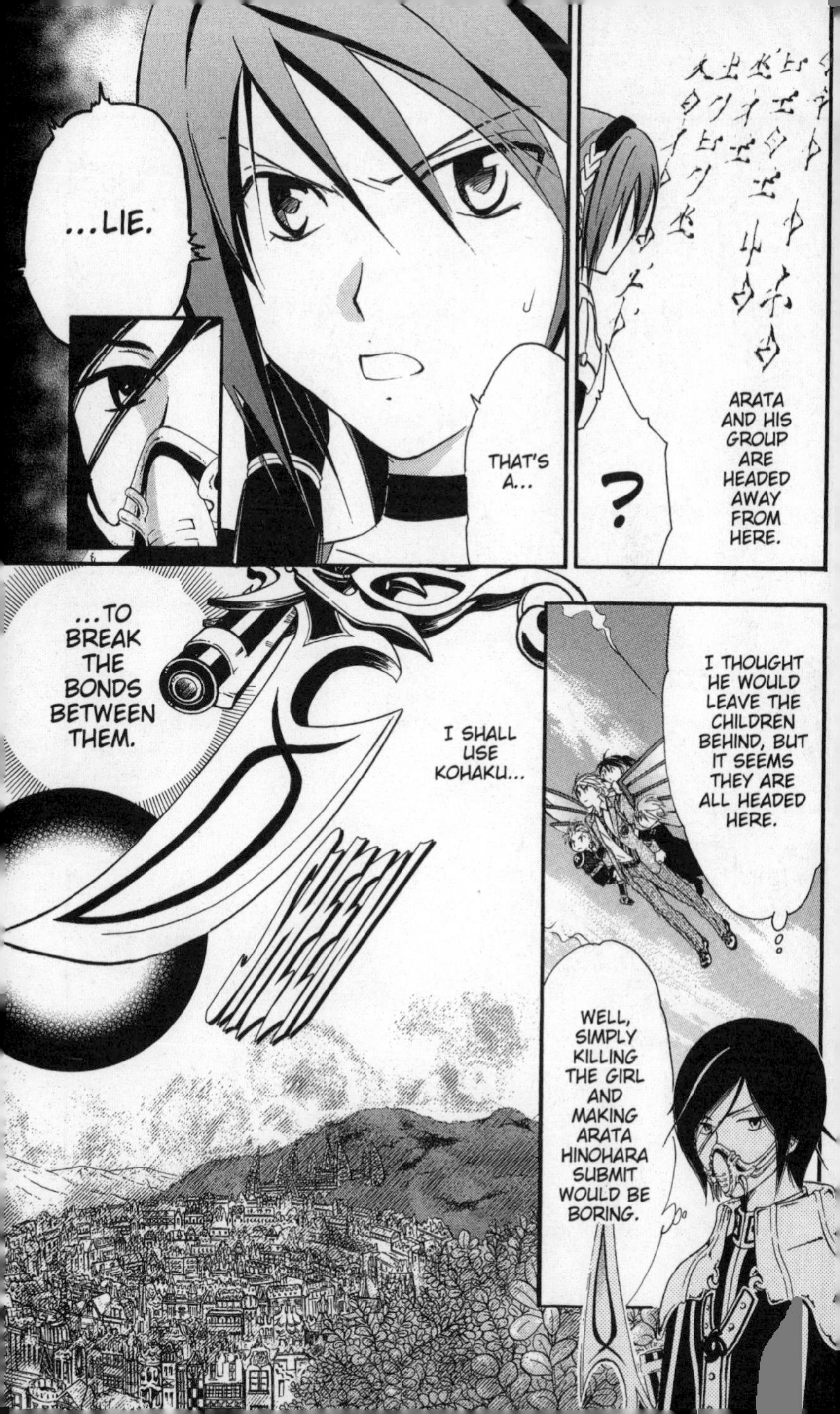
ARATA AND HIS GROUP ARE HEADED AWAY FROM HERE.
?
THAT'S A...
...LIE.
I THOUGHT HE WOULD LEAVE THE CHILDREN BEHIND, BUT IT SEEMS THEY ARE ALL HEADED HERE.
WELL, SIMPLY KILLING THE GIRL AND MAKING ARATA HINOHARA SUBMIT WOULD BE BORING.
I SHALL USE KOHAKU...
...TO BREAK THE BONDS BETWEEN THEM.

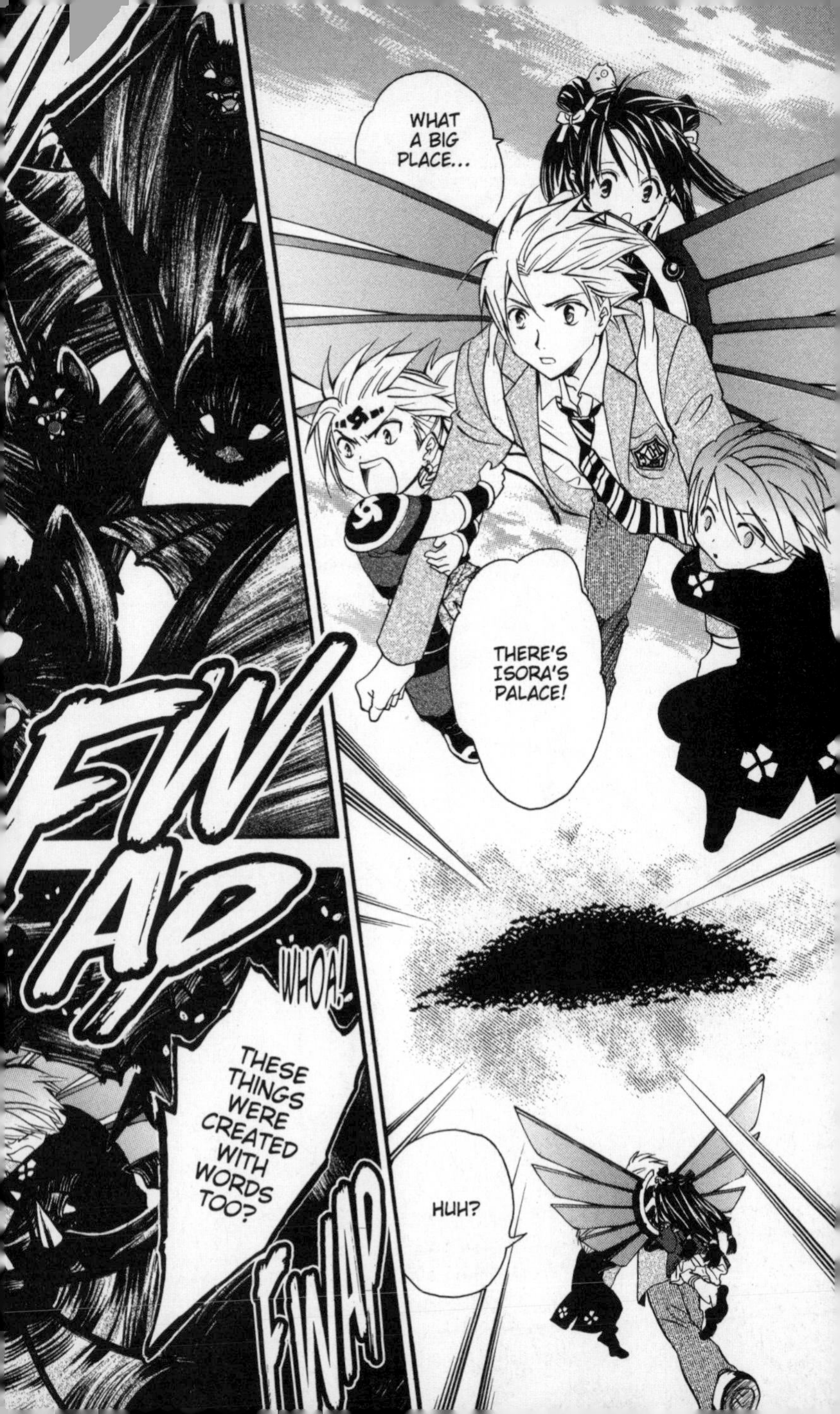

WHAT A BIG PLACE...
THERE'S ISORA'S PALACE!
HUH?
FWAP
WHOA!
THESE THINGS WERE CREATED WITH WORDS TOO?
FWAP

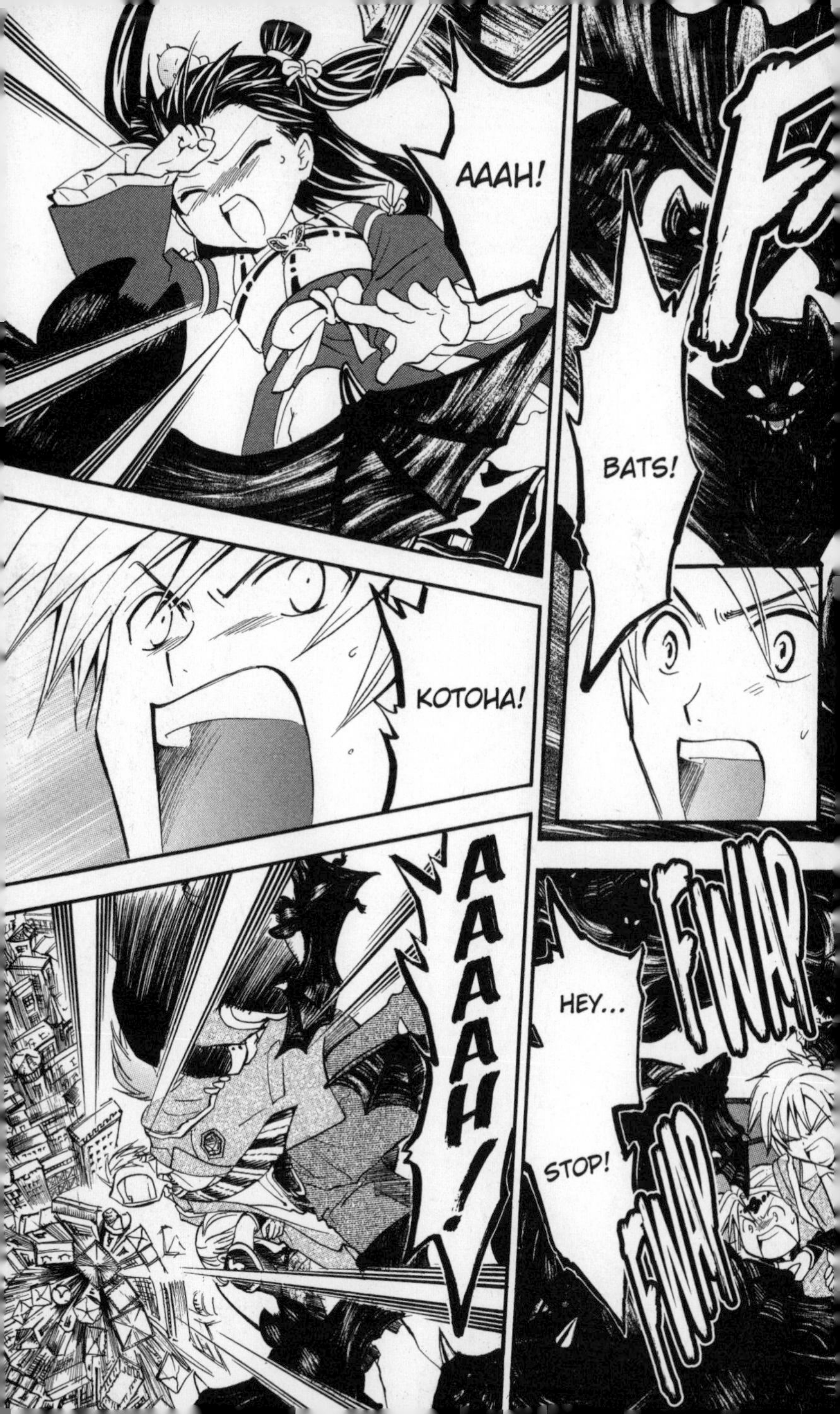
BATS!
AAAH!
KOTOHA!
FWAP
HEY...
STOP!
FWAP
AAAAAH!

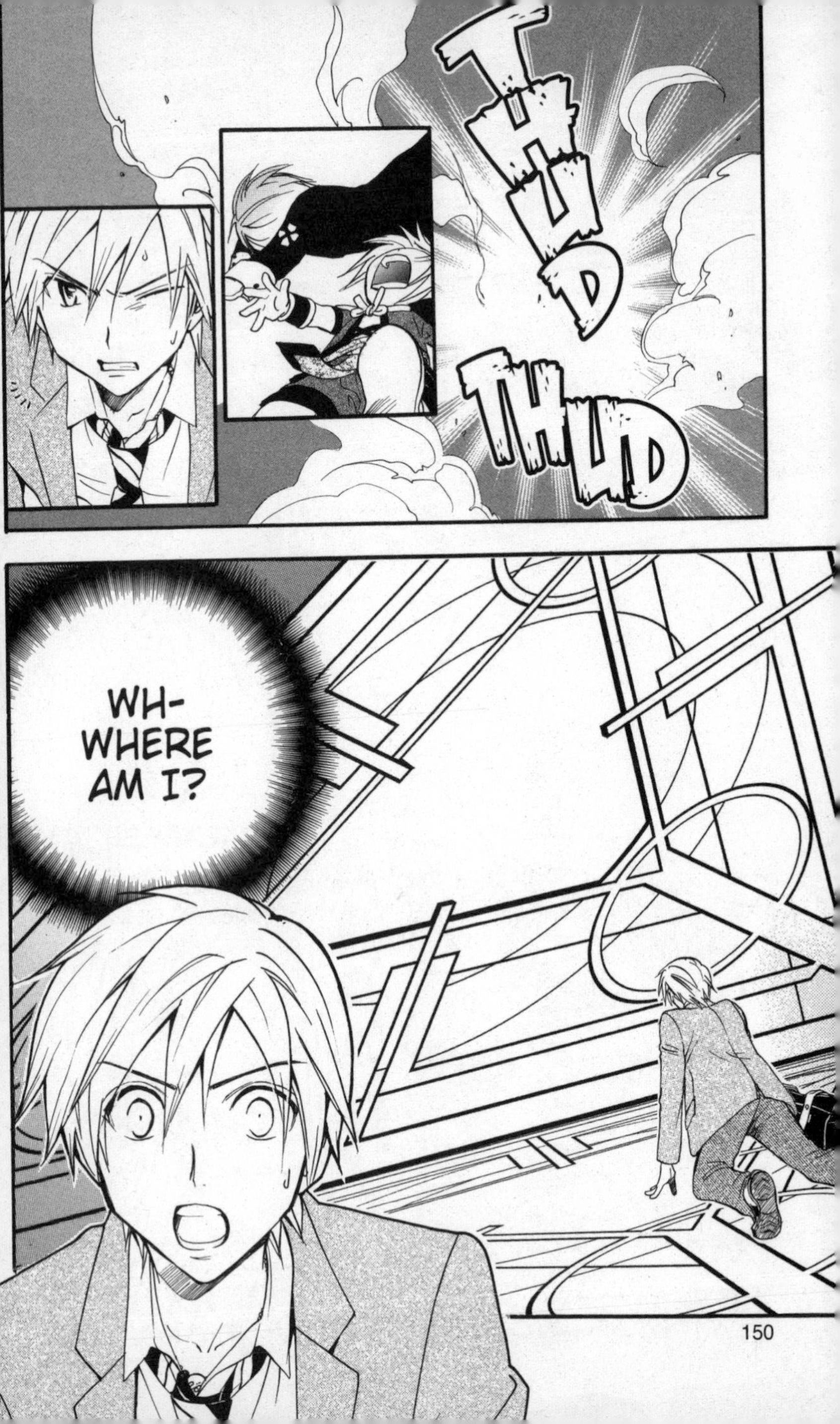
THUD
THUD
WH-WHERE AM I?

CHAPTER 176
ISORA'S TOWN

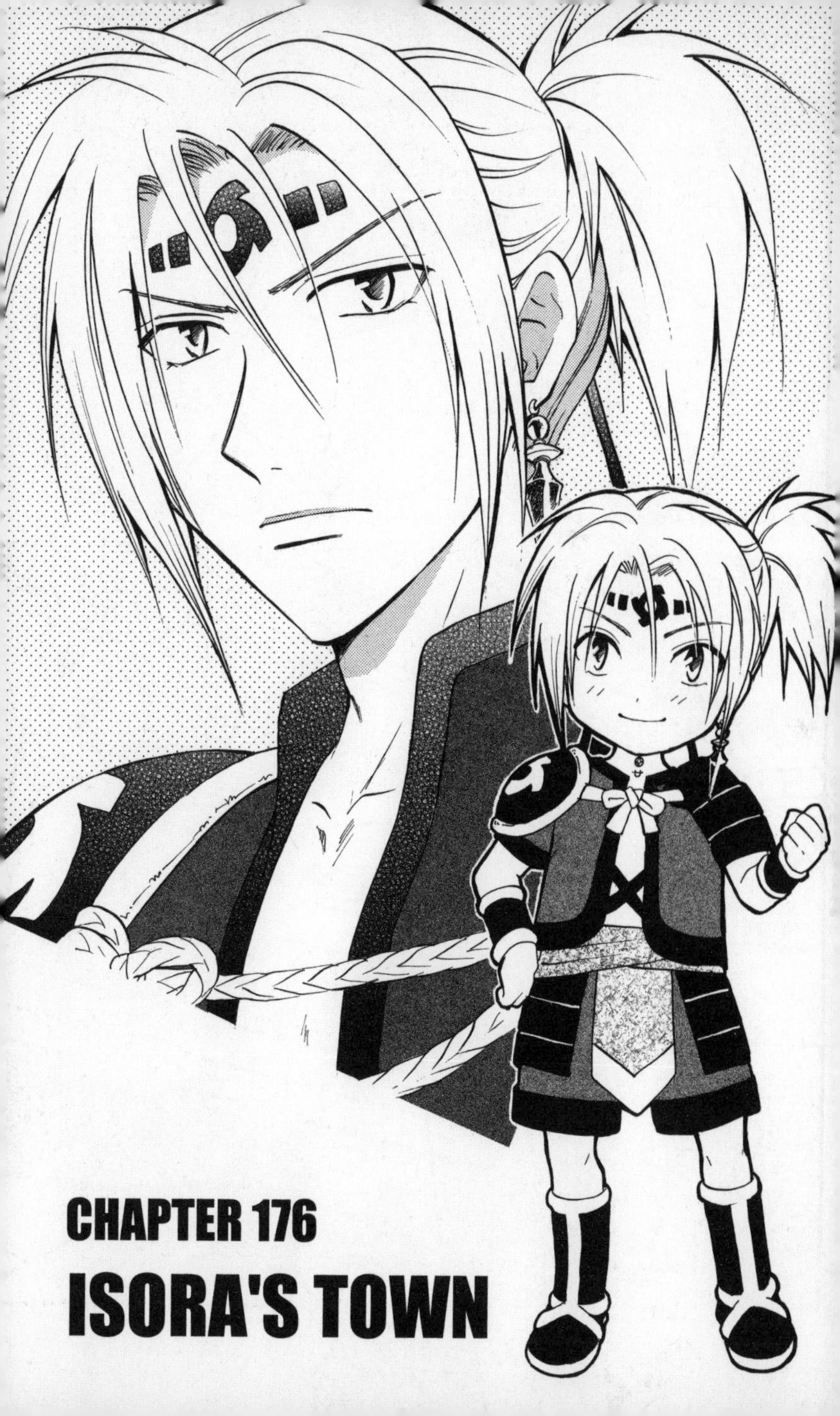

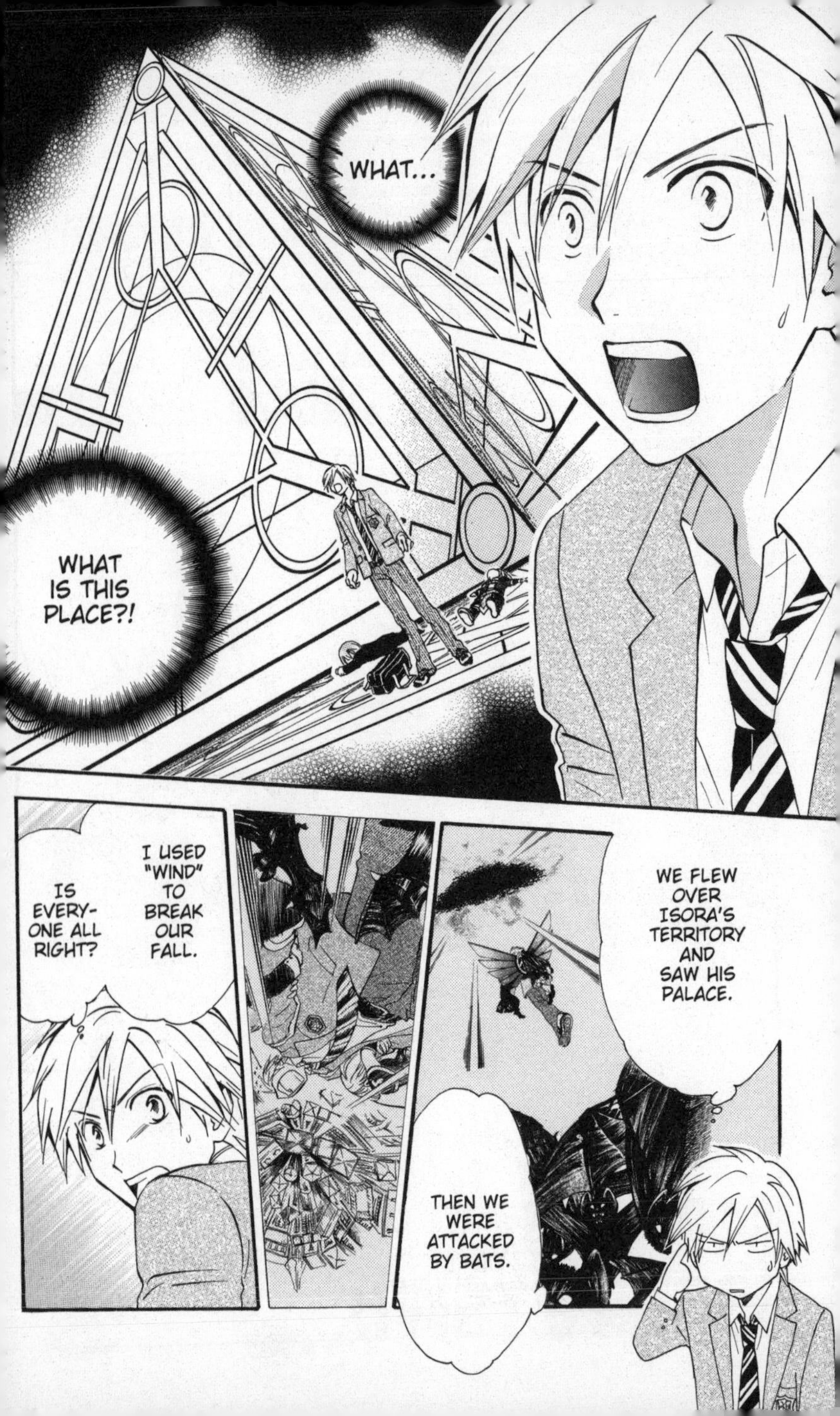
WHAT...
WHAT IS THIS PLACE?!
WE FLEW OVER ISORA'S TERRITORY AND SAW HIS PALACE.
THEN WE WERE ATTACKED BY BATS.
I USED "WIND" TO BREAK OUR FALL.
IS EVERY-ONE ALL RIGHT?

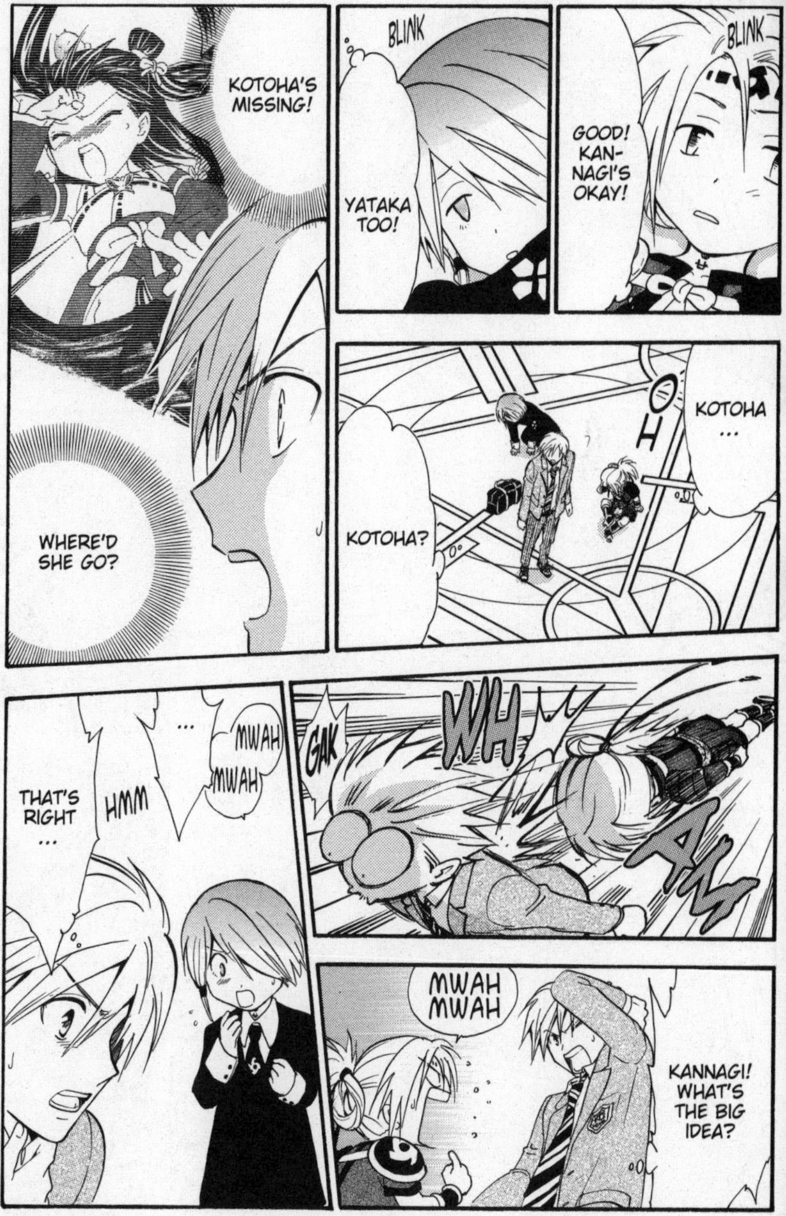
BLINK
GOOD! KAN-NAGI'S OKAY!
BLINK
YATAKA TOO!
OH
KOTOHA ...
KOTOHA?
KOTOHA'S MISSING!
WHERE'D SHE GO?
WHAM
GAK
KANNAGI! WHAT'S THE BIG IDEA?
MWAH MWAH
MWAH MWAH
...
HMM
THAT'S RIGHT ...

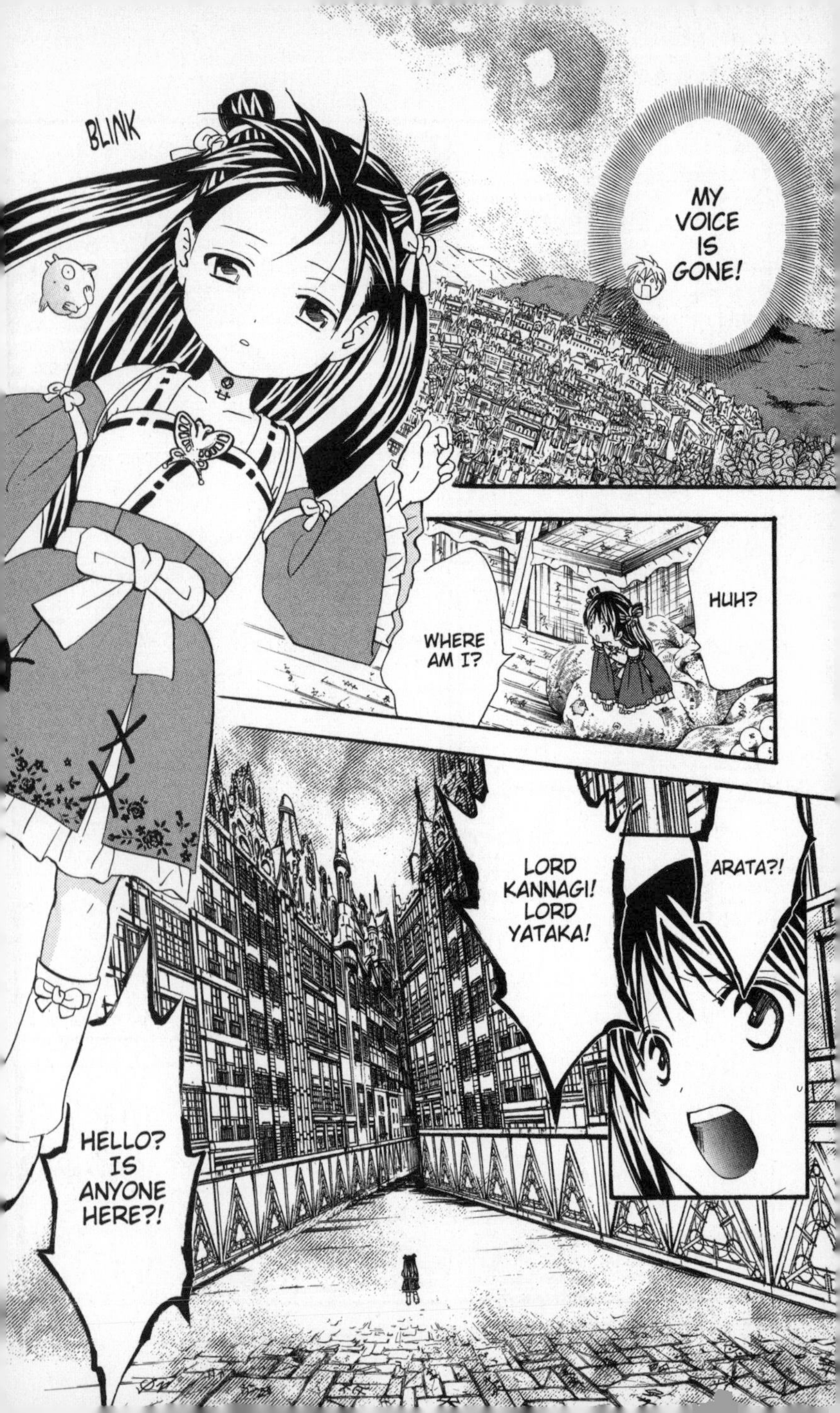
MY VOICE IS GONE!
BLINK
HUH?
WHERE AM I?
ARATA?!
LORD KANNAGI! LORD YATAKA!
HELLO? IS ANYONE HERE?!

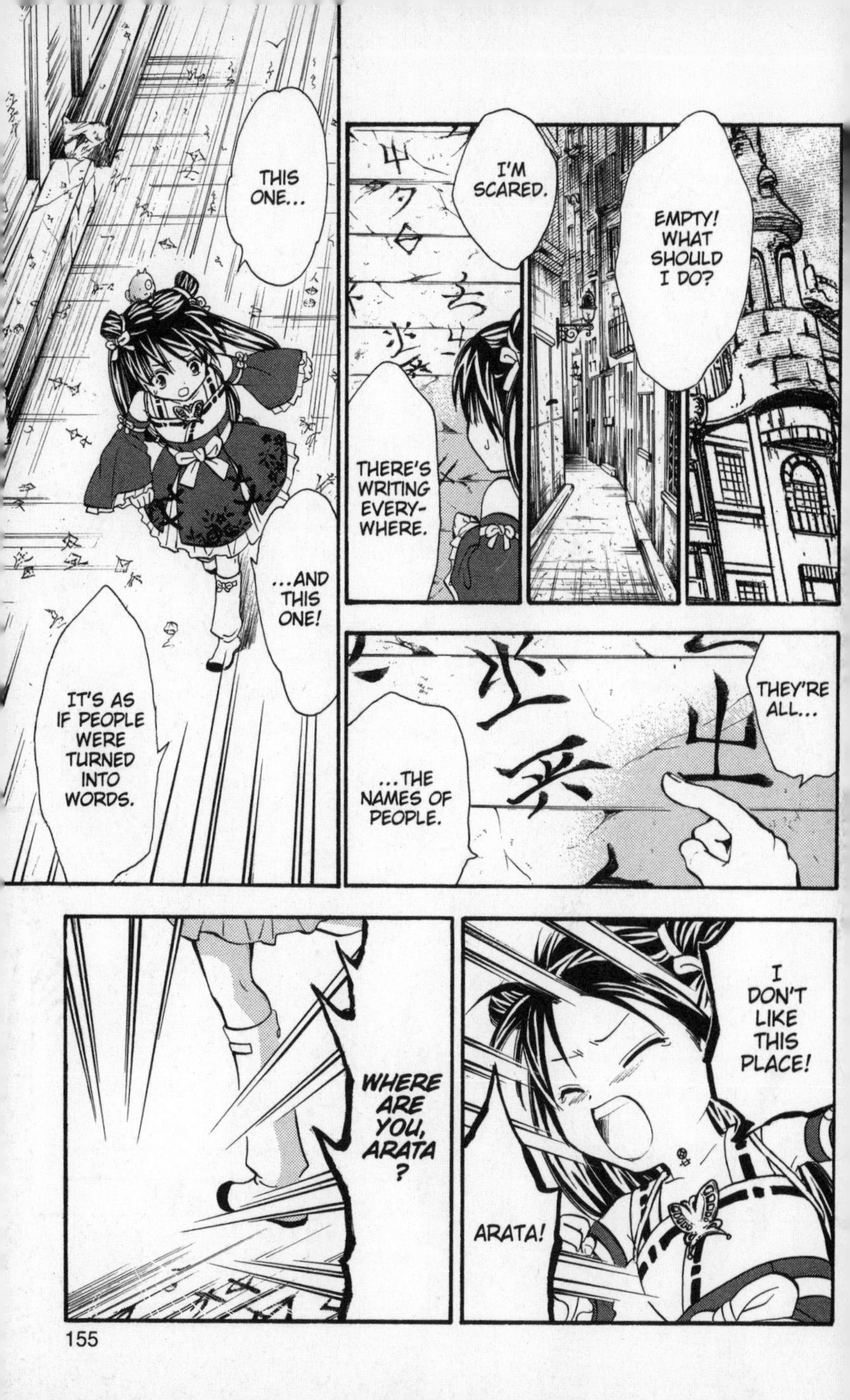
EMPTY! WHAT SHOULD I DO?
I'M SCARED.
THERE'S WRITING EVERY-WHERE.
THEY'RE ALL...
...THE NAMES OF PEOPLE.
THIS ONE...
...AND THIS ONE!
IT'S AS IF PEOPLE WERE TURNED INTO WORDS.
I DON'T LIKE THIS PLACE!
ARATA!
WHERE ARE YOU, ARATA?

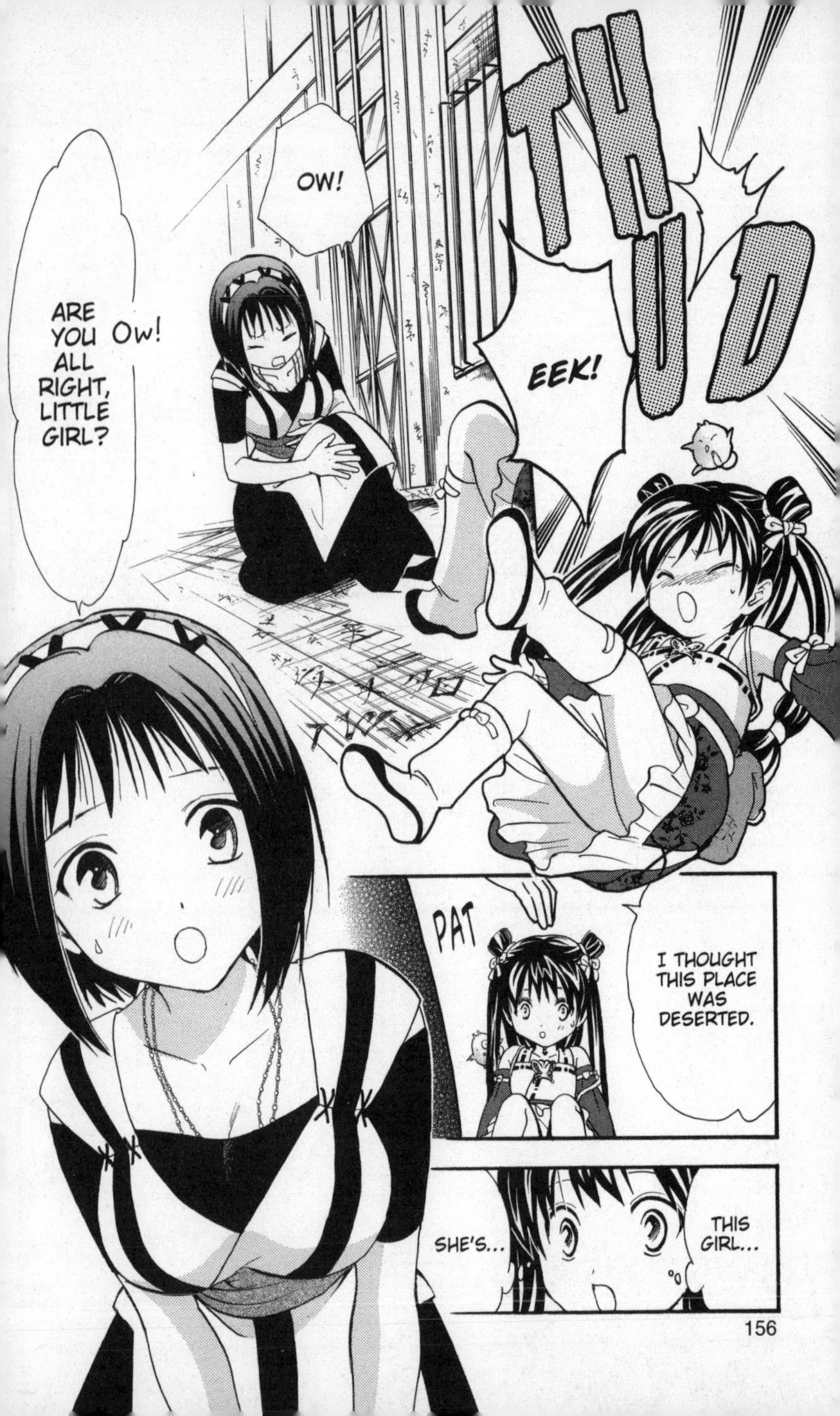
THUD
EEK!
OW!
Ow!
ARE YOU ALL RIGHT, LITTLE GIRL?
I THOUGHT THIS PLACE WAS DESERTED.
PAT
THIS GIRL...
SHE'S...

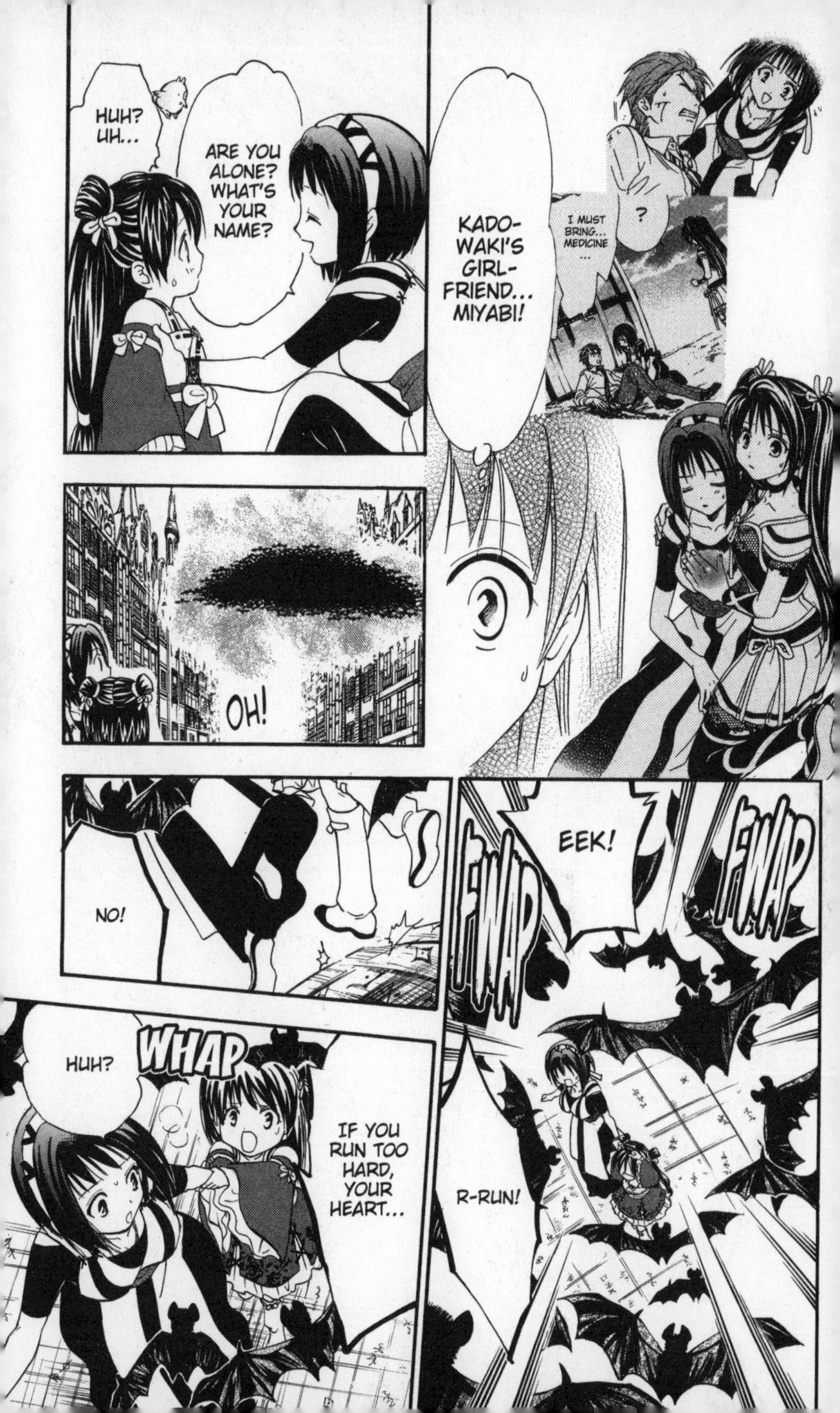

?
I MUST BRING... MEDICINE...
KADO-WAKI'S GIRL-FRIEND... MIYABI!
ARE YOU ALONE? WHAT'S YOUR NAME?
HUH? UH...
OH!
FWAP
EEK!
FWAP
R-RUN!
NO!
WHAP
HUH?
IF YOU RUN TOO HARD, YOUR HEART...

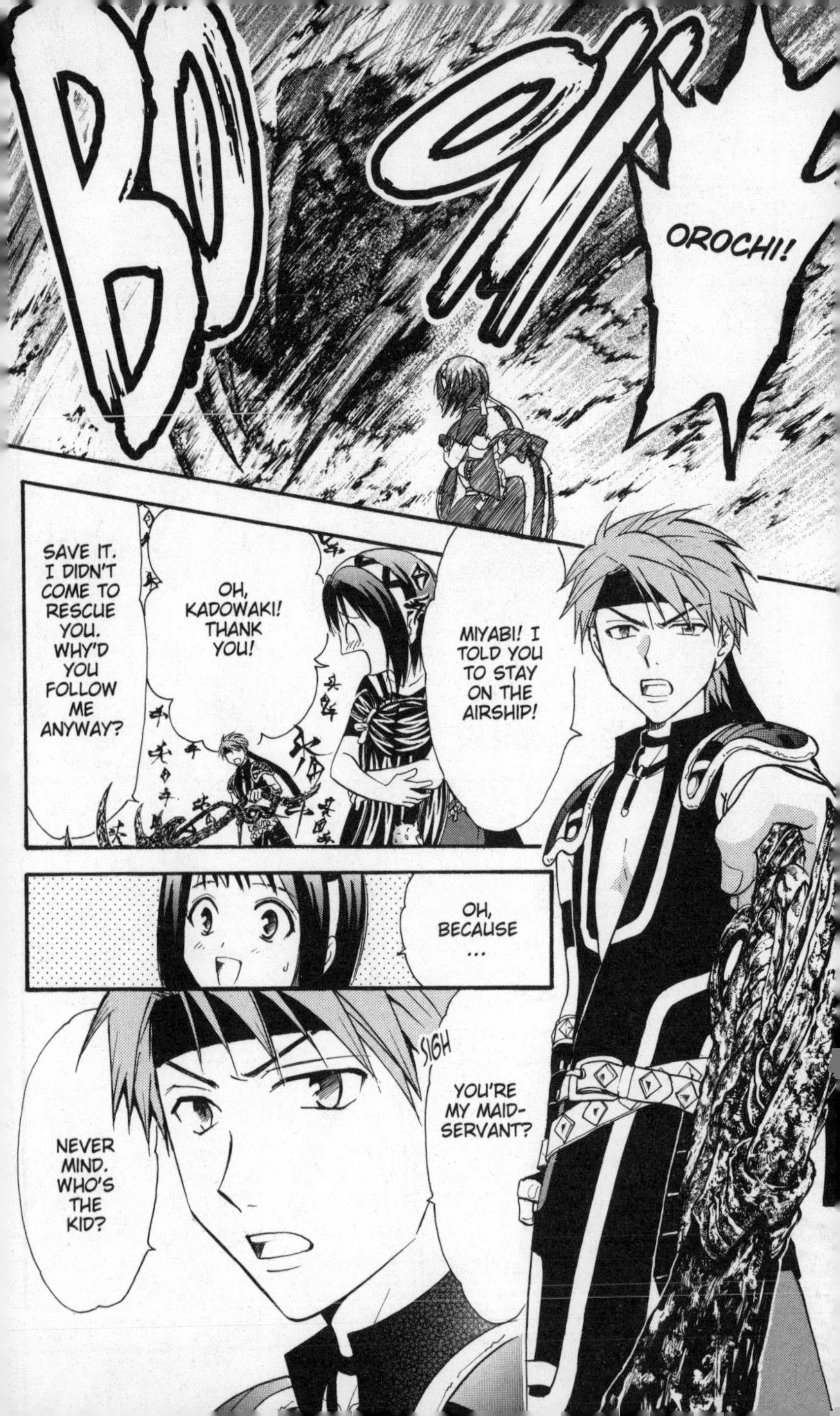
BOOM
OROCHI!
MIYABI! I TOLD YOU TO STAY ON THE AIRSHIP!
OH, KADOWAKI! THANK YOU!
SAVE IT. I DIDN'T COME TO RESCUE YOU. WHY'D YOU FOLLOW ME ANYWAY?
OH, BECAUSE ...
SIGH
YOU'RE MY MAID-SERVANT?
NEVER MIND. WHO'S THE KID?

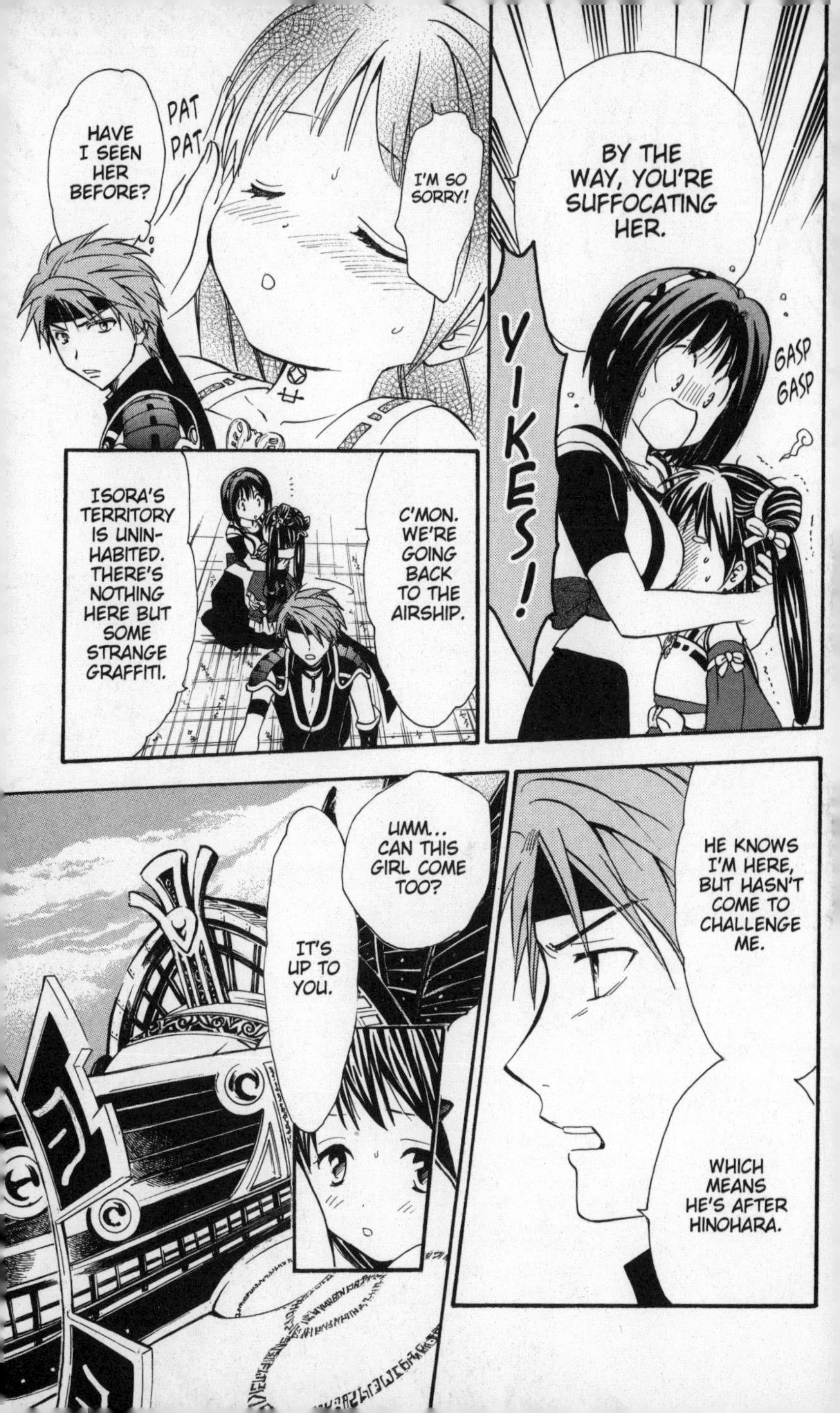
BY THE WAY, YOU'RE SUFFOCATING HER.
YIKES!
GASP GASP
I'M SO SORRY!
PAT PAT
HAVE I SEEN HER BEFORE?
C'MON. WE'RE GOING BACK TO THE AIRSHIP.
ISORA'S TERRITORY IS UNIN-HABITED. THERE'S NOTHING HERE BUT SOME STRANGE GRAFFITI.
HE KNOWS I'M HERE, BUT HASN'T COME TO CHALLENGE ME.
WHICH MEANS HE'S AFTER HINOHARA.
UMM... CAN THIS GIRL COME TOO?
IT'S UP TO YOU.

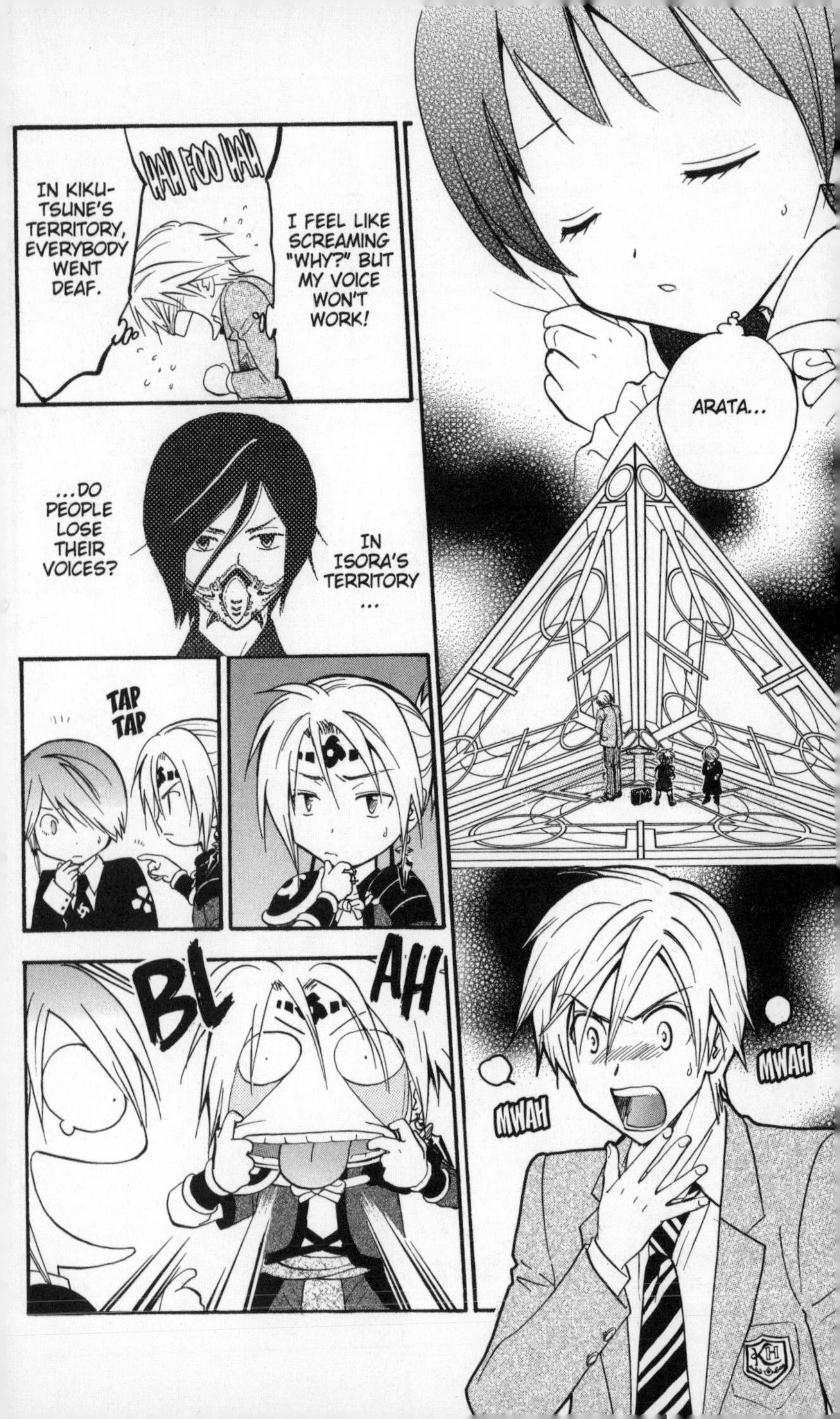
ARATA...
MWAH
MWAH
HAH FOO HAH
I FEEL LIKE SCREAMING "WHY?" BUT MY VOICE WON'T WORK!
IN KIKU-TSUNE'S TERRITORY, EVERYBODY WENT DEAF.
IN ISORA'S TERRITORY...
...DO PEOPLE LOSE THEIR VOICES?
TAP TAP
BL
AH

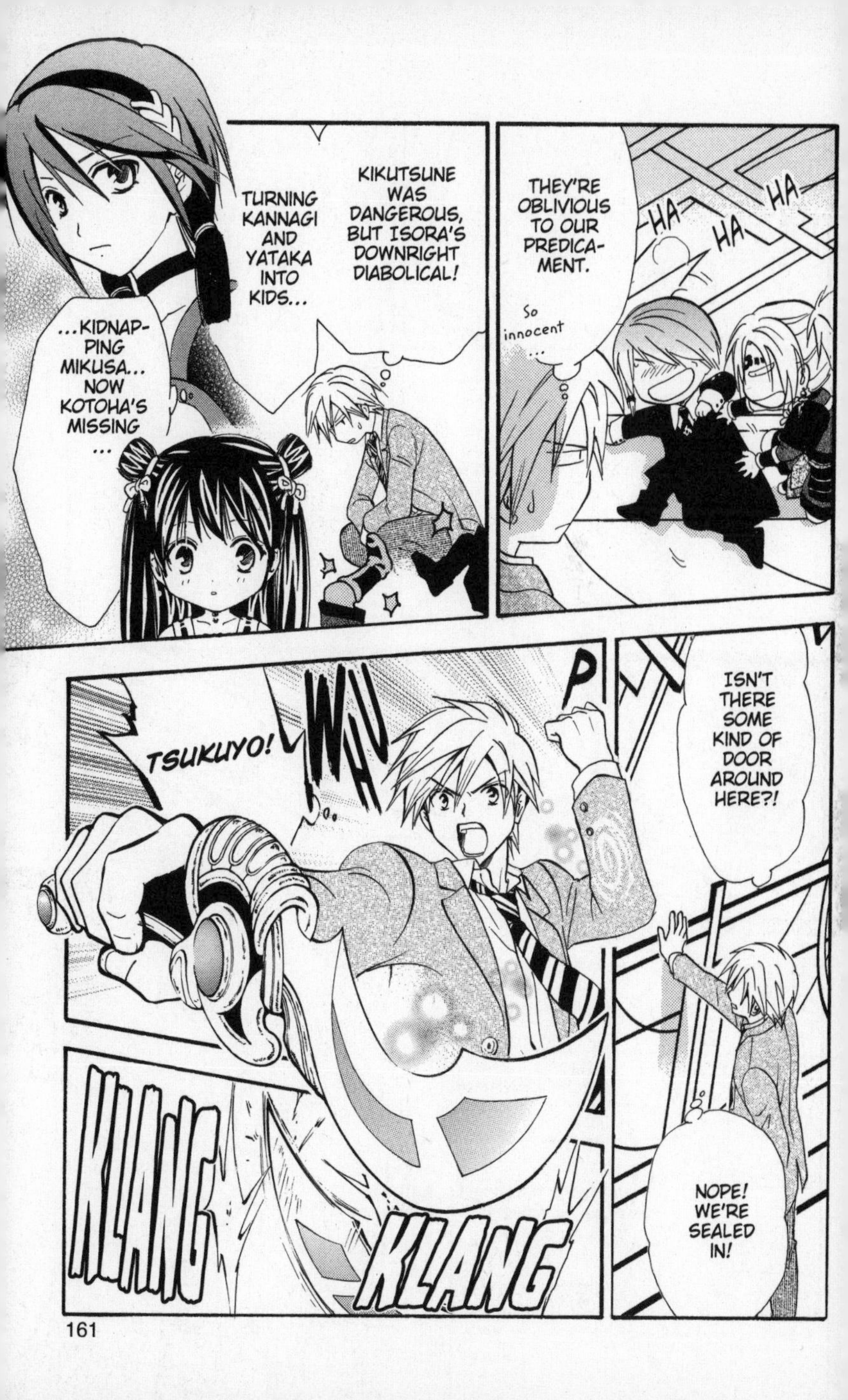
THEY'RE OBLIVIOUS TO OUR PREDICA-MENT.
So innocent...
HA HA HA
KIKUTSUNE WAS DANGEROUS, BUT ISORA'S DOWNRIGHT DIABOLICAL!
TURNING KANNAGI AND YATAKA INTO KIDS...
...KIDNAP-PING MIKUSA... NOW KOTOHA'S MISSING...
ISN'T THERE SOME KIND OF DOOR AROUND HERE?!
NOPE! WE'RE SEALED IN!
TSUKUYO!
WHAP
KLANG
KLANG

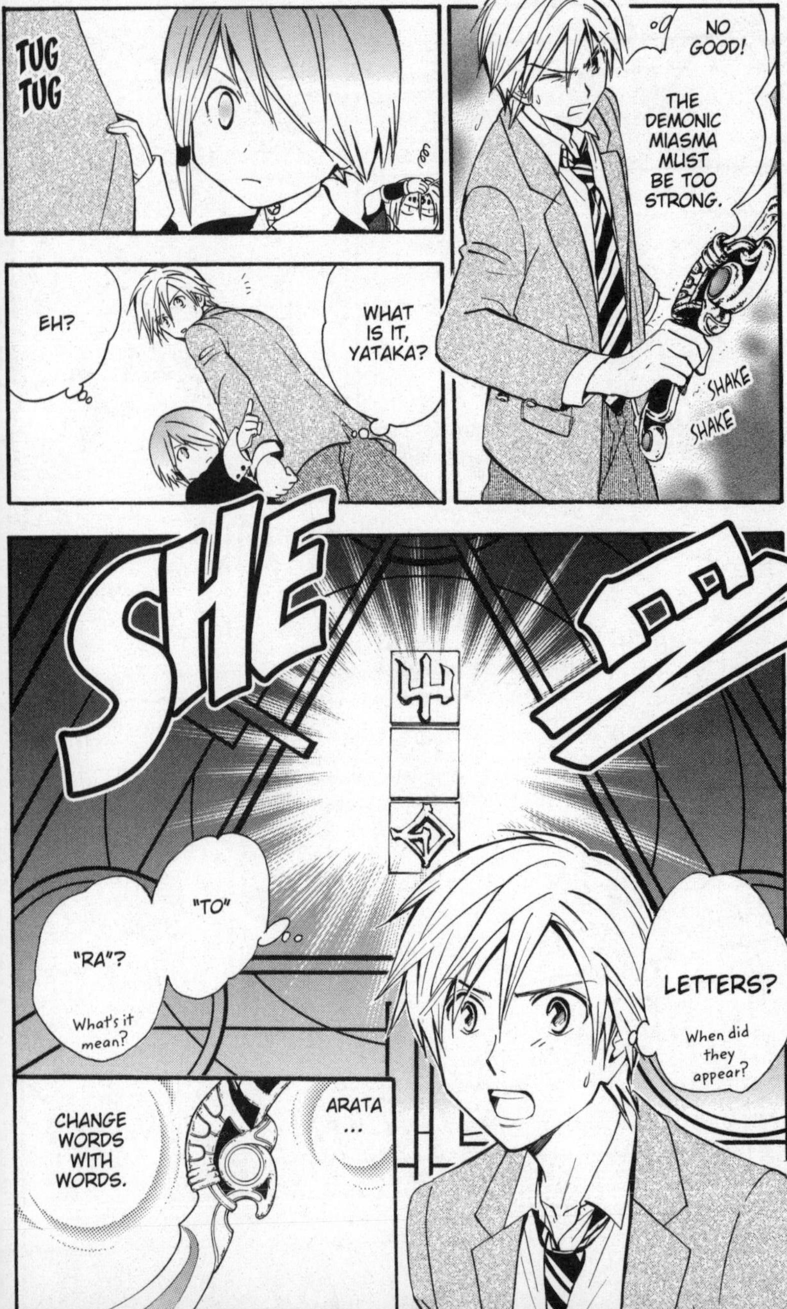
NO GOOD!
THE DEMONIC MIASMA MUST BE TOO STRONG.
SHAKE
SHAKE
TUG TUG
WHAT IS IT, YATAKA?
EH?
SHE
LETTERS?
When did they appear?
"TO"
"RA"?
What's it mean?
ARATA ...
CHANGE WORDS WITH WORDS.

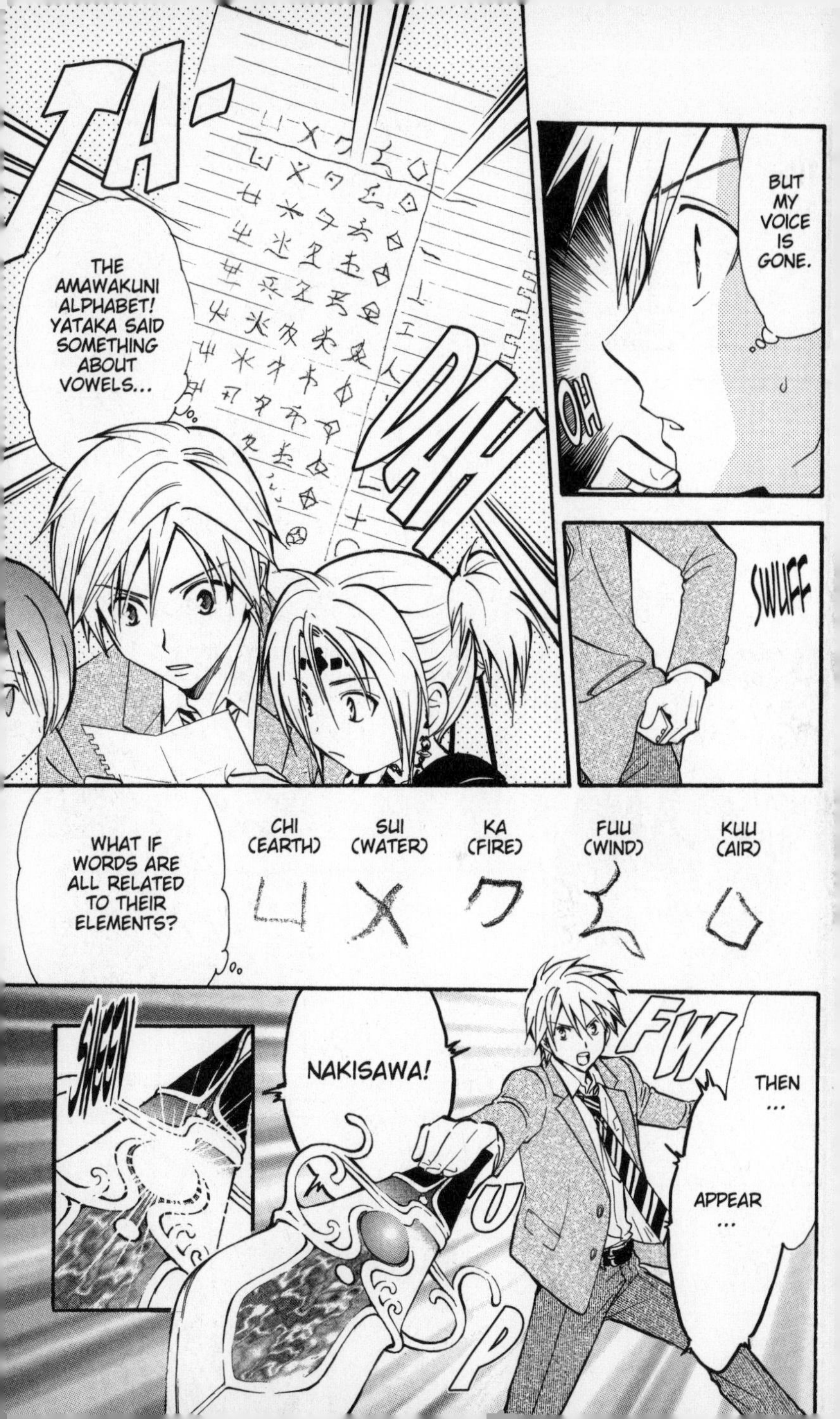
BUT MY VOICE IS GONE.
SWUFF
TA-
DAH
THE AMAWAKUNI ALPHABET! YATAKA SAID SOMETHING ABOUT VOWELS...
CHI (EARTH)
SUI (WATER)
KA (FIRE)
FUU (WIND)
KUU (AIR)
WHAT IF WORDS ARE ALL RELATED TO THEIR ELEMENTS?
FW
THEN ...
APPEAR ...
NAKISAWA!
SHEEN

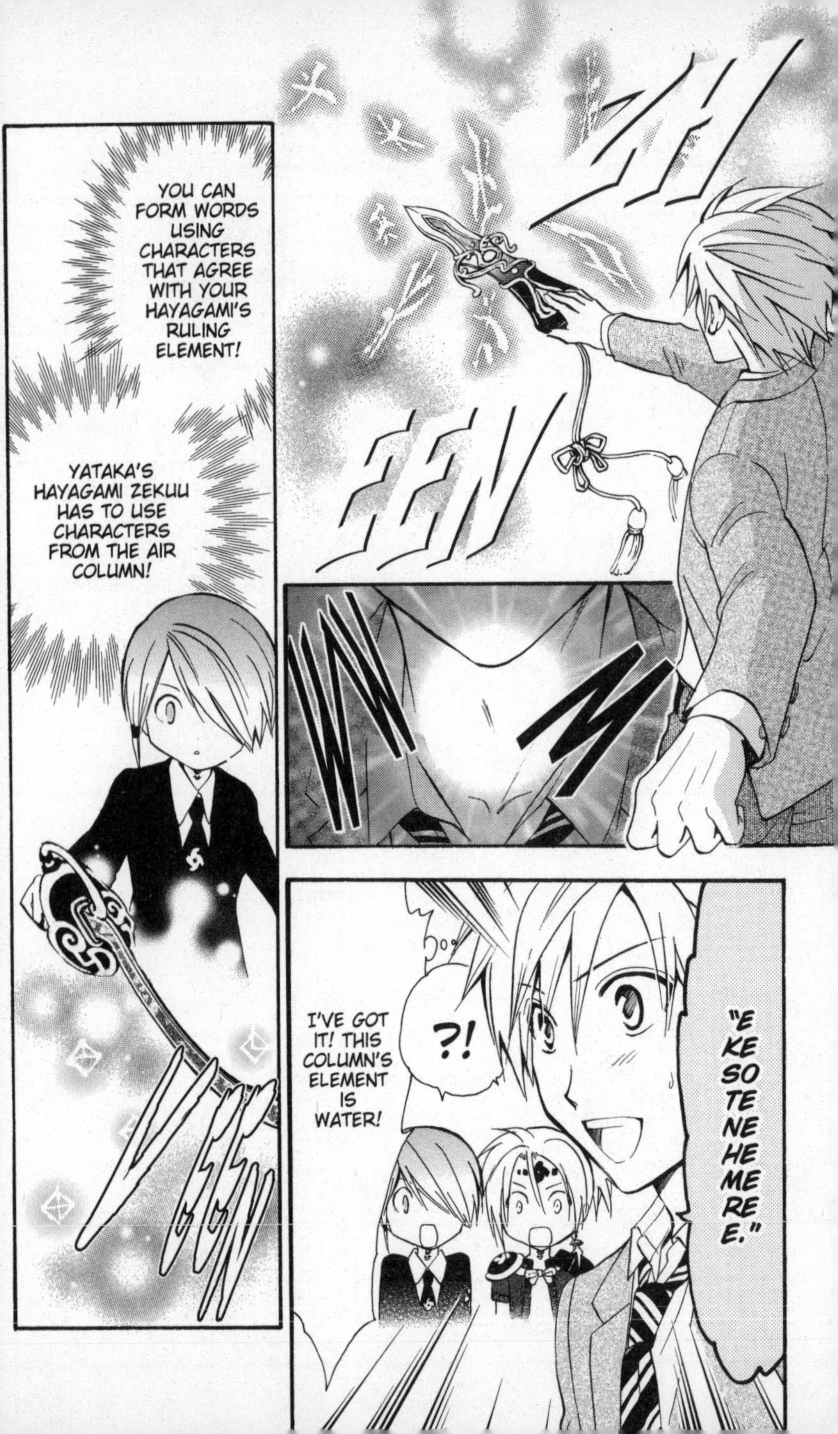
"E KE SO TE NE HE ME RE E."
?!
I'VE GOT IT! THIS COLUMN'S ELEMENT IS WATER!
YOU CAN FORM WORDS USING CHARACTERS THAT AGREE WITH YOUR HAYAGAMI'S RULING ELEMENT!
YATAKA'S HAYAGAMI ZEKUU HAS TO USE CHARACTERS FROM THE AIR COLUMN!

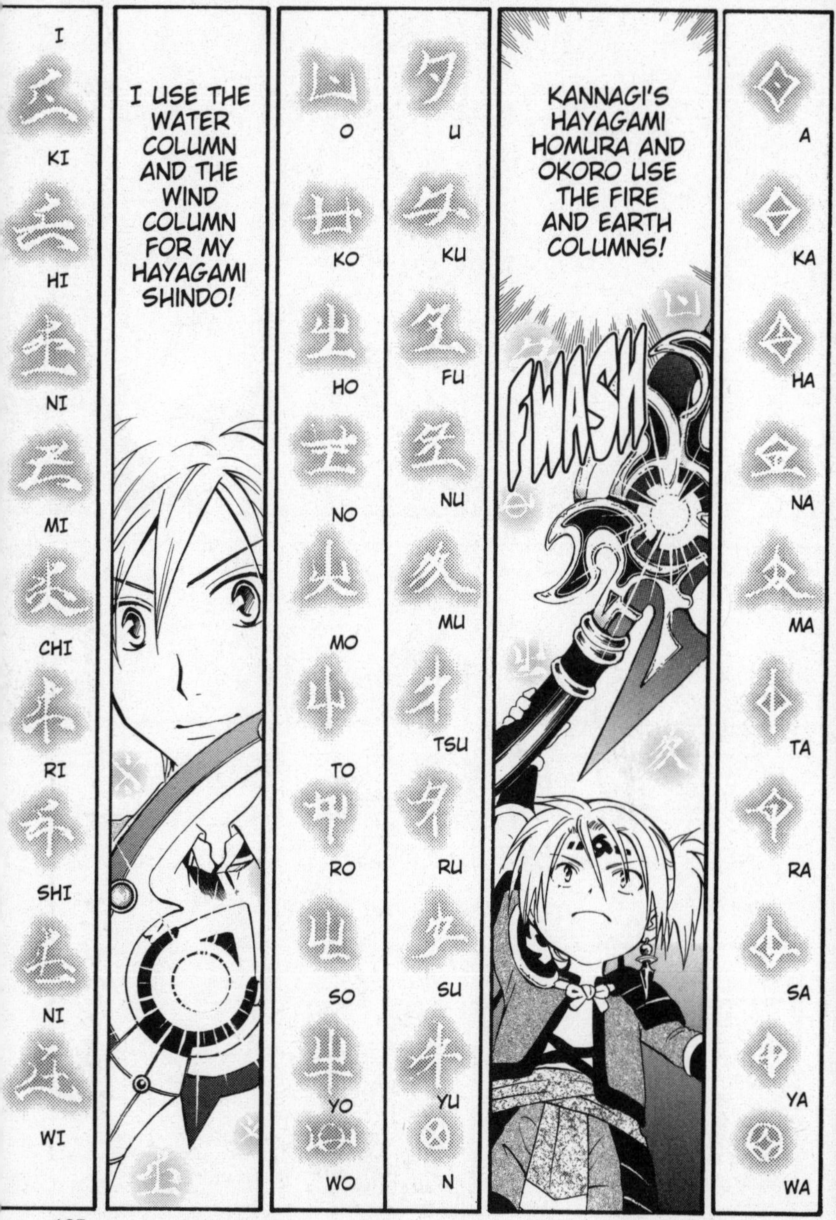
A
KA
HA
NA
MA
TA
RA
SA
YA
WA
KANNAGI'S HAYAGAMI HOMURA AND OKORO USE THE FIRE AND EARTH COLUMNS!
FWASH
U
KU
FU
NU
MU
TSU
RU
SU
YU
N
O
KO
HO
NO
MO
TO
RO
SO
YO
WO
I USE THE WATER COLUMN AND THE WIND COLUMN FOR MY HAYAGAMI SHINDO!
I
KI
HI
NI
MI
CHI
RI
SHI
NI
WI

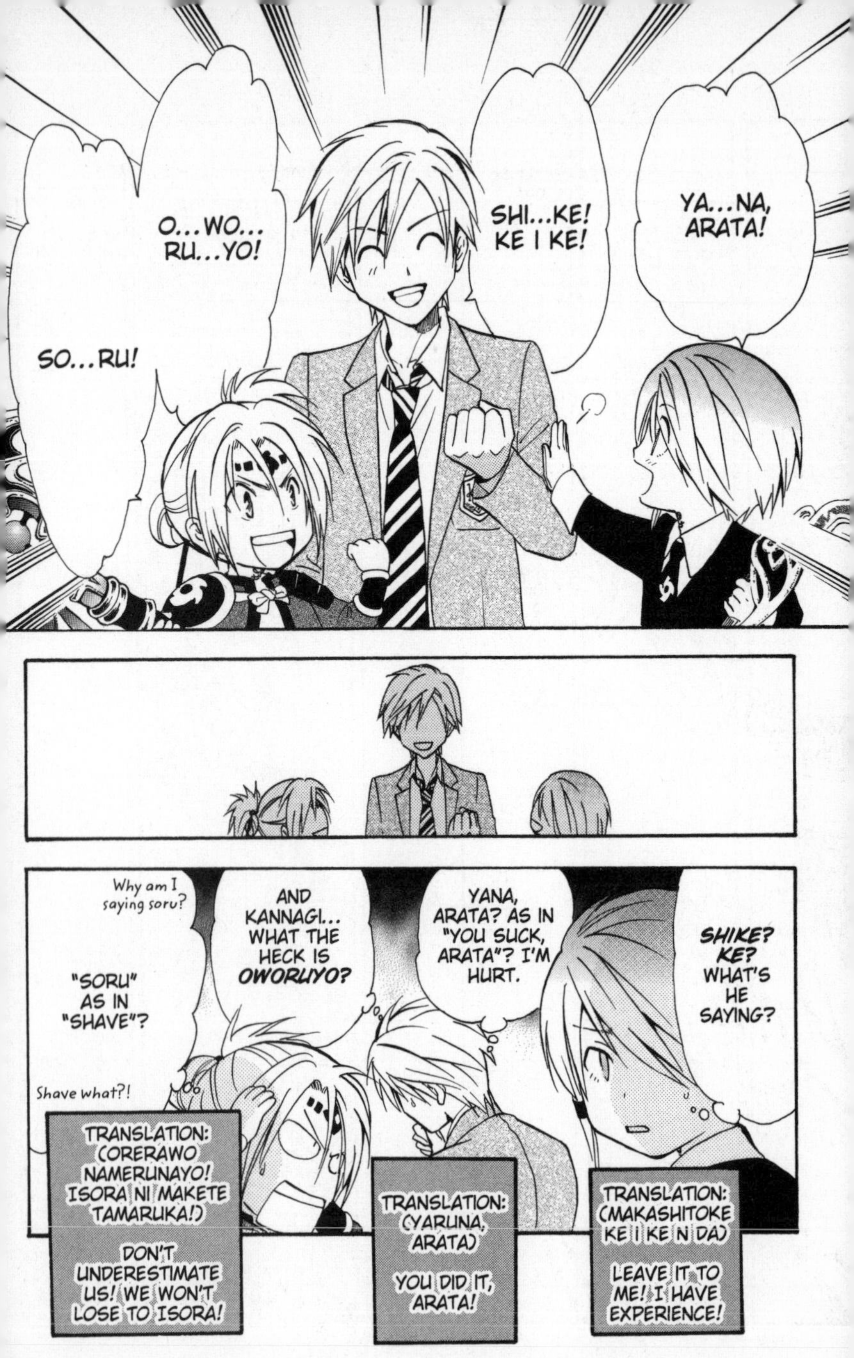
YA...NA, ARATA!
SHI...KE! KE I KE!
O...WO... RU...YO!
SO...RU!
SHIKE? KE? WHAT'S HE SAYING?
YANA, ARATA? AS IN "YOU SUCK, ARATA"? I'M HURT.
AND KANNAGI... WHAT THE HECK IS OWORUYO?
"SORU" AS IN "SHAVE"?
Why am I saying soru?
Shave what?!
TRANSLATION: (MAKASHITOKE KE I KE N DA) LEAVE IT TO ME! I HAVE EXPERIENCE!
TRANSLATION: (YARUNA, ARATA) YOU DID IT, ARATA!
TRANSLATION: (CORERAWO NAMERUNAYO! ISORA NI MAKETE TAMARUKA!) DON'T UNDERESTIMATE US! WE WON'T LOSE TO ISORA!

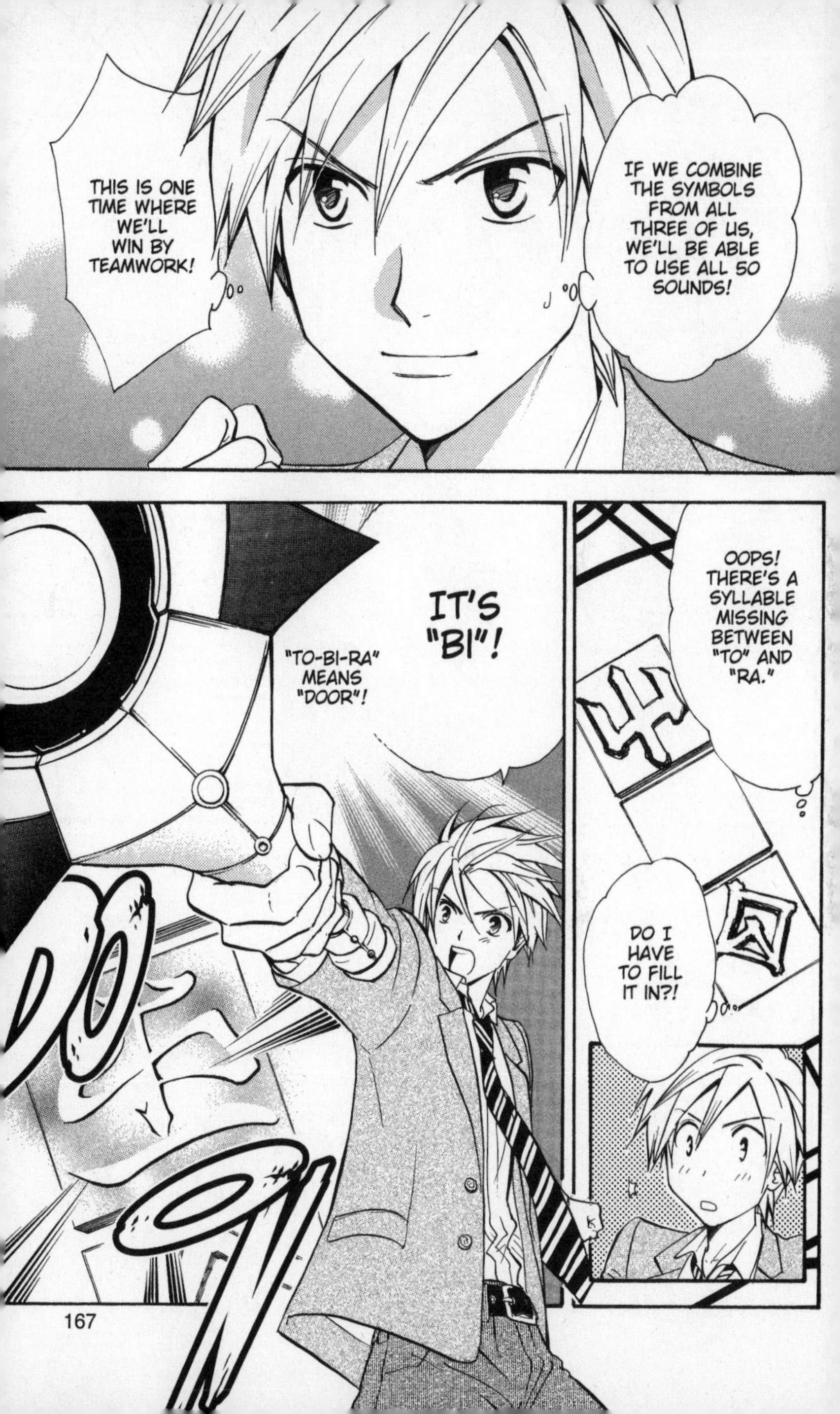
IF WE COMBINE THE SYMBOLS FROM ALL THREE OF US, WE'LL BE ABLE TO USE ALL 50 SOUNDS!
THIS IS ONE TIME WHERE WE'LL WIN BY TEAMWORK!
OOPS! THERE'S A SYLLABLE MISSING BETWEEN "TO" AND "RA."
DO I HAVE TO FILL IT IN?!
IT'S "BI"!
"TO-BI-RA" MEANS "DOOR"!

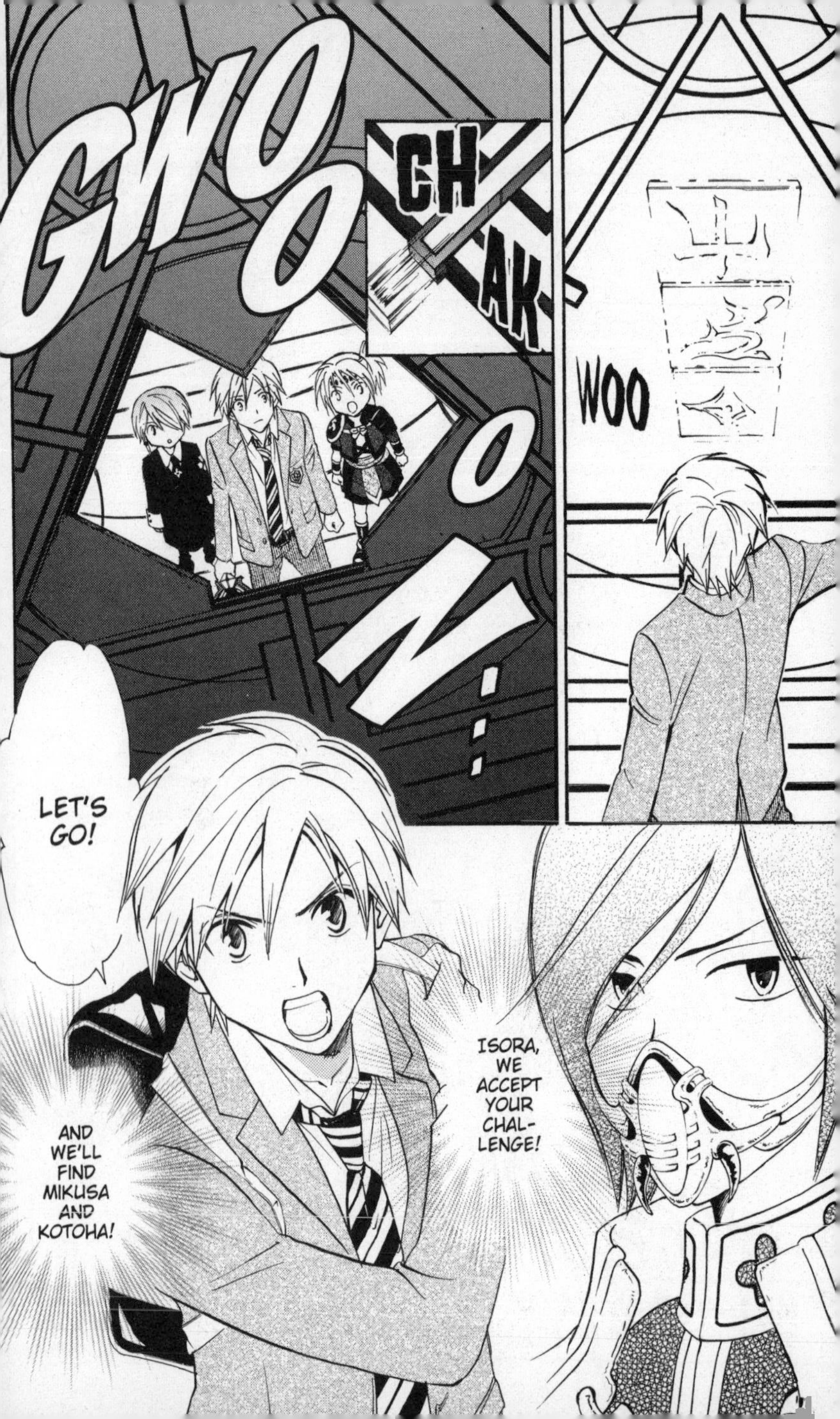
WOO
GWOO
CH
AK
ON...
ISORA, WE ACCEPT YOUR CHAL-LENGE!
AND WE'LL FIND MIKUSA AND KOTOHA!
LET'S GO!

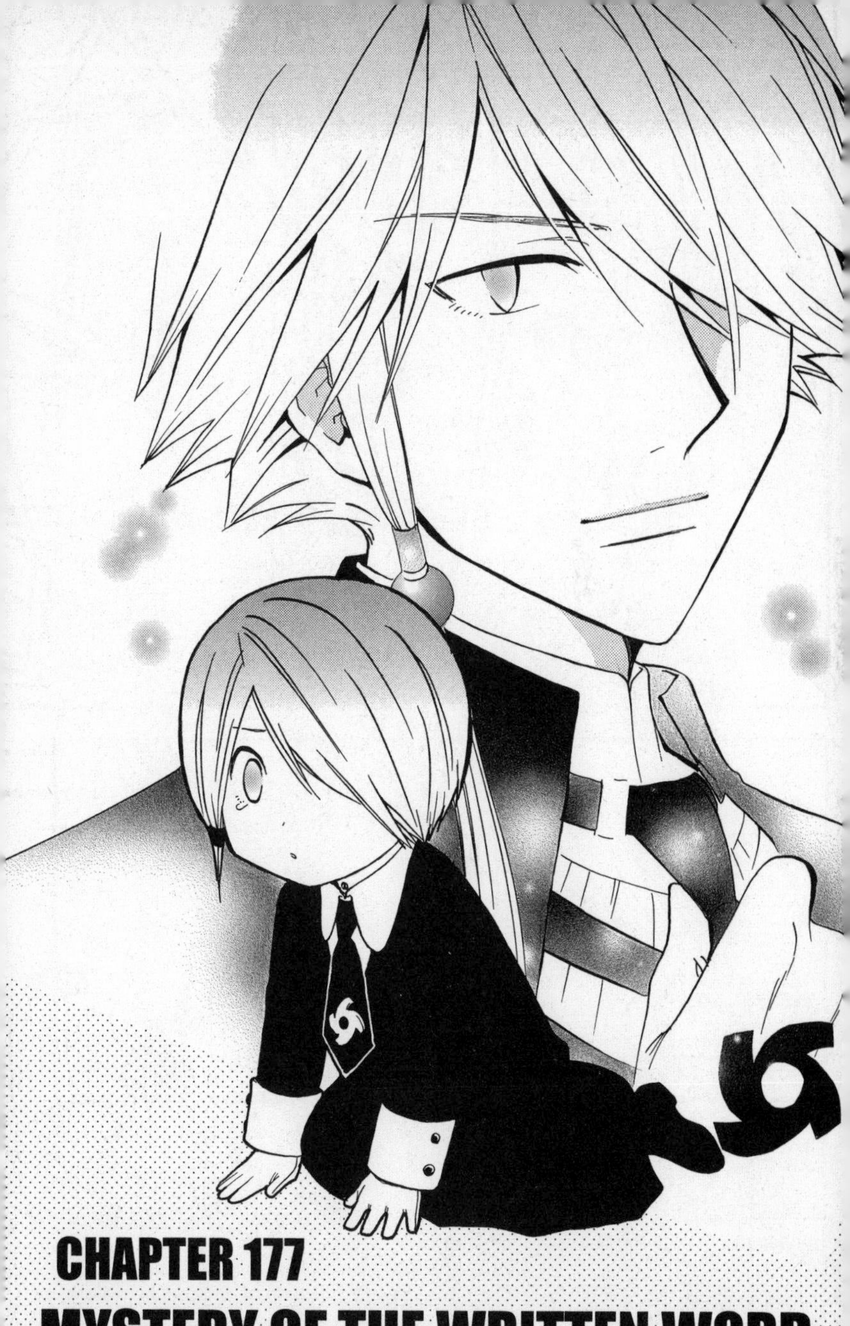

CHAPTER 177
MYSTERY OF THE WRITTEN WORD

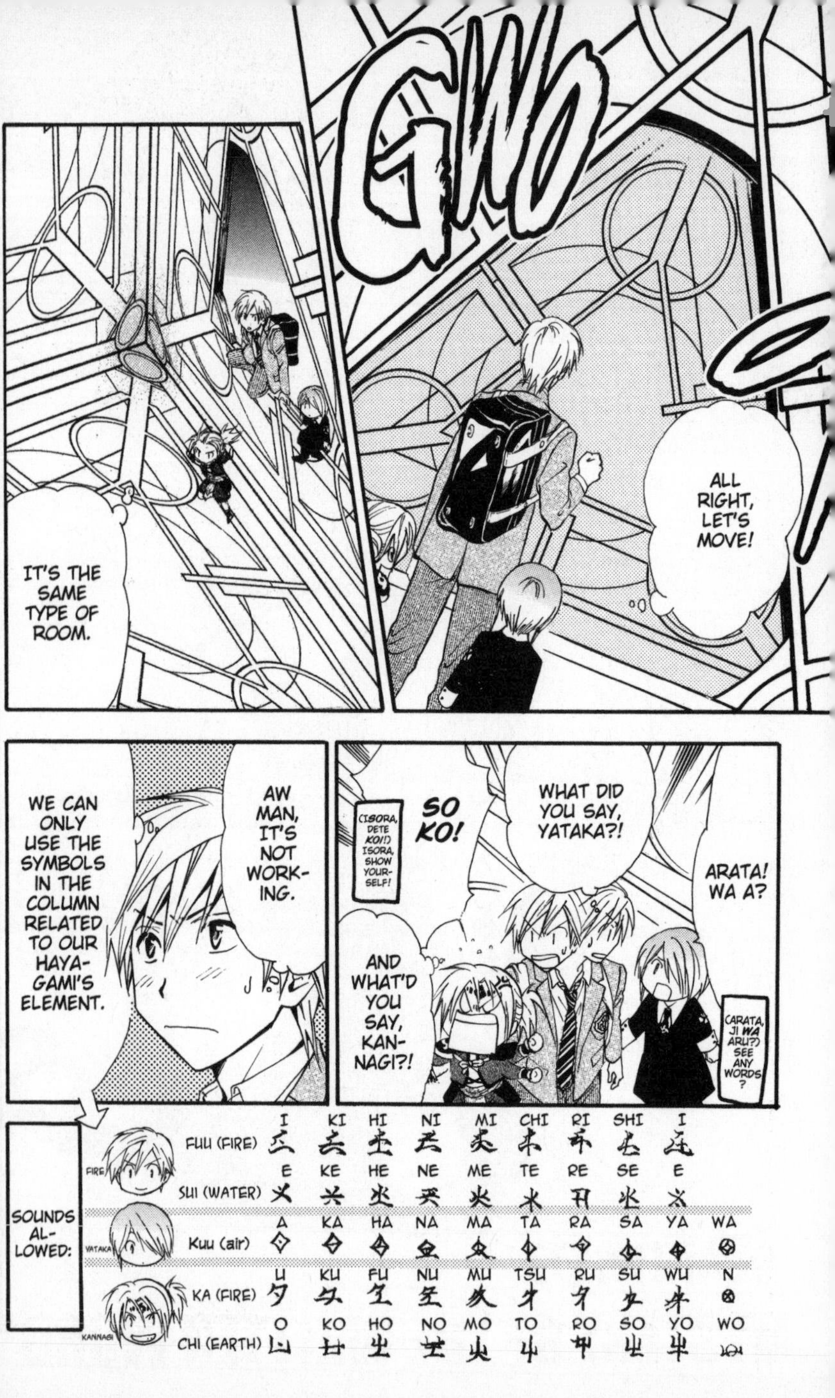
GWO
ALL RIGHT, LET'S MOVE!
IT'S THE SAME TYPE OF ROOM.
ARATA! WA A?
(ARATA, JI WA ARU?) SEE ANY WORDS?
WHAT DID YOU SAY, YATAKA?!
SO KO!
(ISORA, DETE KOI!) ISORA, SHOW YOURSELF!
AND WHAT'D YOU SAY, KANNAGI?!
AW MAN, IT'S NOT WORKING.
WE CAN ONLY USE THE SYMBOLS IN THE COLUMN RELATED TO OUR HAYAGAMI'S ELEMENT.
SOUNDS ALLOWED:
FIRE
FUU (FIRE)
I KI HI NI MI CHI RI SHI I
SUI (WATER)
E KE HE NE ME TE RE SE E
YATAKA
Kuu (air)
A KA HA NA MA TA RA SA YA WA
KANNAGI
KA (FIRE)
U KU FU NU MU TSU RU SU WU N
CHI (EARTH)
O KO HO NO MO TO RO SO YO WO

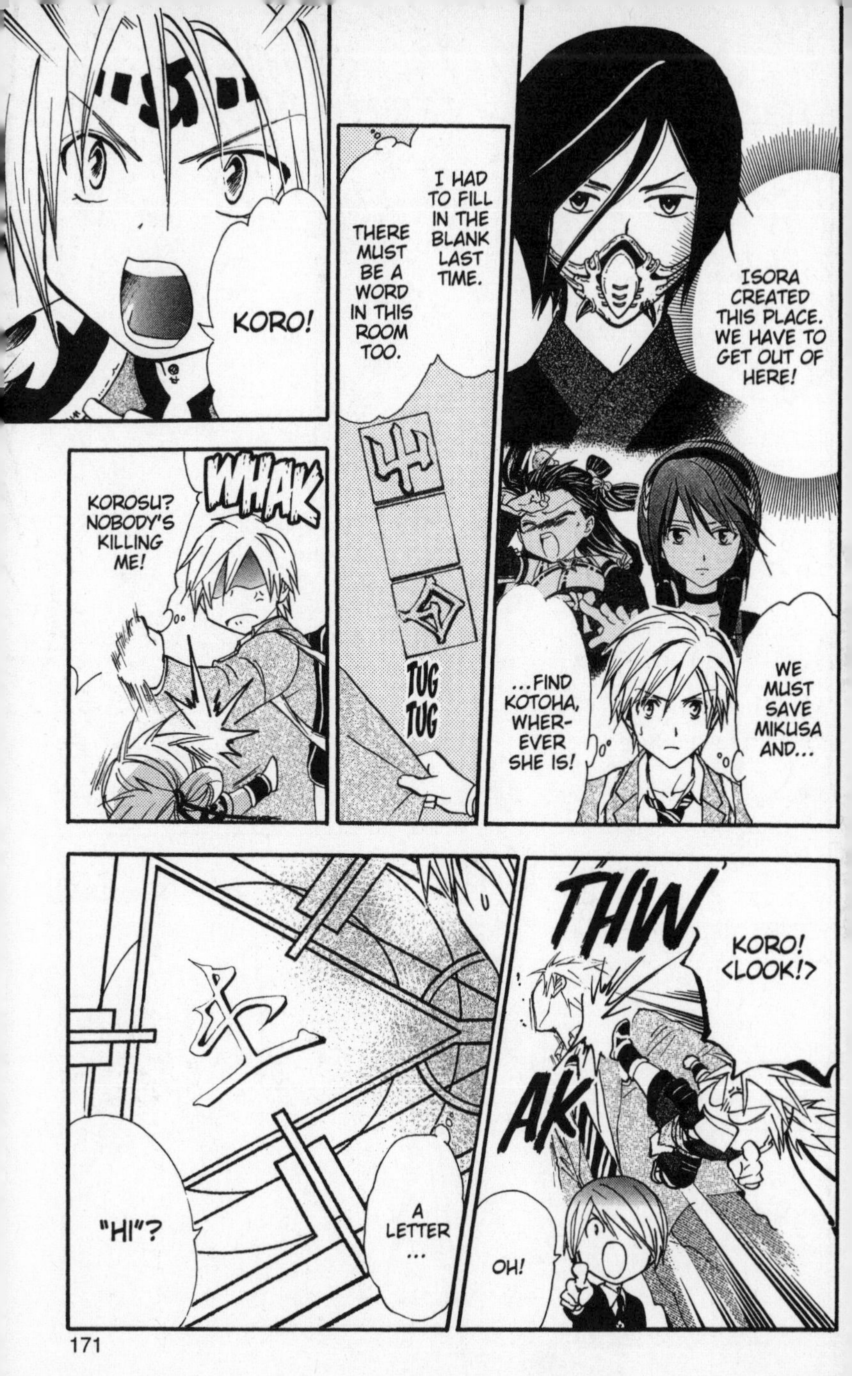
ISORA CREATED THIS PLACE. WE HAVE TO GET OUT OF HERE!
WE MUST SAVE MIKUSA AND...
...FIND KOTOHA, WHEREVER SHE IS!
I HAD TO FILL IN THE BLANK LAST TIME.
THERE MUST BE A WORD IN THIS ROOM TOO.
TUG TUG
KORO!
WHAK
KOROSU? NOBODY'S KILLING ME!
THW
AK
KORO! <LOOK!>
OH!
A LETTER ...
"HI"?

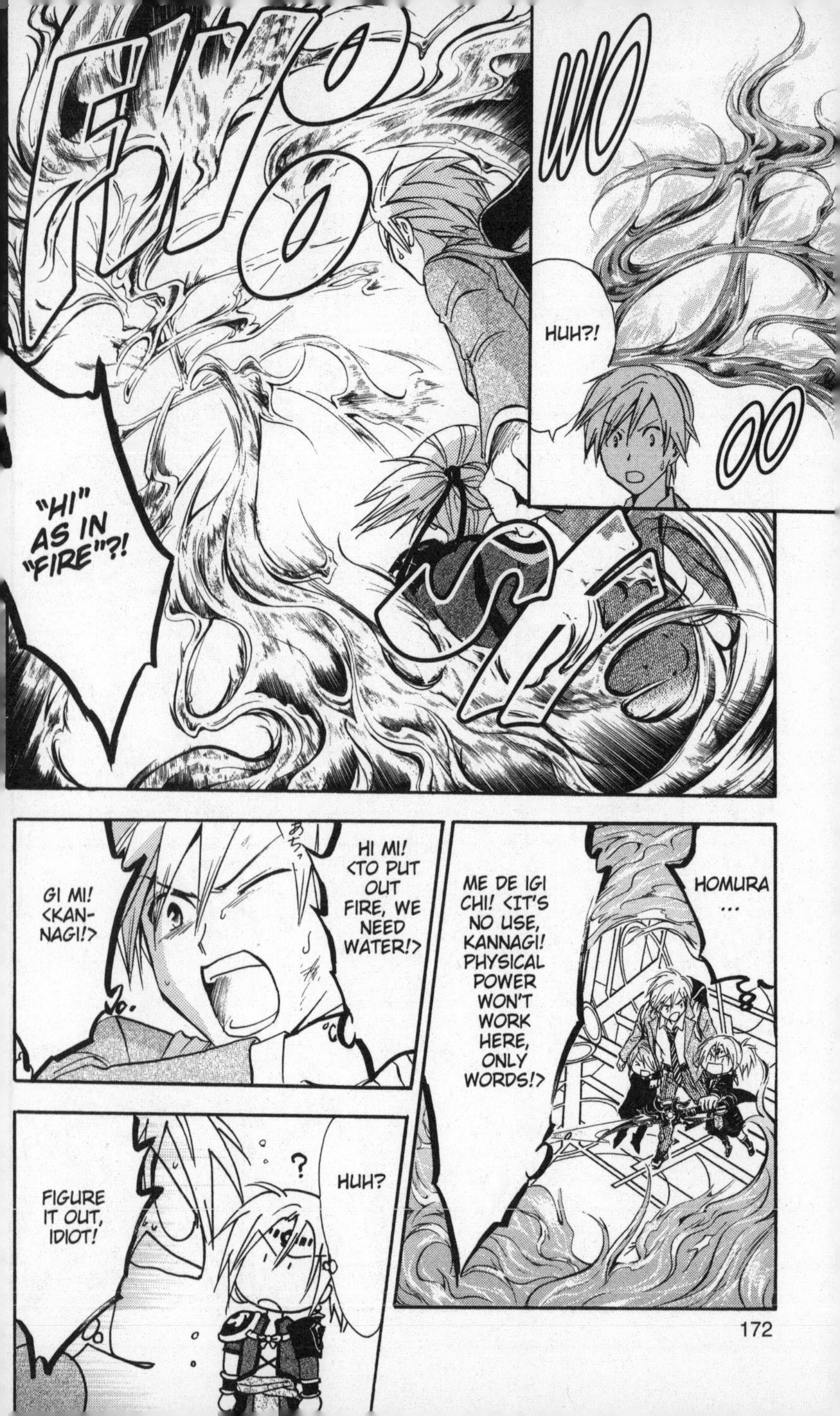
WO
HUH?!
OO
"HI" AS IN "FIRE"?!
HOMURA...
ME DE IGI CHI! <IT'S NO USE, KANNAGI! PHYSICAL POWER WON'T WORK HERE, ONLY WORDS!>
HI MI! <TO PUT OUT FIRE, WE NEED WATER!>
GI MI! <KAN-NAGI!>
HUH?
?
FIGURE IT OUT, IDIOT!

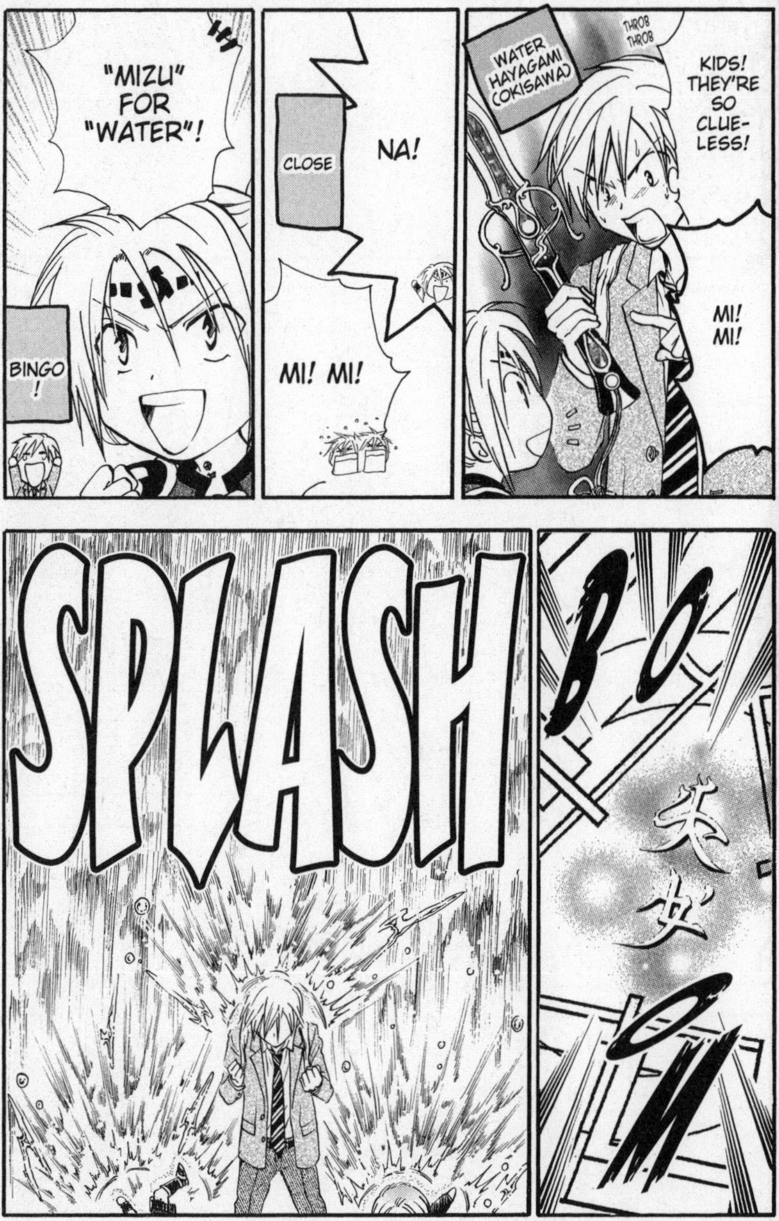
THROB THROB
KIDS! THEY'RE SO CLUE-LESS!
WATER HAYAGAMI (OKISAWA)
MI! MI!
NA!
CLOSE
MI! MI!
"MIZU" FOR "WATER"!
BINGO!
BOOM
SPLASH

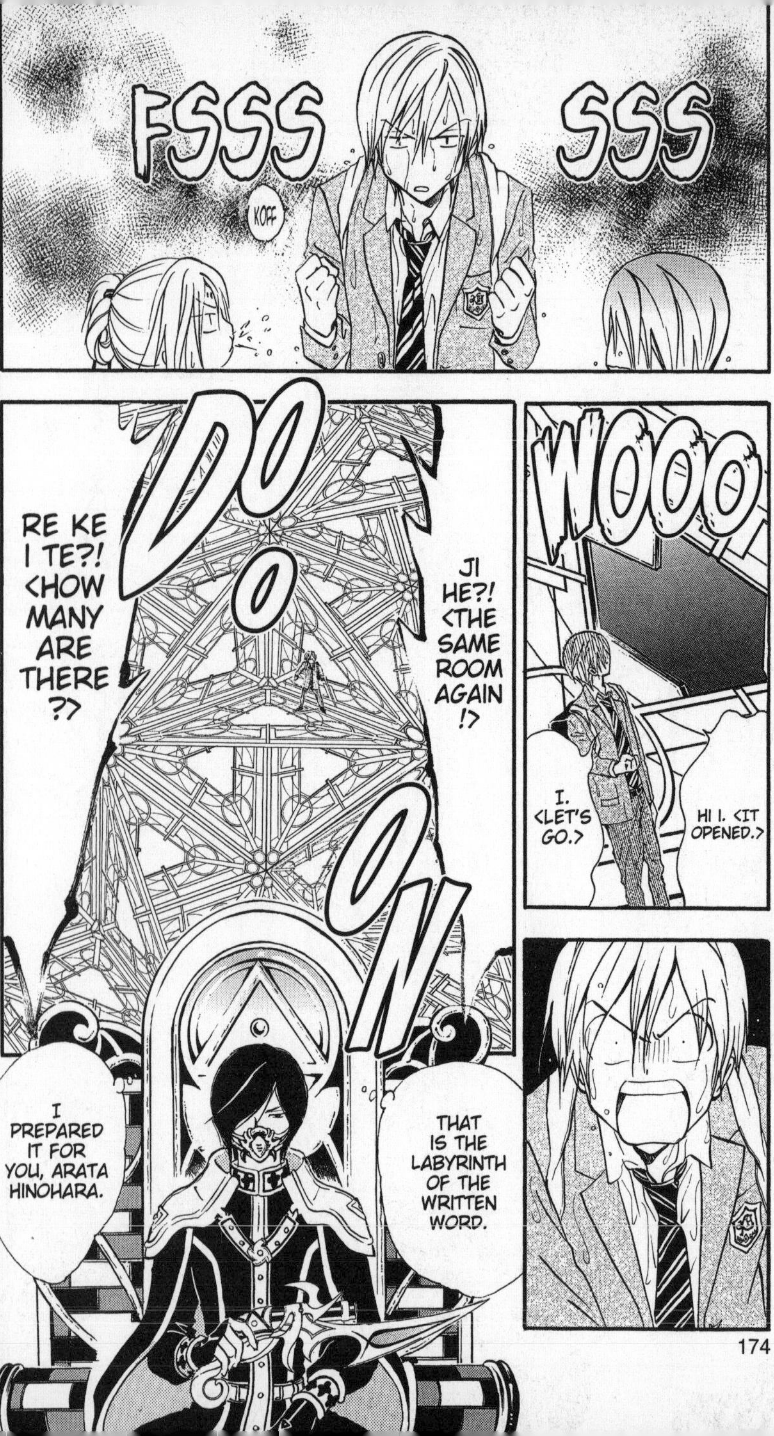
FSSS SSS
KOFF
WOOO
HI I. <IT OPENED.>
I. <LET'S GO.>
DOOON
JI HE?! <THE SAME ROOM AGAIN!>
RE KE I TE?! <HOW MANY ARE THERE?>
THAT IS THE LABYRINTH OF THE WRITTEN WORD.
I PREPARED IT FOR YOU, ARATA HINOHARA.

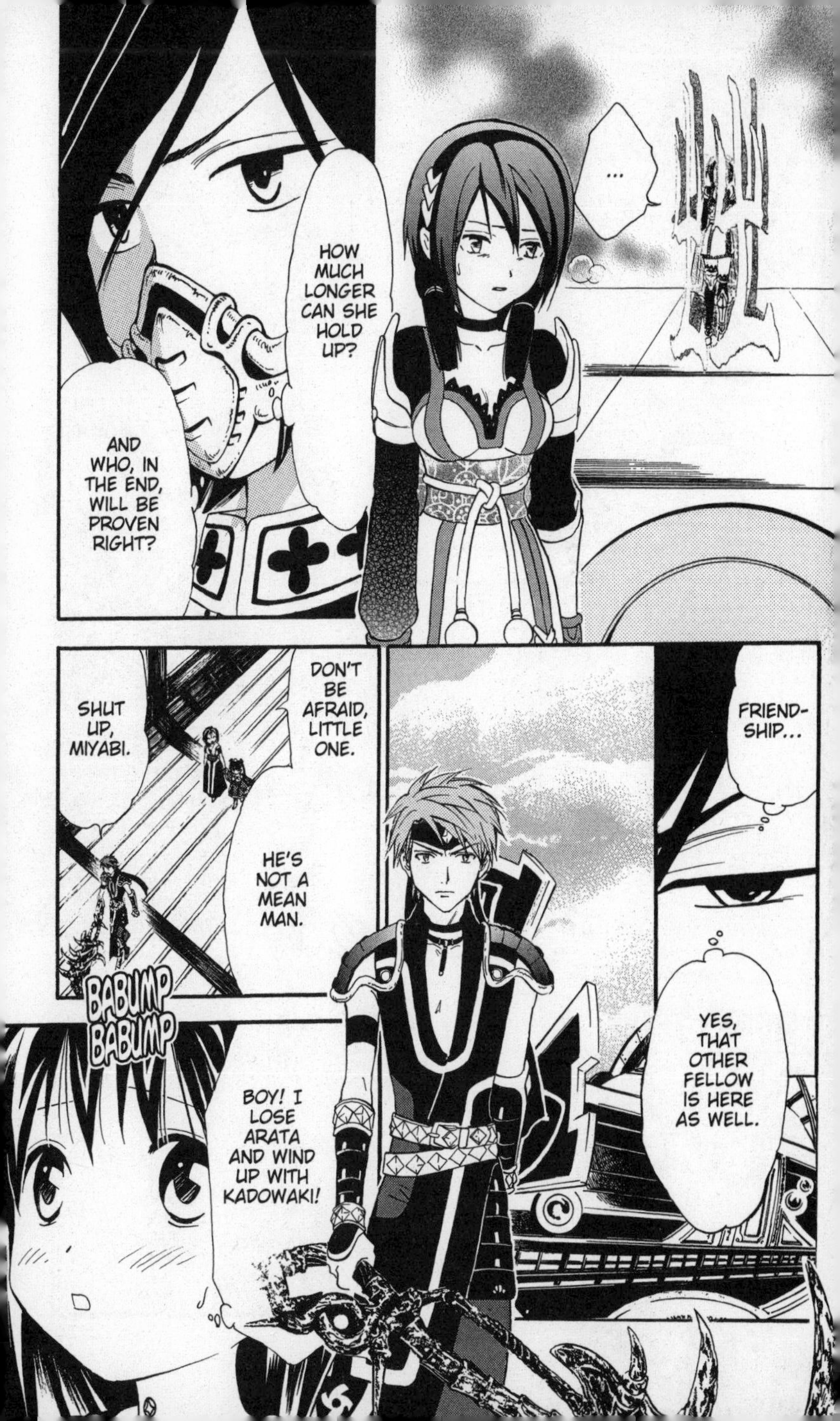
...
HOW MUCH LONGER CAN SHE HOLD UP?
AND WHO, IN THE END, WILL BE PROVEN RIGHT?
FRIEND-SHIP...
YES, THAT OTHER FELLOW IS HERE AS WELL.
DON'T BE AFRAID, LITTLE ONE.
HE'S NOT A MEAN MAN.
SHUT UP, MIYABI.
BABUMP BABUMP
BOY! I LOSE ARATA AND WIND UP WITH KADOWAKI!

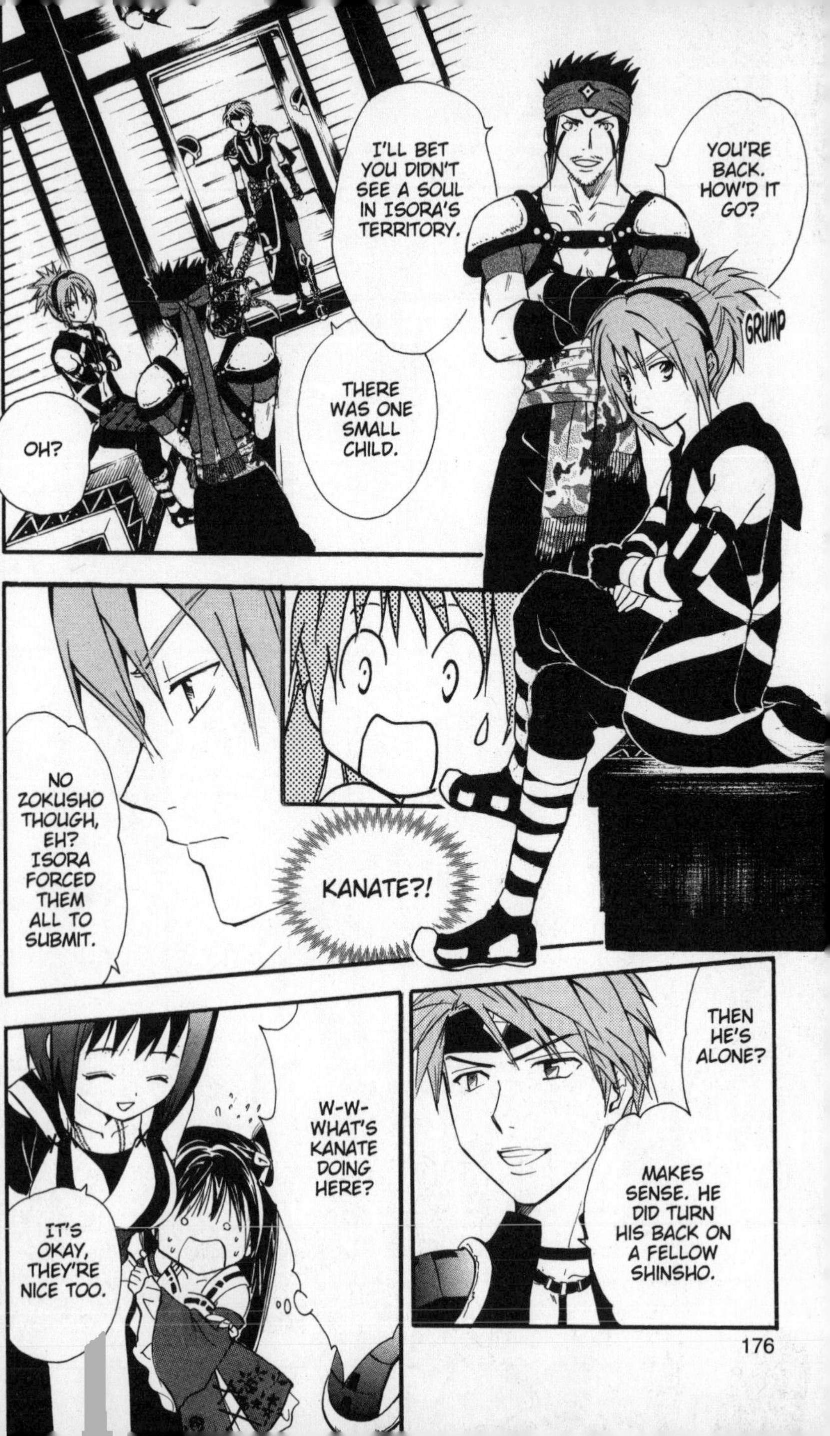
YOU'RE BACK. HOW'D IT GO?
I'LL BET YOU DIDN'T SEE A SOUL IN ISORA'S TERRITORY.
GRUMP
THERE WAS ONE SMALL CHILD.
OH?
KANATE?!
NO ZOKUSHO THOUGH, EH? ISORA FORCED THEM ALL TO SUBMIT.
THEN HE'S ALONE?
MAKES SENSE. HE DID TURN HIS BACK ON A FELLOW SHINSHO.
W-W-WHAT'S KANATE DOING HERE?
IT'S OKAY, THEY'RE NICE TOO.

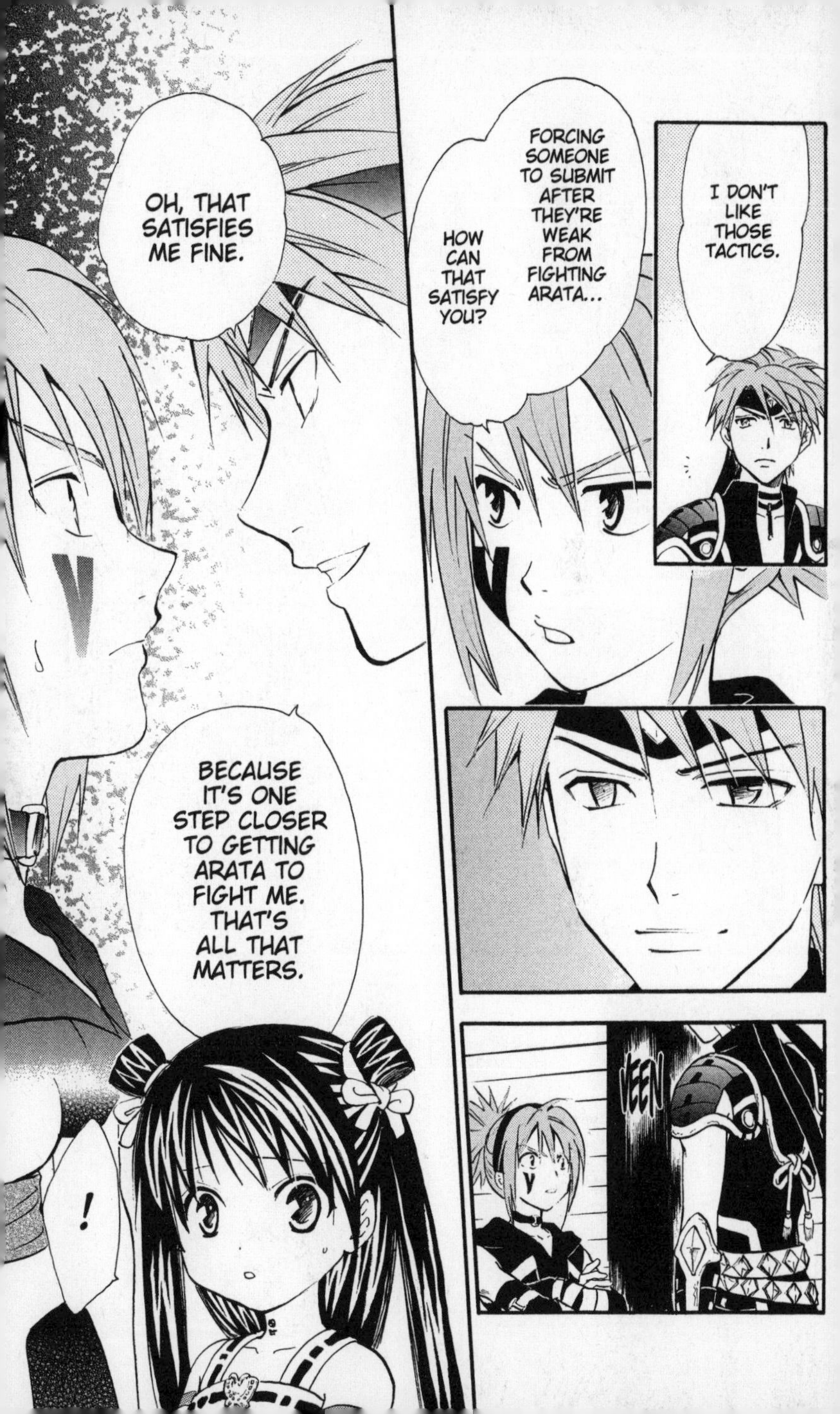
I DON'T LIKE THOSE TACTICS.
FORCING SOMEONE TO SUBMIT AFTER THEY'RE WEAK FROM FIGHTING ARATA...
HOW CAN THAT SATISFY YOU?
VEEN
OH, THAT SATISFIES ME FINE.
BECAUSE IT'S ONE STEP CLOSER TO GETTING ARATA TO FIGHT ME. THAT'S ALL THAT MATTERS.
!

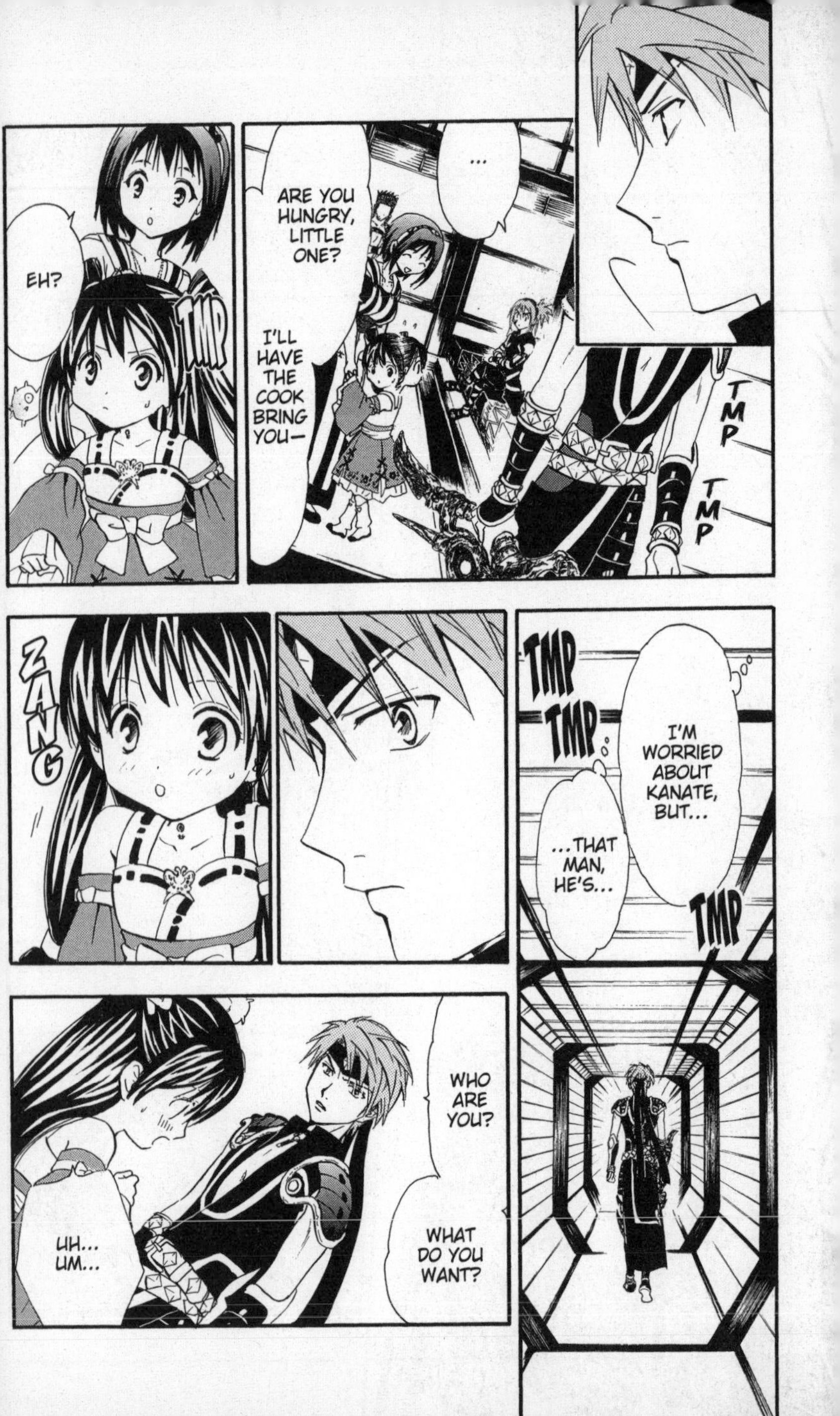
...
ARE YOU HUNGRY, LITTLE ONE?
I'LL HAVE THE COOK BRING YOU—
TMP
TMP
EH?
TMP
TMP
TMP
I'M WORRIED ABOUT KANATE, BUT...
...THAT MAN, HE'S...
TMP
ZANG
WHO ARE YOU?
WHAT DO YOU WANT?
UH... UM...

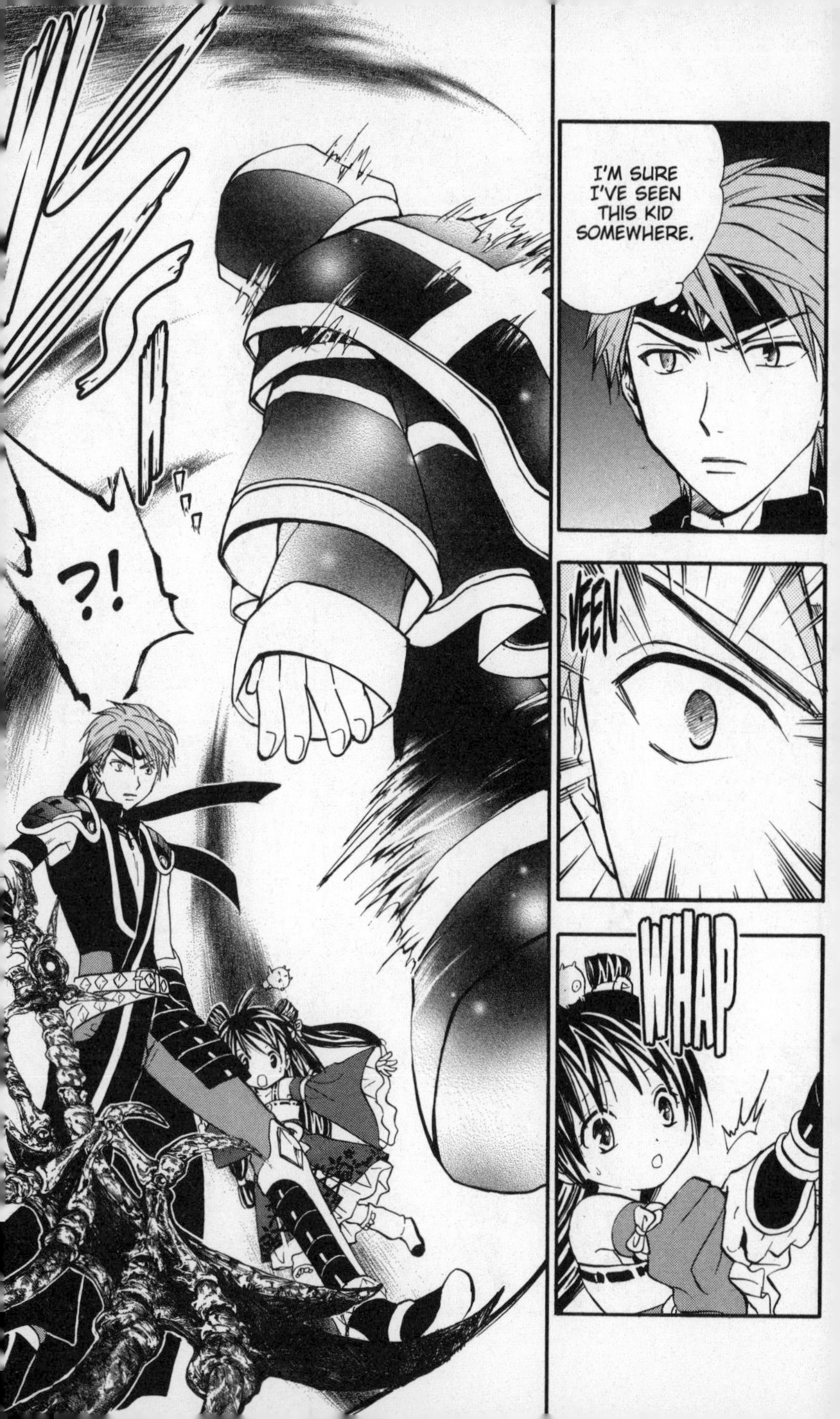
I'M SURE I'VE SEEN THIS KID SOMEWHERE.
VEEN
WHAP
?!

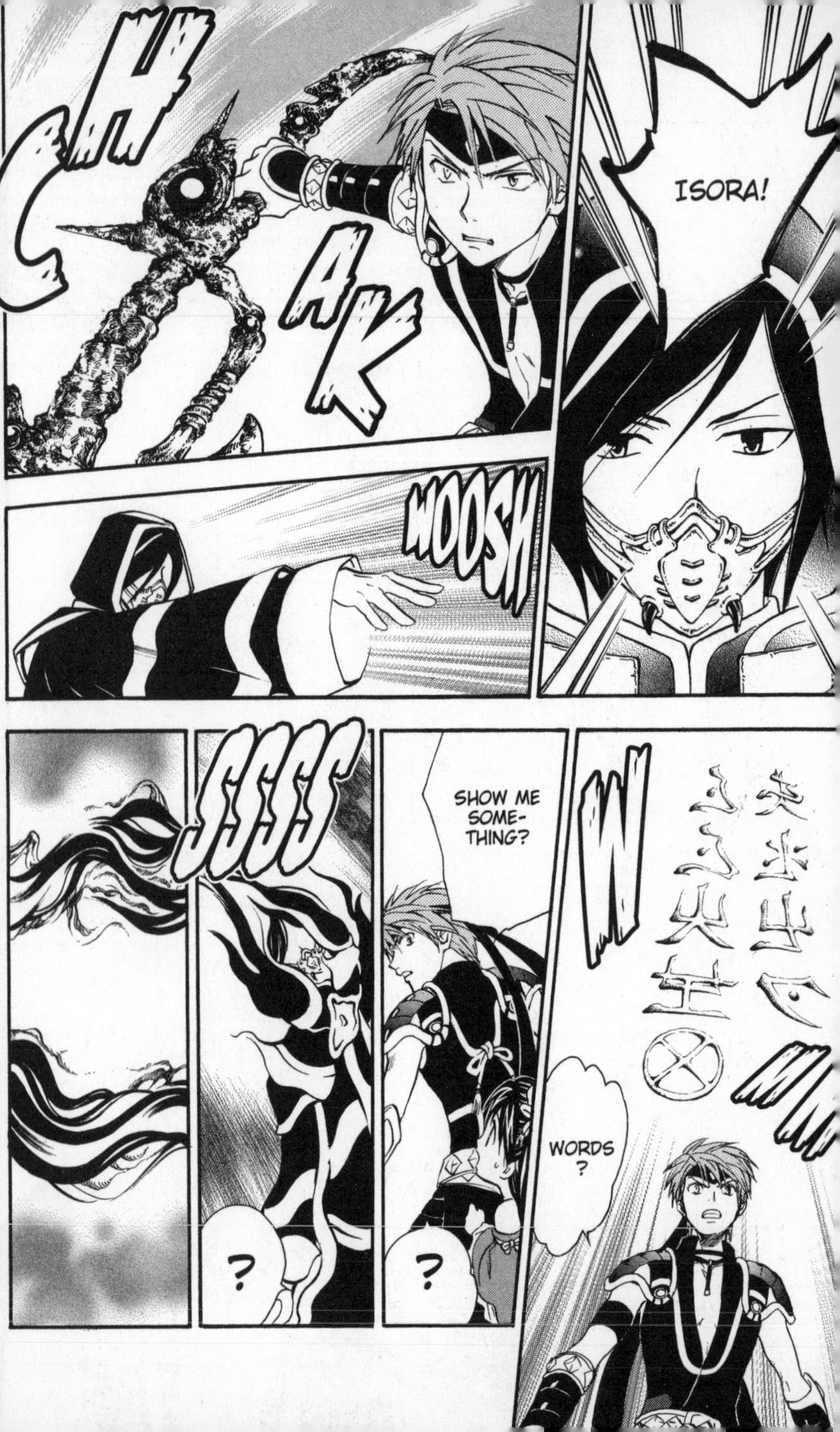
ISORA!
CHAK
WOOSH
WORDS ?
SHOW ME SOMETHING?
?
SSSS
?

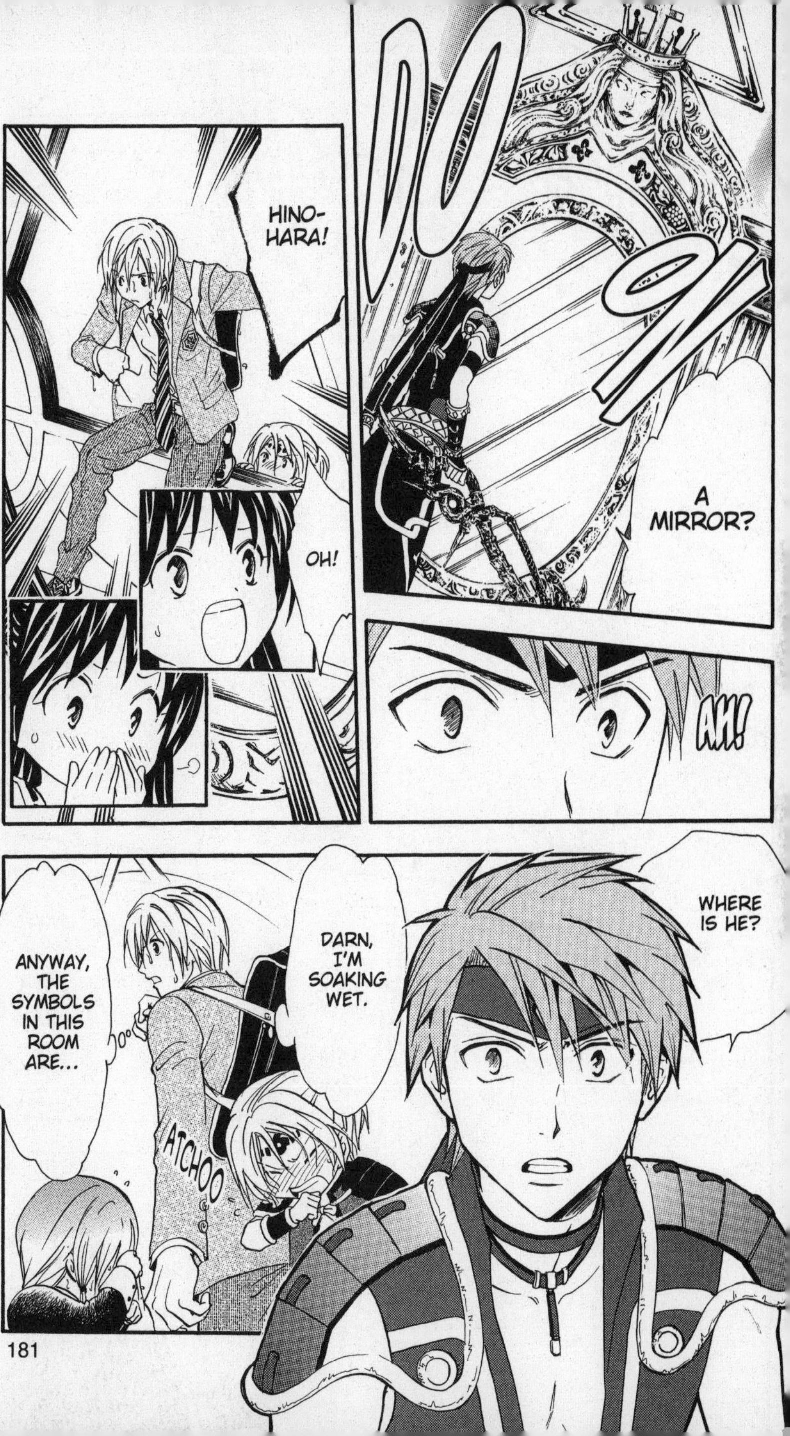
A MIRROR?
AH!
HINO-HARA!
OH!
WHERE IS HE?
DARN, I'M SOAKING WET.
ANYWAY, THE SYMBOLS IN THIS ROOM ARE...
ATCHOO

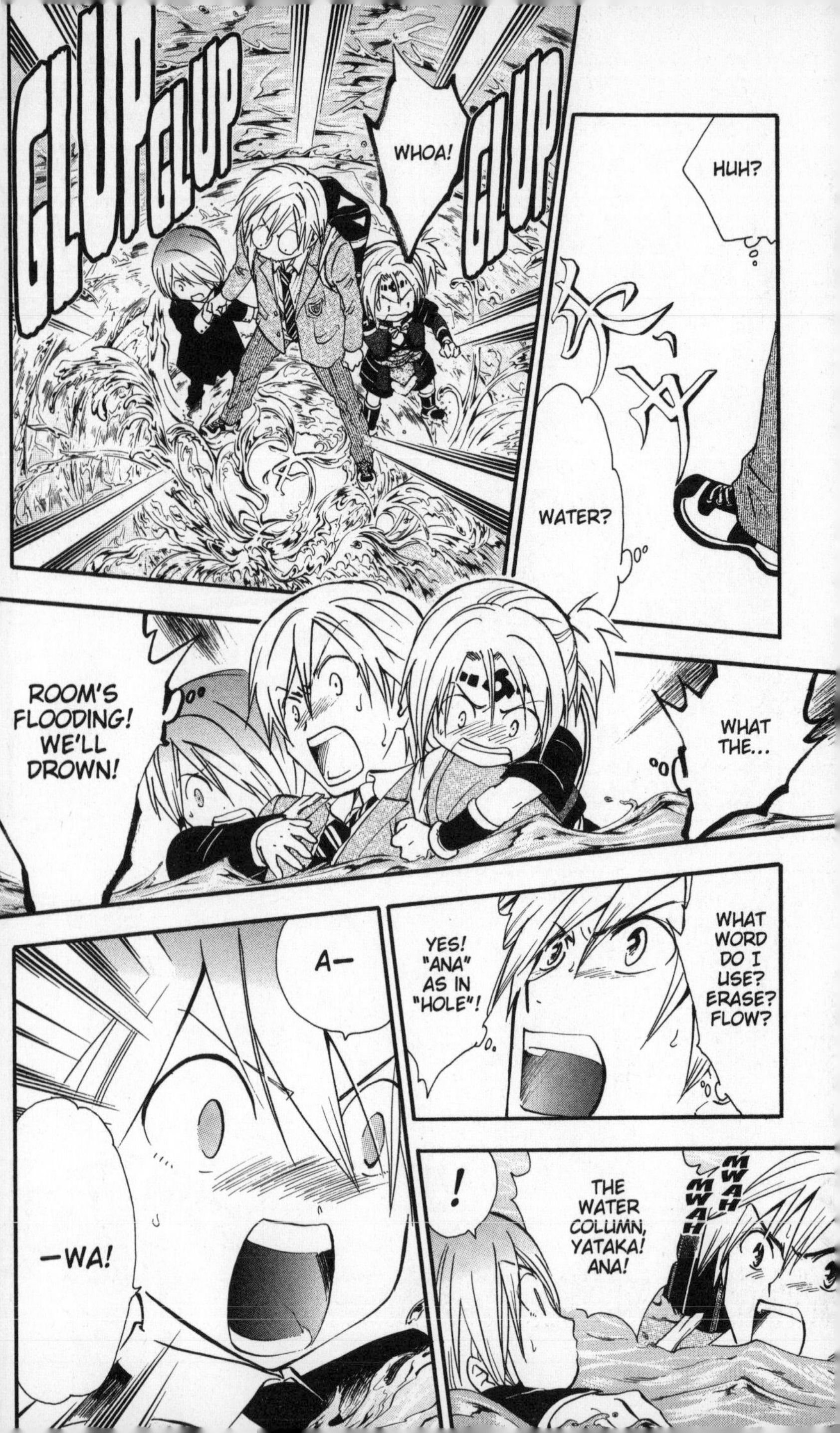
HUH?
WATER?
GLUP
WHOA!
GLUP GLUP
WHAT THE...
ROOM'S FLOODING! WE'LL DROWN!
WHAT WORD DO I USE? ERASE? FLOW?
YES! "ANA" AS IN "HOLE"!
MWAH MWAH
THE WATER COLUMN, YATAKA! ANA!
!
A-
-WA!

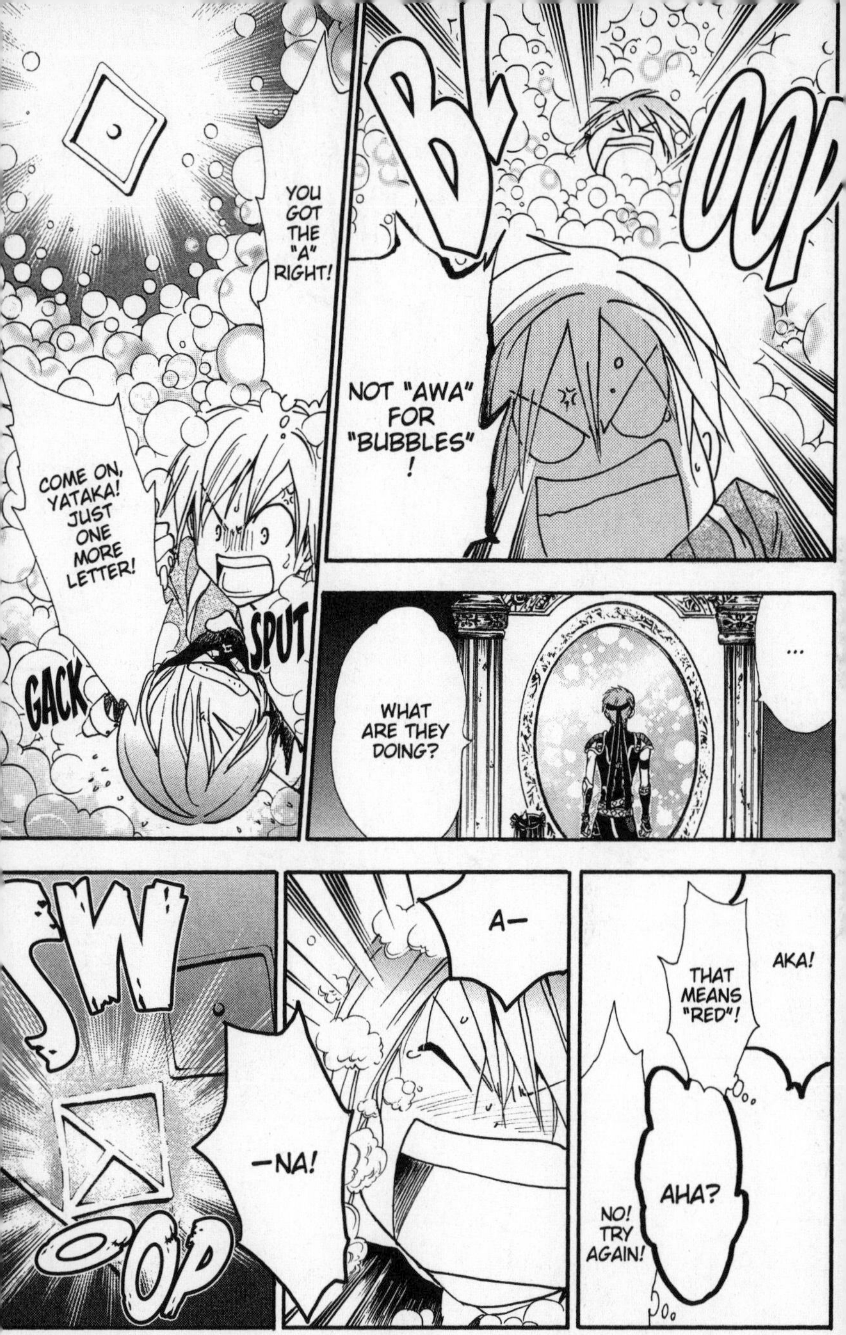
BLOOP
NOT "AWA" FOR "BUBBLES"!
WHAT ARE THEY DOING?
...
YOU GOT THE "A" RIGHT!
COME ON, YATAKA! JUST ONE MORE LETTER!
SPUT
GACK
AKA!
THAT MEANS "RED"!
AHA?
NO! TRY AGAIN!
A—
SWOOP
—NA!

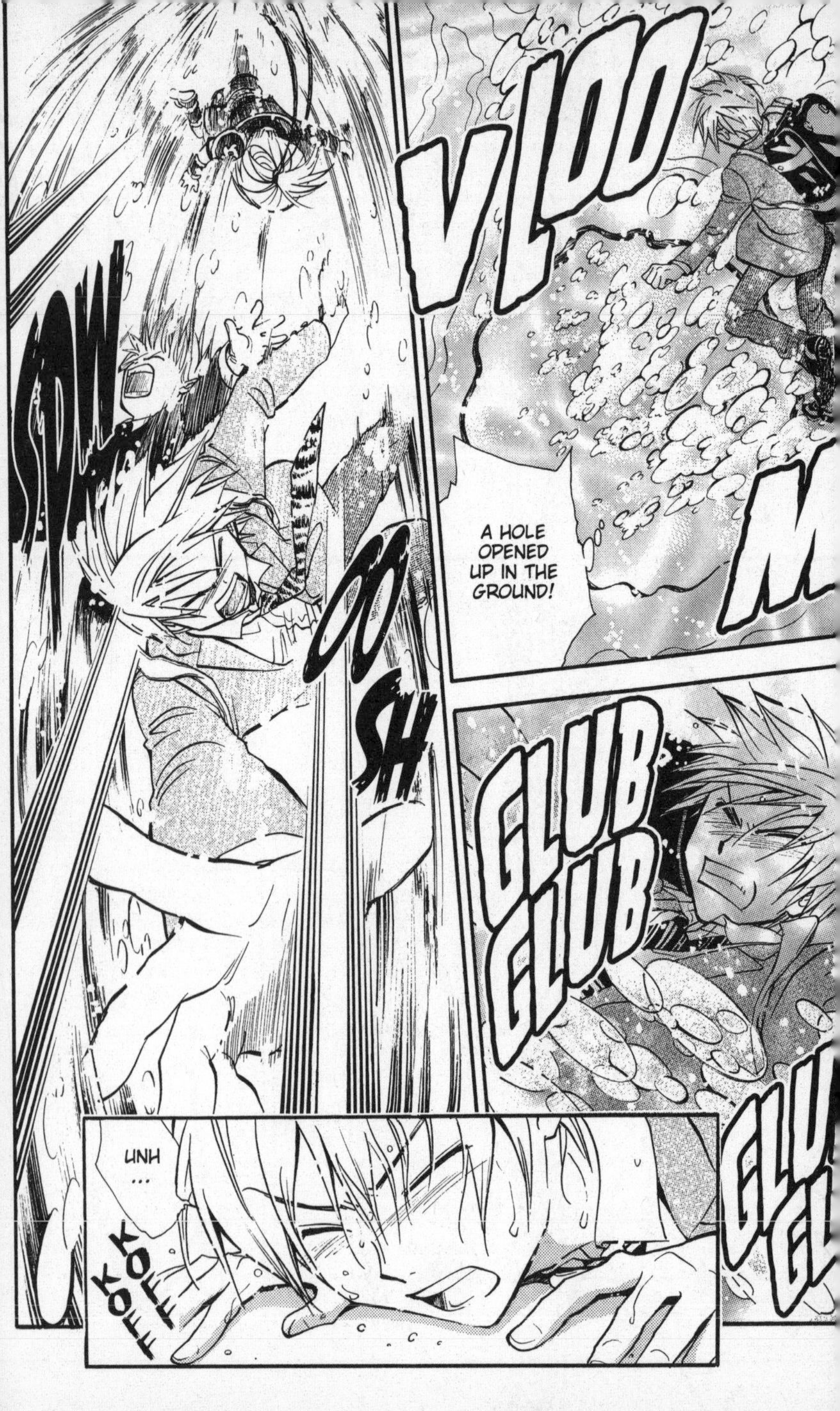
VLOO
A HOLE OPENED UP IN THE GROUND!
GLUB GLUB
SPOW
UNH ...
KOFF KOFF

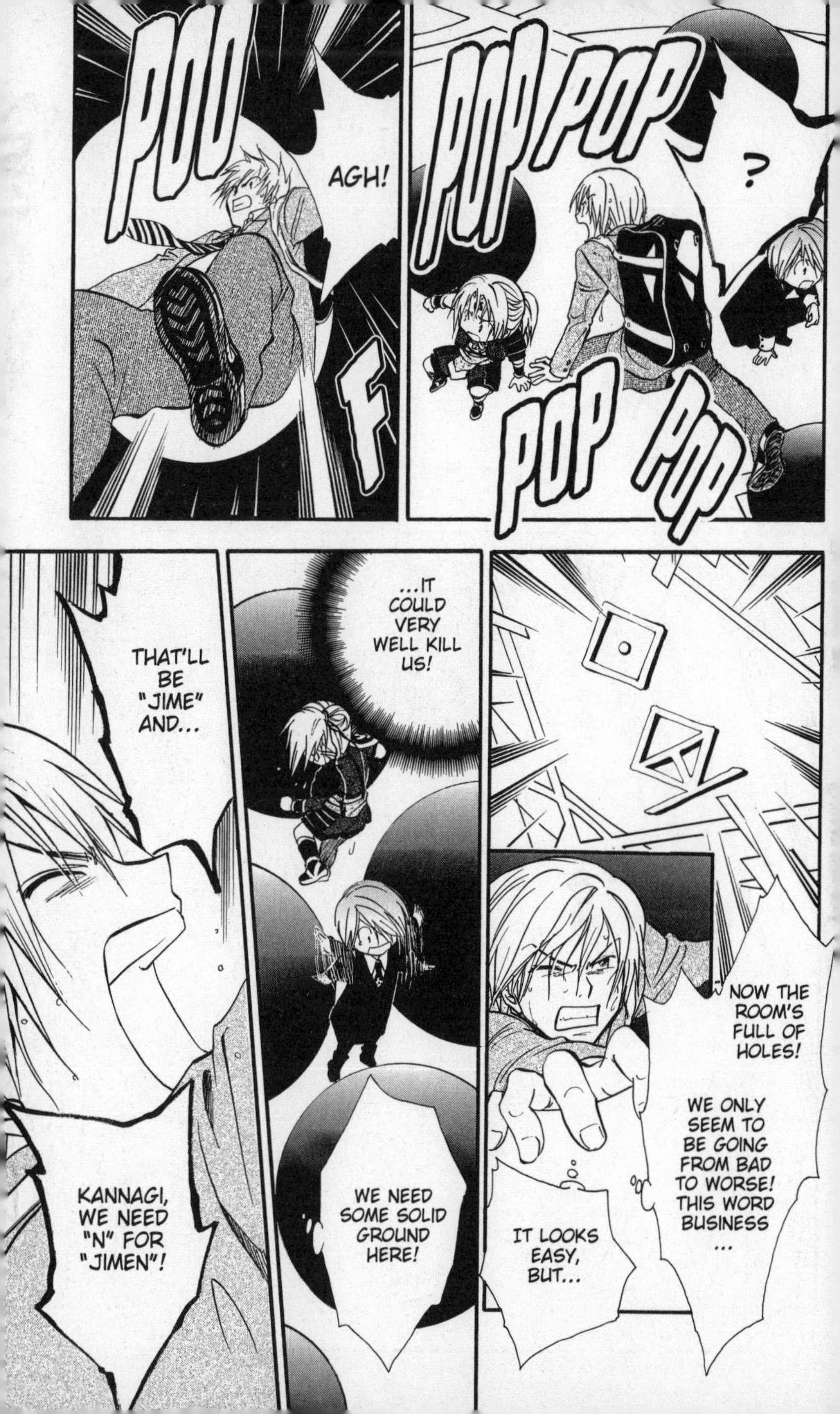
POP POP POP
?
POP POP
POO
AGH!
F
NOW THE ROOM'S FULL OF HOLES!
WE ONLY SEEM TO BE GOING FROM BAD TO WORSE! THIS WORD BUSINESS ...
IT LOOKS EASY, BUT...
...IT COULD VERY WELL KILL US!
WE NEED SOME SOLID GROUND HERE!
THAT'LL BE "JIME" AND...
KANNAGI, WE NEED "N" FOR "JIMEN"!

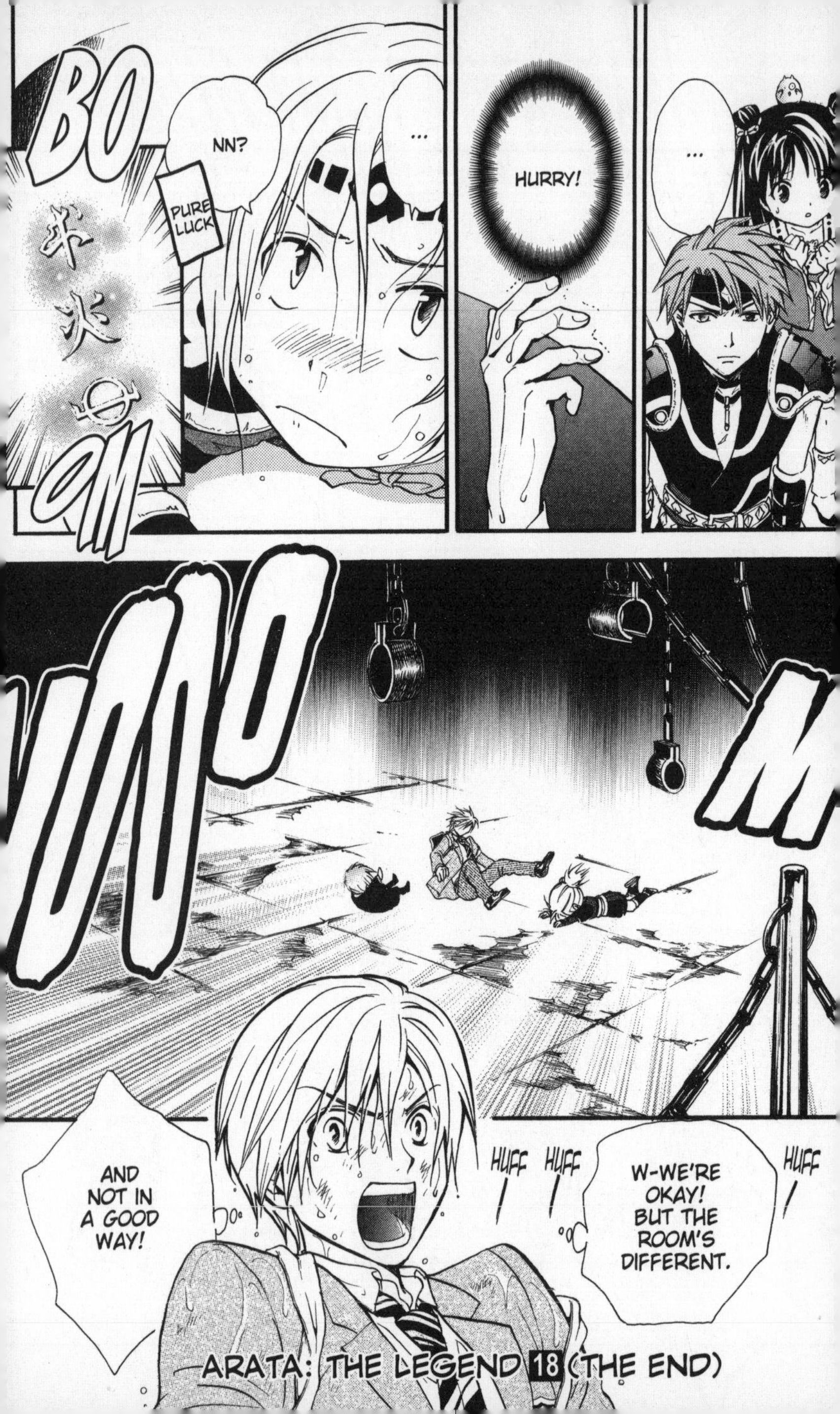

...
HURRY!
...
NN?
PURE LUCK
BO
OM
OOO
M
HUFF
HUFF HUFF
W-WE'RE OKAY! BUT THE ROOM'S DIFFERENT.
AND NOT IN A GOOD WAY!

ARATA: THE LEGEND 18 (THE END)

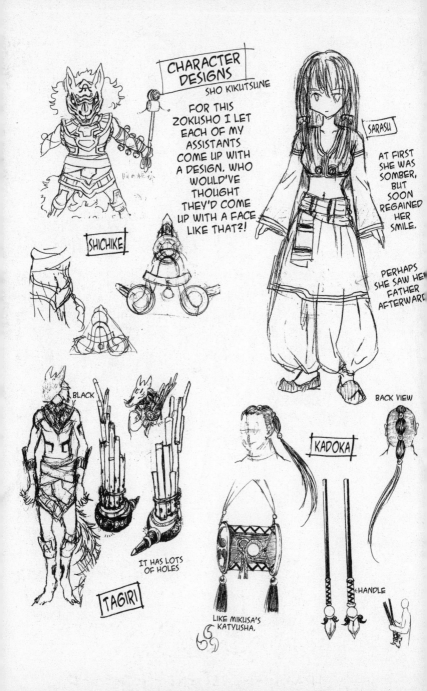

CHARACTER DESIGNS
SHO KIKUTSUNE

FOR THIS ZOKUSHO I LET EACH OF MY ASSISTANTS COME UP WITH A DESIGN. WHO WOULD'VE THOUGHT THEY'D COME UP WITH A FACE LIKE THAT?!

SHICHIKE

SARASU

AT FIRST SHE WAS SOMBER, BUT SOON REGAINED HER SMILE.

PERHAPS SHE SAW HER FATHER AFTERWARD

BLACK

BACK VIEW

KADOKA

IT HAS LOTS OF HOLES

TAGIRI

LIKE MIKUSA'S KATYUSHA.

HANDLE

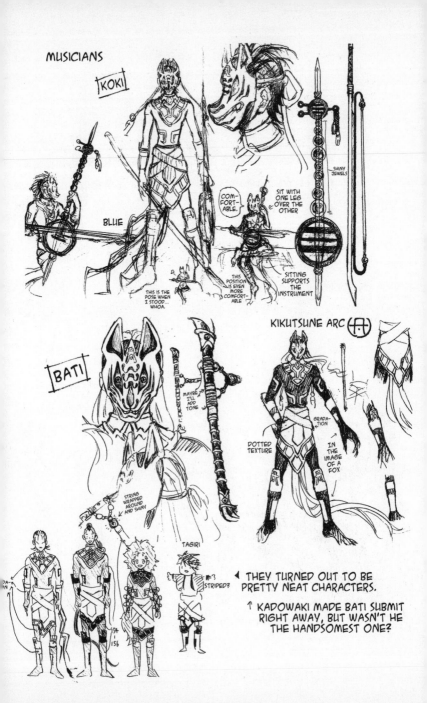

MUSICIANS

KOKI

BLUE

COMFORTABLE.

SIT WITH ONE LEG OVER THE OTHER

SHINY JEWELS

THIS IS THE POSE WHEN I STOOD... WHOA.

THIS POSITION IS EVEN MORE COMFORTABLE

SITTING SUPPORTS THE INSTRUMENT

BATI

MAYBE I'LL ADD TONE

KIKUTSUNE ARC

DOTTED TEXTURE

GRADATION

IN THE IMAGE OF A FOX

STRING WRAPPED AROUND AND SHINY

TAGIRI

STRIPED?

154 156

◄ THEY TURNED OUT TO BE PRETTY NEAT CHARACTERS.

↑ KADOWAKI MADE BATI SUBMIT RIGHT AWAY, BUT WASN'T HE THE HANDSOMEST ONE?

THE KITSUNE

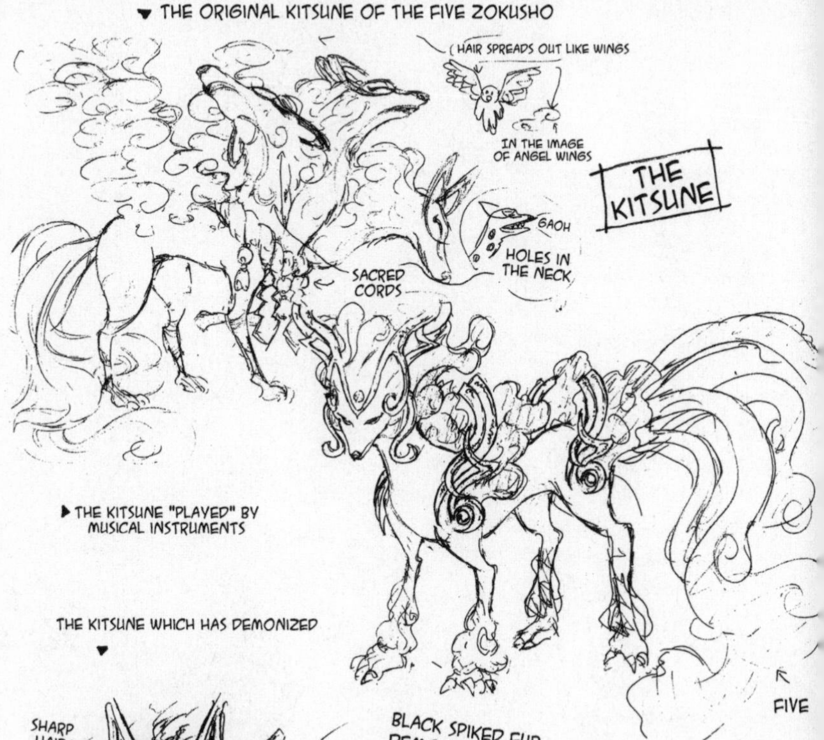
▼ THE ORIGINAL KITSUNE OF THE FIVE ZOKUSHO
(HAIR SPREADS OUT LIKE WINGS
IN THE IMAGE OF ANGEL WINGS
GAOH
HOLES IN THE NECK
SACRED CORDS
▶ THE KITSUNE "PLAYED" BY MUSICAL INSTRUMENTS
FIVE

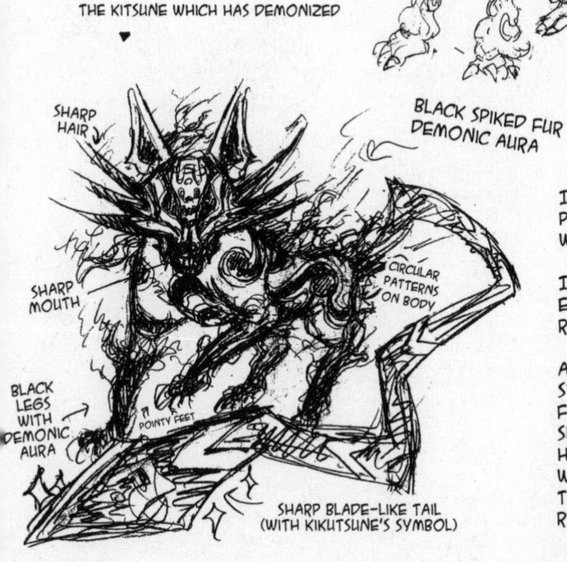
THE KITSUNE WHICH HAS DEMONIZED ▼
SHARP HAIR
BLACK SPIKED FUR
DEMONIC AURA
CIRCULAR PATTERNS ON BODY
SHARP MOUTH
BLACK LEGS WITH DEMONIC AURA
POINTY FEET
SHARP BLADE-LIKE TAIL (WITH KIKUTSUNE'S SYMBOL)

IN THE KIKUTSUNE ARC, I PORTRAYED A COUP D'ETAT AS WELL AS DISASTER.

IT'S LIKE WHAT HAPPENED IN EGYPT WHEN THE PEOPLE REVOLTED.

ALSO, THE WORD "REVIVAL" IS STILL A VERY VALUABLE WORD FOR JAPAN. THE WAY EACH SHINSHO BATTLES DIFFERS AND HAS MEANING. I THINK IT WOULD BE INTERESTING TO THINK ABOUT THAT AS YOU READ.

The *Arata* anime series began airing in April!

From the first meeting to the storyboarding and final planning, through the auditions of the voice actors (and being allowed to make little, final changes as the author), this has been a wonderful education.

Due to the number of episodes, some content and storyline changes had to be made. So some of you may notice that a certain character or a certain episode is missing. But make no mistake, this is 100 percent *Arata the Legend* in concentrated, undiluted form!

Actually the story is very easy to follow! (Ha!) This anime version will be like a review in which there are "Aha!" moments where you suddenly understand what certain things mean. I hope you enjoy it. I'll work hard to make the original story exciting, so please support both versions! Please make sure you wake up every Monday in the middle of the night to watch it! (Hee!)

–YUU WATASE

AUTHOR BIO

Born March 5 in Osaka, Yuu Watase debuted in the *Shôjo Comic* manga anthology in 1989. She won the 43rd Shogakukan Manga Award with *Ceres: Celestial Legend*. One of her most famous works is *Fushigi Yûgi*, a series that has inspired the prequel *Fushigi Yûgi: Genbu Kaiden*. In 2008, *Arata: The Legend* started serialization in *Shonen Sunday*.